FAMILY-CENTERED POLICIES & PRACTICES

Katharine Briar-Lawson,

Hal A. Lawson,

and Charles B. Hennon,

with Alan R. Jones

FAMILY-CENTERED POLICIES & PRACTICES

International Implications

Columbia University Press • New York

Columbia University Press
Publishers Since 1893
New York Chichester, West Sussex

Library of Congress Cataloging-in-Publication Data

Family-centered policies and practices : international implications / Katharine
Briar-Lawson, Hal A. Lawson, and Charles B. Hennon, with Alan R. Jones.
    p.   cm.
    Includes bibliographical references and index.
    ISBN 0-231-12106-7 (cloth : alk. paper)—ISBN 0-231-12107-5
(pbk. : alk. paper)
    1. Family policy.   2. Family services.
    HV697 .F353 2001
    362.82—dc21   00-060257

⊗ Casebound editions of Columbia University Press books
are printed on permanent and durable acid-free paper.

Printed in the United States of America

c 10 9 8 7 6 5 4 3 2 1
p 10 9 8 7 6 5 4 3 2 1

WE DEDICATE THIS BOOK to the millions of

families whose tragedies, losses, and demise could

have been prevented. Their pain has not been in

vain. They have provided important lessons,

which compel strategic action that promises to

protect and strengthen families around the world.

Contents

Foreword

The professionalism of this book makes it fascinating reading. Perhaps as fascinating as the International Year of the Family itself. The unanimous proclamation by the General Assembly of the United Nations of 1994 as International Year of the Family (IYF) was proof of the global concern over the future of the family and the growing interest in family issues around the world. Although there had been a certain "fatigue" with events of this kind, an international year devoted to the family was thought to be the type of subject that lent itself to the setting and achieving of tangible objectives with a common unifying motif: to bring together threads of social life that until recently had been treated separately and disjointedly.

Similar events of the past had stressed a sectoral approach to social problems by concentrating on selected aspects of human development (such as gender equality, children, the elderly, disabled members of families, drug abuse, crime prevention, violence in the family, environmental issues). In contrast, the subject of families offered a much more comprehensive and, at the same time, synthesizing approach, since families represented the fullest reflection, at the grassroots level, of the social and developmental welfare environment. Families bring down several important social issues to a common denominator of action. This proved to be an extremely important function of IYF on the eve of the World Summit for Social Development, held in Copenhagen, Denmark, in March 1995, as well as in the light of a series of other global conferences of the 1990s, notably the World Summit for Children, United Nations Conference on Environment and Development, World Conference on Human Rights,

International Conference on Population and Development, and the Fourth World Conference on Women: Action for Equality, Development, and Peace. Thus, IYF was not an isolated project, one taking place in a vacuum. It had been conceived and pursued in full harmony with the overall development efforts of the international community. In fact, it constituted a major step toward human-centered sustainable development. This intimacy and essentiality of IYF to the global processes became all the more striking in the context of the definition of human development as "development of the people, for the people and by the people."

The theme of IYF, "Family: resources and responsibilities in a changing world," was pragmatic enough, with emphasis on increasing awareness of family issues among governments as well as in the private sector: to highlight the importance of families, encourage a better understanding of their functions and problems, promote knowledge of the economic, social, and demographic processes affecting families, and focus attention upon the rights and responsibilities of family members. Its motto, *Building the smallest democracy at the heart of society,* depicted the everlasting truth that democracy is a way of life that needs to be learned and practiced. Family, as the heart of society, is democracy's fundamental learning place. Families founded on the principles of equality, the inviolability of the rights and responsibilities of the individual, mutual respect, love, and tolerance can be a natural cradle of democracy. Such families are the foundation for the well-being of individuals, societies, and nations. Efforts to build a civil society, based on the principles of human rights and democracy, can succeed only when these principles are learned, practiced, and respected in families. This is both a message and a challenge of a tall order: to work together toward a human society where children and adolescents feel that their voices are heard, and where men and women live in partnership, based on equality and mutual respect. Only then can there be a well-functioning two-way communication between the community at the grassroots level and society at large. Only then can children come to understand the underlying principles of democracy and how to integrate them in their own personalities and daily life.

The rationale behind IYF was loud and clear: families are, and have been, universally present and recognized in some form in all societies. In all cases, they have been fundamentally important to the structure and action of societies of which they are part. Families are basic, fundamental elements of the human experience and builders of social cohesion. They offer an integrated approach to social progress and development, with a view to instituting family-sensitive policies in family-friendly societies.

In what we used to refer to as the "global village," the notion of the family can have many meanings. The world has shrunk. The concept of the family has expanded: from blood relations and ties based on affection, to veritable community of interest, self-support, and mutual advantage. We can also observe this dynamic process in Europe and North America, where family issues remain a "hot topic." In the overwhelming majority of cases, people would still be ready to paraphrase Winston Churchill: *Right or wrong—my family;* or reword another English saying: *My family—my castle.* Yet, it is equally true that too many women, men, and children cannot but conclude: *My family—my drama, my tragedy.* This is why it would be utterly wrong to either idealize or condemn the family institution.

War, violence, extreme poverty, social exclusion, substance abuse, hunger, gender discrimination, domestic violence, and disease are just a few of the numerous specters haunting families everywhere. The recent sociopolitical transitions in many countries have placed millions of families in totally alien situations, left to themselves without support to survive under the emerging mechanisms of market economies. The current number of refugee families is unprecedented in history. Many families, especially those headed by single-parent females, find the constant need to balance work and familial responsibilities to be among the most demanding aspects of daily life. With severe fiscal pressures, social services are cut back, reducing the safety net for the population at the very time when it is most needed.

Fundamental to the notion of family seems to be a dichotomy between the presence of the repressive, hierarchical structures of family life and the absence of a sense of moral obligation, awareness, and solidarity concerning others' needs and rights; the dichotomy between power and control, on the one hand, and the equal and inalienable rights of all family members, on the other; the dichotomy between the major components of what the secretary-general of the United Nations, Kofi Annan, defines as *uncivil society* and the makings of its *civil* antonym. When a family rests at, or descends to, the point where the basic human rights of individual members are endangered by others within the unit, the costs to the individual and the greater society cannot be measured in any currency. When poverty is allowed to become so extreme that parents mutilate their own children to make them more successful as beggars in the street, we have all somehow failed. When a child takes his or her life in desperation and in fear, something important dies in all of us. Life in a repressive family, which has no respect for the rights of its members, can be an experience even harsher than functioning in a repressive society. Both are unacceptable. Societies cannot be healthy as long as families are haunted by the specter of disrespect for duly established international standards. The power of the family, therefore, must be limited by the basic human rights of its individual members.

When, in the late 1980s, in the United Nations, Poland first proposed the proclamation of an international year of the family, there were concerns that a focus on families would polarize debate on family issues and intensify existing controversies. There was also a concern that a focus on families might somehow detract from the positive developments for and by particular social groups, notably women and children.

Ultimately, what we experienced was quite the opposite because the International Year of the Family was built on convictions. It confirmed the centrality of families as the natural, primary, and fundamental group units of society. It firmly placed them on the social agenda and reaffirmed their central importance to understanding and addressing a wide array of social issues. Through a family focus, IYF has offered a powerful integrating factor to social development issues, underscored by the strong interdisciplinary and multisectoral preparations and observances in most countries of the world, involving various levels of society. It has given a renewed impetus to the concepts of empowerment and subsidiarity and thrown into sharp relief the need for international cooperation and exchange of experience through the United Nations system.

The book in your hands is an eloquent plea on behalf of the world's families. It is an appeal for action to governments, international and nongovernmental organizations, societies, and families themselves. Its authors have been consistent in writing it in a pro-family and UN-friendly language. Still, they readily concede that their "suggestions and recommendations should not be interpreted as rigid prescriptions," since families, as the oldest and most enduring social institutions in every nation of the world, "vary across nations and cultures, and they have evolved over time." By closely following the preparations to, and the observances of, the International Year of the Family, the authors have earned additional credentials to deal with what continues to be a sensitive subject of international discourse. Proceeding from the belief that the world's families have more in common than not, they have advanced considerably the search for a common denominator of approach. Their findings, too, sustain the conclusion that "the idea of family advocacy, as a key part of citizenship, is feasible and desirable." The crux of the matter, however, is that "unless advocates and leaders recognize the diversity in each family system's composition, goals, aspirations, and unique ways of knowing and acting, they will not be positioned to help these families." This book is, therefore, a special attempt to understand the significance of families as a follow-up to IYF and tangible evidence that "they can no longer be taken for granted, ignored, and neglected."

The International Year of the Family has made a clear mark on the international consciousness and moved families to the forefront of the debate. Although we have not yet reached our destination and a much longer distance remains to be covered, after 1994 the world is not the same on the subject of families. It remains to be hoped that IYF and its follow-up will have also firmly placed families as an essential focus of social policy action and a foundation upon which we can confidently look to the future we leave the generations to come.

Henryk J. Sokalski
Former United Nations Coordinator
for the International Year of the Family

Preface

The human family, universal and diverse as it is, represents the complexity of a global phenomenon that escapes scientists' attention despite the rhetoric of the Universal Declaration of Rights and varied governmental policies and programs. The family, metaphorically as well as institutionally, symbolizes the hopes and despair of humanity. The postindustrial society has not yet invented a viable mechanism that will sustain the viability and functionality of this universal institution. It can be argued that family needs are both a cause and consequence of massive societal changes that warrant urgent attention before a catastrophic explosion irreparably disrupts the main fabric of society.

Family-Centered Policies and Practices uniquely offers a postmodern perspective on the global experience of a universal concern: a conceptual and practice-based framework to building family supports and policy. Not many books are written in this field with a focus on international family issues, especially signifying their integrative role and patterns in a fast-changing world. This book assumes a special relevance as globalization and its forces continue to impact intra- and interpersonal relationships.

The main body of the text includes twelve well-organized chapters with facts and analyses pertaining to different aspects of family-centered policies and practices. The background, resources, and talents that helped develop concrete scenarios of practice and policy ably represent a new awareness that skill-based helping disciplines can fruitfully utilize in teaching, research, policy, and planning. Citizens, community leaders, social activists, and policy makers across the national and international boundaries need frameworks that truly work. Family-centered policy practice is a viable approach to social development and community building. The chapters unfold family systems, their institutional and preventive aspects; globalization and its forces; social and economic sustainability; differential approaches, policy and practices, and discourses; roles of advocates, practitioners, and helping professionals; and the imminent challenges that abound at the dawn of the new millennium.

The major strengths of this study include its interdisciplinarity and focus on universal issues with a unique emphasis on family-centered policy and practice. Social scientists have used many frameworks for different purposes but—barring a few studies—none has ever encompassed issues, approaches, and contexts that universalize family policy practice as a veritable vehicle of global development and uplift.

In my considered professional judgment, this book makes a significant contribution in a hitherto neglected but fertile field of research. Its significance cannot be overstated. It fills a daunting vacuum that is both intriguing and challenging.

Brij Mohan, Editor
New Global Development: Journal of International and Comparative Welfare

Acknowledgments

Books like this one are often inspired by events and people. The United Nations International Year of the Family (IYF) was an important event in the development of this book. The International Year of the Family commenced in 1992 with the preparatory work, was celebrated formally in 1994, and has continued with follow-up activities. One or more of the authors has been involved at each phase.

The people associated with IYF also were instrumental. We are indebted to the IYF Secretariat, especially Henryk Sokalski and Eugene Rolfe. Henryk and Eugene inspired the authors, and they provided invaluable perspectives and information. The authors also benefited from interactions with other IYF leaders, attendance at international conferences, and access to relevant databases.

Enormous help in preparing this book came from Armand Lauffer, Alvin Sallee and his students, as well as Candy Minchey, Kadisha Khadja, and Ernesto Soto. In addition, Ann Kubisch, John Lanigan, and the Ford Foundation were most helpful in facilitating the authors' research on IYF. We are indebted to all of them.

FAMILY-CENTERED POLICIES & PRACTICES

Introduction

Families matter, and so do economic, social, cultural, and political matters concerning families. After decades of neglect, today there is resurgent interest in families (Boyden, 1993; United Nations, 1992c). Some of this interest derives from publications produced by the academic community (e.g., Burggraf, 1997; Halpern, 1998), including research on the role of families in preventing social problems and filling individual needs (e.g., Kamerman & Kahn, 1978; Kumpfer, 1998).

A second source of interest stems from political mobilizations regarding families, family rights, and gender rights (e.g., Berheide & Chow, 1994). In some cases, historically marginalized, oppressed, and disfranchised groups are helping to foster these movements (e.g., Mah, 1997; Mohanty, Russo, & Torres, 1991).

A third group comprises helping professionals and their professional associations focusing increasingly on families (e.g., Wilcox, Smith, et al., 1991; Family Resource Coalition, 1996; National Association of Social Workers, 1993; National Council on Family Relations, 1993; Schorr, 1997). Policy makers, both national and international, make up a fourth group (e.g., Premier's Council in Support of Alberta Families, 1994; United Nations Council of State Policy and Planning Agencies, 1989; United Nations, 1992c).

The United Nations 1994 International Year of the Family (IYF) was a pivotal event in promoting interest in, and concern for, families (e.g., United Nations, 1991a, 1995a, 1995e). This celebratory year advanced critical perspectives about families, especially their strengths, needs, challenges, and resilience. Local, national, and regional meetings, conducted in conjunction with IYF, convened policy makers, helping professionals, representatives from nongovernmental organizations, and family advocates. Proclamations were offered about the importance of families and new commitments to them. Ultimately, some 140 member nations joined in the work to celebrate and advocate for families.

This resurgent interest is timely, and already its benefits are evident. New frames of reference, policy agendas, and action systems are evolving. Sometimes these new frames of reference produce conflicts because their differences are not reconciled. For example, some advocates speak about reclaiming "traditional values," oftentimes calling them "family values." Others speak about the need to support women and children. Still other persons speak about families as self-appointed groups of interdependent adults who provide unconditional emotional and social support to one another. Some are critical of dominant family-related discourses. They criticize patriarchy and violence within the families and take issue with gender roles and expectations that dominant discourses convey.

Fortunately, the new frames, agendas, and action systems are more inclusive. They promote more consensus and coherence. For example, these new frames and action systems avoid dichotomies, such as nuclear families versus family systems; individuals versus families; and individual rights versus family rights. Proponents of these new frames recognize that dichotomies like these, along with the binary logic that supports them, have impaired understanding of families, hampered policy development, and limited family-supportive action strategies.

This book is intended to serve as an example of such an inclusive approach to families. It offers new frames, agendas, and action systems. It emphasizes policies, practices, and advocacy in support of families. It promotes family-centered policies and practices.

INTRODUCING FAMILY-CENTERED APPROACHES AS A CHANGE STRATEGY

In this book we introduce a very basic idea. When families and their well-being provide the focus for governmental policies and helping professionals' practices, citizens, advocates, helping professionals, policy makers, families and their members, and others will all be better off. We base our pro-family arguments on a growing body of the research literature, which spans many disciplines, about the importance of families.

This literature also demonstrates the folly and dangers of ignoring and neglecting families. So many priorities, so many social institutions, and every helping profession share one important feature: they all depend on families.

Family-centered thinking, policies, and practices promote more integrative conceptualizations and approaches to human needs and rights. Families are integrative units, which provide individual and group identities and promote social cohesion. They defy mechanistic models and industrial-age machine metaphors that have often dominated modern-day thinking and analysis. Above all, families transcend categorical approaches to human needs such as health, housing, employment, and the fragmented professions and policies that have emerged from these categorical frames of reference.

In other words, families do not do only health care; *or* counseling; *or* education. Families have to address them all, often at the same time. Families are comprehensive social welfare institutions. They are like miniature social welfare states (Waring, 1988).

Because families are comprehensive, integrated entities, which defy the categorical, specialized perspectives inherited by the professional disciplines and governmental service sectors, they compel new models of analysis and new kinds of collaborative practices. The long-standing dichotomy between individuals and families simply doesn't stand up under inspection.

Families also call into question the false dichotomy of policy work versus practice. It questions other dichotomies, especially the one between expert (professional) knowledge and "client" (individual and family) ignorance.

A key premise for this book is that families and people from all walks of life have expertise. They know, to some extent at least, what helps and hurts. Families need to become partners with policy makers, helping professionals, and advocates. When families are viewed as experts and treated as partners, policies and practices are more family centered. And when they are family centered, the dichotomy between policy and practice is no longer useful. In fact, this dichotomy may cause problems, not the least of which is catching helping professionals and families in "double binds" involving what policies require and permit and what families and the professionals who serve them really need.

This book thus promotes an integrative approach to policies and practices. Mindful of tensions between them, it sees benefits in these tensions.

Family-centered policies can stimulate like kinds of practices. Or, family-centered practices can promote like kinds of policies. It is not a question of family-centered policies *or* practices; it is both. This integrative approach to policy practice includes multimodal service, support, and resource strategies, and multilevel systems and cross-systems changes in support of them. Segregated, categorical policies and practices will appear to be homeless in this family-centered, integrative, and comprehensive perspective.

PROMOTING FAMILIES AND THE IMPORTANCE OF THEIR WELL-BEING

Families vary across nations and cultures, and they have evolved over time. Despite their apparent universality today, families are not inevitable in structure or function (Collier, Rosaldo, & Yanagisako, 1992). There is no evidence in support of claims that one variety of family arrangement is superior to others. There is evidence in support of claims that families and family arrangements vary through time and in different places and cultures.

Sometimes families have represented choices people continue to make about how they wish to live; about how they garner and give support; and about the social, political, cultural, and economic arrangements they find most suitable. Sometimes these decisions have been made by governments and powerful authorities. Here, coercion has outweighed free choice. Even under coercion, families have demonstrated their capacities to resist and subvert decisions that are not in their best interests. Individuals and families are usually active agents in co-determining their own lives.

Despite diversity in their composition and organization, families across cultures typically share similar duties and challenges. For example, families provide economic resources; create and consume products and services; address the health and emotional needs of their members; provide shelter, food, and other essentials for survival; enforce moral codes and norms of behavior; and promote local, regional, national, and international economic growth and social development.

Families constitute the largest social welfare institution in the world. This is not to suggest that all groups considered as families serve as optimal units of a social welfare system. Nor does it imply that families want and need to perform all these social welfare–related functions. When all of the facets of social welfare are weighed—e.g., health, education, social supports, etc.—and when families are viewed as the largest social welfare institution in the world—their centrality and multidimensionality become apparent. Families gain new meaning and significance within and across nation-states. Nonetheless, families are not inevitable. Nor are they indestructible.

Preserving and strengthening families requires consistent attention to their needs and aspirations. It requires close monitoring of their well-being. This monitoring involves governments, both individually and collectively, as well as families, policy makers, professionals, and advocates.

Families are points of convergence for grand issues involving politics, economics, and social-moral philosophy. Using families as a lens, evaluative questions can be addressed about power and its distribution (politics); about the allocation of resources and rewards (economics); about the contributions of government to the good, just society and to individual and family well-being (social-moral philosophy); and especially about the relations among families, governments, economics, morals, and ethics.

We will raise some of these questions in this book. The questions we ask may be as important as the answers and implications we provide. Our work is grounded in shared concern about the present and future well-being of the world's families.

FROM DANGERS AND CRISES TO OPPORTUNITIES

Most of the nations in the world have economic development agendas, social development agendas, or some combination of them. Development has tended to be uneven because nations have not been equal players or beneficiaries. Development also has been competitive. Some nations and their families are like winners, while others are losers. When an economic calculus reigns, the human costs and some stark realities may be lost from the public eye.

We authors take as our point of departure four basic assumptions:

1. Many of the world's families are experiencing crises, and others are in danger.
2. Crises and endangerment erode individual and family well-being.
3. It is possible and desirable to prevent these crises, dangers, and declining well-being.

4. Crises, dangers, and declining well-being are opportunities to act strategically, especially to invent innovative, more effective, family-centered policies and practices.

RECURRENT THEMES

These four assumptions have framed our examination of the world's families. Despite international diversity, recurrent, pervasive themes are evident. For example, families are experiencing transformation.

Transformation

The twentieth century has witnessed the transformation of over 95 percent of the world's families (Henderson, 1996). For some families, such as those in high-income nations, this transformation has been occurring over a century or more. For others, such as those in low-income nations, this transformation is accelerating. For example, long-settled families and extended family systems have been fragmented.

Once sustainable agriculture has been eroded along with the arable land. Rural families, faced with survival challenges, have had more children to survive, and many have moved to cities to find minimum and low-wage employment in the informal sector of the economy. Rural to urban flows challenge nations, as they transform families.

Families and Work

Waged jobs are in decline in many parts of the world, owing in part to technology development and in part to the deindustrialization caused by the mobility of transnational corporations. Once vibrant indigenous agriculture, crafts, and microenterprises have been undercut by requirements associated with structural adjustment and economic development policies. As discussed earlier, inequalities are growing, both within and among nations (e.g., Bradshaw & Wallace, 1996).

There are now more than 800 million workers out of work or under-employed worldwide. This pervasive unemployment involves many more workers than were affected by the world depression of the 1930s (Rifkin, 1995). As millions of workers and families fall victim to the predictable human costs of joblessness and the fracturing of their families, irreversible family scarring takes place. Cycles of addictions, abuse, depression and mental illness, and related health problems rise. Even genetic changes may occur as a result of the pollutants and industrial hazards or deteriorating health habits in the home and community.

Despite aggressive policies to shore up "human capital" in support of competitive advantages in the luring of transnational corporations (TNCs), the fact of the matter is that formal sector jobs, which provide good wages and benefit programs, are in short supply in many nations (International Labour Office, 1998). Although official unemployment figures may be low, they are low because a growing number of people are employed in informal sector jobs, ones that do not provide employment security, appropriate wages, and benefit programs.

Children's Aspirations and Schooling

Awareness is growing among children and youth that staying in school and completing a degree will not automatically translate into a good job, let alone a permanent one. This loss of hope and aspiration is itself a cause of declining well-being, especially for vulnerable and marginalized families, especially in the high-income nations (e.g., Wilson, 1997; Fine & Weis, 1998).

Poverty, Inequality, and Families

World poverty is rising in some nations, despite some impressive gains in a small group of nations (Ghai, 1997; Woodward, 1996). Poverty is a cause of migration. It is not just poor families who have been hard hit. The 1980s ushered in a world phenomenon of decline in developed economies such that many families have seen their incomes plummet as income redistribution and inequity have grown (Reich, 1993).

Patriarchy is a persistent problem in families. It looms beneath the surface, often concealing gender violence as well as child abuse and neglect. It plagues social and economic development. And, it denies to girls and women their rights and fundamental freedoms.

National Debt and Corporate Profits

At this time, every nation except one is in debt. Only Norway reports a surplus, and its unemployment rate is growing (Jordan, 1998). These debts are one small measure of the level of decline that many nations experience. In the midst of such declines, super profits are being realized by an identifiable minority of people and corporations. New forms of investments involve paper profits, with few if any new jobs being created (International Labour Office, 1998; Thurow, 1996). Many TNCs are wealthier than entire nations (Bradshaw & Wallace, 1996).

Rising Perils

As the perils for many of the world's families grow, challenges to sustainable living and health-enhancing environments grow. The governmental planning and decision-making infrastructures and action mechanisms families require are not in place. The nation-state is too small for some matters, too big for others (Giddens, 1990). The United Nations lacks the supports and mandates to do all that it might.

Welfare states are certainly a key part of the solution. However, they need to be reinvented to keep up with the new challenges. Otherwise, they, like many families, may experience more crises and dangers. Above all, governmental leadership is needed, the kind of collaborative, strategic, imaginative, democratic leadership that serves families locally while keeping a firm international perspective. Serving families means assessing their strengths, meeting their needs, and seeing families as worthy social investments.

NEEDS FOR AN INTERNATIONAL SOCIAL MOVEMENT FOR FAMILIES

The International Year of the Family (IYF) demonstrated that worldwide advocacy on behalf of families is feasible and potentially powerful. It is just one example of how leaders of nations, individually and collectively, can make families important focal points for investments and how they can advance policies and practices that honor, promote, and support families. The International Year of the Family marked a beginning of work that must continue.

The International Year of the Family illustrated the ways that supports and policies for families have the potential to transcend the cultural and national diversity of the world community. Against wide diversity, there are important points of convergence and agreements. Above all, IYF called attention to the meaning and significance of families. And, once the significance of families is understood, one hopes that they will no longer be taken for granted, ignored, and neglected.

There are many signs of need. Each day individuals and their families come into harm's way. Chapter 1 provides a compelling list of challenges to their well-being.

To reiterate, many of these needs can be met. Many of these harms can be prevented. When families experience harm and need, there are ways to respond to, and help them. Knowledge, skills, and intervention-improvement strategies are not the primary problem. The real problem involves the political will of governmental leaders, especially their commitments to individual and family well-being. Rhetoric in support of families is nice, but it is not enough.

In both national and international contexts, policy leaders, helping professionals, and family advocates face identical challenges:

1. Reaffirming the importance of families
2. Finding common grounds amid political, economic, and socio-cultural diversity
3. Designing, implementing, and evaluating pro-family policies and practices
4. Integrating concerns for families with agendas for sustainable living and economic development.

This book attempts to respond to these related challenges. It is but one contribution to an emergent international movement in support of the world's families.

FAMILY-CENTERED VISIONS

The imagined tomorrow is today's idea (Polak, 1973). In this time of postmodern criticism of utopian schemes and themes (e.g., Lyotard, 1984), visions of the possible are more important than ever before. These family-centered visions need not become locked up in the grand ideological and political struggles of the past, ones that pitted capitalism against socialism, and both against communism. Family-centered visions help chart the course into a more desirable future. "Better than before" is an apt slogan for citizens in a democracy (e.g., Rorty, 1998). It signals that some improvements may occur at glacial speed, but also that there are no predetermined destinations beyond improving individual and family well-being.

This book is not an agenda for cultural imperialism and colonialism. Its title signals its orientations. It calls for policies and practices, indicating plural needs for a diverse and complex world. It emphasizes implications, not "one size fits all" prescriptions and broad-sweeping generalizations. This book is structured to encourage family-centered visions.

What visions do you have for families? In other words, what do you want families to be, experience, and do (after Collier, Rosaldo, & Yanagisako, 1992, p. 46)? Ask yourself these two questions, just as the authors did. Then ask this one: *How can family-centered policies and practices help make these visions materialize?* This book presents our collective exploration of these questions.

Imagine a world united in its commitments to and investments in families. Imagine a family well-being index that shows steady worldwide gains, nation by nation, year after year. Imagine semiannual local, regional, and international meetings that are devoted to monitoring progress and sharing lessons learned about family-centered policies and practices. Imagine integrated social and economic development policies and practices in which families are viewed as cornerstones, and in which they are provided tailored services, social supports, and economic-occupational resources. Imagine, in short, an international social movement that makes every year "an international year of families."

Olympism as an Exemplar

Despite their limitations, the Olympic Games are an example of the ways in which the world community can rally around shared visions. Most world leaders have demonstrated their abilities to put aside their other differences and agree upon shared norms and values that make up Olympism. Nation-specific policies and practices in support of it have followed. If the world community can initiate and sustain a social movement in support of competitive play, then why can't it mobilize a world movement for families?

As in the Olympic Games, some competition is involved. All pro-family advocates are joined in a race against time because individuals and families are dying for attention. Informed advocacy and policy on behalf of families can help unite the world community. Local communities, states, provinces, and nations can reap benefits. Investments in families bring dividends.

Like athletes competing in a relay race, the authors of this book have benefited from other pro-family advocates. We accept their torch of knowledge and understanding about families, together with examples of important policies and practices. The race on behalf of families will continue after we finish our leg. In other words, this book represents another torch that can be accepted and improved upon by others.

We authors have not always agreed. Some differences have been reconciled, while others remain. We "see" the world differently, and our gazes may reflect our disciplinary orientations. We represent health, education, family studies, and social work, and each of us is attracted to interdisciplinary perspectives. In the end, we decided to identify the authors for each chapter. This was one way to reconcile our differences and honor academic ethical imperatives.

On the other hand, the book has conceptual integrity and overall value coherence. It is not merely an edited book with separate chapters in search of common themes and shared assumptions. Our differences notwithstanding, we authors are united with others in the global village by a firm advocacy for families and deep commitments to improving their well-being.

Value Orientations

One of the most important challenges for policy and practice leaders is to gain more understanding of why some families are not able to meet their own expectations, achieve their own goals, and discharge all of their duties—despite their desires to do so. New, pro-family investment strategies require family-centered and responsive frames of reference. It is time to discard language and practices that are deficit and problem oriented, ones that label and stigmatize families in need as "dysfunctional" and "pathological." The authors promote in this book an orientation that emphasizes family aspirations, strengths, and resilience. This orientation can be approached by asking and addressing several key questions.

For example, if families are asked what they want and need, are their answers dramatically different from what policy leaders expect? Similarly, do families receive the services, supports, and resources they need to meet their own expectations and achieve their own goals? Are families, in essence, blamed for their needs and challenges, or are their problems and stress viewed as the absence of sufficient investments in them? Are individual nations and their leaders being blamed and held responsible for declining individual and family well-being indices when some of the root causes are, in fact, outside of their control?

Are helping professionals doing for families what families could be doing for themselves if they had the requisite services, supports, and resources? Do families develop a strong sense of collective efficacy, or do professionals foster in them patterns of learned helplessness and dependency? Are families seen as having expertise? Since they are the persons closest to the problem or goal, have they been recruited to be part of the solution? Are "natural helping systems" promoted, whereby individuals and families are supported and strengthened to help themselves and each other?

Exploring Dimensions of Family-Centered Policies and Practices

The authors are committed to policies and strategies that facilitate responsiveness to what families say they want and need. This means working with, and for, families. It entails giving voice to all of their members, especially to girls and women. It means granting them effective jurisdiction over their own lives and honoring their expertise, especially with regard to what helps and harms them. It also means shifting away from top-down, one-size-fits-all policy edicts. Good intentions notwithstanding, family-centered policies and practices must be co-designed, implemented, and evaluated with the families they are intended to help. Only then will these policies and practices become appropriately tailored; only then will they respond to family, contextual, and cultural uniqueness. It is time to build upon good intentions and seek pathways to family-centered and family-supportive policies and practices.

This book explores these and related dimensions of family-centered policies and practices. The intent is to help policy makers and family advocates develop new understanding, allowing them to work more strategically. Ideally, they will gain knowledge, values, skills, and abilities needed to help develop better policies and improved practices because the choices they make are more strategic.

For example, categorical (also called "sectoral"), single-system, and single-profession approaches make it likely that both policy leaders and professionals will focus on just one area of human need and family well-being. Binary logic resides underneath categorical policies, and oppositional thinking dominates. Hence, health priorities are pitted against education; education and health against criminal justice; and so on. By contrast, when families and family well-being are the focus, and when families are involved in policy designs, single-sector, categorical thinking, planning, and programming are problematic. Individual and family well-being help integrate policies in a more coherent and cohesive fashion. Counterproductive policy and practice competitions are prevented.

Theoretical Orientations

No single theoretical frame dominates this analysis. The subject of families and family-centered policies in the international community is simply too broad, complex, and innovative. Our subject outstrips the descriptive, explanatory, and predictive powers of any one theory, or theoretical frame. World systems theory (Wallerstein, 1974), while compelling, does not meet our needs.

Just as these policy leaders, helping professionals, and advocates must reach compromises—sometimes uneasy ones at that—so, too, have the authors worked to develop compromises. The result is a theoretical hybrid, together with all the benefits and limitations associated with it.

The authors have tried to blend and integrate relevant aspects of systems theory; social ecological theory; critical theory; postmodern theory; economic resource dependency theory; democratic political theory; globalization theory; and emergent kinds of "family theory." The language, constructs, and concepts the authors employ reflect this hybrid theoretical framework. Theoretical purists may find fault with this. The authors understand and accept whatever criticism follows from this decision to mix theoretical perspectives.

THE UNDERLYING LOGIC FOR THE CHAPTER PROGRESSION

Several key questions have been asked of the authors; and, in turn, the authors have asked them of others. The International Year of the Family also raised and addressed some of these same questions—for example:

- What exactly is a family? Is there a definition that encompasses diversity worldwide?
- How and why should society's leaders invest in families? What are the benefits? What are the consequences of ignoring, neglecting, harming, eroding, and destroying families?
- What indices exist for family well-being and for the development of pro-family policy practices?
- How do investments in families double as investments in democracy and, at the same time, in integrated, equitable, sustainable, and culturally responsive social and economic development?
- What unmet needs do families experience, and how much say should families have in determining how these needs are met?

- Can family-support agendas also enhance the well-being of individuals and groups such as children, elders, women, and men?
- How best can family-centered policies and practices be designed, implemented, and evaluated?
- How much gender balance is necessary to truly "hear" what families and all their members need?
- To what extent can the concept of "family" help integrate now-separate policies and practices for individuals, such as those for children, women, and persons with disabilities?
- To what extent can families become enfranchised as partners and joint authors of these policy practices?
- What future directions and challenges for families should leaders and advocates consider and promote?

These and other practical, important questions have helped the authors plan the chapter progression.

CHAPTER PROGRESSION

Chapter 1 introduces the meanings and significance of families in the world community. The authors address the challenges of defining "family." They also emphasize the importance of family systems—their functions, duties, and significance. The concept of family well-being is introduced, along with indices to assess it.

Value-laden issues surrounding the definition of families are addressed. Here, the authors, like this book's readers, face important ethical-moral issues. The authors decided that they could not impose personal definitions of families upon readers. This decision stemmed from collective commitments to honor and respect cultural and national diversity in policies and practices on behalf of families.

On the other hand, the authors are not committed to the dictum that "anything goes." Respect for cultural and national diversity must be weighed against nonnegotiable human rights and protections, which transcend any one cultural system or nation-state. These human rights, promulgated by the United Nations and adopted by many nations, are inseparable from a concern for families. Practices that honor these rights must be enacted in families, and national as well as international indices of family well-being must incorporate them. These individual and family rights include equitable and just treatment, regardless of gender, age, and developmental status; freedom from violence, abuse, and involuntary exploitation; freedom from oppressive, discriminatory, and repressive practices; religious, political, and economic freedoms; and protections from individual and family harms. The problems that patriarchy brings are of paramount concern.

Why invest in families? Chapter 2 begins a book-long response to this question. This chapter sets the stage by identifying and defining key ideas and concepts. Here, and elsewhere in this book, families are identified as comprehensive social welfare institutions. They are also the "engines" for economic development. Family work, especially women's work, goes unrecognized and unremunerated. This chapter focuses on the work that families do and the need for social accounting and resources, supports, and services to aid them in their critical roles. Unfortunately, a key point is often forgotten, if it is understood at all. *Most large companies and businesses once started out as small family businesses* (Burggraf, 1997; Fukuyama, 1995). Advocacy for families, especially in the political arena, must attend to these realities. Effective advocacy also means addressing implicit images that politicians and other leaders may have, images that act as obstacles to family-centered policies and practices.

Families are presented as part of a social investment strategy, rather than a narrow, categorical, economic development strategy. For, at the same time that families enhance economic development, they promote democratic government and civic participation. National health, education, and crime-related agendas all benefit when families are supported and strengthened.

In chapter 3, the idea of gender-equitable, meaningful employment is emphasized. Related economic concepts are introduced, including unemployment and underemployment. Three different economic sectors for family work are identified. The argument is that conventional social and health services have not addressed employment needs and economic development. And, because they have not, families have not been served effectively. The various people- and family-serving helping professions have key roles to play in this work, especially if they build capacity in families by creating mutual aid societies and neighborhood or village support networks. This entails building from families' needs and wants tailored services and resources that are supportive of them, rather than having professionals dictate to families without asking them. Barter systems and support networks also are important.

If families are to continue their key roles in economic systems, especially their roles as economic incubators, they need to receive their fair share of economic investment dollars. In addition, they must receive tailored, appropriate services, supports, and resources. Nowhere are these needs more apparent than with families' caregiving, social support, and mutual assistance functions. As leaders at the 1995 World Summit in Copenhagen concluded (UNDP for Sustainable Human Development, 1998) this means working to eliminate poverty, providing full employment, and increasing income equity for women, especially in relation to their caregiving roles.

It also means understanding the economic costs and social consequences associated with poverty, unemployment, and "runaway economic development policies" that are structured without reference to individual and family well-being. Based upon due recognition of the harms and costs associated with poverty, this agenda signals needs for the fair distribution, and redistribution, of the investment dollars associated with economic development.

Chapter 4 introduces questions and issues about governmental responsibilities for families and their well-being. Are families and their well-being key foci in the agendas that leaders establish? How are family needs and issues framed and named? Drawing on responses to these questions, a family-centered policy continuum is identified and described. In addition, a frame of reference is provided in which the rights and entitlements of individuals are no longer viewed as competing with pro-family agendas. To the contrary, the needs of individuals and the needs of families can and should be aligned with each other. The chapter also calls attention to needed congruence and cohesiveness across often-separate policy domains (e.g., education, health, environment, economic development). Pivotal questions are raised about the democratization of policy making—the extent to which families are enfranchised and empowered as partners in design, implementation, delivery, and evaluation of policies and practices aimed at them.

The authors try to walk the fine line between sensitizing readers to the issues and possible solutions, and offering prescriptions that are insensitive to national and cultural diversity. Mindful that national context and cultures always must be taken into account, the authors explore some of the predictable factors that most powerfully affect policy making on the behalf of individuals and families. We authors are action oriented. Like Putnam (1993), "We want government to *do* things, not just *decide* things" (p. 8). Examples of policy proclamations from IYF are provided to indicate how some governments decided to frame and name family needs, issues, and concerns, and perhaps to do things.

Readers are reminded in chapter 4 that familiar frames of reference bring yesterday's language; and that tomorrow's new practices may require a new language to help structure new frames for thought and action. Moreover, it emphasizes agenda setting, reminding readers that policies and practices are effective to the extent that they are based upon accurate and ecologically valid assessments of what's right that needs strengthening and what's wrong that needs fixing.

Chapter 5 picks up where chapter 4 leaves off. It emphasizes the importance of strategic decision-making and actions amid political inertia and multiple choices. The important roles of research and intervention logic in policy development and practice improvement are emphasized. Approaches to policy borrowing are described, together with some cautions and recommendations. Innovations involving service integration and interprofessional collaboration are sketched. A family impact assessment inventory is introduced to facilitate policy analysis, implementation, evaluation, and learning systems that accompany them.

Chapter 6 promotes family-centered collaboration and, in turn, broad-based collaboration among all stakeholders in the community. Key features of family-centered collaboration, policy, and practice are identified. For example, families are viewed as experts, treated as partners, and no one, especially helping professionals, depersonalizes them by calling them "clients." A family-centered policy and practice planning framework is identified, including its key phases (e.g., forming a vision, establishing missions, determining accountabilities, framing action plans). Examples derived from family-centered work in Florida provide concrete examples of the products this framework may yield.

Chapters 7, 8, and 9 are skills-based contributions. Chapter 7 focuses on how to structure a policy dialogue. Using four key examples, it illustrates how a family-centered perspective can be fostered by means of dialogue. Chapters 8 and 9 combine policies and practices. They describe policy-practice skills and abilities for developing family-centered agendas, developing working alliances, promoting widespread support, and engendering advocacy.

Chapters 10 and 11 take the analysis to an international scale. The focus is globalization and its companion processes, correlates, and consequences. These two chapters are, in fact, several chapters condensed into two. Chapter 11 introduces globalization and focuses on economic globalization. It explores challenges, changes, and opportunities associated with economic globalization. The effects on the welfare state are emphasized, especially the unfortunate tendency of the economy and its free markets to gain supremacy over government (the polity) and the needs of the people.

Chapter 11 picks up where chapter 10 leaves off. It addresses some of the psychological, social, cultural, and social-geographic correlates and consequences of globalization. It describes and explains the significance of people migrations and cultural flows. These twin flows produce a new polyculturalism and are responsible for the growing number of divided family systems and their long-distance neighborhood communities. Intercultural contact zones, called "scapes," are introduced, along with their new possibilities for grassroots social action. The chapter concludes with two frameworks for policy in the global world and key development principles that derive from chapters 10 and 11.

Finally, chapter 12 presents a summary call to action. It presents key propositions, or change theories, for family-centered policies and practices. Together these propositions signal future possibilities for a family-centered theory of action. Such a theory of action requires a new world ethic. Key transitions that will make up this ethic are identified briefly. This chapter and the book conclude with the call for a worldwide Family-watch, along with attendant commitments to action.

A FINAL NOTE: THE CHALLENGES OF GLOBAL DIVERSITY

Human cultures are inventive, resilient, and adaptable. It is possible in theory to conceive of surrogate social institutions other than the family. Such a theoretical possibility does not, however, square with the present-day priorities in the majority of nations and cultures. Nearly without exception, the family as an institution is assigned the same, exalted levels of importance. Certainly families' duties and responsibilities vary, just as their memberships do, but perceptions about their social, economic, and political significance are shared among nations.

The title for this book indicates the authors' intent to respond to international diversity, while building from successful exemplars and lessons learned. Our narrative is sometimes strong and forceful because the authors also are family advocates with clear, firm, pro-family value commitments.

On the other hand, the authors' suggestions and recommendations should not be interpreted as rigid prescriptions. For cultural diversity and culturally responsive practices are consistent themes in the narrative, and these twin themes signal needs to tailor and accommodate key ideas to local cultures and contexts.

Similarly, the authors' approach to family-centered policies and practices is process oriented. In fact, the chief contribution of this book may lie in its sensitizing perspectives (i.e., analytical frameworks). This is especially likely if these sensitizing perspectives and analytical frameworks facilitate critical assessments of past/present policies and practices; and if they help leaders and advocates to think, talk, act, and interact more effectively and appropriately.

In today's turbulent and rapidly changing world, basic values are being called into question. Are families important? Do they need to be supported and strengthened? Will they have food, decent housing, jobs, and related supports for their well-being? Will they be safe from the harms of patriarchy in their family and society? The answers seem so obvious, the need so important, that it seems redundant to raise these questions.

We authors, like you, want to live in a world in which these kinds of questions no longer need to be raised. The authors hope that this book reinforces new-century dialogue, action planning, and successful policy and practice innovations that prioritize and address family needs and wants. We aim to make a contribution to an international social movement, one that will result in a family-centered and family-supportive world community.

Katharine Briar-Lawson
Hal A. Lawson
Charles B. Hennon
Alan R. Jones

The Meaning and Significance of Families and Threats to Their Well-Being

Katharine Briar-Lawson, Hal A. Lawson,
and Charles B. Hennon, with Alan R. Jones

As a new century begins, the world community faces unprecedented challenges and changes (e.g., Bruce, Lloyd, & Leonard, 1995; Leidenfrost, 1992; Mason, Skolnick, & Sugeraman, 1998; Stoez & Saunders, 1999; United Nations, 1995e). For example, individuals and families are migrating and fleeing at unprecedented rates (Cohen & Deng, 1998), and families are affected as people move (Henderson, 1996; UNDP, 1999). Some families are becoming fragmented, and others are becoming destabilized (e.g., Booth, Crouter, & Lanvale, 1997). This unprecedented number of migrants, immigrants, and refugees challenges nations, especially ones that were once more culturally homogeneous. These nations now face the challenges of growing ethnic and cultural diversity. Families are affected as their nations address these new cultural and social geographic challenges, along with other new social, economic, political, and cultural realities. Social, cultural, and economic inequalities impose special difficulties and cause stress.

Life is certainly better for some families, especially some nations in the northern half of the globe (e.g., McMichael, 1996). Questions remain, however, about the sustainability of these families' lifestyles. Moreover, there are increasing insecurities about employment and growing inequities among individuals and families (Blau, 1999).

Three-quarters of the world's families are struggling to survive, especially families in the southern half of the globe (McMichael, 1996). As their well-being is threatened, families experience stress. Others experience violence, terror, and death. For example, new parents may wonder whether their baby will survive. Other family members may worry about the burdens of caregiving for their frail elders and children. Parents may worry about whether there will be enough jobs that provide sufficient income and important health benefits. Women may agonize over domestic violence and child abuse in their homes (Van Soest, 1997).

Vulnerable families may wonder whether concerned citizens, helping professionals, and policy makers are aware of their needs and will help address them. Their question is: Does anyone care about my plight? Stressed families often despair, because they assume that nobody cares. As families experience stress, there are ripple effects. A plethora of related challenges and problems arise, and they affect family members, other families, communities, states, provinces, entire nations, and regional alliances among nations.

What exactly is a family? Why are families so important? What is family well-being? How is family well-being threatened? Why are family rights important? These basic questions frame the following discussion. The purposes of this chapter are to enhance readers' understanding of families and family systems; to alert them to threats to families' well-being; to foster their understanding of the need for family-centered policies and practices; and to explore beginning parameters for pro-family policy and practice agendas.

The chapter begins with a sketch of some of the threats to family well-being. Then several definitions of families and family systems are presented. After individual and family rights are identified, the discussion turns to the special needs of girls and women under a system of hierarchical power relations called patriarchy. The chapter concludes with indices of individual and family well-being. These indices serve as goals for family advocates, helping professionals, and policy makers.

INDICES OF THREATS AND HARMS TO THE WORLD'S FAMILIES

Family well-being is threatened in many communities of the world. Many families are in crisis (United Nations, 1995e). To facilitate understanding of threats and harm, selective categories and indices are provided below. These indices also reflect how integral families are to many other societal institutions and service sectors. For example, health planning is also family-related planning.

Indices Related to Health, Well-Being, and Life Expectancy

- Conflicts in fifty-six countries where UNICEF works make it impossible for workers to deliver vaccines and provide immunizations to children in need (UNICEF, 1999).
- Every *day,* 35,000 children die from hunger and preventable-treatable diseases (Bradshaw & Wallace, 1996, p. 15).
- Every *day,* 11,000 children die, one every *eight seconds* from hunger and malnutrition (*New York Times,* November 13, 1996).
- In parts of sub-Saharan Africa, one woman dies for every fifty live births (versus Scandinavia where the death rate is one per 20,000 births).
- Of the 100 million children between the ages of seven and twelve who are not in school, two-thirds are girls (United Nations, 1993b). This inequitable access harms individuals and families because the schooling, education, and support of girls and women is one of the best ways to combat excessive poverty, population growth, and environmental destruction (Dasgupta, 1995).
- One-seventh of the world (840 million people) does not get enough to eat (Bender & Smith, 1997).
- 11 million young people between the ages of fifteen and twenty-four are suffering from AIDS (UNICEF, 1999).
- Each day some 6,000 persons die from AIDS in sub-Saharan Africa, resulting in an estimated 10.4 million orphans (Masland & Norland, 2000).
- Approximately 540 million children—one in every four—live in dangerous situations (UNICEF, 1999).

Poverty Indices

- Profound poverty affects at least 1 billion people; many earn less than a dollar a day (Kung, 1991).
- 35,000 children die each day because of poverty and the lack of access to life-saving technologies (United Nations, 1993j).
- The poorest three-quarters of humankind face growing malnutrition, starvation, resource depletion, unrest, enforced migration, and armed conflict (Hoogvelt, 1997; McMichael, 1996).
- The stresses of poverty and the associated demands of survival are responsible for rapid and uneven population expansions in areas al-

ready impacted by too many people and high poverty. Adults may have more children than usual to expand their labor pool; and as food-producing lands decline, more and more families migrate to cities already impacted by poverty (Bender & Smith, 1997; Dasgupta, 1995; Ray, 1998).

- Nations with the highest levels of social, political, and economic inequalities—many associated with poverty rates—tend to have the lowest average life expectancies (Sen, 1999; Wilkinson, 1996).

Environmental Degradation Indices Associated with Family Poverty

- Population pressure in many developing countries is depleting local agricultural resources, while more farm output is needed for feeding growing numbers of people (Dasgupta, 1995; Kennedy, 1993, pp. 12–13). Examples include the overgrazing of the African savannas, the erosion of the Amazon rain forests, and the salinization of land from India to Kazakhstan.
- Every year, huge sections of tropical forest are destroyed, some lost forever (Kung, 1991); in turn, deforestation causes the erosion of precious soils necessary for plant growth. Food and oxygen production are reduced.
- If present global warming trends continue, the temperature of the earth's atmosphere could rise dramatically each succeeding decade —between 1.5 and 4.5 degrees Celsius—with a resultant rise in sea levels. Global warming presents disastrous consequences, particularly for the coastal areas of all the earth's landmasses (Kung, 1991, p. 2).

Economic and Technological Indices of Need and Misplaced Priorities

- In 1992, world military spending totaled $815 billion, equaling the combined income of 49 percent of the world's people. Developing countries spent $125 billion. By allocating 25 percent of this $125 billion, the developing nations could have met many of their needs for health, education, and family planning. Twelve percent of this amount would have provided basic health care, immunization, and safer drinking water; and it would have reduced malnutrition. Four percent would have halved adult illiteracy, provided universal public education, and addressed educational inequities between girls and boys. Eight percent would have provided all men and women with a family planning pack, contributing to the stabilization of the world's population (Goldthorpe, 1996, p. 82).

- Every month, the world's economic system adds more burdens to the catastrophic debt that debilitates people of the developing nations. As debts increase, social and health services are reduced, currencies are devalued, and the purchasing power of individuals and families declines. So does their well-being. (Bradshaw & Wallace, 1996; Goldthorpe, 1996; McMichael, 1996).

- The technology revolution involving computers is taking place overwhelmingly in economically advanced nations. These nations have slow-growing or declining populations. At the same time, developing nations with burgeoning populations lack resources, trained personnel, needed funding, and appropriate investment strategies. In some cases, nations most in need have governing elites and ideological prejudices oriented against technological change (Kennedy, 1993). The result is a growing gap between the "have" nations and the "have-not" nations (Athanasiou, 1996; Reich, 1993). Individuals and families in have-not nations—many in the global south—are disadvantaged, and as technology growth and development continue, their disadvantaged position is exacerbated.

- The gaps between "have" and "have-not" nations are growing—and so are the gaps between "have" and "have-not" families within some of these nations (e.g., Hoogvelt, 1997; Jordan, 1998; Reich, 1993; UNDP, 1999). As these gaps grow, the well-being of millions of the world's families will continue to deteriorate, absent appropriate policy changes (Kennedy, 1993).

- Technologies employed by multinational corporations based in economically advanced nations may exacerbate harm to poorer countries and their families. Although these technologies may promote industrialization and employment initiatives, they also promote monetarized economies in substitution for indigenous, cooperative exchange networks (Bradshaw & Wallace, 1996; Goldthorpe, 1996; Kennedy, 1993; McMichael, 1996).

- As companies become "exporters" in a global economy, and as production technologies eliminate needs for semiskilled workers, middle-income workers (often men) lose their jobs and an informal employment sector grows, usually employing women and children. Families often lack living wages and health benefits.

- Rapid population growth, diminishing resources, insufficient food and inadequate food supplies, unemployment, poverty, and lack of education are responsible for significant migrations to cities (Dasgupta, 1995; McMichael, 1996; Ray, 1998). Forced migration may detract from well-being. It fragments families, and it contributes to environmental deterioration and destruction.
- In turn, these problems may trigger conflict and war over boundaries, water, and grazing rights. In fact, more armed conflicts among nations may be expected, including the prospect of another world war (Kennedy, 1993).
- Sufficient amounts of food are being produced, and there is potential to produce more. All of the world's people, especially its children, can be fed. The problem lies in the distribution and use of food, not in its availability (Bender & Smith, 1997).
- Four-fifths of the world's 5 billion people produce food and consumer goods for the well-to-do one-fifth, but the majority lack the income and resources to enjoy the food and goods they produce (McMichael, 1996).

Indices of Family Stress, Safety, and Security

- At least 26 million refugees experience stress, destabilization, and related health and mental health problems (Henderson, 1996).
- In addition to individuals, many refugees are families; 80 percent of refugees are women and children (United Nations, 1995d).
- The social and economic development agendas of developed nations often compete with the cultural and religious factions of developing nations. Resistance follows, including rising terrorism (Barber, 1996).
- In world conflicts, families—especially women and children—are the targets and victims of violence. Since World War II, 20 million people have died and 60 million have been wounded. Eighty percent have been civilians, most of them women and children. Children have been conscripted into military and paramilitary forces. Sometimes they have been required to kill members of their own families. Land mines have been disguised as toys and placed on playgrounds and schools.
- 1.5 million children have been killed by wars, and 4 million others have been disabled (United Nations World Conference on Human Rights Preparatory Committee, 1993).

- Caregiving responsibilities are increasing worldwide as the "graying of wealthy nations" increases—that is, as the number of elders grows (United Nations, 1993f). Caregivers, usually women, may have responsibilities for as many as four or five generations of family members. In brief, aging issues also are family concerns and women's issues. Stress increases because women caregivers also are required to work outside their home full-time.

Indices of Governmental Capacities and Willingness to Invest in Families

- The number of industrialized nations dismantling their social welfare programs is growing (Geyer, Ingebritsen, & Moses, 2000; Goldthorpe, 1996; Jordan, 1998; Pierson, 1996). In their joint quests to attract and maintain multinational corporations and promote economic development, industrialized nations are revoking the policies that once supported poor and vulnerable individuals and families.
- Global economic development and exchange networks, in combination with loans through international monetary bodies, create long-term dependency patterns in developing nations. Faced with inflationary spirals, developing nations are often required to borrow more; and as they do, their currencies are devalued. For families, this pattern translates into decreased purchasing power and discretionary economic resources; their well-being is eroded (Bradshaw & Wallace, 1996; Goldthorpe, 1996; McMichael, 1996; Midgley, 1997).
- Deregulation of environmental and labor standards, in combination with subcontracting, encourages a significant increase in labor and production in the informal sector of national economies, especially in the developing nations. Concentrated in cities, the informal sector is built on domestic, low-wage labor performed disproportionately by women and children—who frequently do not receive social and health benefits for their work (Dangler, 1994; Nuralamin, 1996; Parker, 1994; Sanyal, 1996).
- Even when families do not move, and jobs are maintained, real wages and associated benefits for many workers in the well-to-do nations actually decline against the rate of inflation (Reich, 1993; Thurow, 1996). The trickle-down effects of economic growth do not automatically mean improvements in individual and family well-being.

- Indigenous economies, especially culturally proscribed microenterprises and cooperative exchange networks, increasingly are replaced
by transnational corporations and trade agreements that deregulate
standards for clean air, water, working conditions, and safe and
healthy consumer goods. Environmental deterioration, pollution,
and deteriorating workplaces follow (Henderson, 1996).

Family Threats and Crises Signal Public Policy and Practice Needs

Individually and collectively, these indicators serve as reminders of
unmet needs and as warnings about the future well-being of the world's
families. Although it is tempting to assume that these problems are restricted to the developing nations of the world, the evidence suggests
otherwise (Sen, 1999).

Dramatic changes—locally, regionally, nationally, and globally—
provide important opportunities, policy, and practice for learning and
development. To benefit from these opportunities, governmental leaders,
policy makers, helping professionals, family advocates, and citizens at
large need to be better prepared for the important challenges at hand
(United Nations, 1995a, 1995e).

Strategic and effective action depends in part on understanding family-
centered policies and practices (e.g., Baker, 1995; Cass & Cappo, 1995;
Hartman & Laird, 1983; Hooper-Briar & Lawson, 1995; United Nations, 1995c, 1995e). Strategic and effective action on behalf of families
also requires firm commitments to evaluate policies and practices. Evaluation designs are needed that facilitate learning and continuous improvements (Argyris & Schön, 1996; Schön & Rein, 1994).

A basic question must be addressed first. Why invest in families?

THE SIGNIFICANCE OF FAMILIES

Families are important social institutions. Social institutions are culturally prescribed and inscribed, meaning that most institutions—especially
families—bear the "signature" of their surrounding culture(s) (United
Nations, 1993b). Different in some ways because of their cultural con-
text(s), social institutions such as the families also may share common
features.

Family as a Social Construction

A social institution results when *a* way of doing things becomes *the* way (Berger & Luckmann, 1967). The "family" is thus one way to organize individuals. It is not the only way. In other words, families are socially constructed and constituted entities. They are not inevitable.

Families as social institutions are powerful agents of socialization (e.g., Kamerman & Kahn, 1978; National Commission on Families and Public Policies, 1978; United Nations, 1992c, 1993b). Social institutions, and especially the family, tend to typecast people, social relationships, and practices. They imply history and social control. Through socialization and social control strategies, institutions structure and reward standardized cultural practices. These practices are taken for granted and viewed as "natural" cultural traditions (Berger & Luckmann, 1967).

On the other hand, nations and their societal cultures differ. So do their social institutions. And so do their families.

For example, in some societal cultures the practices associated with marriage are viewed as structuring "a family." In other places, this idea of the traditional nuclear family is not evident. If it is evident, it may be accompanied by other ways to structure a family, such as developing a committed relationship. For example, in nations such as Sweden and Belize, partners engaged in committed relationships make up half, or more, of families. In still other societal cultures, the family is associated with nature, including corn and other plants (Trzcinski, 1995). In other words, families are viewed as parts of the natural environment and as enabling and sustaining life. In short, just as culture is selective, so are families as social institutions.

Analyzing Families as Social Institutions

Social institutions can be analyzed by means of three categories of questions. Policy makers, practitioners, and advocates can inquire into family forms, contents, and relations (United Nations, 1992c).

Questions about the *forms* of families address the ways in which they are defined, especially the criteria for inclusion and exclusion into the category "family." For example, who or what is a family? As a newcomer to a societal culture, how would you identify a family? (One approach to these questions is presented later in this chapter.)

Questions about the *contents* of families as social institutions address the meanings and knowledge conveyed through families as socializing agents (United Nations, 1992c). What is learned and conveyed via family membership? What roles, duties, and assignments are involved, and who must learn and perform them? Where duties are concerned, who does what, when, where, and why? What are the behavioral rules in families? Who has the ultimate authority, and how does religion influence this cultural power? What are the rules for family membership?

There are two sets of questions about *relations*. One set addresses the ways in which power, authority, rewards, and other resources are distributed in families. Who has access to power and other resources? Who benefits most and least from family life? Who sets the rules in families? These are questions of family politics (United Nations, 1993g).

In addition to micropolitics in the family, families are subjects for macropolitical questions. Macropolitical questions address the relationship between families and other cultural, political, and economic institutions. How do families affect the economy, the political system, and the educational system? In turn, how do these and other societal institutions impact the family?

In short, these three kinds of questions (about form, contents, and relations) create a framework for understanding and analyzing institutionalized family systems. Place and context matter. In other words, the questions may be the same, but the answers will vary as a function of unique community, societal, national, and regional world contexts. In turn, local differences and uniqueness help to promote an understanding of cultural, national, and regional history and diversity. Indeed, the growing diversity of families and family systems is a cornerstone for family policies and practices (Hennon, 2000).

DEFINING THE FAMILY

So, what exactly is a family? How would you know one if you saw one? As with so many questions, the answers depend upon whom you ask, where you ask, when, under what circumstances, and why.

Diverse Families

Families around the world exhibit various kinds of forms and living arrangements (United Nations, 1993c). These daily living arrangements are expressed primarily in simple daily tasks and negotiations, which family members perform. In many cases, family members co-determine these arrangements and functions (United Nations, 1993c). They know who does what, where, when, why, and how. Family members gain meanings and identities through these arrangements and duties (after Knowles, 1996, p. 13).

Families and their individual members develop unique ways of communicating, perceiving, behaving, and making meaning of their experiences. Sometimes these family meaning systems and knowledge structures are implicit, not explicit. In other words, families' beliefs, knowledge, and action systems may even be specially "coded." In some cases only the family itself may understand these codes. These coded meaning systems and knowledge structures help constitute profound differences among families, both within and across cultures and nations.

To put it another way, families are not once-and-for-all, static or rigid entities, nor are families islands unto themselves. For example, there are multiple dynamics within family systems. There are dynamics involving each family's internal and external environments; dynamics involving other families; dynamics involving other social institutions and organizations; and dynamics involving the larger society and even the global community (Milardo, 1988).

For many families, these tasks and arrangements are private matters, not public concerns. Therefore, one way to define, and inquire into, a family is to use the definition, identities, and meanings of its members. In many cases, family members know best their boundaries and meaning systems. These boundaries and meaning systems are self-defined and also help define them. Their stories of experience, or narratives, are rich sources of knowledge and understanding (e.g., Becker, 1997; Knowles, 1996).

Lived Experiences as Framing Definitions

Family members' answers to questions about what a family is, and does, reveal family forms that include nuclear families, but also transcend them (United Nations, 1992c). When members are asked what they mean by a family, their responses often differ. Moreover, families' responses may diverge from predetermined meanings and categories that survey researchers and demographers impose upon them. For example, single adults engage in familial relationships beyond their own birth families (Eichler, 1997).

Although individual and family responses are diverse, there tend to be four common elements in these responses, i.e., in members' accounts and life stories. Individuals are connected with their families because

1. they have a shared sense of history;
2. they experience some degree of emotional bonding;
3. they have constructed their individual identities in relation to one another, meaning that their personal identities are inseparable in some ways from their family identity; and
4. individually and together they devise strategies for meeting the needs, wants, and aspirations of individual family members, the group as a whole, or both.

Any working definition of families incorporates these four elements. At the same time, however, those definitions must be flexible and adaptable to diverse societal cultures. They must accommodate the lived experiences of diverse people around the world. In other words, these four elements may be universal, but other elements are particularistic. Diverse families in diverse parts of the world must be understood in their surrounding contexts. So rather than forcing outsiders' definitions on families, analysts need to ask family members, and to expect diversity.

For example, box 1.1 offers examples of families rendered through the eyes of children and one elder. These examples show how families, as defined by their members, may differ from definitions derived from legal codes, textbook definitions, or sociological jargon.

In brief, "family" is not a simple social institution, especially in an international context. Amid so much diversity, it is necessary to proceed beyond the singular, traditional idea of "family." It is helpful to focus on the broader concept of "family system."

The Idea of Family Systems

Clearly, some reserve the concept of "family" to mean the nuclear family. Once a global perspective is adopted, however, the need arises for a more comprehensive and inclusive conception of families (United Nations, 1992c). This conception must encompass the nuclear family and, at the same time, transcend it. The cultural selectivity and limits of the nuclear family must be avoided. *Ethnocentrism*—viewing and evaluating diverse cultural practices and people through the lens provided by personal and local practices—is an ever-present danger.

BOX 1.1

FAMILIES IN THE EYES OF CHILDREN

Juputu, like countless other nine year olds, considers himself part of a family; however, his family consists of three other children and four adults. Three of the children are those born of his parents; his other sister was brought into the family when her parents (his aunt and uncle) and other siblings died in war. The two other adults are good friends of his parents. Their children also died in war. These eight people reside together, and all the adults take turns in caring for the children and their socialization. Because each adult is a caregiver, Juputa thinks of all four as his parents. He sees all the members of his household as being part of his family system. He treats them like family and they treat him likewise.

Saia, sixteen years old, lives in a commune. She has fourteen other children around her. There are several adults who help support and supervise these fifteen children; the children also beg and do odd jobs to bring in money. Everyone does housekeeping chores. On some weekends Saia goes home to be with her biological parents. The time she spends with the commune results in her having a sense of two families, because both her own parents and the other adults and children in the commune perform similar functions. Both, in similar ways, provide food, shelter, clothing; set and enforce rules and a moral code; provide care for the sick; and give love, support, and security to Saia and the other members. Saia's family system, then, includes two groups equally important—her parents and the commune.

Jason is also sixteen. His parents divorced soon after his birth. While Jason lived primarily with his mother over the years, he and his father remained close. Jason has always considered his dad as part of his family, and resided in his household on weekends and school vacations. His father remarried twice and additional children were born. Jason lived with his "half-sibs" and stepmothers, and grew to accept and love them. These people gave him support and provided care when he needed it. Even with the divorce of his father from his second wife, Jason still considers these siblings to be family and has fond memories of them and his stepmothers. Jason's definition of family includes his father's two subsequent wives, his half-sibs, and his biological mother.

Sarah lives in a home in which she, at age nine, is the oldest of two children born to her mother, whom she now calls Mommy One. Mommy One is living in an intimate relationship with Mommy Two. The Mommies became partners after the death of Sarah's father. The household contains two foster-care children both Mommies are seeking to adopt. Sarah sees both Mommies, her sister, as well as the two foster children, as her family. She also thinks of Sandy, the neighbor who is with them daily, as part of her family system. Sandy takes Sarah to school each day and on weekend adventures once in a while. Sandy also helps with the other children, who go to her house after school while both Mommies are working. Sarah knows she can count on Sandy. Sometimes Sandy gives money to Sarah's Mommies when there is not enough to make ends meet.

Mona is seventy-six. She has been single all her life. She considers her family to be her three neighbors who look after her daily as she recovers from hip surgery. She lost most of her kin in war and was able to migrate to a western European community where health supplies were available to treat her diabetes. While her household consists of her and her cat, she defines her three neighbors as her family.

The concept of a *family system* defined by members themselves helps prevent ethnocentric thinking, and it accommodates international diversity in family forms, contents, and relations. This international perspective on family systems offers an important benefit. Policy leaders, helping professionals, and family advocates may be able to avoid endless and conflict-producing debates about the criteria involved in determining what "real families" are, or must become (Hennon, 1981; Trost, 1996).

Family system is, of course, a metaphor.[1] It involves seeing individuals and families selectively—in systems terms (e.g., Anderson & Sabatelli, 1995). Family system is a global concept that helps to foster an understanding of the diversity found in families as well as some of the universal functions that families perform. In other words, despite international diversity in their composition and organization, families are alike in fundamental ways. They often have the same basic needs, share many of the same duties, and confront similar challenges (e.g., National Commission on Families and Public Policies, 1978; United Nations, 1992c).

As the process of globalization acts to shrink the world community, families also may become aware of their similarities, commonalties, and differences. Increasingly families may begin to define themselves as others around the globe have defined themselves.

Family systems, on the other hand, are not simple structures, but open and ever evolving. They are socially constructed by their members and socially constituted by other people and institutions (after Hennon & Radina, in press).[2]

Nor are families easily isolated for analysis and intervention apart from their environments or ecologies. Families shape, and are shaped by, their ecologies or near environments (United Nations, 1993b). Families also are adaptable. They may reconfigure themselves over their life courses as they strive to accommodate to internal changes and the pressures of the external environments (Bruce, Lloyd, & Leonard, 1995).

Thus, the family systems concept emphasizes family structure (i.e., the composition and organization of families) as well as the duties families perform (Anderson & Sabatelli, 1995). It calls attention to family members' interactions, internal relationships, external relationships, and surrounding environments and cultural contexts. Moreover, family members define their family systems, and, in turn, these systems help define their members.

Another Analytical Frame: Social and Ecological (Relational) Analysis

Socioecological analysis (e.g., Lawson, 1992; Trzcinski, 1995) is a close companion of systems thinking. Both kinds of thinking and analysis focus on relationships, especially on patterns of dependence and interdependence. Each frame is selective. Each emphasizes some features of families and family systems at the expense of others. For example, systems frames derive from the machine metaphor, and this metaphor influences perceptions and language (e.g., Schön & Rein, 1994). Socioecological frames derive from the metaphor of harmonious, symbiotic relationships among bio-natural, social, and cultural ecosystems.

Socioecological analyses attend to interactions among people and their social institutions and their natural environments. Place and context do matter, and they are weighed in to every analysis. That is, socioecological analyses of families take into account their social geographies (e.g., Curtis & Jones, 1998).

For example, the social ecologies of families can be both external and internal. Internal social ecologies refer to relationships among members. External social ecologies refer to families' physical and social environments, especially families' interdependence with other social institutions (United Nations, 1993c).

For example, it is possible to trace ripple effects associated with a plant closing. These ripple effects begin with the layoff of a worker (parent). They continue when the parent is considered unemployed—and begins to define herself in this way. Family stress follows, and so do personal-social problems. In turn, family stress often is associated with children's school problems, child abuse and neglect, and possibly substance abuse (Benoît-Guilbot, 1994; Briar, 1988; International Network on Unemployment and Social Work, 1987; Vosler, 1996).

The social aspect of socioecological analysis emphasizes power and authority issues and relationships. Sometimes socioecological analysis is given a shorthand definition—*relational analysis*—because it emphasizes power and authority relationships.

Regardless of the label, the analytical lens is the same. This lens focuses on intra- and interfamilial negotiations and contests for control related to cultural authority, social power (power in social, political, and economic structure; power over resources; power to act or agency), and economic power and privilege. There are pivotal questions to be asked.

Whose knowledge, rules, values, meaning systems, and cultural practices have the highest priority? How will they result in ideals regarding just societies, especially improved individual and family well-being? How do practices and policies, families, and other social institutions relate to one another? Do they support one another or do they work at cross-purposes? What power and authority do families enjoy in the policy-making process? In practices and policies that affect them?

Relational analysis usually involves power and authority differentials within and among families. For example, it involves power differentials between men and women, a problem that is explored later in this chapter.

Relational analysis also paves the way for empowerment-oriented helping strategies. As the idea of empowerment implies, relational analysis involves needs for power sharing with families (United Nations,

1993g). Similarly, families are active agents who also exercise their power (United Nations, 1995c). That is, individuals and families are not powerless; they can make changes. Relational analysis makes it possible to understand why some individuals, groups, and families conform to policies and practices; or, make mutual accommodations; or, temporarily comply (postponing firm decisions and commitments); or, resist passively; or, actively sabotage. Systems analytical frames tend not to emphasize these important power dynamics.

On the other hand, dichotomies are not helpful. It is beneficial to integrate relational, socioecological frames and systems frames. A hybrid theoretical frame results. This hybrid frame enhances understanding and analysis because of the relationships it emphasizes and the patterns of interdependence it illuminates. It helps to foster an appreciation of how families may change and improve. It may encourage a view of families as active agents, able to exercise control over their lives and able to help others and themselves (United Nations, 1995c). It also prevents an inappropriate dichotomy, one that pits individuals against families.

Beyond the Individual-Family Dichotomy

Planning, policies, and practices in many nations are predicated on a problematic dichotomy. Policy makers and helping professionals often tend to focus on individuals (e.g., children, *or* women, *or* elders) *or* families.

A hybrid analytical frame emphasizes *relationships* between individuals and families. It prioritizes policies and practices that attend simultaneously to individual *and* family systems needs, wants, and aspirations.

For example, all individuals need social support networks, and families may be the most important of these social support networks (Eichler, 1997; Milardo, 1988). As they act as social support networks, families reflect and shape individuals. Children are obvious beneficiaries, especially when their families promote healthy growth and development. Families also give children a strong identity. Through families, children, elders, and other individuals gain a sense of "self," a reflective, connected identity, of who they are relative to their physical and social environments. Furthermore, families play an important role in how adults come to know themselves and, in turn, how they define themselves.

Families are rich sources of language, other important symbols, traditions, rituals, and stories. All give meaning to the past/present experiences, identities, and orientations of the individual and the family. For example, individuals learn about their histories, their cultures, and heritage in family systems. Through family interactions, individuals learn to make sense of the world around them. The learning and interaction of the family are continuous, and they often change over time and in different contexts.

Together, this interaction and learning make up the process of socialization. The family is an important agent of socialization in most societies today. Family socialization is not, however, limited to children (United Nations, 1993c). In fact, children socialize their parents and other family members. Similarly, adult parents may socialize their parents (i.e., their children's grandparents). In short, families are strong socializing agents, with all family members being influenced by the interaction and learning that occurs among them (United Nations Economic Commission, 1993; United Nations, 1994f). Who one is or wishes to become; how one thinks, communicates, and behaves; the values, norms, and beliefs one endorses; conceptions of knowledge and how it is obtained—all these and countless other characteristics of each person frequently originate in families.

One's sense of human rights also may originate in families. Indeed, the rights of individuals need to be expanded to encompass family rights. Family rights may safeguard both individual and family well-being.

FROM INDIVIDUAL RIGHTS TO INDIVIDUAL AND FAMILY RIGHTS

Individual and family rights are relevant building blocks for improved policies and practices. Family rights are cited in United Nations documents (e.g., Center for the Study of Human Rights, 1994, 1996; United Nations, 1988a, 1988b, 1991b, 1992d, 1992e, 1992f, 1993i, 1995a; United Nations Commission on Human Rights, 1989). Individual and family economic, social, cultural, civil, and political rights need to be viewed as connected and interdependent (United Nations, 1995a).

Once these rights (and documents that proclaim them) gain legitimacy, legal action may be taken when they are violated. Litigation is important. It often provides the equivalent of a back door to changes in policy and, in turn, improvements in practice. For example, rights can be translated into governmental entitlements for individuals, groups, and families (e.g., United Nations, 1993j). Similarly, families may help safeguard their members' basic human rights. In some nations, family rights and human rights may become indivisible.

For example, the democratic rights of citizenship, including freedom of speech and freedom of belief, are inseparable from each individual's and each family's rights to well-being. Especially in democracies, well-being, evidenced in *freedom from* want, basic necessity, and moral exclusion, is a prerequisite for *freedom to* act as a citizen (Sen, 1999). Many governmental reforms aimed at promoting individual and family self-sufficiency—reforms that may relieve governments of social welfare responsibilities—miss this important relationship between well-being and effective citizenship. Individuals and families who are not free because they lack the basic necessities of life and the employment opportunities that provide them dignity and equality cannot be expected to act as independent, strong citizens who promote civil society, strengthen democracy, and enjoy self-sufficiency (Bauman, 1998; Sen, 1999). Said another way, vulnerable individuals and families cannot be expected to "pull themselves up by their own bootstraps" if their basic needs for well-being are not met, and when they do not enjoy freedom from oppression, repression, and moral exclusion (e.g., Jordan, 1998; Sen, 1999).

This view of rights is relational, and it is as important in so-called industrialized or high-income nations as it is in developing nations. Leaders in developed nations may decry the lack of political rights for families in developing nations, while remaining silent on the rights of individuals and families inside their own borders. At the same time they offer social development and aid programs for other nations, they may ignore social and economic development needs of their own. In the United States, for example, the social development challenges confronting vulnerable children and families in urban segregated areas may be as formidable as some of the development challenges in developing nations (e.g., Jordan, 1998; Sen, 1999).

Comprehensive individual and family rights agendas may be viewed as universal (United Nations, 1993j). They need to guide policy and practice. For example, the following are some operational categories of individual and family rights set forth in United Nations documents. They provide concrete foci for the implementation of individual and family rights agendas.

Family Formation and Marital Dissolution

- The rights of men and women of full age, regardless of race, nationality, or religion, to marry and form a family

- The right to determine how many children a family wants to bear
- Full equal rights of men and women to marry and to divorce

Family Well-Being

- The right to a standard of living adequate for the health and well-being of the self and the family—including food, clothing, housing, and medical care and necessary social services
- The right to social security when a decent standard of living cannot be assured because of, for example, unemployment, lack of livelihood, sickness, disability, widowhood, and old age
- The right of children to enjoy healthy, harmonious development in a family environment of happiness, love, and understanding; the right to be protected by family, society, and state; and to be separated from families only as a last resort
- The rights of families to be protected and assisted in the care and education of children; and, for parents, to keep their children unless their safety and security is compromised

Family Equality

- The family as a fundamental human right; the family as a basic instrument for existing individual human rights
- The rights of girls and women to expect and secure equality in families and in society
- The equal rights of all family members

Clearly, these rights are intended to be international and national in scope. For example the right to stay together as a family, including the right to move to another nation when the corporate employer moves (Jordan, 1998), is both national and international. Some depend upon other requisite rights.

Similarly, freedom from poverty is a requisite right (e.g., Bauman, 1998; Jordan, 1998; Ray, 1998; Sen, 1999). Individual and family well-being, as well as social and economic development, depend fundamentally on alleviating poverty and its correlates. Full equality requires role changes among men and women and their sharing of responsibilities—for example, for children's upbringing and caregiving of frail elders.

Moreover, a focus upon individual and family rights involves more than a discussion of human entitlements, which are mandated, or provided outside of family systems. Families and family systems also are mechanisms for the expression, implementation, and evaluation of these rights (United Nations, 1995a). In other words, both the internal and external ecologies of families—their micropolitics, social norms, and rules—should be structured in relation to individual and family rights.

For example, it is counterproductive and harmful when women elders enjoy rights in society writ large, but are denied them in their families. Children may enjoy rights and entitlements outside the family, but be denied them in family systems. Thus, families are not merely beneficiaries of rights and entitlements. They also are developers and enforcers of rights and entitlements (United Nations High Commissioner for Refugees, 1991). Where rights are concerned, ethnocentrism is a key problematic. The world community continues to struggle with cultural diversity and difference.

In this perspective *universal individual and family rights* are important. They provide a global standard, a criterion measure, against which to assess efforts to enhance individual and family well-being. When individual and family rights are weighed, it is not an "anything goes" situation. If children are neglected, if women are exploited and abused, if elders are not supported or cared for, then appropriate corrective actions must be taken. These universal standards do not allow individual and family harms to be excused and justified as culturally appropriate and congruent. Once individual and family rights are deemed universal, and then violated, intervention strategies are warranted.

Gender equality and equity issues are especially important to this individual and family rights agenda. Many women's issues double as individual and family policy, rights, and practice issues (e.g., Dornbush & Strober, 1988).

WOMEN'S NEEDS AS FAMILY SYSTEMS ISSUES: THE CHALLENGE OF PATRIARCHY AND GENDER VIOLENCE

Patriarchy is a system of power relations that privileges men. Patriarchy involves the negotiation of gender roles and relations, including the allocation of power, authority, and privilege. It is pervasive in families, communities, and nations around the world (Riley, 1997). It invites controversy and is interpreted in different ways.

For example, some analysts view patriarchy as a foundation of civilization (Fuchs, 1972). For others, it is a destructive force (Moghadam,

1996). Some analysts link patriarchy with the growth of poverty (Brai-dotti, Charkiewicz, & Wireinga, 1994). Still others associate patriarchy with the rise of the work ethic, the industrial revolution, and the industrial welfare state (Bauman, 1998; Giddens, 1994).

Despite these differences in analysis and interpretation, common elements can be identified. To begin with, when patriarchy reigns, women and girls are second-class citizens (e.g., Lerner, 1986). Patriarchy also serves to deny to girls and women their universal individual and family rights. They may be viewed as property, as objects owned and controlled by men. Even worse, women may be viewed as commodities. Furthermore, patriarchy is a root cause of violence, especially violence against women. It is also a leading correlate of poverty and declining well-being in family systems (Riley, 1997).

Patriarchy lurks beneath the surface of observable, daily interactions and routines. It is embedded in the private spheres of the family. Men exert pressures and apply sanctions to keep these power relations intact. They work to control women and girls, requiring them to remain quiet, obedient, and compliant.

Thus, women and girls are forced, or persuaded, to view intrafamilial issues as private matters. All issues, especially gender equity and equality issues, are to "remain in the family" because they are personal and interpersonal issues. They are not to be shared with outsiders. Domestic violence, child and elder abuse and neglect, inequitable access to food, resources, schooling, and other important issues—all must be concealed, kept within the private domain of the family. Women and girls are often required to "normalize" harmful and unjust practices controlled by men and in service of their power.

For example, the distribution of food at home is both a patriarchal and family policy issue. In spite of many feeding policies and programs to address starvation, anemia, and malnutrition, women and girls are profoundly more at risk than boys and men. Preferential feeding patterns in families put the food needs of men and boys ahead of the needs of women and girls (Ray, 1998; Riley, 1997). These practices often are deeply embedded in other cultural traditions. Policy problems also may contribute to them.

Women do 90 percent of the world's food gathering. Yet, they and their daughters have inequitable access to food (e.g., Ray, 1998; Riley, 1997; Wetzel & Campling, 1993). Malnourished, lactating mothers along with their babies may suffer irreversible and permanent consequences. Disabilities, retarded growth, and the death of infants are all correlates of poor nutrition among mothers. Young girls denied access to food and nourishment are less likely to bear wellborn children. Their children may become permanent dependents as impairment takes a toll on health and independent functioning. Dependency often tracks into poverty. The poorest of the poor around the world tend to be women and girls.

Advocates need to be alert to other signs of patriarchy. One such sign is the objectification and depersonalization of women. For example, a husband refers to a woman, even in her presence, as "the wife." Another sign is treating women and girls as a commodity—as a sexualized product to be exchanged and used in markets. A third sign is the treatment of women as property, including the process of selling their labor.

Gender violence is a fourth sign of patriarchy. Domestic violence (stripped of some of its patriarchal connections in the labeling process) is a worldwide phenomenon, affecting up to half the women in the world (Van Soest, 1997). Gender violence refers to the harms done to women because they are women. Examples include rape, female genital mutilation, female infanticide, burning new brides, and sex-related crimes (Schuler, 1992, p.10). Other harms involve physical and psychological abuse, deprivation of resources (nutrition, education, livelihood supports), and feelings of inferiority caused by hierarchical relations. In addition, when women's labor in the home is seen as separate from economic productivity, this exploitation is a form of gender violence (Schuler, 1992).

In some nations and cultures, the community and the state legitimate and provide the mechanisms by which men acquire proprietary rights over women. In short, some social policy actually structures the conditions for gender violence (Van Soest, 1997). To reiterate, patriarchy is constructed by men. When it is maintained and supported by men and by the compliance and consent of women, it serves men's interests.

Relational analysis signals solutions: power and authority must be redistributed (United Nations, 1993g). Redistribution involves micropolitics in the family and macropolitics in each nation and in the international arena (United Nations, 1991a, 1993i). Both local, bottom-up strategies and national-international, top-down strategies are needed.

Indeed, the slogan for the United Nation's International Year of the Family (1991a; 1993f) heralded the family as the "smallest democracy" at the heart of society. This slogan implied that the relationships among family members should be democratized—all members, especially women, should have equal voices and power. It follows that democratized family policy and practices should address patriarchy and its correlates. In other words, patriarchy is not inevitable, nor is it "the natural order of things."

For example, Levinson's studies in central Thailand (1989, cited in Schuler, 1992, p. 17) yielded an important finding—namely, that such hierarchical and violent relations did not exist. Sexual division of labor did not occur. On the other hand, in seventy-five out of ninety societies in which female battering occurred, patriarchy was implicated (Levinson, 1989). The predictors of battering were sexual economic inequality; the routine use of physical violence to solve problems; male authority in family decision-making; and divorce restrictions for women. The United Nations has played a pivotal role in attempting to eliminate gender violence and patriarchy. Beginning in 1945, a United Nations charter stated that men and women have equal rights (Pietilä & Vickers, 1996).

Considerable challenges remain for policy makers, helping professionals, and family advocates. The basic idea that women's challenges double as family challenges and needs is new to some people. Although the manifestations and implications of patriarchy are not new, it will not be easy to convince men in diverse cultures around the world to change —especially when patriarchy is viewed as inseparable from religious beliefs and traditions (Fuchs, 1972).

A new-century agenda for individuals and families must center on issues of inequality in the family and society and globe (e.g., Baber & Allen, 1992; Berheide & Chow, 1994; Burggraf, 1997). Foreshadowing the specific recommendations and alternatives that follow, in subsequent chapters, this one concludes by identifying key indices of individual and family well-being.

EXPLORING THE PARAMETERS OF INDIVIDUAL AND FAMILY WELL-BEING

Earlier in this chapter, indices of threats to individual and family well-being were presented. Here, indices of individual and family well-being are identified. These indices may be viewed as standards for effective policies and as targets for effective practices. These indices also may facilitate the implementation of individual and family rights, both national and international.

The categories and indices for individual and family well-being offered below are derived from several sources (e.g., Arendt, 1958; Brandon, 1996; Radin, 1996). Like all categories and indices, they are unavoidably selective and incomplete. In other words, those indices are merely examples. Policy makers, helping professionals, and advocates are invited to amend and expand this list.

Nurturance

- Satisfactory emotional, cognitive, and social supports, such as nurturing relationships; being well treated by others; having access to networks for help and support
- Positive kin and nonkin affiliations and attachments that nurture development throughout the life cycle, creating trust, social supports, problem-solving resources

The Conditions for Optimal Development

- Satisfactory physical supports such as food, shelter, safety
- Freedom from oppression, repression, discrimination, patriarchy, and moral exclusion
- Freedom to act as an agent on the behalf of the self and one's family and community
- Access to developmental supports, including being well born, with adequate prenatal care, freedom from toxins, inequities, or harms such as unequal feeding patterns in the home, unequal access to jobs, wages, and education
- Ability to access requisite resources, services, and supports to prevent unnecessary stress and harm
- Equal access to food, social supports, educational, economic, recreational, and political opportunities
- Protections from violence and crime
- Meaningful employment, broadly defined, that provides a satisfactory standard of living
- Health-enhancing social and natural environments, including clean air, good water, and suitable food
- Prenatal care and supports for mothers and children
- Low or minimal placement of children in foster care or institutional settings
- Successful aging and its related societal and family supports

Efficacy and Self-Worth

- Satisfactory expression of one's talents and gifts in family, school, community, and work life
- Ability to contribute to the betterment of self and others
- Ability to feel effective in what one does
- Ability to develop oneself in one's work and play
- Ability to have meaningful and valued work roles both in and out of the home
- Low levels of suicide and suicidal preoccupation among youth and adults

Caring Communities

- A community of residence able to nurture the ability of families and individuals to obtain the above goals
- A general public that is knowledgeable about well-being and adopts its improvement and maintenance as a societal goal
- Caring communities that strive to help every family and its members achieve their collective potential rather than being satisfied with basic necessities and minimalist goals
- Vibrant community associations and family-to-family support networks that reflect and promote civic voluntarism
- Ability to sustain these attributes of well-being over time, resisting pressures that threaten it and mobilizing assistance, resources, and supports when any measure of well-being becomes unsatisfactory

Reduced and Eliminated Inequalities

- Sustained gains among historically disadvantaged and marginalized populations, closing the gaps between them and the most advantaged groups in society
- Sustained gains for girls and women, ending patriarchal structures, their correlates, and consequences
- Supports for caregivers and domestic laborers, especially girls and women
- Improved life expectancies related to successful aging, and a corresponding decline in life-threatening preventable diseases, especially among historically marginalized and disfranchised groups
- Minimal levels of unemployment and underemployment

Both systems thinking and socioecological thinking are implicit in this conception of well-being. It focuses on reducing and preventing social and economic inequality, especially its individual and family costs.

An anti-poverty agenda also is implicit in this list. Family-centered policy and practice must address poverty and its close companions. Absent this agenda, it may be impossible to achieve ideals for individual and family well-being and to achieve individual and family rights.

Well-Being, Equity, and Equality as Issues for Family-Centered Policies and Practices

Social inequality is a special concern. The case of personal health illustrates the importance of social inequality and its ripple effects. To begin with, each individual's health status is inseparable from her or his learning and development and well-being. Health status is also nested in the family system. For example, health risk factors (e.g., obesity, substance abuse, violent behavioral tendencies) associated with children's and adults' health problems are also likely to be found in their families, and one family may transmit health problems to the next generation (e.g., Farmer, 1996).

Furthermore, in any given society, not only does social class predict health status, but health status determines social class. The lower the social class standing, the higher the rate of health risks and problems (e.g., Farmer, 1996). As Wilkinson (1996) observes: "The higher the social class standing, the healthier are the individuals and families. For example, poorer people in developed countries may have annual death rates that are two to four times higher than for richer people in the same society" (p. 3). In brief, social inequalities within nations reflect and may determine the health status of both the individual and family.

Class inequalities also impact individual and family well-being. Research on cross-national differences expands this line of analysis. For example, Wilkinson's (1996) research in high-income nations tracks relationships among inequalities, social class determinations, and health status. Wilkinson suggests that it is possible to measure indices of healthy and unhealthy societies. He indicates that the crucial questions are (1) how much of a gap is there between "haves" and "have-nots" in a given nation? and (2) what proportion of the population falls into the "have-not" category?

The relative distribution of income, goods, services, and supports has major impacts upon individual health and well-being (and, by extension, family health and well-being). Moreover, health is affected by social position and by the scale of social and economic differences among the population. Wilkinson concludes that the high-income nations with the best health profiles are not the richest ones. They are the most egalitarian ones.

This integrated conception of well-being, especially its relationship with poverty and social inequality, has important policy and practice implications. For example, with this expanded definition, it is possible to begin talking about, and planning for, *social accountability,* in addition to *personal accountability* (Brandon, 1996). Social accountability for family well-being entails the responsibilities of policy makers, especially their responsiveness to individual and family needs and well-being.

Thus, social inequality and poverty compel the redistribution of power, authority, and resources. Both legal issues and moral obligations are involved. For example, the well-being of individuals and families depends upon two systems of distributive justice (see also Jordan, 1998).

The first system involves the economy and the polity. The political economy must provide equal access to jobs, education, and developmental supports. Men, women, children, and families depend on effective and responsive government. When governments are family responsive and effective, well-being is promoted.

The second system depends on distributive justice inside the family. This system includes efforts to eliminate patriarchy. It involves power sharing, equal rights, and equal access to supports and resources, including access to food, education, and health services (Dasgupta, 1995; Ray, 1998; Riley, 1997). It encompasses caregiving and other family roles, ensuring that these burdens do not fall disproportionately on women (Moghadam, 1992).

Subsequent chapters build on this platform. They provide specific alternatives and recommendations. They reinforce the claims about the importance of families in every societal culture. And, they demonstrate that many policies and practices must take into account the well-being of individuals and families. In short, policies and practices need to become family centered.

NOTES

1. The family systems metaphor, like all metaphors, is unavoidably selective and somewhat limited. It emphasizes relationships and interdependence

—an advantage. But it pays less attention to other important influences upon family well-being—for example, differences in cultural power and authority.
2. This systems perspective is not intended to be closed and deterministic. When open family systems become the unit of analysis, the focus is upon their commonalties and similarities in organization and function.

CHAPTER 2

Families as Comprehensive Social Welfare Institutions and Preventive Systems

Katharine Briar-Lawson, Hal A. Lawson,
and Charles B. Hennon, with Alan R. Jones

Family structures, systems, and dynamics vary. Despite their diversity, the world's families share similar responsibilities and challenges (United Nations, 1993c). For example, families are involved in educating, counseling, nurturing, socializing, healing, feeding, and sheltering. In fact, in comparison to any social and health service system, families have more duties and responsibilities. Unlike these service systems, families usually perform these duties without appropriate recognition and rewards.

In the same vein, families are often expected to function without supports, services, and resources from their communities and nations. And sometimes families are viewed as "deficient and dysfunctional" and blamed for problems outside their control. For example, families may "get named" as the problem and then may be blamed for it. Crime, drug use, teen pregnancy, school failure, child abuse and neglect, and other social ills all may be blamed on families (e.g., Sklar, 1995; United Nations, 1992b). Families are challenged in circumstances like these.

Given these difficulties faced by families, how should policy makers, practitioners, and citizens think about, talk about, and plan for families? How and why should policy leaders invest in families? What are the benefits and drawbacks? What are the challenges and opportunities associated with political arenas in which politicians and advocates may have competing agendas? What does family advocacy entail? These questions are addressed in this chapter. It explores some of the needs of policy makers, helping professionals, and advocates.

The chapter is structured with another need in mind. People may have selective and limited images of families (Coontz, 1988; United Nations, 1993c). Some of these images stem from their direct experiences as family members. For example, many people tend to view families through the lens of their childhood memories. Others acquire images through the mass media. Still others acquire their images from professional training about families (Zlotnik, 1998). Images of families are transmitted through cultural norms and values, some of which are expressed in stories and myths. Politicians and religious leaders frequently offer normative expectations about families, including implicit definitions, duties, gender roles and responsibilities, and family structure. Their images and expectations may influence others. In brief, there is a continuing need to understand and effectively address these images, including how they are played out in political arenas.

Family-centered policy makers, helping professionals, and citizen advocates must be able to address these diverse images (Family Resource Coalition, 1995; United Nations, 1994g). They must be able to help others transform implicit images of families, which may be selective and inappropriate, into more inclusive views of families and family systems.

This chapter has been structured with all of the above needs and priorities in mind. It emphasizes families' duties, responsibilities, resources, and needs. Families are portrayed as comprehensive social welfare institutions. In other words, families are comprehensive service, resource, and support systems. Viewed in this light, families are public goods. They are associated with multiple benefits. They are, therefore, worthy public investments (Midgley, 1997, 1999). Families are indispensable for the common good (e.g., Moroney, 1986).

In fact, when families are supported they can prevent individual, family, community, and national problems (e.g., National Commission on Families and Public Policies, 1978; United Nations, 1992b, 1995c). Their invaluable, indispensable contributions become evident when a hypothetical possibility is introduced: *Imagine what would happen if families, especially parents and adult caregivers, went on strike!* It takes little imagination to conclude that families are key preventive systems.

PREVENTIVE SERVICES, RESOURCES, AND SUPPORTS PROVIDED BY FAMILIES

To reiterate, families are comprehensive service, resource, and support systems. They continuously care for, and work on the behalf of, their members. Families cannot say: "We only do health care." Nor can they say: "We're done now."

In most communities families perform, for example, most of the child care, elder care, health care, teaching, counseling, norm enforcement, and justice work (National Commission on Families and Public Policies, 1978; United Nations, 1993c). They do not have the luxury of vacations away from their duties and obligations. When families are supported, healthy, and strong, many individual needs and social problems are prevented (United Nations, 1993d).

Women perform a disproportionately heavy share of domestic labor and family work (e.g., Mies, Bennholdt-Thomsen, & von Werlhof, 1991; O'Connell, 1994; Pietilä & Vickers, 1996; Wetzel & Campling, 1993). Women's work is, for the most part, unpaid domestic labor (e.g., Fox, 1980; Minton & Block, 1993; Oakley, 1974; Waring, 1988; Warness, 1983; Strasser, 1982). New views on women's work and their accompanying power and authority in families are required (e.g., Dangler, 1994; D'Aluisio & Menzel, 1996). To return to the previous chapter, patriarchy must be addressed because it affects individual and family well-being. These new views and policies and practices in support of them are among the most important challenges for the twenty-first century (e.g., Bauman, 1998; Giddens, 1994, 1995). The discussion that follows lays some of the foundation for these new policies and practices.

Indices of Families' Strengths and Contributions

Policy makers typically report on the number of services they provide and some of the beneficiaries. For example, how many children were educated in schools the past year? How many children were immunized? How many elders had hot meals delivered to them in their homes? Unfortunately, most policy makers and governments are silent on families. What would it be like if these same social welfare indices were simultaneously gathered for, and from, families? For example: The popular "kids count" data surveys currently underway in each state in the United States chart progress in helping children.[1] Without family well-being indices, it is difficult to determine the extent to which any one family is a resource or a problem. Moreover, when the data are child centered, they tend to generate child-focused policies and practices. Families count, too; data surveys need to attend to the well-being of both children and families (Smith, 1995). Family data may generate more family-centered policies and practices.

For example: The services, resources, and supports provided by families in a small town can be charted (see table 2.1). Governmental or nongovernmental programs sponsored 1,000 hot meals for elders in a com-

TABLE 2.1. Services, Supports, and Resources for One Month

EXAMPLES OF SERVICES RENDERED, SUPPORTS OFFERED, AND RESOURCES UTILIZED	BY FAMILIES AS UNWAGED WORK	BY GOVERNMENTAL AND NONGOVERNMENTAL PROGRAMS AS WAGED WORK
Hot meals to elders	9,990 to 111 people; 85% by women	1,000 to 33 people; 75% by women
Number of persons receiving 24-hour health care	300; 75% by women	60; 90% by women
Average hours devoted to helping preschool children learn to read and write	5,000; 68% by women	240; 100% by women
Encouraging and providing recreational activities for children	8,000; 65% by men	1,000; 85% by men

munity. This chart also reveals that families provided an additional 9,990 meals to others in need. While the government-sponsored hot meals at lunchtime were primarily delivered to elders living alone, additional data show the level of prevention and support that families give to their members all day long. Governmental provision of twenty-four-hour health care, a labor intensive and expensive item for both governmental and nongovernmental institutions, is rather meager compared to that provided by families. The same pattern is evident when the reading and writing services provided to children by their families are contrasted with those provided in schools.

Because family work is often overlooked or hidden, it is usually not captured as part of asset-based ledgers for social welfare accounting (e.g., Burggraf, 1997). Nor is family work included in national economic indicators such as the gross national product, or domestic national product (e.g., Henderson, 1996). The example provided in table 2.1 depicts the value of recording the socially and economically relevant work that families do. It helps to build recognition of families as agents as well as beneficiaries of social and economic investments and development (United Nations, 1995c).

When families are provided the services, supports, and resources they require, they are more likely to perform their duties and meet their responsibilities as comprehensive social welfare institutions and prevention systems (e.g., Dunst, Trivette, & Hamby, 1996; National Commission on Families and Public Policies, 1978). By contrast, when they lack the necessary requisites, and when they are harmed by problems such as poverty, war and violence, and health and mental health challenges, their capacities to meet their own expectations, to achieve their own goals, and to satisfy others will diminish (Family Resource Coalition, 1995). The story of Paolo and his family, in box 2.1, illustrates family stress.

Paolo's family, like many others, may not have enough money, time, and energy to come close to meeting each individual's needs. Like Paolo

---

BOX 2.1

PAOLO AND HIS FAMILY

Paolo is three years old. He has dysentery. He is hungry a good deal of the time. His parents, Jaime and Maria, are both in their late twenties. Recently both were maimed in a mine accident. Jaime was working in the mine and Maria was delivering meals that she sold to the workers, when the tragic explosion occurred. Sonya, Jaime's mother, is ill and frail with heart problems.

Significant costs and expenses would have to be undertaken to care for their needs one person at a time. Governmental or nongovernmental organizations would have to identify and address each person's needs independent of the others' and perhaps without regard to the environment and conditions in which they live. In some countries, Paolo might be able get the help of health or social services, or get this help in an orphanage if he was separated from his parents. Jaime and Maria might get help through disability insurance and income supports. Sonya might be aided by being in an institution for frail elders. All this would be costly, and in some nations such services might not exist for persons like Paolo, Jaime, Maria, and Sonya. In some more "developed" nations, if these people have recently immigrated or are not citizens, they might not qualify for services or resources. Many people around the world face these same challenges and experience the same kinds of stress.

and his intergenerational family, the Roso family also depends on inter-generational family supports and services. The Rosos live in the same community. Their similar tenuous situation, described in box 2.2, can be assessed from another perspective.

Collectively, all the members of the household make up the Roso family system. The efforts of the older child and the uncles may be one key to this family's survival. Viewing these people as a family rather than as individuals emphasizes their relationships and interdependence. It calls attention to this family system as a natural support system, to relations among members, and to the family's relations to others.

Like Paolo's family, the Rosos are in crisis. Without aid from the outside, the survival of the impaired and dependent family members, as well as the family unit itself, may not be possible. Individual members will suffer and may even die. In addition, the family system of care may be destroyed.

The Roso family illustration shows how a mine explosion impaired the parents so that they cannot work and thus cannot perform the role of economic providers for their family. The relocation of the factory that might take away the uncles is likely the final devastation for the Roso family, unless they all move. Where are the workplace policies that might protect persons who are so vital to the sustainability of their families and their members? Where are the policies and practices to support and enhance this family? Beyond the Roso family, how many more of the victims of the mine explosion, and how many of the relocated workers, play pivotal roles in their families' future well-being and even survival? What alternatives in policy and practice might have been in place to mitigate the harms to this family and to others?

EXPLORING DEFINITIONS OF SERVICE, RESOURCE, AND SUPPORT

What services, resources, and supports help families? What is the relationship among services, resources, and supports? Once again, diversity and variability are evident. A service for one family may be a resource for another. As in the case of what it means to be "a family," definitions of services, resources, and supports must correspond to the lived experiences and meaning systems of families—in the cultural and national contexts (e.g., Boyden, 1993; Pinderhughes, 1995). So the following definitions are offered as points of departure. They are not rigid categories.

BOX 2.2

THE ROSO FAMILY HOUSEHOLD

The Roso family consists of four children, two parents, and two uncles. For a few years this household has been pooling its resources. Together, they managed to fashion the resources needed to survive. Although they did not have much money for extras, they had basic necessities and social supports. Recently both Roso parents were injured in the same mining accident that affected Paolo's father and mother (see box 2.1). Yet because both uncles had relatively good jobs working in a factory that builds and repairs mining equipment, they were able to help tide the family over.

However, the Roso family circumstances have begun to worsen. Shortly after the mining accident, the uncles learned that their local factory is relocating to another site, some 900 kilometers away. The owner offered employees who wanted to transfer equivalent jobs in the new location. The two uncles are unsure about this move because it is the second time they have had to move due to a plant closure or relocation.

The oldest Roso daughter (age thirteen) tries to work sporadically at whatever jobs she can find while also trying to attend school. However, unless there is some other source of income she will be unable to continue her schooling.

This fragile family caregiving system may be all that keeps the dependent members supported. The relocation of the uncles may signal the final unraveling of available supports and services. It may present the final crisis for all of them. If the uncles move, they will take most of the resources with them. If they stay, they will not be able to find work. The family system cannot afford to support two households in two separate locations.

What should the Rosos do? Should they all move to a new location where the factory is being relocated? Should the family system be divided? What are the consequences of each choice? What kind of resources, services, and supports should have been available to them from the mine, the factory, the welfare state?

Services are assistance strategies involving counseling, health, education, law enforcement, and other activities to improve overall individual, family, and social welfare. Services are the activities and practices provided by some people, especially helping professionals, to help others. They are regarded as "services rendered" to preserve, assist, and strengthen families and their individual members. In high-income nations, services are usually planned, organized, and delivered by state-recognized and -supported agencies who employ an array of helping professionals (e.g., Kahn & Kamerman, 1975, 1982).

Services also originate in local, community-based organizations and neighborhood associations (e.g., Family Resource Coalition, 1995). Family-centered, community-based services may be offered by schools, social services, health care providers, employers, and law enforcement agencies. These services may include education of children and adults, emergency health care after an accident, alcoholism awareness and treatment, and prosecution of people arrested for committing crimes.

Families also deliver services such as child care and counseling. One family may help another. Or, larger networks may be structured for self-help, mutual aid, and assistance. Family members may give services to others as part of their occupational development. For example, they may perform paraprofessional roles and receive formal training (e.g., Alameda, 1996; Apple, Berstein, et al., 1997; Foree, 1996; Lipscomb, 1996). These examples are drawn from the United States, and they do not exhaust the possibilities.

Every nation has the opportunity to plan for innovative approaches for families to help other families and, at the same time, to help themselves. Two kinds of service systems are warranted: professionally delivered and family delivered. Complementary and symbiotic relationships between these two systems are essential (e.g., Briar-Lawson, 1998; McKnight, 1997).

Resources are tangible and intangible assets found in, and available to, families. Resources provide for the most basic of human needs such as shelter, food, and clothing, as well as transportation, employment, communication, and medicines. Resources also include economic provisions aimed at enabling greater self-sufficiency in families. Examples of economic provisions include loans for small businesses, income subsidies, and discretionary funds that families may use in pursuit of goals, aspirations, and needs.

Technological resources are also important. These resources include telephones, computers, typewriters, vehicles for transportation, and vacuum cleaners, as well as resources for personal functioning such as hearing aids and eyeglasses. These resources preserve and protect families, while enabling greater self-sufficiency. Families challenged by poverty may evidence special needs for these resources.

Unfortunately, helping professionals often ignore or neglect resource needs. In the United States, for example, few helping professionals have had income, jobs, or housing-related resources available for individuals and families in poverty (e.g., Halpern, 1998). Such resources are not in their helping repertoires. For the most part, these helping professionals view and perform their work in accordance with their training and the resources prescribed by social policy. Poverty is reinforced because economic structures and politics promote the provision of in-kind services rather than income supports, jobs, and housing. Helping professionals thus often struggle to become more effective. They need to learn why and how to assess families' resource needs and, in turn, to support resource development (e.g., Vosler, 1996; United Nations, 1995c).

Psychological resources also are important. For example, love, commitment, and cognitive abilities are psychological resources. Love and nurturing behavior are affective resources. Like money, they are sometimes scarce. They also may be viewed as intangible. However, an intangible resource can be as important as a more tangible one. For example, in a child's mind, a sense of security and of feeling wanted may be more important than money for another toy (e.g., UNDP, 1994).

Cognitive abilities are another resource that families can tap. Informed people can make informed decisions. Know-how that is shared or used can help families to function better and be supportive of their members' needs and aspirations. Resources, then, are opportunities one can use. Families can use these resources to solve problems and care for people.

Supports are social, cultural, and political provisions (i.e., services and resources) that buttress family well-being. Obvious examples include meaningful employment, environmental quality, and home- and neighborhood-based mutual aid networks. Other examples are new values, ideologies, and institutional planning frames that are mindful of, and responsive to, family duties and needs.

Supports exist when families feel a sense of caring and concern (e.g., Family Resource Coalition, 1995). Supports can build upon families' capacities; supports may be experienced when there are tangible, emotional, and informational strategies for families in which nations create a pervasive sense of caring and concern for their well-being. Successful aging, for example, may be enhanced by access to social supports (United Nations, 1992c, 1994f). Both aging and elder issues double as family issues. In the same vein, discourse about universal human rights often doubles as discourse about family supports (e.g., United Nations, 1995e).

For example, a child's right to vaccines doubles as a family health issue. As in the case of services and resources, governments share responsibilities for supports, sometimes involving large-scale bureaucracies and specialized helping professions. Supports also can be conceptualized as a caring community, village, and neighborhood, with families or other groups working to enhance the well-being of others (e.g., Kagan, 1996; Kagan & Weissbord, 1994).

There are many types of supports. Some are tangible, while others (e.g., emotional and informational supports) are less visible. The richness and quality of support is an important aspect of both individual and family well-being (e.g., Dunst, Trivette, & Hamby, 1996; Vosler, 1996).

To summarize: Social support can be symbolic, substantive, or emotional, giving a feeling of being accepted, defended, sustained, valued, and part of a group. Such support is essential in helping individuals and families be resilient to stress. Families can supply all types of social support to their members, and families function better knowing that they can call upon others for the support they need and want (Vosler, 1996).

Combinations of Services, Resources, and Supports

From a dependent family member's viewpoint, the provision of love or food is a service rendered. Both love and food are resources, but their provision is a service. Simply stated: When there are no resources, no services are rendered. But one can have resources and still not use them to meet needs (of the self or others).

Sometimes there are resources but no services because of lack of caring about someone or self-interest, or because there is no way to tap into the resources to use them. Having parental leave available in one's workplace is a resource. Getting help from the personnel office to be able to use that leave is taking advantage of a service. Leave time (a resource) becomes a service when the parent cares for and nurtures a child. The result is that the child feels supported (because of the parental care) and the parent feels supported (because of the resource available from the employer or government, as well as because the human resources personnel helped the parent to tap this resource). In this sense, support is both tangible and intangible; it involves physical care and the feeling of well-being one gets from the appropriate access to and use of resources and services.

Sometimes needs, stresses, and consequential social ills result more from a lack of, or selective distribution of, intangible resources than from a lack of tangible ones. Alcoholism and drug addiction, domestic violence, and child abuse may be related to not feeling wanted, needed, or valued as much as to a lack of money and housing insecurity (e.g., International Council on Social Welfare, 1986). This view does not imply that tangible resources are not needed. They are. For example, when families lack resources such as adequate income and housing, there can be intolerable and wrenching violations of human rights and needs, many involving vulnerable children and elders (Jordan, 1998).

Another example has been provided by members of the United Nations International Year of the Family Secretariat (H. Sokalski & E. Rolfe, personal communication, Vienna, August 1994). In Uzbekistan, thousands of children have been living in holes in the ground for which they have fashioned temporary covers. When it rains, these children must survive under miserable conditions. They and their families may live in mud up to their knees.

Elsewhere in the world countless thousands of children and elders are without adequate family care, or they have lost their families entirely. These children and elders often survive in the streets, or alongside dirt roads (e.g., Lusk & Mason, 1995). They and their families lack services and resources. Even in wealthy nations like the United States, there are many homeless families who live in their automobiles. Others live in makeshift tents in public parks, in cardboard boxes in alleys, or in temporary shelters for the homeless. In these and similar instances, children are unable to regularly attend school, and their health and emotional needs are not met. Elders in the family system may not receive support or, if needed, family caregiving.

Sometimes when family members lack services, resources, and supports and feel they are failing as providers, the stress may become too great. Problematic coping responses may also aggravate their stress (e.g., Van Hook, 1987; Vosler, 1996). Helping professionals such as social workers and family advocates may attempt to offer families whatever services and resources are available. But there may be a mismatch between what families need and what help is available (Ray, 1998; United Nations, 1995e).

In actual practice, then, services, resources, and supports are interrelated. Already policy makers, practitioners, and advocates from nations around the world have learned that services alone will not automatically solve social problems and improve the well-being of families (United Nations, 1995a). They have also learned that more is not necessarily better. If the service strategy is flawed, there is little to be gained by intensifying, expanding, and allocating more funds in support of it. Policy makers, practitioners, and advocates are also beginning to learn that the best strategies for nurturing and promoting the well-being of families are ones in which family members are joint designers, implementers, and evaluators (United Nations, 1995c).

EXAMPLES OF SENSITIZING PRINCIPLES

A family-centered approach to policy and practice is founded upon firm value commitments. These value commitments may be expressed as family-centered principles, and include the following:

- Respecting family pluralism, diversity, and different conceptualizations of family; while seeing families as systems embedded within multiple contexts and confronting issues internally and externally involving unequal power and authority
- Allowing that policy cannot "force" families to act in certain ways, nor can it "fix" them—families are active agents who choose to take what they perceive as rational courses of actions that appear to further what they define as important goals
- Intervening when family rights are violated, risks to family members are identified, and harms are documented
- Addressing needs and wants and formulating solutions as close as possible to families
- Building upon family strengths, aspirations, goals, and competencies, while seeking ways to build better family functioning
- Empowering families by their inclusion and enfranchisement in the process of negotiated change (especially, allowing families to name and frame their needs and preferred solutions; empowerment means making them "inside" experts or persons with "expertise" in policy

making and implementation, giving them a sense of personal agency and importance, allowing them to design their own futures, and giving them a sense of autonomy rather than feeling dependent on government alone)

- Encouraging and rewarding collaboration between families and "outside" experts such as helping professionals and governmental leaders
- Linking plans for integrated, equitable, sustainable, and culturally responsive economic and social development to plans for promoting individual and family well-being
- Seeing families as guides and agents for, and beneficiaries of, sustainable social and economic development
- Integrating service, support, and resource strategies in response to family needs and goals and ensuring collaboration among helping professionals

TOWARD INVESTMENTS IN FAMILY-CENTERED POLICY AND PRACTICE

Families and family issues are viewed as private domains in many nations (United Nations, 1995c, 1995e). It is assumed that families must either remain protected from state-initiated interventions, or that families survive on their own. There is a tension between the responsibilities of individuals and families to advance their own well-being and the duty of governments to safeguard the well-being of all individuals and families (Moroney, 1986). Debates over this dualism in thinking and acting often become deadlocked. When nothing is done to help families, they often suffer.

Traps, Tensions, and Unintended Consequences

An additional reason for harms is that, in some nations, policies are not implemented with fidelity. In still others, well-determined policies may have unanticipated consequences. In yet other nations, policy makers may frame policies for a sector (such as education or housing) without considering families and understanding the burdens these policies impose. In other words, policies addressing, say, more effective schooling for children may simultaneously erode the influence of parents and families. For example, educators may blame parents for the learning and developmental problems of their children, and parents may blame the educators. Also, what is learned in school may contradict and erode family-based knowledge and understanding, both of which may have their own value.

Similarly, families may get caught in "policy traps or dilemmas." One sign of this problem is, for example, when well-meaning policies for health contradict those for education, housing, or employment. By conforming to the requirements of one sector, the family loses out, or is harmed, in the other. For example, families may lose their housing subsidies when they get a job, but insufficient wages may make them homeless. They must choose between a job or housing (Ooms & Binder, 1993).

Families as Public Goods and Building Blocks for Strong Democracies

Families are the most important building blocks of democracy: strong families, strong democracy (e.g., Putnam, 1993). Families in all of their forms provide the foundation for civil society (Popenoe, 1994). As indicated earlier, leaders for the United Nations International Year of the Family promoted an important image about families: "Building the smallest democracy at the heart of society" (United Nations, 1991a). This promotional slogan has symbolic value. It conveys important information about the meaning and significance of families. It also conveys values supporting democratic, equitable and just, and nonpatriarchal families and societies.

The Promise of Family-Centered Policy and Practice

What would happen if families could plead their respective cases for what each needed and wanted? What would policies, programs, and practices look like if societies wanted to respond to each family? Imagine some of the possibilities for tomorrow's world as opposed to today's.

Instead of families being eroded and children being raised in foster care and orphanages, imagine a world without surrogate child-rearing institutions, or at least with fewer of them. Instead of children dying before the age of five, or mothers dying in childbirth, imagine a world in which the longevity and well-being of children and adults are enhanced. Instead of depression, substance abuse, interpersonal conflict, domestic and neighborhood violence and crime—some of the by-products and corollaries of rising poverty and unemployment—imagine full employment agendas that may help prevent personal and social problems and nurture families' roles in social and economic development. With these imagined possibilities in mind, policy makers, helping professionals, and advocates face critical challenges in setting agendas.

FIRST CALL FOR FAMILIES AND THEIR MEMBERS

Families, especially the most vulnerable ones, merit significant social investments (e.g., Midgley, 1997, 1999). Both current families and future generations of families merit "first call" on available services, supports, and resources. As families are given this top priority, policies and practices become more family centered. Family well-being is promoted and crises involving them are prevented.

There is need for a family investment inventory. This inventory may guide policy development and practice. Table 2.2 provides an example of a family investment inventory. It provides a point of departure for policy makers, helping professionals, and advocates. Clearly, each community, nation, and region might add or substitute items to this list.

TABLE 2.2. Toward a Family Investment Inventory

- Are family needs for services, supports, and resources featured prominently in all governmental and community missions?

- Are families treated like valued members of society and in their communities as they interact with schools, law enforcement, social services, health systems, recreation systems, housing authorities, and transportation systems?

- Do governmental budgets reflect and support investments in families?

- Are families and their needs a top priority in the governmental budgetary process?

- Are lobbyists for big business and military concerns relegated to secondary status while families and their advocates are given voice and preeminence in the policy-making process?

- Are communities and nations measured on how well they fare in their family investments and well-being indices?

TABLE 2.2. (*Continued*)

- Are these family investments and well-being indices routinely published worldwide?

- Are the poor, women, and minorities treated well as special investments for the nation and communities?

- Are prevention and early intervention emphasized in addition to crisis-oriented, remedial services?

- Is every policy decision scrutinized for its investment messages about families; for example, is every dollar invested in prisons, home, and community safety systems (such as alarms, walled communities) treated as a dollar that could have been better spent on prevention and early intervention?

- Are social workers, teachers, child care providers, health care providers, family life educators, and other helpers relegated to a high status in society as key family builders and supporters of social and economic development?

- Are economic growth, environmental protection, and community development treated as separate policy categories apart from families? Or, are they integrated in relation to their separate and combined effects on family well-being?

- Are families' capacities to bear children aligned with their communities' and the earth's capacity to support them?

- Is population policy family friendly and gender equitable?

- Are sustainable development strategies arrived at jointly with families, or are they imposed on them?

- Are indigenous family lifestyles and cultural traditions supported?

- When indigenous lifestyles and cultural traditions threaten, or impede, gender equity and family well-being, do individuals, families, and communities receive educational and developmental supports for change?

- Are these educational and developmental supports also provided when the environment is being destroyed?

- Are local and national efforts to eliminate poverty informed by international efforts? Is the aim of eliminating family poverty an enduring commitment?

FAMILY ADVOCACY AND CONTESTS FOR CONTROL
IN THE POLITICAL AREA: COMPETING IMAGES
OF FAMILIES AND FAMILY SYSTEMS

Clearly, even the most persuasive and effective advocate for women, girls, elders, and other family members, and for democratized family systems, cannot solve alone the problems presented by patriarchy and gender violence. Political supports and mobilization are required, and practitioners and advocates must enter the political arena. This arena reflects diverse interests, and the interests of men dominate (United Nations, 1993g).

The multiple social realities for families, policy makers, helping professionals, and family advocates pose other challenges. For example, competing images of "family" may be passionately defended and hotly contested. The lives, lifestyles, reputations, values, and religious beliefs of practitioners, advocates, and politicians are embedded in these competing images. Because men are disproportionately represented in policy-making bodies, and many may be predisposed to patriarchy, it is likely that patriarchal views will be represented (United Nations, 1995e).

Patriarchy looms beneath many images of "the family." All such images reflect the values, vested interests, preferences, and commitments of the persons who framed them. These persons are competing to become "reality definers." They want their views of what families ought to be like and do to become the dominant vision. These views often are implicit, not explicit. They need to be unpacked from what policy makers say and do not say and how they say it.

Images of Families as Mental Models

Culturally constructed and contested images are embedded with conventions, stories, and even myths. For example, Anderson and Sabatelli (1995) suggest that views of "the family" are accomplished through a synthesis of interrelated myths. These myths are often tied to nostalgic memories, selective perceptions, and attention to biased information. Myths are carriers of personal beliefs and cultural values about what is "correct, normal, and true" about families. Ethnocentrism is ever present. The term family often conjures up warm thoughts of nurturance, caring, and love—"families" means child-bearing and child-rearing institutions. Or, families are households where groups of people spanning more than one generation reside and interact. Or, family is a code word for women and children. Or, family serves only the power and vested interests of men. These examples do not exhaust the views and competing interests regarding families.

When images and perceptions of families are firmly entrenched, the key is to create conditions under which implicit images can be made public and interrogated. In other words, it is essential to provide public forums in which mutually beneficial dialogue can facilitate co-teaching and learning. To put it yet another way, the challenge is to create settings in which it is difficult for people to remain satisfied with limited images (e.g., Argyris & Schön, 1996; Bruce, Lloyd, & Leonard, 1995). This dialogue is an important part of democratic politics. It promotes dialogical understanding—i.e., understanding that derives from listening to divergent views on the same issue and weighing the needs and interests of other individuals, groups, families, and organizations (Hoogvelt, 1997).

In a most fundamental way, family-centered policy and practice involves gaining privileges in defining "families and family systems." Important questions can be raised about all "reality definers," and their contests for control. Whose rules, interests, values, and perspectives matter most and why? Whose images, views, and voices are not heard? (United Nations, 1991a, 1993f) By skillfully using the political process, pro-family practitioners and advocates can position new, more inclusive and appropriate definitions of family systems and pro-family policy and practice.

The intent is to build family capacity in political, social, economic, and cultural systems (Sen, 1999). Capacity-building efforts should aim for sustainability. In other words, pro-family commitments, agendas, images, and definitions should have "sticking power" and "staying power." Sustainability of this kind requires gaining and keeping the attention and support of the majority and competing successfully with the opposing views of other groups.

Thanks to the growing popularity of the ideas of organizational learning, development, and continuous quality improvement (e.g., Argyris & Schön, 1996; Schön & Rein, 1994), awareness also has grown about the importance of so-called "paradigms," also called "mental models" (Senge, Kleiner, et al., 1994). These mental models provide perceptual and conceptual boxes. They are selective and limited. They are like images because people may not be aware of them. The key idea is this: *If you wish to get people to think, act, and interact differently, in turn promoting learning, development, and continuous quality improvement, then you must get them to change their mental models, i.e., their paradigms.* In other words, people need help in seeing the limitations in their mental models. They need to get outside—and think and act outside—their boxes.

Three categories of images, or mental models, operate in the political arena. These are dominant, emergent, and residual mental models (Williams, 1977). There can be more variations in each model or image, and they may be categorized differently in diverse societal cultures.

Dominant mental models are the ones preferred by the majority, often those with political and economic power, at any given time and place. Dominant conceptions and definitions of families, especially of "normal families," are more implicit than explicit in most societal cultures. These definitions (mental models) are culturally prescribed and inscribed. They carry lots of ideological baggage from other social institutions—the economy, the polity, religion, and education.

For example, in many societal cultures, conceptions and definitions of "normal" childhood are inseparable from definitions of families (Knowles, 1996, p. 15). Similarly, gender roles and responsibilities are often connected to childhood and families. Men's roles and responsibilities, especially "fatherhood," are bound up in images of families.

Emergent mental models are new. They are advanced by interest groups seeking to challenge the status quo. For example, they challenge dominant assumptions about the role of men and women in families. They address issues such as patriarchy and gender violence. They may take issue with images of families as restricted to persons with the same bloodlines. They may claim that cohabitation constitutes a family system.

Residual mental models linger from the past. They are associated with cultural traditions and the interest groups that continue to advocate for them. For example, the nuclear family (often thought of as a legally married man and woman with a child or children) in some societal cultures is offered as the only family, despite social and policy changes to the contrary. "Family values" mean the values of advocates for these nuclear families. In these contexts, the nuclear family is part of a residual mental model, and it may be influenced by religious beliefs. Or, the residual mental model involves indigenous people and their family forms and relationships (Boyden, 1993). Every residual model will continue as long as it has advocates and supporters and continues to recruit and socialize new candidates.

Once these mental models are recognized as limited and selective—

that is, as normative, moral, evaluative, and political boxes, or categories that are often ethnocentric—they may be contested and changed. Moral judgments often are involved. Nowhere is this more apparent than in instances where policy makers, family advocates, helping professionals, and concerned citizens make claims about "normal, dysfunctional, and dangerous families."

Normal and "Abnormal" Families

Families are institutions for public surveillance, judgment, and intervention. As Knowles (1996) observes:

The family is a focus for analysis, intervention, and commentary. Many different kinds of narratives—psychological, social policy, legal, medical, moral, and popular—converge upon it and shape it into its present form. Each of these narratives has its own social, political and professional agendas, but the overarching result is to make the family one of the most highly pressured arrangements in contemporary society. (pp. 18–19)

In this sense, the very idea of family is part of the public, governmental forum in many societal cultures (e.g., United Nations, 1987). The mere fact that some families, especially poor and vulnerable ones, are center stage in political arenas guarantees that families and family boundaries will be contested (e.g., Abramowitz, 1996; Coontz, 1988). Moreover, when some families become "public problems," their privacy and freedom may be jeopardized (United Nations, 1992c).

Private family matters become public issues when things appear to go wrong. For example, expectations are not met. Norms and standards are violated. Taken-for-granted assumptions and implicit beliefs about families are threatened and contested. Rights are denied. People, especially vulnerable ones, are harmed (e.g., women are abused; children are neglected). During these times, ideas about "normal" families surface, not so much in the form of concrete definitions, but in the form of "not-this" and "not that" frames of reference (after Knowles, 1996).

In other words, so-called normal families are often defined by the absence of needs, problems, and challenges. The phrase "no news is good news" signals that all is well and that the family is "normal." By contrast, key disruptions, disturbances, and violations are viewed as cause for alarm. Then the labeling process begins (United Nations, 1992c).

Families perceived to threaten and violate ideals for "normal families" fall under increasing public scrutiny because they and their practices are viewed as "at risk or dysfunctional." Subsequently, surveillance, inspection, and regulative activities are commenced by helping professionals and by the police to enforce the boundaries of "normalcy" (Foucault, 1977; Knowles, 1996; Ransom, 1997). Contests for control follow, including families' efforts to regain or maintain their privacy.

In many societal cultures, there are never-ending tensions between families' privacy rights and public expectations, norms, surveillance, and enforcement practices. Significant constitutional and legal issues are embedded in these tensions. For example, the rights of women and children are often weighed against the rights of families to privacy and freedom (United Nations, 1992c). To reiterate, there are nonnegotiable standards regarding the rights of children, women, and elders, which have been adopted by the United Nations and observed by many countries around the world. These standards involve rights of individuals within their families and the rights of families (United Nations, 1995a, 1993i).

Policy advocacy and family helpgiving will be appropriate to the extent that policy makers understand and appreciate family diversity, aspirations, strengths, and needs. The various helping professions (education, health, social welfare, law, and medicine) and their social organizations are, in many societal cultures, deeply enmeshed in addressing such rights and some of their inherent tensions. They are among the "reality definers" and "rights balancers" of families (United Nations, 1992c).

The knowledge these helping professionals claim and use in their work is not value neutral or value free. Oftentimes, this knowledge is self-serving. It helps guide researchers and practitioners alike, simultaneously justifying their special status as helping professionals. Professional education programs and practice standards are carriers of norms and values regarding "normal" and "at risk or dysfunctional" individuals and families, together with recommended strategies for how to identify and work with them (e.g., Dunst, Trivette, & Hamby, 1996; Hooper-Briar & Lawson, 1994; Lawson & Briar-Lawson, 1997). For example, many of these helping professionals are prepared to focus on child maltreatment, neglect, and abuse. Others address domestic violence, education, and mental health. When specialized helping professionals perceive these needs, they may view families as "at risk" or perhaps as "dysfunctional," and therefore as needing expert professional assistance (Mc-Knight, 1995).

Family well-being is, in this sense, inseparable from the vested interests of helping professionals. Their "gazes" into family life, and their organizations' missions, responsibilities, and accountabilities are very important. Their mental models structure their gazes (e.g., Lawson, 1999b). Therefore, the challenge of strengthening and protecting families is simultaneously one of preparing helping professionals to "see" families in a variety of ways (Briar-Lawson, Alameda, & Lawson, 1997; Pinder-hughes, 1995), to work with expanded, multiple mental models. For example, helping professionals must ensure that family members are not harmed, while safeguarding them against unnecessary and unwarranted intrusions into their private lives. A balancing act is involved, and striking a reasonable and appropriate balance is often tricky (United Nations, 1992c).

In contrast, these same characteristics and behavior can be viewed paradoxically as strengths—as signs of special expertise—and as starting points for supports and assistance (Briar-Lawson, Alameda, & Lawson, 1997). For helping professionals to view difference and needs as strengths, they must rid themselves of their ethnocentric gaze. Once families are viewed as having expertise, and helping professionals are able to view needs and even problems as strengths and points of departure for helping, the stage is set for "paradoxical practices." Individuals and families presenting needs and challenges are used as opportunities to build on strengths and to build capacity (Briar-Lawson, Alameda, & Lawson, 1997). For example, families whose children have the most head lice are viewed as experts, and they are mobilized, as partners for helping professionals, to address the head lice problem. Solving this problem together paves the way for future, collaborative problem solving (Alameda, 1996; Briar-Lawson, 1998).

Families as Victims

When helping professionals do not have this kind of understanding, and when they have limited mental models, they may act insensitively. In turn, families may blame themselves. The case of child abuse is instructive (e.g., Knowles, 1996). The mother is sometimes unable to protect the child because she is also a victim of abuse. Upon closer inspection, there may be co-occurring causes—gender inequality in the family, the father's stress over unemployment, and the mother's low wages (e.g., Gil, 1970). Because children learn through what they experience, an abused child may become an adult abuser (e.g., Kessler, Mickelson, & Zhao, 1997).

Moreover, research reveals that where there is domestic violence there likely is also sexual and physical child abuse (O'Keefe, 1995). The point is, relational, socioecological, and systemic analyses help pinpoint some of the sources of stress and causal connections that result in coping dynamics within the family as well as the triggers that may be reinforcers or shapers from the outside (e.g., Vosler, 1996).

Every family has the potential to become one in need. Families will become stressed if they lack appropriate resources, and if they are isolated without supports. Severely stressed families cannot meet their expectations, achieve their goals, or perform all of their duties (e.g., United Nations, 1995c). When families experience crises, individual members may be harmed; and as individuals are harmed, their families are affected.

Families as Natural Support Systems

Informed and responsive family-centered policy and practice builds from organic, natural views of families and family systems. Families across the world are the foremost system for the production of goods and services as well as for the care and support of their members. In this sense, families are like small communities within much larger societal circles. Families are also the generators of most small businesses (Burggraf, 1997; United Nations, 1995c). Moreover, families have impacts on their political, economic, social, and cultural environments, and, reciprocally, these environments affect families (United Nations, 1993b).

Families as Active Agents: Rights, Resistance, and Mobilization for Change

When family members—individuals and groups—have clear needs, issues are raised about their responsibilities and accountabilities. On the other hand, excessive surveillance, unwarranted intrusions, and excessive governmental controls raise issues about families' rights. Other persons' images of family and "normality" can mobilize resistance. Families who feel excluded, and who perceive potential harms, will ignore these images, labels, and definitions (passive resistance). Or, they actively resist by means of political and social action strategies. For example, in some places, gay and lesbian families have successfully resisted definitions of the nuclear family, and they have gained benefits and entitlements once denied them (United Nations, 1995a). In other places, women have resisted definitions that automatically make them caregivers in family systems dominated by men (United Nations, 1993g).

TOWARD EFFECTIVE FAMILY ADVOCACY

This chapter has introduced key concepts and issues. These concepts and issues are like building blocks. Once they are cemented, they help form the foundation for new mental models. These new mental models may facilitate innovations related to individuals, families, and communities. They may also foster more effective advocacy in political arenas and in everyday affairs.

Advocacy is the relentless pursuit of improvements in the well-being of individuals and families. Advocacy is a democratic concept, with both local and global reaches. It begins at home, but it does not stop there. Grounded in understanding of global interdependence, this concern for individual and family rights and well-being spans, and connects, the world community. Informed, dedicated practitioners and advocates are able to promote more helpful policies and practice, all in support of the world's families.

These agendas will be tailored to the needs and characteristics of each culture. At the same time, they will address cultural prescriptions that inadvertently result in harm to individuals (especially women and children) and families. As universal rights for individuals and families are accepted as the standards, patriarchy, gender violence, and the exploitation of children, elders, and women cannot be justified as "culturally appropriate and congruent." These violations and others of basic human freedom limit every social development agenda (e.g., Sen, 1999).

Policy and Practice Tools for Effective Advocacy:
Learning to Think, Talk, Act, and Interact Differently

Mental models for family-centered policies and practices are determined in large part by language, cultural values, and policy traditions. Over time, policy makers develop patterned ways to think, talk, act, and interact in relation to families. They develop language preferences, which are sometimes difficult to change. When families are in need and crisis, it is often timely to introduce different language or discourse, which helps change mental models (Kinney, Strand, et al., 1994). Practitioners and advocates can take the lead in introducing new discourse and frames of reference. They can address past/present ethnocentrism and silences, asking penetrating questions and employing language differently (Family Resource Coalition, 1995).

It is, therefore, necessary that practitioners and advocates help policy makers examine their mental models, discourses, definitions, and assumptions about families. For example, practitioners and advocates can help leaders examine the evidence—the facts—against their espoused beliefs. Advocacy also entails mobilizing families and working with their mental models. With the idea of family-centered policies and practices, it is imperative that families' voices be heard, especially the voices of its most vulnerable and often-oppressed members (e.g., children, women, and elders).

Looking Ahead: Vicious and Virtuous Family Cycles as Choices

Families and family systems can be at the center of virtuous, self-reinforcing cycles. Or, when families are neglected, ignored, and insufficiently supported, vicious cycles develop. In short, crucial choices are involved.

First, the virtuous cycles. Families help make democracy and peacekeeping work (e.g., United Nations, 1991a). An otherwise strong economy is not likely to be sustained when a growing number of families do not enjoy well-being (United Nations, 1993e, 1993g). When families are supported and strong, their children have a greater chance to thrive. Elders may be more likely to enjoy successful aging, and family members with severe disabilities receive in-home care, reducing the burdens on governments (United Nations, 1994b). In turn, strong, peaceful democracies, economies, and civil societies foster and reinforce strong, healthy families and ensure well-being.

By contrast, when families are ignored or neglected, unintended consequences and harms result. Vicious cycles develop. Women, children (especially girls), members with disabilities, and elders are harmed the most. The economy is weakened because of intergenerational crises and unmet needs. Democracy is eroded because disfranchised people do not join in community associations; nor are they as able to make contributions to schools. As schools are weakened, children are not served, reducing their chances for productive citizenship and risking the possibility that their children—the next generation—also will be harmed.

These vicious and virtuous cycles tend to be self-renewing and self-reinforcing. They can be passed on from generation to generation (e.g., Felitti, Anda, et al., 1998). They ensure continuing benefits and well-being, or they wreak havoc, affecting the well-being of people and the vitality of entire nations and regions.

NOTE

1. These reports are available from the Annie E. Casey Foundation, Baltimore, Maryland.

CHAPTER 3

Meaningful, Gender-Equitable Work and Family Well-Being

Katharine Briar-Lawson, Hal A. Lawson, and Charles B. Hennon

Economic and employment development priorities and policies affect families. In many cases, services, resources, and supports are responsive to families to the extent that their income and employment needs are met. Full and gender-equitable employment is a key contributor to individual and family well-being (Briar, 1988; Briar-Lawson, 2000-a). When employment is provided, it is a key social investment and family support strategy. This claim leads to two related claims: (1) families are important workplaces, and (2) workplaces outside the family need to be family supportive (United Nations, 1994c, 1995c; United Nations Economic and Social Council Commission, 1993).

Unfortunately, many helping professionals in the fields of education, social work, health, and justice, as well as policy makers and family advocates, are unprepared to engage in policy and practice discourses about full and equitable employment. Similarly, helping professionals often do not assess, or address, needs for employment and employment supports when they address family needs and goals. Most have not been given in their professional preparation, or in their on-the-job training, the knowledge, skills, values, sensitivities, and understanding needed for employment-related services, supports, and resources (e.g., Halpern, 1998; Briar-Lawson, Lawson, et al., 1999). It is not surprising, therefore, that many policy makers and helping professionals do not view jobs, occupational rights, and income supports as relevant to family well-being. In fact, the International Year of the Family data and the inventory of action plans for member nations were relatively silent on the importance of meaningful work and employment for families.

The purpose of this chapter is to address, in a preliminary way, some of these voids and gaps in practice and policy discourses. The chapter is structured to enhance understanding of the importance of full and equitable employment, and "meaningful work." Meaningful work does not mean just any job, and it is different from the concept of commodified labor. Commodified labor is dehumanizing (Gil, 1998a, 1998b). It exacts human costs. By contrast, meaningful work is, as the label suggests, rewarding and satisfying. People gain a sense of accomplishment and efficacy. They are remunerated appropriately, and they are provided social and health benefits.

This emphasis on meaningful work includes special attention to women's challenges, needs, and opportunities. Women's domestic labor, especially their role as caregivers, is a key issue in the global economy and in social welfare planning. Domestic labor needs to be shared and allocated equitably, viewed as meaningful work, and supported and remunerated accordingly. In other words, domestic labor is not inherently or automatically "women's work." Domestic labor is a family systems issue, one that includes gender relations, cultural norms, values, and expectations. Domestic labor is, in addition, a national and international social welfare policy issue (Abramowitz, 1996).

Men's needs, like women's, also are family issues. Their needs for meaningful work also are important, especially as their employment opportunities may change and decline (United Nations, 1995c).

Furthermore, the relationship between men's work and women's work is crucial. To begin with, gender roles and relations in the family, as well as in surrounding societal cultures, often are constructed in relation to employment opportunities and priorities. Women's employment and work roles are also related to patriarchy. Patriarchy is a relatively recent social construction that some believe is attributable to or reinforced by rising industrialization, with wage-based labor (e.g., O'Connell, 1994; Degler, 1980). Families' sociocultural, political, and economic standing in the local community and in the nation often depends on the employment status of adults. Relationships involving power and authority in the family also depend on employment status and its corollaries, such as place and kind of residence, income-generating capacity, level of education, opportunity structures, and lifestyles (United Nations, 1994c).

Indeed, two concepts in social, political, and economic analysis, *socioeconomic status* and *social class*,[1] derive in part from employment differences. Socioeconomic hierarchies, i.e., social and cultural stratification systems based on differential income, education, power, and prestige, derive from the kind of employment individuals and families have. Their social and economic position also is influenced by the sector of the economy in which their employment is located. It matters to individuals and families if their employment is in the *formal sector*, the *informal sector*, or the *home and family sector*.

Similarly, *unemployment* and *underemployment* affect individual and family well-being, gender relations, and the family's location in these stratification systems (e.g., Wilson, 1997, 1999). Both conditions are also associated with strong national and cultural norms, standards, and sanctions. Unemployment may compel governmental policies intended to support individuals and families in need. Even so, families that are burdened by unemployment and underemployment often experience hurtful and harmful practices such as social marginalization and negative labeling (e.g., Benoît-Guilbot & Gallie, 1994; Wilson, 1997, 1999). In some communities and nations, unemployment and underemployment are inseparable from poverty and the dynamics of social and cultural exclusion (Hooper-Briar & Lawson, 1995). In others, survival, not just well-being, hinges on sustainable solutions to unemployment and underemployment (International Council on Social Welfare, 1986).

Every analysis of employment and economic sectors must be placed in a context, one that includes the diversity of the world community and its family systems. In the vast majority of nation-states, employment issues, like economic development, have traditionally been national concerns. Owing to the effects of a growing global economy, today they are increasingly international concerns as well. The global economy provides a mixture of new opportunities for some women, men, and their families at the same time that it presents significant challenges and problems for others (e.g., Hennon & Jones, 2000; Hennon & Loker, 2000; International Network on Unemployment and Social Work, 1987; UNDP, 1999). It invites controversy at the same time that it presents important new-century challenges for policy makers, helping professionals, and families (e.g., United Nations, 1975, 1986e, 1987; Vickers, 1991; Ward, 1990).[2]

The chapter progression is as follows. First, the concepts introduced above are defined. These concepts are basic building blocks for more responsive and effective policies and practices for families and helping professionals alike.

Then follows a discussion of unemployment, underemployment, and employment. Finally, the chapter examines the need for full and gender-equitable employment, including the remuneration of roles that contribute to the family, community, and society. Family-centered, occupational development skills are introduced in conclusion.

DEFINING THE KEY CONCEPTS

It is one thing to advocate for full, equitable, and meaningful employment. It is another to define it. The chapter thus begins with definitions.

Meaningful Work Versus Commodified Labor

Meaningful work is different from unhealthy, dehumanizing labor (Arendt, 1958). Labor is unhealthy and dehumanizing when workers who produce goods, services, and commodities are treated and feel like commodities (Radin, 1996). Commodified labor is dehumanizing, and it often does not bring sufficient income or benefits. When people perceive that they are merely labor-related commodities and feel like production units, not human beings, they feel devalued, their work is not meaningful, and their well-being declines (Lerner, 1986). Nowhere is this syndrome more evident than in cases involving the commodified, unhealthy labor of vulnerable women and children (e.g., Sen, 1999). As the well-being of women and children is compromised, so is family well-being (e.g., Lerner, 1986; Shore, 1987).

Definitions of meaningful work vary through time and across cultures, and they are dependent on material circumstances. National and international policies may exert a significant influence on whether activities such as domestic labor, caregiving, and community service are viewed by the persons who perform them, and by other citizens, as meaningful, socially valued work (e.g., Abramowitz, 1996). Individual preferences and the sense of rewards (intrinsic and extrinsic) for different kinds of jobs also vary within the same family system.

Despite this seemingly infinite variation, meaningful work has some important, defining features, including equity. Work is meaningful when it serves to maintain and enhance individual and family well-being. It is an identity sign. A person's work helps define one, in one's own eyes and the eyes of others. Meaningful work also hinges on norms and standards for equity, dignity, inclusion, and citizenship (Arendt, 1958; Gil, 1998a).

Work must be equitable in at least six important ways. First, ideally every citizen in a nation needs to have equal access to, and opportunities for, meaningful employment. Second, men and women, younger and older adults, need to receive equal compensation and benefits for the same kind of work.

Third, work opportunities, compensation, and benefits should be non-discriminatory (Wilson, 1997). Race, ethnicity, gender, sexual orientation, age, marital status, family system status, religious preference, presence of disabilities, and prior health and previous employment should not prevent current employment access, opportunity, and equity. Fourth, employment is equitable when international individual and family rights are honored, rights that prohibit child labor, slavery, indentured servitude, involuntary bondage, sweatshops, and unhealthy work policies and workplaces (United Nations, 1995a).

Fifth, employment is meaningful and equitable when it ensures an acceptable standard of living. It enables workers and their families to maintain and improve their well-being. They enjoy the rights, responsibilities, and dignity of being treated as important and feeling like important citizens. In this sense, employment promotes sociocultural, economic, and political inclusion. Sixth, employment is equitable when work hours are equitable. Work, whether in the home or out of the home, is equitable to the extent that it is the same for men as it is for women. Access to work as well as to wages and subsidies, both in the home and outside, also must be equitable. Wages must be equitable for all work that is performed, whether in the home or outside it.[3]

Short-term and Long-term Unemployment

Unemployment usually means being without a paid job of any kind. Unemployed persons are denied the benefits of employment and other meaningful work. On the other hand, unemployment, like "family," has different meanings in different nations. In turn, nations have different assumptions about unemployment. In some nations, unemployment is assumed to be temporary (also called "frictional unemployment"), and this assumption influences who gets counted as unemployed (e.g., Aronowitz & DiFazio, 1994).

In nations such as the United States, it is assumed that there always will be a small percentage of the unemployed who are temporarily jobless. They may be in between jobs, or returning to work after time in school or in family caregiving roles. Persons who have given up looking for jobs, i.e., those who are among the long-term unemployed because of failed job searches, hopelessness, and despair, may not be counted as "unemployed" (Briar, 1983).

The concept of temporary unemployment is sometimes based on the assumption that people want good jobs and that there are enough for everyone if one really wants to work. For example, social welfare benefit programs such as unemployment insurance in the United States are viewed as short-term "fixes," as temporary assistance, to assist individuals and families through the "transitions" from a lost job to a new one. The attendant stress on individuals and families also is viewed as temporary. Despite such perceptions, the reality is that at one time over 90 percent of the United States workforce had access to unemployment benefits. Such access has dramatically declined in the past two decades. Thus, even a short spell (less than fifteen weeks) of unemployment may be catastrophic for some individuals and families.

Structural unemployment and *chronic unemployment* present entirely different scenarios. Both signal equitable job creation needs and challenges.

Job loss may be the result of several factors. For example, technological innovation (e.g., robotics in industry, mechanization of agriculture) may make some jobs obsolete or redundant. In a growing number of nations, jobs may be lost forever because of changes in the employment sectors such as manufacturing declines, and the flight of business and industry to other nations. Economic recessions and depressions may cause businesses and companies to close, or to reduce their labor forces (Reich, 1993). Governments may downsize their departments, offering early retirements for employees without replacing them. Whatever the reason, the result can be the same. Structural unemployment runs the risk of consigning jobless workers to a permanent condition. When livelihoods are lost forever and, at the same time, work is transformed, the unemployed run the risk of becoming "the unemployable" (Briar, 1988).

Oftentimes, chronic unemployment is related to, and caused by, structural unemployment. Like structural unemployment, chronic unemployment may be long-term. It may be a by-product of job rationing—e.g., jobs for majority males, not minority males or women (Briar, 1988; Wilson, 1999).

Sometimes chronic unemployment in individuals and families is associated with health and mental health challenges such as substance abuse, depression, domestic violence, and child abuse and neglect. Disabling conditions, whether at birth or caused by circumstance, also influence employability and chronic unemployment. Individuals may want to work but lack essential employment-related supports and resources such as child care, caregiving supports, transportation assistance, housing, and attendance assistance. All may be both causes and consequences of chronic unemployment. In other words, unemployment is often accompanied by circular causal chains. Each need and problem link may be associated with the others, if not in the here-and-now, then eventually.

In brief, long-term unemployment, both structural and chronic, is often a root cause for many individual and family needs and presenting problems, which will be described later in this chapter. For now, two key points about chronic unemployment must be emphasized.

First, individuals (and their families) who are classified as unemployed, especially those who are chronically unemployed, are often blamed by others and even sanctioned by governments for their unemployment. When they are, the seeds are sown for social exclusion and marginalization. Employment challenges mount under these conditions.

The second point is related to the first. When structural unemployment is not understood, and there are no national and local monitoring mechanisms for it, structurally and chronically unemployed families may be blamed for a problem that was not of their own making. To put it another way, these individuals and families are casualties of economic policies and conditions that do not ensure jobs and income (Gil, 1999).

Underemployment

Underemployment has two meanings:

1. When persons have knowledge, skills, and abilities that their jobs do not tap, they are underemployed (e.g., Briar, 1988).
2. When persons are employed, but their jobs do not provide sufficient income and benefits to maintain individual and family well-being, they also are underemployed (e.g., Hoogvelt, 1997).

Both kinds of underemployment conflict with ideals of meaningful work. Both may be associated with commodified, dehumanizing labor. Like structural and chronic unemployment, both may be accompanied by economic, health, and mental health problems, which affect individuals and family systems (Briar, 1988). In fact, structural unemployment may compel individuals to take jobs that make them underemployed in both senses.

As noted earlier, the very concept of unemployment is market driven and even gender-role driven. Imagine, for example, what it would be like if families as workplaces were also covered in unemployment statistics and benefits. While the concepts of unemployment and underemployment are important to national and international policy and practice, exclusion of family work and "gendered" roles reflects some of the causes of the worldwide growing feminization of poverty and the impoverishment of households headed by women.

THE COSTS OF POVERTY, UNEMPLOYMENT, AND UNDEREMPLOYMENT

As millions of workers and families fall victim to the predictable human costs of joblessness and the fracturing of their families, irreversible family scarring may take place. Cycles of addictions, abuse, depression, and mental illness and related health problems rise (Briar, 1988). Genetic changes may occur over time as a result of the hazards of deteriorating health (self-medicating behaviors) compounded by environmental pollutants. Despite aggressive policies to shore up "human capital" in support of competitive advantages in the luring of transnational corporations (TNC), there are in fact job shortages everywhere (e.g., International Labour Office, 1998). Awareness is growing among children that going to school and completing degrees does not automatically translate into a good job, let alone a permanent one (Watts, 1984). This loss of hope and aspiration is itself a cause of declining well-being, especially for vulnerable and marginalized families (Fine & Weis, 1998).

Commodified, dehumanizing labor and workplaces that are harmful have adverse impacts on individuals, families, and, in turn, communities (Lerner, 1986). Many of the human costs of harmful workplace practices seem to be universally shared by workers and their families around the world (e.g., International Council on Social Welfare, 1986). Unemployment of an adult worker usually creates an economic crisis in the family. There are now more than 800 million workers unemployed or underemployed worldwide (Rifkin, 1995). Problems stemming from structural, long-term unemployment are being evidenced, for example, in every nation in the European Union (Benoît-Guilbot & Gallie, 1994; Geyer, Ingebritsen, & Moses, 2000; Jordan, 1998; Reyneri, 1994).

Not all persons who experience job layoffs, underemployment, workplace toxins, accidents, and stresses suffer irreparably. Some people can turn to their families, communities, and governmental services for help in coping.

Others are able to move freely into a new, more desirable job. Still others derive satisfaction and recover from psychosocial and economic injuries through religious or civic involvement and activism. Some become union organizers or work to build better services to mitigate the afflictions of others. They turn their pain into action. They seize the opportunity to talk about human rights and engage in democratic mobilization. They ask corporate, labor, and governmental leaders to consider their social responsibilities and accountabilities to individual, family, and community well-being (M. Lerner, 1986).

Most nations do not provide sufficient supports and resources to laid-off workers, their families, and communities. In developed nations there may be a modest unemployment or welfare benefit. Many of these supports are being dismantled or reduced (Midgley, 1997, 1999). In some nations (e.g., Scandinavian countries), income supports may be sufficient to sustain the family's wage-based standard of living, even when the wage was low (Ginsberg, 1983). However, in many developed nations policy makers tend to keep income assistance below wage levels to ensure that workers will work rather than become dependent on some form of government-provided income assistance.

In a few Western European nations (e.g., Sweden), ones that have active and intensive labor market policies, a laid-off worker may appear the next day in a governmentally provided public sector job until a new private sector job opportunity emerges (Ginsberg, 1983). Under the best circumstances, evidenced primarily in Scandinavian countries, these workers can maintain their homes and standards of living.

Many persons around the world who are the only provider of wages for their family and who face layoffs also experience some form of downward economic skidding because, without wages, they and their families have few other income sources to which to turn. Social isolation and marginalization may grow. As a result, there may be the loss of housing, resources, or other goods. Even their family may splinter as members go in search of jobs or cope by self-medicating though alcohol or drugs. In some countries, families may be driven to place their children in an orphanage, while others may send their children out to help by wandering the streets, begging for money or food. In extreme cases, children may be sold so that they and their family can survive (Bales, 1999). Some children starve and die along with their parents and other family members.

Despite this, adults who are jobless and poor are often stigmatized and blamed for their unemployment and problematic functioning. Their families are blamed and stigmatized, too. All members may be considered different, inferior, and irresponsible, and they may be subjected to the dynamics of moral exclusion (Opotow, 1990). This exclusion increases the social inequalities of a society and their consequences (Gallie, 1994a; Giddens, 1995; Wilkinson, 1996).

The absence of welfare state supports for families can have devastating and irreparably damaging effects on individuals and the family as whole. For example, loss of a job may lead to the loss of the home, and then the family may become homeless. Stopping and reversing vicious downward cycles takes time. Tragically, it may be too late for some individuals and families.

The dynamics of unemployment and its effects on families vary. Some families become stronger emotionally because they have weathered pain and challenges with their relationships in tact. However, many families cannot.

Box 3.1 presents the case of Jan and Marv Bordsy. The pervasive effects of their layoffs are ones found in other families who experi-

---

JAN AND MARV BORDSY

When Jan and Marv were laid off from the pharmaceutical company, they went through a very painful time. Jan was depressed and even suicidal, and Marv began drinking heavily. To deal with their desperation, Marv moved 550 kilometers away to find work in another transnational corporation. Only recently has a garment factory opened near their home. Jan now works there about ten hours each day, plus takes home piecework to complete in the evenings.

A few of the former pharmaceutical plant employees got employment with the garment factory, but at much lower pay. In fact that is one reason the factory opened in this village. The owners knew people would be desperate for work and could be hired for low wages.

While it is not talked about openly, Jan suspects that some of her friends and co-workers are victims of domestic violence. People miss work, and then she sees the bruises they try so hard to cover up. The husband of one of her friends died one night in an accident after drinking heavily. Jan worries about her friends and village, but she is trying so hard to take care of her own family that she doesn't have much time to fret or try to help.

BOX 3.1

TABLE 3.1. Phases in Unemployment

Typical stresses and coping responses involving long-term joblessness (15 weeks or more)

Phase I:

- Loss of self-esteem
- Loss of self-confidence
- Increase in anxiety, irritability
- Rising economic fears

Phase II:

- Rising debt
- Problematic interactions with family and friends
- Self-medicating behaviors
- Stress-related health problems
- Job seeking may involve rejection, heightening depression and withdrawal
- Stress reactions increase

Phase III:

- Increasing loss of relationships
- Debt-ridden with reclaimed property
- Withdrawal
- Reduced job seeking

Phase IV:

- Loss of home
- Loss of family and friends (caused by stress-induced or abusive interactions)
- Loss of economic credit
- Loss of support network necessary to support successful job seeking
- Rising disabilities (mental and physical health problems, substance abuse leading to addictive behaviors)
- Many engage in criminal acts to survive

ence the dramatic shift from employment to unemployment and under-employment.

Sometimes families reject and in effect "lay off" the already laid-off worker. Consider, for example, the case of a male who was once the chief wage provider for his family. His job and income loss and his consequent coping responses (depression, abuse) may make him a threat to the family. And so, he may be rejected or "laid off" again. Because the family faces an economic crisis, the former provider is no longer seen as an asset but a liability (Briar, 1988). The other family members may see him becoming a problem and want to move away. He may be barred from the home. Now two households face a crisis.

While coping responses and behavioral orientations are influenced by the presence or absence of welfare state supports, a predictable pattern of responses occurs. This pattern can be thought of as occurring in phases, which may overlap and recur. Table 3.1 presents these phases.

Figure 3.1 depicts renewing and downward cycles of individual functioning that may accompany unemployment. Both the renewing as well as the more likely downward cycle have significant associated social and economic costs. These costs might have been prevented.

Table 3.2 depicts some helping strategies that can be used to foster family supports as strategic help to the jobless family member. These strategies are merely examples. They do not exhaust the possibilities, nor do they meet every need. The table illustrates what helping professionals might do differently and better with families challenged by employment-related needs. As employment challenges continue to grow around the world, employment-related skills and abilities will be essential for helping professionals. Presently, most helping professionals do not possess them, nor are they emphasized in professional education programs or in agency accountability and supervisory policies and practices.

In brief, helping professionals need to understand, look for, and address employment needs (Briar-Lawson, 2000-a). With policy makers and advocates, they also must begin to mount strategic efforts in support of employment- and unemployment-related policies and practices that are family mobilizing and family centered. Unfortunately, for some families and communities, it may be too late.

Hysteresis

Hysteresis is a term associated with the word "history." It signals that, for every problem and vicious cycle of problems and needs, there

Unemployment
↓
Demise Syndrome
↓

Jobless worker personalizes job-seeking rejections, compounding effects of layoff.	Subsidized unemployment enables worker to hold out for desirable job.
↓	↑
Joblessness compounded by lack of unemployment benefits, causing economic crisis.	Successful networking with family and friends reinforces job acquisition prospects.
↓	↑
Jobless worker engages in self-recriminating and abusive behaviors.	Social skills and livelihood options increase chances of job-seeking affirmations.
↓	↑
Jobless worker tends to punish self and support network; family and friends experience some of the symptoms and then withdraw or recoil.	Jobless worker seizes unemployment as opportunity to have a vacation to reconsider work options.
↓	↑
Jobless worker may "disable" self, unable to work; may be institutionalized for health, mental health, crime-related activities.	**Rejuvenating Opportunities** ↑ **Unemployment**

Figure 3.1 Unemployment: Crisis or opportunity

may be a history or a chain of cause-and-effect relationships. Hysteresis denotes a condition or state beyond which these problems and chains cannot be reversed.

Take, for example, a father who is experiencing discrimination and harassment at his job. His despondency and depression overtakes him. He quits. His wife is pregnant, or ill, and therefore cannot work outside the home. There is no money coming into the family. His children start having emotional problems, and their school attendance and performance plummet. The father becomes so despairing that he wants to give up. He turns to drugs or alcohol. Finally he becomes ill with heart

TABLE 3.2. Family-Centered Occupational Problem Solving

SUGGESTED STEPS	RATIONALE
Helping professional's initial remarks convey acceptance of and supportive feelings toward jobless member and family.	Given the stress of joblessness, the helping professional seeks to "normalize" some of what the jobless family member and family are experiencing.
Helping professional seeks jobless member and the rest of the family's perception of the causes and nature of the income and employment problems currently being experienced.	
Helping professional assesses the extent to which expectations, experiences, reference or support group, and family dynamics may impede or facilitate job search and employability.	
Helping professional explores with jobless member and family how their developmental needs might be best addressed by their occupational problem-solving effort.	
Helping professional assesses jobless member's and family members' current affective, cognitive, and behavioral functioning as a possible barrier to employment or as debilitated by rejections from a job search.	Helping professional is aware of human costs of joblessness and probes for any of its debilitating effects (e.g., substance abuse, irritability, violent interactions).
Helping professional attempts to "enter the family's culture," sensitively addressing age, ethnic, gender, sexual preferences, and occupational-related concerns and rights.	If such debilitating effects are pervasive, they may need to be the "presenting problem" until these job-seeking barriers are minimized.

Occupational Problem Solving

Helping professional assesses prior work history and competencies derived in the home, community, and in paid work.

continued

TABLE 3.2. (*Continued*)

SUGGESTED STEPS	RATIONALE
Helping professional assesses the chain of stressors and coping responses derived from the impact of joblessness, underemployment, and unemployment on the jobless worker and his or her family.	
Helping professional normalizes anger while assessing how the jobless worker and family cope with frustration, hurt, and anger.	
Helping professional addresses the losses and grieving that may be occurring in a supportive and family-centered manner.	
Helping professional pinpoints presenting problems (such as increased use of alcohol or drugs) and weighs whether they are barriers to employability or can be ameliorated with a job.	With increased risk factors, like an increase in "self-medicating" behaviors, the helping professional assesses whether a job search will exacerbate the situation or be a productive protective factor.
Helping professional normalizes joblessness, underemployment, and income problems as increasing by-products of changing economic and family structures.	
Helping professional helps jobless member to recall lost dreams, generating possible short- and long-term occupational goals.	
Helping professional structures occupational assessment to focus on strengths (prior work history, education, enduring a long, hard job search); blaming is avoided whenever possible.	
Helping professional assesses whether the jobless member is in a prevocational state or is in a job search/career planning process.	Many jobless workers seek any job and lose sight of the aspirations they once had. The helping professional can help the worker and the family think about

TABLE 3.2. (*Continued*)

SUGGESTED STEPS	RATIONALE
Helping professional assesses whether livelihood loss has occurred and the extent to which occupational diversification is possible.	a plan (even a long-term plan) to address these aspirations if they are potentially realistic.
Helping professional assesses the degree to which occupational problem-solving knowledge exists in the family, especially the consequences of multigenerational marginalization and exclusion from waged work.	
Helping professional helps jobless member to reconceptualize barriers as workable goals to be addressed, which may become employability plan goals.	
Helping professional helps family assess the degree to which the family's emotional, social, and financial resources support or impede a job search or the creation of a small business or microenterprise.	In some cases, barriers to job-seeking or microenterprise development may involve family members. For example, a father may want the mother home and not working, thus increasing the barriers to her job search.
Helping professional helps jobless member to prioritize goals and to select various options for achieving them.	
Helping professional addresses feasibility, if applicable, of fostering a microloan application and the development of a business plan.	
Helping professional is prepared for the jobless member to experience a "stuck" phase or two; is able to help jobless member examine the advantages and disadvantages of impasse, especially involving the return to a livelihood in demise, the issues that keep him or her stuck, and solutions to move beyond impasse.	

continued

TABLE 3.2. (*Continued*)

SUGGESTED STEPS	RATIONALE
Helping professional explains in detail what the various options entail, including taking a vocational interest inventory, pursuing informational interviews, joining a job club, pursuing a microloan, working and attending school, etc., while encouraging the jobless member and family to select preferences that fit their needs.	Many jobs sought by workers have low probability of attainment. This is because there may be many more workers seeking the desired job. Thus a "probability assessment" is essential. This involves labor market research by the helping professional, worker, and even family members.
Helping professional helps jobless member develop a manageable timetable for achieving these steps.	
Helping professional conveys expectation that jobless member and family will succeed at steps in process.	
Helping professional and jobless family member collaborate on a plan to make the process of a work search or small business application a tool for self-development and instrumental to both short- and long-term employment and career.	
Roles are explored for family members to be helpful with self-assessment, labor market research, and self-promotion.	
Roles are explored in terms of gender equity and balance: e.g., how can women and girls have equal access to school and jobs and microloans and not have to do both household and waged work without more equitable sharing of loads across both genders in the family.	The helping professional assesses the need for role realignment in the family and support network so that gender role equity is fostered whenever possible.
Helping professional, jobless family member, and family assess possible	

TABLE 3.2. (*Continued*)

SUGGESTED STEPS	RATIONALE
stumbling blocks in carrying out "work search" or microloan application plan. Helping professional attempts to minimize failure of plan by ensuring that the jobless member and family have the resources, skills, and cognitive, affective, and behavioral supports and capacity to carry it out.	Many job searches require up to 100 applications and 15 interviews prior to job acquisition. This "job rejection" pattern is aversive and may reduce job-seeking behavior. Helping professionals can foster a realistic understanding of the dynamics and probabilities associated with job applications. It is essential that family members and others in the support system understand the job search rejection process to be supportive and do not despair with job rejections.
Agreement is reached about the tentative nature of the plan and flexible expectations for its achievement based on family members; and about preferences on how to proceed, scaling down or changing steps in the plan as a way of minimizing failure or behavioral, cognitive, or affective relapse.	
Jobless worker's and family members' resources for energy and self-care are assessed.	
Helping professional's role in mobilizing resources and in occupational "mentoring" will be identified.	

Team Building: Case Management

Helping professional convenes all service providers, with family members present and empowered as much as possible to be in charge.

Helping professional reviews commitment to helping family succeed in its occupational problem solving and related goals.

Family members state their expectations from service providers; service

continued

TABLE 3.2. (*Continued*)

SUGGESTED STEPS	RATIONALE
providers state their expectations and plans; helping professional pinpoints any areas requiring more problem solving or alternative service plans.	
Helping professional examines time-table for all involved and sets realistic expectations for when changes can occur, especially job acquisition or job creation activities.	In many cases, a successful job search or job creation requires other supports, from child care professionals, teachers who might not understand the support role of children, microcredit lenders, and so forth. Having all of these stake-holders meet to pledge support and to foster additional help and ideas may reinforce the worker, family, and job generation process.
Helping professional provides continuity between service providers and family.	
Helping professional serves as advocate for jobless member and family with service providers, resource systems, credit organizations, schools, and employers.	
Helping professional provides support and feedback on a regular basis.	

problems. His children are now neglected; they suffer emotionally. These children have dropped out of school and are in and out of juvenile detention. They cannot reclaim their youthful rights and years as they are incarcerated with others who are teaching them even more aggressive criminal lifestyles and brutalizing them. The father cannot regain his health, nor can the marriage survive the stress. The family problems have taken such a toll that after a while the parents separate.

Hysteresis characterizes the situation for this family. It implicates negative consequences for the family, helping professionals, and policy makers. Hysteresis can be prevented, and it could have been prevented in this case.

Appropriate intervention policies, welfare state supports, codes of conduct and accountability standards for employers, full and gender-equitable employment agendas, and other measures help prevent hysteresis. Instead of driving children to jail, a father to a heart attack, and a relationship to a divorce, policy makers might have had in place job placement, retraining, family business incubator programs, or micro-enterprise schemes for the father and the children. Children's or family allowances might have also helped to sustain this family. Or, caregiver benefits might have been provided.

Because these and other family-responsive policies were not available, hysteresis took root. Hysteresis adds to the sense of crisis governments may experience. Decades of neglect may create intergenerational health and mental health needs in families, addiction, and violence-related consequences (Briar, 1988).

Permanent injury, inequality, and declining well-being have long arms that reach through time. When hysteresis is evident, many generations of family members are affected. For example, there is a growing body of research that documents how childhood abuse, for example, is associated with preventable diseases and adult longevity problems (e.g., Felitti, Anda, et al., 1998).

Nation-state analyses also parallel such findings on the ripple effects of injury and harm to classes and groups. For example, it may take decades, if not a century or more, to eradicate all of the harmful effects of apartheid in South Africa. Similarly, the enslavement of African Americans in the United States has harmful effects even 150 years after the abolition of slavery. For example, African-American men are disproportionately represented in prisons and jails. The life expectancy of African-American families challenged by poverty and clustered in American cities is lower than that of their counterparts in developing nations (Sen, 1999). In the same vein, it may take decades and centuries to eradicate the harms of castes in nations such as India.

Similarly, it is difficult to reverse traditions that support gender-based atrocities, such as female genital mutilation; the delivery of girls into marriage, as property, with a dowry or bride price; and bride burning. Rapes, female genocide, and other atrocities are all related to patriarchy and gender inequality. Despite attempts to promote equitable rights for women (e.g., the United Nations Decade for Women), the harms associated with patriarchy and inequality are omnipresent, and include inequitable access to good jobs, income, and education. These gendered harms also implicate children, increasing their vulnerability, poverty, and diminished hopes for a better life. They perpetuate poverty and the rising feminization of poverty worldwide (O'Connell, 1994; Vickers, 1991).

To help frame new-century challenges and opportunities, the discussion now turns to three work sectors. The third such sector, the home and family, which often is neglected in policy discourses, is especially important when addressing the feminization of poverty.

THREE WORK SECTORS: AN OVERVIEW

As discussed above, conventional economic thinking often focuses upon two dominant work sectors: the formal sector and the informal work sector. This thinking overlooks a third important sector: the home and the family. All three sectors are important shapers of family functioning.

The formal work sector includes work organizations in both the private and public sector. It encompasses the production of consumer goods, along with the industries associated with their production, marketing, and consumption. It also includes service sectors, both public and private. Employment in this formal sector includes formal wages, social and health benefits, and perhaps governmental protections and entitlements. Wages usually are subjected to taxation. Governments know who is employed in this sector.

Labor unions, nongovernmental organizations, and professional associations have advanced workers' rights and working conditions in formal sector jobs. This formal sector is associated with the rise of industrial economies and the accompanying development of the welfare state in developed nations. In fact, the formal sector is a strong correlate of the welfare state (e.g., Pierson, 1996).

The informal economy is both a historical artifact, which predates the welfare state, and a growing contemporary employment sector. It encompasses a broad range of jobs, including those related to the production of consumer products and work performed in the expanding services industry. So-called cottage industries, "sweat shops," also are informal sector enterprises (e.g., Nuralamin, 1996).

As in the formal sector, employment in the informal sector is performed for wages. However, these wages are often lower than those received for comparable jobs in the formal economy. Moreover, wages in the informal sector do not include benefits and entitlements. Nor are workers automatically taxed, because governments may not know about the jobs or the employers. Similarly, protective policies for workers in the informal sector are absent. Workers in the informal sector are power-less to unionize. Many are women and children. Their workplaces and working conditions often are unhealthy. Many such workers are under-employed because they have knowledge, skills, and abilities that their jobs do not tap and because their jobs do not provide wages and benefits that support an adequate standard of living. They and their families ex-perience multiple kinds of stress and insecurity related to income and their jobs.

The home and family sector centers on domestic labor, family roles, and responsibilities such as caregiving. The key points about this sector are that women perform the bulk of the work and that they do so with-out wages, benefits, and other employment supports (e.g., O'Connell, 1994). Because their work is hidden in the household and it is not valued, women who perform these jobs thus present classification problems (e.g., Oakley, 1974). They are not considered employed, but neither are they considered unemployed (unless they recently lost a job). Yet they often are used as a surplus labor pool (Abramowitz, 1996). Their work value, domains, and opportunities often are regulated by patriarchal policies.

Moreover, women's wages in the formal sector may be a function of patriarchal standards and expectations in a community or nation. A woman may work in the formal sector, but her wages will be less than a man's for the same job. This may be reinforced by the fact that she is expected to contribute her wages to the family controlled either by father or husband (e.g., Ward, 1990).

THE FORMAL WORK SECTOR

Unlike caregiving and other domestic roles in the family, jobs in the for-mal work sector are wage based. This formal work sector comprises pri-vate sector corporations, plants, and factories, as well as public sector governmental programs such as schools, prisons, and social services. This formal sector is dominated by workplaces located in transnational corporations (TNCs) and other organizations that are part of market economies. These workplaces are the evolutionary consequences of the industrial revolution, the rise of wage-based labor, and the commodifi-cation of work and workers. They are also the generators and reinforcers of the sexual division of labor involving waged and women's unwaged work (Mies, Bennholdt-Thomsen, & von Werlhof, 1991).

As Pierson (1996, pp. 36–37) observes, a cluster of related forces making up "modernization" fueled and accompanied the rise of this formal sector. These forces include (1) the rise of capitalism; (2) the commercialization and commodification of economic relationships; (3) the growing social division of labor; (4) transformations in modes of thought and planning as instrumental rationality, especially scientific modes of thought, replaced tradition, affect, and value rationality; (5) urbanization; (6) demographic shifts; and (7) democratization, especially expansion of political participation and the provision of new opportunity structures to greater numbers of people.

Gender differences are most evident in the formal economy. Men tend to have more of these jobs than women. For example, in TNCs women make up only 28 percent of the workforce (Ward, 1990). Some of these jobs have recognizable personnel policies, some have benefits (both material and psychosocial), and some have access to union protections.

Today, the formal work sector is changing rapidly and dramatically. Once constrained by the boundaries of nation-states and under the control of national governments, global forces have freed it from these constraints and controls. New global finance strategies, together with the rapid movement of economic capital, are characteristic features of this economic globalization (Thurow, 1996). Another key feature is accelerating development of the global production organization, especially the rise of the TNC.

Today TNCs are found in nearly every part of the world. They shape both the formal work sector and much of the informal work sector. As Pierson (1996) argues, TNCs make talk about "national economies" nearly anachronistic and obsolete. Changes in the formal work sector and the emergence of a growing informal sector are defining components in the new "economic globalization."

The impacts of economic globalization on the world's families and their well-being are being documented. Some are identified in chapter 10. One family scenario is presented in box 3.2. The situation described in this box is not atypical. Many workers around the world are increasingly lured or recruited from agricultural roles into the formal economic sector with its factories, labor laws, and employment benefits. (Chapters 10 and 11 will provide another frame for understanding this pattern.)

Men establish a wage base in the formal economy that makes their

BOX 3.2

SINGH AND LIM MUNG AND THEIR FAMILY SYSTEM

Lim Mung is ten years old. He and his mother, Singh, go to a garment factory each day. They sometimes take Lim's three-year-old sister with them when their grandmother is unable to care for her. Grandmother often does domestic work outside the home. When this happens, Singh carries the three-year-old on her back for up to ten hours. She makes the equivalent of $1 an hour, while Lim makes 65 cents an hour. Lim's father, Ming, works in a transnational corporation far away. He sends money to the family and returns home as often as he can.

Singh works up to seventeen hours a day. Ten of her hours are in the garment factory, four hours with piecework that she takes home, and an average of at least three hours in food gathering, meal preparation, child care, and socializing and educational activities for the children. Singh is not unlike many women worldwide whose work may span all three sectors—the formal, informal, and household domains —involving up to nineteen hours a day (Hossfeld, 1990). Some nights she is awake attending to the children's coughing and asthmatic attacks. Several times a month she has to help her mother with bouts of weakness, shortness of breath, and what seem to be increasing circulatory problems.

Two of the children have been born with disabilities because of the pollutants in their community. They are being reared by Singh's sister. This family had worked earlier for a pharmaceutical company that closed. The family moved after it was revealed that harmful toxins were affecting the well-being of children. Now Singh and Ming despair about their future as they worry that they cannot support themselves, or Singh's sister, including all of her home-based caregiving. They also worry about their frail grandmother, who increasingly is unable to work or to care for their three-year-old.

For generations, both Singh's and Ming's families had been farmers who grew rice and tea plants. While Singh and Ming feel a sense of productivity from being good and able workers, they have become very frightened by the rupturing of their family systems. They lament the loss of the old family farm ways, the ruination of ancient soils, and the increasing inability to have a sense of hope about the future. They feel very insecure. They are getting by for now, but the layoff of any one of them could send the family into abject poverty and hunger and perhaps result in the death of family members. Many other children in their village have been shipped off as contracted workers for carpet weaving and prostitution in the big cities. Their family system is "hanging on" as best it can.

earnings of primary value to their family, because they are usually paid twice what women earn (e.g., Baber & Allen, 1992; O'Connell, 1994). By contrast, many of the roles of women are regulated by the state in accordance with customs and desires of the corporate sector; in addition, these roles often reflect patriarchal traditions and practices. Corporate supervisory, hiring, and retention policies and practices are carriers of cultural stereotypes and prescriptions for women; most are discriminatory (e.g., Abramowitz, 1996; Baker, 1995; Burggraf, 1997; Ridgeway, 1997). Women's responsibilities for children or elder care weigh heavily upon the wages they receive (e.g., Waldfogel, 1997), including their decisions to seek full-time employment in lieu of welfare, if it is available (e.g., Edin & Lein, 1997).

On the other hand, the global economy poses problems and challenges for men as well. Men's work roles are also changing with the global economy. Two causes stand out. First, globalization in concert with technology has resulted in fewer jobs in the formal sector. Second, as the plight of rural families has worsened, a growing number of men have migrated to the cities to find employment (Dasgupta, 1995), or families in cities see their members go to rural areas for work in agriculture (e.g., in the Ukraine) (Jordan, 1998). Families are divided in the process, and the challenges they face intensify. In the informal work sector, men may not be any more financially supported than women.

THE INFORMAL WORK SECTOR

Economic globalization is associated with growth in the informal work sector. The informal work sector involves ancillary jobs that are temporary. These jobs lack social and health benefits and labor protections. As noted earlier, this informal sector includes cottage and street industries and sweatshops, which tend to exploit the labor of women and children (Ward, 1990; Mies, Bennholdt-Thomsen, & von Werlhof, 1991). As in the industrial era, in this globalization process men may disproportionately bypass the informal work sector and move directly into the formal work sector, into transnational corporate work roles as technicians, laborers, and managers (Mies, Bennholdt-Thomsen, & von Werlhof, 1991; Ward, 1990).

The growth in this informal sector is enormous in some parts of the world. For example, at least 60 percent of the employed workers in sub-Saharan Africa work in this sector; 40–60 percent in Asian nations are in this sector (Haruo, 1996). The rapid expansion of this sector is so new, and its growth is so pronounced, that researchers and community developers are still examining ways to study and plan in relation to it (Nuralamin, 1996). For example, many community-development strategies do not work as planned with families in the informal sector because they underestimate the extreme vulnerability and uncertainties of living faced by these families, especially those headed by women (Mies, Bennholdt-Thomsen, & von Werlhof, 1991; Ward, 1990; Sanyal, 1996).

Women's work in the informal sector is interwoven with their domestic work roles in the home (Mies, Bennholdt-Thomsen, & von Werholf, 1991). In some cases it is an extension of it. Working in the informal sector, for some, means that their work is done in their living quarters. Working in close quarters may intensify family stress. It also means that health-enhancing home and family environments may be compromised in the face of economic necessity. Nonetheless, women's access to employment in a TNC may not be a guarantee of better wages, living standards, or esteem (Ward, 1990).

Gender and child oppression is also compounded by age, race, and class discrimination (Ward, 1990). Hiring practices reflect cultural traditions and patriarchy. These practices may discriminate against people based on their age, gender, race and ethnicity, and religion. Young and older populations are relegated to the least desirable jobs in the informal sector or become locked out of jobs entirely. These groups, along with women, may be regarded as a surplus labor pool.

WOMEN, DOMESTIC LABOR, AND INCOME ISSUES IN THE THIRD ECONOMIC SECTOR

As discussed in chapter 2, the world's families provide the vast majority of the work involving caregiving, peacekeeping, counseling, education, health care, and justice. Women tend to perform this work in their homes. The United Nations *Human Development Report* (UNDP, 1995) has estimated the value of women's work in the home to be 11 trillion dollars. Men's domestic work is valued at 5 trillion dollars (United Nations, 2000).

Moreover, studies sponsored by the United Nations found that women do two-thirds of the world's work but receive only 10 percent of its income and own only 1 percent of the world's means of production (e.g., Bennholt-Thomsen, 1991, p. 159). There are other signs of inequity. Although women produce half of the world's food and run 70 percent of the world's small businesses, women actually own only 1 percent of the world's property (Henderson, 1996).

Women represent two-thirds of the world's poor (Wetzel & Campling, 1993). In the developing nations, women make up 80 percent of the poor in rural communities (Jordan, 1998). One source of their poverty is their unpaid labor. Women's domestic labor, the oldest form of work in the world, is essential to family support and care and to the economic, social, and cultural foundations of a nation.

Waring (1990) and others argue that women and children will remain property as long as their labor is appropriated by those who regulate it, and as long as outsiders decide whether to acknowledge and remunerate it. This framework ushers in one definition of slavery. Giddens (1994), moreover, indicates that ideas about productive citizenship and productivity derive from gendered divisions of labor. These citizenship ideas fail to acknowledge that domestic labor, performed primarily by women, is important work. When caregiving and other domestic functions are not performed effectively, and when the health and well-being of individuals and families decline as a result, a more complete picture emerges of the benefits and costs of domestic caregiving and related family roles and jobs (e.g., Minton & Block, 1993).

Caregiving is often a full-time job. Like other forms of work, it can bring a sense of satisfaction. It also can cause stress. Because many caregivers lack sufficient supports, stress and isolation take a toll. Caregiver "burnout" is the best predictor of the placement of an elder in a nursing home (e.g., Briar & Kaplan, 1990; Briar & Ryan, 1986). Caregivers also double as employers when they hire aides, child care providers, and attendants.

The isolation, impoverishment, and resource shortfalls stemming from unpaid labor may erode families' capacities. Stressed caregivers may cause harm instead of nurturing and protecting loved ones. Abuse, neglect, and domestic violence are common responses to excessive stress (United Nations, 1992c). Furthermore, stressed caregivers may be just one "caregiving crisis" away from skidding into abject poverty, dependency, and declining health while caring for another. Ironically, caregivers involved in long-term care may need the help of other caregivers because of the tolls exacted from them (e.g., Briar & Ryan, 1986).

Women and children face special challenges. It is estimated that some 50 percent of the subsistence needs of families worldwide are met through the labor and substandard wages of women and children, who dominate informal labor markets (Ward, 1990).

However, statistics like these do not adequately explain family experiences and impacts. Women's well-being and, in turn, that of their children and other dependent family members, derives from the priorities assigned them in the political economic order (e.g., Doyal, 1995, p. 5). For example, a survey in Kenya showed that women are responsible for 80 percent of the cereal production, yet the training facilities are entirely for men. Similarly, the Beti men of Cameroon labor seven and a half hours a day and are seen as active laborers by the International Labor Organization, a UN agency, but the Beti women work eleven hours a day and none of their work is deemed "active labor." Such work becomes productive only when it is remunerated.

Children are also affected. Many are exploited and harmed. Child labor laws either do not exist, or they are not enforced. Despite the United Nation's protective child labor regulations adopted in 1976, large numbers of children are employed, many in insidious jobs. It is estimated that there are now 250 million children, ages five to fourteen years, employed; half of them work full time. Of the more than 250 million children who are employed, 153 million are at work in Asia, 80 million in Africa, and 17.5 million in Latin America (International Labour Office, 1993). Many work in hazardous industries. For example, in the Mung's village (box 3.2), millions of children and youth are sold or contracted out as laborers, including some in the "sex trade." Child trafficking for sex industries is on the increase. Reportedly, millions of children are hired or enslaved as child prostitutes. Obviously, practices like these do not tap the human potential, and they are associated with intergenerational patterns, which also may multiply and spread. Clearly, there is a need for new policies and practices that support and strengthen families and promote human freedom, dignity, and well-being.

TOWARD A PRO-FAMILY POLICY AND PRACTICE AGENDA THAT PRIORITIZES MEANINGFUL WORK

To summarize, meaningful work taps the human potential and facilitates learning and healthy development (Gil, 1999). It allows adults to have productive and contributing roles, benefiting in turn their families, co-workers, and communities. And, when adults work with others in health-enhancing workplaces, there are other benefits. Co-workers may offer supports that are critical to individual and family well-being. For some, the workplace is like a healthy family (Briar, 1988). Even in the informal sector, women may find that their work gives them means to resolve gender-related and gender-based economic stress and power conflicts with their partners (Ward, 1990).

Unfortunately, economic globalization and the global economy do not bode well for all of the world's families. As Burggraf (1997) observes, problems for families are rooted in political and economic decisions, and increasingly these problems are bound up in globalization. Families, she argues, are the most important components in economic development, but they have never been recognized and supported as such. Said differently, if the well-being of families is privileged over the relentless and blind pursuit of profits, many of today's "social problems" involving, or related to, families can be prevented. Effective social and economic development policies will build on this basic finding.

TOWARD NEW INVESTMENT STRATEGIES FOR WOMEN AND FAMILIES

The preceding analysis implicates a host of related policy and practice questions. For example: Is meaningful work a right or a privilege? At what point does meaningful work gain a higher priority than cost-saving production technologies? What are the sociocultural and political consequences of economic determinism? Who will arrest "runaway capitalism" and its commodification of human beings? These kinds of questions pave the way for an integrated approach to development, one that is social, equitable, political, and economic.

These questions, and others that they suggest, indicate that in nations throughout the world a critical, new investment strategy is needed. *The various roles family members play (e.g., caregiver or student) must be defined as meaningful work and remunerated appropriately.* A conceptual shift is involved—namely, that the important work families perform—

especially women members—is given due recognition, is measured, and then remunerated and rewarded.

Families and Women as Social Investments

This line of reasoning is consistent with the basic premises that families are comprehensive service, support, and resource systems; and when they discharge their duties and meet their responsibilities, essential work is being performed. This conceptual shift thus involves recognition of family work roles, sees families not merely as consumers of goods and services but as producers of goods and services. Goods and services include, for example, the education of children, caregiving for elderly and disabled persons, and family support work on the behalf of neighbors (United Nations, 1995c).

In short, in this pro-women and pro-family policy frame, two things are done at the same time. The work spheres of families are preserved and their achievements are recognized, remunerated, and rewarded. Gender equity in both role allocation and income supports then needs to follow. This conceptual shift entails viewing achievements such as healthy, educated children and disabled or elderly persons who do not require institutional care as demonstrable public goods, public goods that can be assigned economic and social value.

Remuneration for these family-produced public goods can take various forms: such remuneration can be viewed as a *social investment,* complete with identifiable human development, economic, political, and sociocultural benefits.[4] Such a social investment can be contrasted with a *social expenditure,* which drains resources and does not provide identifiable returns.

However, many nations are reducing their social investments. As nations are encouraged by the World Bank, International Monetary Fund, and other lending institutions to cut their welfare expenditures, freeing up more money for economic investments, they are working at cross-purposes. In fact, welfare expenditures can be deemed investments that are responsive to the caregiving and related tasks performed by families without which entire societies would fall apart.

Women's and families' futures are consigned to precariousness unless nations shoulder some of the responsibilities for caregiving costs, as is the case in parts of Europe (Folbre, 1994). Moreover, Folbre (1994) argues that by not remunerating family labor, the welfare state's future is threatened.

Universal Demogrants for Caregivers and Families

Industrialized countries in Western Europe, and Canada, have found ways to aid families with the costs of the care and raising of their children. Children's (and Family) Allowances, called *demogrants,* have been integral to their welfare states since the end of World War II. These demogrants provide modest supports to families. They are based on the recognition that wages do not respond to family size. However, some argue that these supplements reinforce sexism and the gendered division of labor (e.g., Abramowitz, 1996; Mies, Bennholdt-Thomsen, & von Werlhof, 1991).[5]

Controversy notwithstanding, demogrants are universal entitlements. That is, they are provided to every family with children regardless of income needs. Unlike in the United States where welfare grants were provided only to the poor, the universal reliance on such demogrants in Western Europe may make the dismantling of them far more problematic. In contrast, consider the relative ease with which policy makers in the United States have attacked and dismantled the welfare program, leaving poor and vulnerable families without any safety net after maximum time limits (less than five years in some states) are up. There are exceptions, however. A few states in the United States are exempting from welfare termination parents who care for disabled children.

NEEDS FOR INTEGRATIVE THINKING IN POLICY AND PRACTICE

Imagine how policy making and professional practice would change if family needs were placed at the center of economic investments and were framed in relation to them. Equitable and democratized workplaces and family ecosystems would produce multiple social and economic development dividends. In short, comprehensive, integrated policies have "ripple benefits" for individuals, families, communities, and entire nations. By contrast, nations that perpetuate laissez-faire policies toward workplaces permit labor and wage discrimination against women and perpetuate inequitable policies and practices.

Patriarchy has to be weighed into this integrative thinking and planning in relation to vexing problems. Its persistence impedes the reduction of poverty and social inequality and obstructs sustainable development. Indices adapted from Wetzel and Campling (1993) for the mitigation or elimination of patriarchy include:

- Equal responsibility across both genders for family caregiving
- Equal wages for the same work
- Equal access to education and to economic loans and supports
- Equal access to requisite food, clothes, shelter, health
- Freedom from sexual harassment at the workplace
- Women's political development seen as an essential component of social and economic development (Wetzel & Campling, 1993, p. 24)

Gender and sex role development would be seen as a universal aspect of human development and a direct result of global economic development (Wetzel & Campling, 1993). Indeed, the Technical and Evaluation Division of the United Nations Population Fund has promoted a gender role analysis for all programs. This analysis can be adapted for all pro-family policies. Role analysis includes creative activity; control over resources; access to money, materials, goods, and services; decision-making power; training opportunities; and access to knowledge (Wetzel & Campling, 1993, p. 36).

Toward a Family-Centered Gender Equity Index

When families' needs move to center stage, gender equity becomes a top priority. The distribution of rights, the allocation of resources, the ability to give voice to family needs and wants—all must be equitable. Equity must be developed in families and among them. Violence, discriminatory practices, and gender inequality, often "hidden in the home," must be eliminated. Promoting this pervasive gender equity is a key challenge for family policy and practice.

A family investment index was presented in chapter 2. This investment index needs to be accompanied by a gender-equitable support index for families. Table 3.3 provides an example of such an index. This gender-equitable family support index (or variations) may serve as a reminder and guide that gender-equitable labor, investments, supports, and rights need to be central organizing frameworks for family investments, work, employment, and income policies and practices. This index can be used to chart progress in the promotion of this key component of equity in family well-being.

With this context in mind, the discussion now turns to full employment as a family support strategy. Full employment may also serve to mitigate some of the effects of patriarchal norms.

**TABLE 3.3. Toward a Democratized,
Gender-Equitable Family Support Index**

- Are democratized families given high status in society and by policy makers and helping professionals?

- Are men held accountable for charting and advocating for democratized and gender-equitable rights?

- Are decisions regarding family matters made in democratized ways, with all stakeholders consulted and involved, especially the women in the family, e.g., mother, daughters, elder women?

- When members are asked to give voice to their families' needs and wants, are women's voices required? Are women's needs and views respected and used in framing policy and practice?

- Are work roles across the formal, informal, and home equitably distributed so that the hours of work are gender equitable within the family?

- Are women and girls able to make independent decisions about their careers, marriages, and choices about partners?

- Is access to school, jobs, and civic roles supported in the home so that there is gender equity?

- Are girls and women allowed to seek careers, and do they have the same rights as men?

- Are there protections for women and children and elders from abuse, especially domestic violence, child abuse, and elder abuse and neglect?

- Are the hours devoted to caregiving, family home maintenance, and food gathering and preparation equitably distributed?

- Are work hours outside the home in the informal or formal work sectors equitably distributed?

- Is food distribution in the family equitable and appropriate for each member's age and developmental stage? Does each member receive the kinds of foods and calories he or she needs to maintain well-being?

- Is there equitable gender access to health and education?

- In nations with strict population controls, are infant girls valued and supported as much as infant boys?

FULL AND EQUITABLE EMPLOYMENT
AS A KEY FAMILY SUPPORT AGENDA

The realities of meaningful work in the home, especially the work done by women, must be acknowledged and rewarded. Domestic labor, including home-based caregiving, must become a recognized and wage-based third work sector. This third sector employment should include remuneration for work that provides family supports and community services. This employment development and support strategy will help define postscarcity societies of the future (Giddens, 1994, 1995).

Unfortunately, today's societies create artificial job scarcity. Paid employment is limited, jobs are rationed, and the unemployed are labeled and marginalized. Such "manufactured unemployment" is critical to capitalism and to anti-inflationary strategies and suppressants to wages and workers' power. However, social and economic costs accompany this manufactured unemployment. Leaders in the postscarcity societies of the future will need to address these costs by promoting a full and equitable employment agenda, in turn, expanding conceptions of meaningful work and providing income supports for it. They will support individuals, women, and families in the process. They will recognize that meaningful employment is a basic human right, promoting freedom, equality, equity, and social development (Jordan, 1998; Ray, 1998; Sen, 1999).

Some of these strategies include the redesign of the work week and work year, so that work is equitably shared. Microenterprises (small businesses) and family-based enterprises also contribute to full employment (e.g., Hennon, Jones, et al., 1998; Hooper-Briar & Lawson, 1994). These small businesses often require financial supports (e.g., Otero & Rhyne, 1994), and these financial supports are crucial to the success of microenterprises of poor persons. Box 3.3 provides an example of an innovative approach to financing microenterprises. It is called the Grameen Bank.

The Grameen Bank experience has demonstrated that women tend to reinvest their money and profits into their families. Men, on the other hand, are more likely to invest profits elsewhere—i.e., their families may not benefit (e.g., UNDP, 1999).

The Grameen Bank model is not a substitute for job guarantees. It does not, for example, address the needs of the poorest of the poor (Ray, 1998). Figuring out how to meet the needs of the most vulnerable families in the world is a crucial new-century challenge.

BOX 3.3

THE GRAMEEN BANK

An economics professor in Bangladesh was frustrated by conventional loan policies. He realized that many of the poor women in Bangladesh were extraordinary investments. They had good ideas, a strong work ethic, and knew how to develop microenterprises that could be tailored to the needs and characteristics of their local communities.

But these women could not get started because conventional financial institutions did not view them as worthy investments. These women were poor, and therefore lacked conventional resources such as savings accounts and real estate that lending institutions could accept as collateral (i.e., a safeguard for their loan). Moreover, lending policies were oriented toward individuals or one family.

The professor wanted to help these women. Starting with some of his own money, he developed an innovative lending institution. He called it the Grameen Bank. He focused its lending and other financial policies on the needs, wants, and aspirations of poor people, especially poor women. And, he formed advisory committees consisting of other women who would help make lending decisions and who would serve as "social collateral" for these loans.

Unlike conventional lending institutions, which focus on individuals and one family, this professor encouraged groups of women to apply for loans and launch their microenterprises. In other words, he recognized that one person confronted by poverty is often vulnerable, and the risks and pressures associated with a business and a loan may be overwhelming. In contrast, when a group of women is constituted, each person's vulnerability is reduced somewhat because of the social supports and shared responsibilities assumed by other members of the group. Moreover, the risks and responsibilities associated with each loan are collectivized, in turn reducing the probability that any one person will default on collective responsibilities for the loan. In this model, social collateral is assessed at the front end, interest rates are held low, and as loans are repaid, the funds are quickly redeployed to encourage other microloans and investments (Mizan, 1994).

In short, the lending policies of Grameen derive from an under-standing of poor women's social support and social capital networks, and they also serve to reinforce and support them. For, when these women are successful in their small businesses, their supports for one another are reinforced. In turn, these groups of women help stabilize their communities, perhaps encouraging others to do what they have done. Indeed, they often create advisory committees of other women who serve as the social collateral for their loans. The loans have helped to create many small businesses. Both the Grameen Bank and the small businesses it supports are examples of local innovations that benefit individuals, families, and communities.

The Grameen Bank has demonstrated that strategic investments in the poor, especially women, are cost effective; and, that these invest-ments produce multiple benefits. The Grameen Bank experience has helped to spearhead an international movement for microcredit and microloan strategies. The goal is to foster 100 million microcredit ini-tiatives worldwide (Microcredit Summit, 1998).

This impressive scale-up of the Grameen Bank has been made possible, in part, by external financial supports (Ray, 1998). After all, each new bank station requires staffing supports and facilities. In other words, significant start-up and infrastructure costs are involved. A con-ventional lending institution would calculate these costs and fix the interest rates on their loans accordingly, and rates would be higher as a consequence. High interest rates (e.g., 17–20 percent) would be counterproductive to the Grameen Bank's aim. Thus, governmental and international financial supports keep interest rates low because they offset start-up and scale-up costs.

Community cooperatives provide another way. For example, Wilkin-son and Quarter (1996) describe in considerable detail both the success stories and the two failures of community cooperatives on Prince Ed-ward Island, Canada. Some of the key facilitators are listed in table 3.4.

As in the Grameen Bank model, strong communal ties among in-dividuals and families were essential parts of effective cooperatives. It

TABLE 3.4. Facilitators for Cooperatives: The Evangeline Experience

The following six features and their components facilitated the development of successful cooperatives:

1. The positive attitudes, perspectives, and actions of initiators and members of the organizing committees, especially

   • a strong sense of attachment and cultural identity;

   • a strong sense of agency, a prevailing "can do" attitude;

   • strong trust networks and trust in the local community;

   • a strong sense of commitment—"kitchen table meetings" brought others on board and served as fact-finding vehicles; and

   • a strong emphasis on building self-reliant individuals and communities.

2. The positive responses of community members and organizations to initiators' actions.

3. The key contributions of institutional leaders (e.g., governmental officials) from the community, especially the roles they played in providing access to funding, serving as researchers and resource persons, providing technical assistance, and enabling capacity-building supports.

4. The key contributions of community development organizations in providing support and helping to legitimate the effort.

5. The role of external agencies and organizations, especially provincial and national governments.

6. The manner of project preparation: Leaders in Evangeline were especially adept at planning and building broad-based supports.

also was important that community members knew what they were up against—e.g., loss of jobs and the need to support local businesses and the families supported by them. It also was important that these cooperatives were voluntary organizations, inclusive in their membership, and democratic in their governance. Members educated one another, supported one another, and knew that they depended on one another. Other key features of cooperatives are listed in table 3.5 (New Economy Development Group, 1993; Wilkinson & Quarter, 1996).

TABLE 3.5. Key Features of Cooperatives

1. There is local ownership and control, either by a geographically defined community or a community of common interest.[1]

2. The cooperative focuses on the interests of individuals, but goes beyond them to include the needs of the entire community.

3. Community economic development is undertaken in a manner compatible with community culture and values.

4. Community economic development involves the creation of local institutions and the initiation of long-term self-reliant processes that aim to make communities more environmentally and financially sound.

5. In addition, community economic development may involve the development of a community vision; the enhancement of individual and collective skills; development of local leadership; support to local entrepreneurs; and the creation of partnerships both within and outside the local community.

[1]A community of common interest comprises people who share the same purposes or calling. A social movement, for example, is a community of common interest. A local collaborative for "at-risk" kids is another example.

In short, when successful cooperatives are demonstrated, it also is demonstrated that families can act strategically on their own behalf. Their strategic action is enabled by governments, especially when governments promote and support employment and the development of cooperatives and microenterprises.

A FINAL NOTE

Microloans and other microcredit strategies, microenterprises, and women's cooperatives are not panaceas for poverty (Berger, 1989; Djamiga, 1981; Hall, 1988; McKee, 1989; Ray, 1998). Income investments in families are needed. Family and child allowances, caregiver stipends, and other measures designed to provide living wages provide the foundation for full employment agendas and anti-poverty strategies. Family-centered policies and practices to support these agendas and practices will make important contributions to each nation's social and economic development agendas. And, they will help address the preventable harms caused by unemployment and underemployment. They are thus essential foci for integrative social and economic development agendas.

NOTES

1. Each concept has an attendant policy discourse that affects the well-being of individuals and families. Socioeconomic status is a liberal democratic concept; it is associated with equal opportunity. It is a here-and-now construct. It suggests that stratification systems are flexible and adaptable over time. It minimizes conflicts, power relations, and differential cultural meaning and identity systems. By contrast, social class is a historical concept. It is associated with long-term, or structural, inequality. Social class emphasizes differences in class cultures, and the differential power and authority of the classes in social structure and over social structure. For social class theorists and practitioners, equality of opportunity is improbable without measures to provide equality of condition.
2. Chapter 10 explores globalization and the global economy and provides more details.
3. One can argue that there are flaws in conventional thinking about equity and unemployment. For example, the conventional notion of unemployment is flawed because it is based on labor market participation or lack thereof. It does not take into account nonlabor market work roles such as family roles and work performed primarily by women in the household.
4. For a somewhat different, but complementary, perspective on social investment strategies, see Midgley, 1997, 1999.
5. In France and Germany, demogrants originally were designed to increase birth rates.

CHAPTER 4

Key Sensitizing Concepts, a Family Policy Continuum, and Examples from the IYF

Hal A. Lawson, Katharine Briar-Lawson,
and Charles B. Hennon, with Alan R. Jones

Family policy is a coherent set of principles and practices that influence, and are influenced by, services, supports, and resources provided by families and helping professionals. Family policy calls attention to the roles and responsibilities of governments and their departments, agencies funded by governments, and nongovernmental organizations. Family policy entails developing laws, policies, rules, and regulations that affect families. And ultimately, policy is what families experience, every day, at the same time that it may shape the practices of helping professionals.

Family policies include the following (Baker, 1995, p. 5):

1. Laws relating to family rights and issues such as marriage, adoption, and child custody
2. Economic strategies related to family income and resources (e.g., tax rebates, family income supplements, transportation assistance, and child support supplements
3. Direct service strategies such as child and family preservation services, child care, and maternal-child health
4. Open entitlements, such as subsidized housing, nutrition programs, and maternal and child health benefit programs

The best family policies result when the needs and wants of families are moved to center stage and families become policy and practice partners. These policies and practices may be called family centered. Even if they are not family centered, other policies and practices can be improved if they become more family sensitive, family focused, and family supportive. In fact, a policy continuum can be developed to reflect these alternatives, or choice points. They suggest a developmental progression in which family-insensitive policies and practices are replaced by ones that take families and their well-being into account.

Issues surrounding the legal rights of families are important to all family policy and practice agendas. Unfortunately, where family rights are concerned there may be contradictions and silences in many nations, states, and provinces. For example, Lahav (1997) has identified the contradictions among international charters and national policies regarding family reunification involving migrants, immigrants, and refugees. International charters and past legal decisions favor and support families. On the other hand, national policies, rules, and regulations often contradict and undercut international rights and legal mandates. The United States Constitution, for example, emphasizes individual rights; families are not mentioned (e.g., Farber, 1973). So, family rights legislation and enforcement is needed in many nations.

There is also a need to design and promote family-centered policies. How, then, can advocates frame family-centered policies? How might family-related policy discourse be developed? What is the role of the state in family life? Are families' voices invited and heard in the policy making, implementation, and evaluation processes? *Which* families are heard? Which family members' voices are heard? Are they gender-balanced voices free of patriarchal control and silencing? Who decides? Who decides who decides? Are women equal partners in decision making? This chapter is structured in response to questions like these, as are the next three chapters.

The progression for this chapter is as follows. The first section focuses on the framing and naming of family needs, wants, and goals. Two case examples illustrate the importance of family-centered policies and practices, and lessons are derived from these cases. Then three essential questions about family policy, governments, and family involvement are presented. A section on setting policy and practice agendas follows. After distinctions are made between two kinds of policies—categorical and relational—a family policy continuum is presented. Each point on the continuum may facilitate policy planning and evaluation.

Then examples of practice orientations are compared with policy orientations. The intent is to illustrate how policies can change practices and vice versa when the two are "out of sync," and to emphasize the need for both policies and practices to be family centered.

Examples are provided in this chapter and the next. These examples are derived from nations' self-reported policy initiatives in connection with the International Year of the Family (IYF); these make up the last section. These examples are like snapshots; they are incomplete, selective, and time-limited. On the other hand, they facilitate important comparisons between and among nations. They illustrate international diversity and indicate multiple policy pathways for improving family well-being.

FAMILY NEEDS AND GOALS: PERSONAL TROUBLES OR SOCIAL ISSUES?

As policy makers, helping professionals, and advocates act strategically in the political arena, they must be aware of a new "politics of welfare" and an accompanying policy discourse (e.g., Jordan, 1998; Walby, 1999).[1] The new social welfare discourse is evident in the United States, Canada, and the United Kingdom, though it is not confined by their borders. There is an enduring tension in this new discourse between the rights and responsibilities of individuals and families, on the one hand, and, on the other, the obligations, resources, and commitments of individual nations, or coalitions formed among them, such as the European Union. In this new policy discourse, leaders often focus on the most vulnerable individuals and families, especially those supported over the long term by the state.

Some leaders have concluded that governments should divest themselves of key responsibilities for individuals and families in need. Promoting the idea of family self-sufficiency, they doubt whether vulnerable individuals and families are worthy of social investments (e.g., Midgley, 1997, 1999). They also criticize many universal, or "blanket," entitlements. And, they are convinced that individuals' and families' long-term dependence on the state, in substitution for self-sufficiency provided through employment, is not a good or viable alternative.

A policy pattern has followed this rationale. Universal strategies and entitlements, i.e., ones that provide blanket coverage, now are in decline. Increasingly, these universal entitlements are being replaced by targeted, or selective, entitlements and strategies. At the same time, all governmental entitlements are becoming more difficult to access. In a growing number of nations, individuals and families in need must meet strict eligibility criteria. They must document that they are truly vulnerable and deserve governmental support. All in all, then, vulnerable and potentially vulnerable families may wonder whether they can expect lasting, essential assistance from governments (e.g., Geyer, Ingebritsen, & Moses, 2000; Jordan, 1998; Pierson, 1996). Indeed, they may be victims of adverse labels and moral exclusion (e.g., Bauman, 1998).

These new social welfare discourses must counter effectively the policy discourse that absolves governments of social welfare responsibilities; that in essence blames the poor for being poor; and that minimizes and neglects social investments in vulnerable individuals and families. Every alternative discourse must effectively frame family needs and goals without blaming poor families for their vulnerability.

Framing Family Needs and Goals

Thirty years ago, the sociologist C. Wright Mills (1969) provided a useful distinction for addressing questions about these individual and family needs. *Personal troubles* are different from *social issues*. Different social action strategies accompany this key distinction.

Personal troubles are private matters. They reside in individuals and families because of their decisions and behavior. In turn, social action strategies (solutions) are their responsibility. Family members may view many of their needs as personal troubles. For example, in every nation, families are surrounded by religious and secular meaning and value systems. These systems may encourage people to see family needs, problems, and conditions as private matters, as personal troubles. At the same time, family members may seek privacy from surveillance by the state. In other words, families may choose to view their needs, wants, and goals as personal troubles for which they alone will assume responsibility.

By contrast, social issues provide a different frame, implicating different policies and social action strategies. With the social issue frame, problems, needs, and conditions in individuals and families are viewed as the equivalent of "symptoms." That is, they are signs of deeper, root problems. Institutional strains and policy dilemmas cause these needs and problems. For example, problems such as substance abuse, poor mental health, and domestic violence may be related to or caused by structural unemployment, underemployment, and economic insecurities (Briar, 1988). To return to the foundation provided in chapter 3, when structural unemployment is implicated, the family's needs are signs of root causes of social issues. Pervasive unemployment, created partly by governmental policies, partly by the permanent loss of jobs as TNCs move, and in part by technological innovation, is a social issue.

When needs are framed as social issues, multilevel action strategies often are implicated. For example, two parents in a family in an Eastern Europe nation may be struggling with unemployment. In their country unemployment rates are 30 percent or more. These parents may become substance abusers, and they may require tailored substance abuse interventions. At the same time, changes in policy and service delivery may be needed.

Here, the family is viewed in the context of policy needs, service gaps, and interorganizational relationships. Its members are not blamed for their presenting needs. Policy makers, helping professionals, and other families know that the family is, in essence, coping as best it can. In fact, while substance abuse needs to be addressed, these parents and their family are also victimized by policy gaps and limitations. Institutional and organizational design problems and policy limitations are implicated. In other words, social issues become public and governmental priorities, which require new policies and action strategies.

Social issues and personal troubles are not dichotomies. When a need or want is framed as a social issue, the private spheres of families should be maintained, and their rights and aspirations should be honored unless they violate international human rights (United Nations, 1993j). The social issue frame necessitates viewing families as "public goods." Families are public goods, in part, because of their pivotal roles in healthy economies, politics, and societies (e.g., Putnam, 1993). To put it negatively, when large numbers of families are in trouble, so are their nation's governments, economies, and other social institutions (United Nations, 1992b).

Unfortunately, many nations have an enduring history of viewing family needs, problems, and conditions as personal troubles. Religion, social norms, and cultural traditions weigh heavily in their views and treatment of families. Their leaders view family needs as private matters for which the family alone is responsible. In these nations, policy makers and other leaders are able to absolve themselves from responsibilities for these families and excuse themselves from policy change (United Nations, 1992b). Leaders may blame families in need, attributing their needs to deficits in moral character and work discipline.

For example, policy makers may recommend punishment in lieu of support. Their reasoning might go something like this: If family needs are personal troubles, then why should government support them? Why should governmental leaders listen to them? In effect, these attributions of responsibility, capability, and culpability have often silenced families and placed them at the political margins because others have framed their needs as private concerns, as personal troubles. In turn, these families may feel marginalized. Families at the margins often are unable to plead their case for resources, supports, and services.

Moreover, when their needs are not addressed, one family's unmet needs may become another's. Moreover, children may develop the same needs as their parents and other members of their family systems. In other words, intergenerational patterns of need, involving, for example, health and mental health challenges, may be evident (Felliti, Anda, et al., 1998). These multiplier effects demonstrate that one family's needs are important social issues.

Two Case Scenarios

Two case scenarios involving the same South American family illustrate some of the differences between personal troubles and social issues. They indicate how policies and practices may change and how outcomes for families may differ.

In the first case scenario (box 4.1), the family is viewed as "an island unto itself." The family is left on its own to meet its needs and challenges and to build its capacities. In this scenario, policy makers and other leaders have absolved themselves from responsibility.

By contrast, in the second scenario (box 4.2), family-related policies provide services, supports, and resources that directly impact the family's well-being. Different outcomes are associated with each scenario, emphasizing that there are identifiable consequences associated with the decisions, choices, and attributions of policy makers.

In the scenario presented in box 4.1, the family is blamed for needs it presents and the problems experienced. Yet, many of this family's problems, especially stress and inappropriate ways to channel depression and anger, are predictable by-products of resource shortfalls in services and supports. The family will suffer more resource declines if Garcia moves away and establishes new familial relationships. In this case, Garcia and Roberta's country does not mandate child support, nor does it require that help be given to them. The entire extended family becomes more vulnerable because of these policy silences.

Imagine how appropriate services, supports, and resources might have made a difference in the lives of Roberta, Garcia, and their family. What

ROBERTA AND GARCIA

Roberta and Garcia have three children, and they care for his ailing mother. From time to time, Roberta's nieces stay with them, especially when her sister works shifts in a garment factory three towns away. Several nights each week Roberta and Garcia go without food to ensure that the children eat. The family endures frequent bouts with dysentery. Medical resources are scarce, compounding the stresses they endure. Roberta and Garcia had two children die of dysentery before they were five years old.

Roberta and Garcia face immense housing challenges, especially in the winter. A bone-chilling cold affects the entire family. Their home might be warmer in the winter, but damage caused years ago by high winds is still not repaired because it is too costly. Both Roberta and Garcia work. Sometimes both are absent from the home. Oftentimes they are gone because they are both searching for a second job. Both feel the stress associated with their living conditions and resource needs.

Roberta and Garcia's stress finally takes its toll. He begins to consume excessive amounts of alcohol. He then becomes violent with her and their youngest child. Roberta's hospitalization for injuries stemming from this violence results in court-ordered protections for her and her family. Garcia is now banned from the family. This decreases the resources for the family. The children and frail grandmother are affected adversely.

Roberta feels exhausted, and then experiences despair. Once again, she is hospitalized. Health, social service, educational, and law enforcement personnel see her as being ineffective, even failing, as a parent and caregiver. Some entertain thoughts that her children should go to an orphanage. Roberta knows this. The castigation and blame is hard for her to accept because she feels as if she has done the best she can given her circumstances.

BOX 4.1

BOX 4.2

ROBERTA AND GARCIA: AN ALTERNATIVE VISION

Roberta and Garcia have a family resource center in their village. Thanks to this center, they are able to take their family for recreational activities, including vacation-like outings and overnights. Their first outing together was remarkable; it was the first time they had ever had a vacation together. Their youngest child said that it was the first time that they had ever been seen by others as laughing and playing together. Garcia's frail mother also assists in their family play time and vacation; she interacts with another elder who entertains her and offers more sedentary recreational enjoyments.

The center's educational programs also help the family. Roberta learns how to develop her own small business (microenterprise), and she is connected to a support network of entrepreneurs. This gives her an alternative to the long and vast distances that she and her sisters must travel for their jobs at the garment plant. She becomes interested in developing a special clothing business in which she can adapt what she's learned in the garment plant. By making and selling special clothing, she also can help maintain some of the cultural heritage of the village and neighboring communities.

Both Roberta and Garcia learn at the center new knowledge and skills about parenting and stress management. Garcia begins to examine his alcohol use in a more constructive way; he comes to understand better how alcohol provided an escape from realities too painful for him to face. He also sees the ways in which his pain and stress make him violent toward Roberta, especially when he has been drinking. He learns that he has been hurting the children as well as Roberta. He learns, much to his dismay, that his youngest son is very frightened of him because of excessive use of punishment and spankings. He seeks alternative ways to interact with his family, learning ways to manage his anger and resolve conflicts in nonviolent ways.

The family comes to see this center as a lifeline and support system. It helps them bring more resources to their livelihoods and adds new dimensions to their family interactions. Roberta learns about her rights to a restraining order if Garcia's abuse does not stop. She commits to helping Garcia with his substance abuse, recognizing ways in which she unintentionally facilitated his drinking. She also commits to giving him time to learn new ways of handling his anger. They re-commit as partners to build their family. Together, they pledge to find ways out of their impoverished conditions and long travels to jobs.

This family's future remains uncertain, even with the center. They still face profound health needs and worry about the medical needs of their youngest son. Nonetheless, they have in this center a base and a support system that allows them to move forward in a constructive manner. They feel more valued as a family, and, as a consequence, they value each other more. Because of the services, supports, and re-sources provided, this family remains intact, enhancing the well-being of the children and the grandmother.

would have happened if Roberta and Garcia had been provided with re-sources such as food supplements and housing assistance? How would their circumstances have been different if they had been provided sup-ports and services such as job development skills, caregiving help for their elder, a vacation, and substance abuse counseling for Garcia? In short, what would it have taken for this family to feel supported and valued by governmental and civic leaders, as well as others in their com-munity? How would their everyday experiences have led them to believe that there are people who care about their well-being; and that there are identifiable places where they can find help and assistance? In what ways would this family have gained a sense of their importance?

An alternative scenario for this same family is presented in box 4.2. Here, governmental policies result in services, supports, and resources that yield more desirable outcomes.

Some Lessons Learned from These Cases

These two case scenarios illustrate the importance of responsive, ef-fective, and appropriate policies. These policies influence the quality and quantity of services, supports, and resources for families.

Family-centered policies and practices are developed in the second case. Some of these policies and practices focus on individuals. Others focus on children and families. Still others encompass the multigenerational family system. In addition to services, adults are provided economic and employment resources, including jobs. They are given choices about where to work. These resources support the economic provider roles of parents and caregivers.

Although the family's needs are viewed as social issues, the immediate, presenting problems of family members are addressed. In this second case, assistance focuses on the personal challenges of stress management, anger, and substance abuse. Roberta's depression is temporarily relieved. Moreover, family members have continuous access to the family support center, which helps to ensure that they have extended support as they cope with their challenges.

In the first scenario (box 4.1), the family's needs are perceived as personal troubles. Here, the family is a closed system where supports are limited to what family members are able to provide until a crisis occurs. Closed systems tend to reproduce themselves. For example, parents treat their children as they were treated. Absent service, supports, and resources, when these children become parents, they may pass on their maltreatment dynamics to the next generation.

In the first case, this family's strengths were not identified or developed. Its members' capacities to learn and to develop were not assessed. The family's interactions and relationships were not subjected to a thorough assessment. In the first case, Roberta's and Garcia's children may learn and "normalize" domestic violence and abuse, along with unequal power relationships.

By contrast, in the second case scenario, family support and services provided by the family resource center staff help Roberta and Garcia to evaluate and then change their interactions with each other, their children, and the frail elder in their care. Thanks to responsive supports and services, they begin to examine gender and power issues. They consider giving their children more of a voice in the choices the family makes. As violent interactions between Garcia and their youngest son are reduced and violent interactions are ended with Roberta, the family is helped to build a more peaceful, humane, democratic system.

An important lesson can be derived from these cases. When families are national and international priorities, and when governments enact family-centered policies, individuals and families both are beneficiaries. Investments in families double as improvements in individual well-being and social development (Cassen, Wignaraja, & Kingdon, 1997; Galtung, 1995; Ghai, 1997; Hennon, Jones, et al., 1998; Hennon & Jones,

2000; Hennon & Kopcanová, 1996; Hooper-Briar & Lawson, 1995; Midgley, 1997; United Nations, 1995c; UNDP, 1994, 1995).

TOWARD POLICY MAKING FOR FAMILIES—AND WITH FAMILIES

Three important questions may drive the policy process:

- What do policy makers, helping professionals, family advocates, and families want their governments to do for them?
- What do policy makers, helping professionals, and family advocates want their families to be(come) and do?
- How will national leaders, policy makers, helping professionals, and advocates involve families in making policies that affect them?

Clearly, these questions are related, and perhaps interdependent. They need to be addressed simultaneously.

How, then, are family-centered policies and practices developed? Both bottom-up and top-down approaches are needed. These two approaches are twin building blocks for effective, appropriate policy and practice changes. Together they help respond to policy makers' requirements for new ways to think about, discuss, design, implement, and evaluate family-centered policies and practices. New-century policies need to transcend present-day tendencies to force-fit family needs and conditions into existing bureaucratic programs and requirements (e.g., Family Resource Coalition, 1990). Moreover, policies must be evaluated continually to facilitate learning and continual improvement (e.g., Schön & Rein, 1994).

Commitments to Families: Rhetoric or Ideology?

The IYF demonstrated that nations are able to herald their families. Some nations have established new policies and programs in the aftermath of IYF (United Nations, 1995b). These are meritorious achievements.

On the other hand, questions remain about the staying power of all governmental proclamations (e.g., Baker, 1995). Political climates and leaders change. The new policy discourse on welfare reform, cited earlier, provides a case in point. Some of the same governments that promoted families and family well-being in connection with IYF now appear to be headed in another policy and practice direction—if, indeed, they ever changed toward family-centered policies and practices.

In short, some new policies appear to have high symbolic value in the short term. Unfortunately, they have minimal practical impacts because they lack staying power and sticking power. They may not have penetrated into the system; or, if they did, they did not last. Baker's (1995) thorough analysis of changing Canadian policies indicates how fragile some good initiatives really are. In other words, it is easy to make policy proclamations. It is much more difficult to secure sustainable funding supports and to build the infrastructure for policy implementation and evaluation. When symbolic appeal triumphs over de facto policy change, a critical appraisal of policy makers is required. Two sensitizing concepts —rhetoric and ideology—are useful assessment tools.

The first need is to establish a context for all assessments. The world community is diverse in its forms of government. International advocacy for family-centered policies and practices must proceed against this reality. While policy makers in democratic governments are compelled to be more responsive (because voters can hold them accountable), their peers in other kinds of governments operate with different constraints. In all governmental forms, leaders' values are pivotal, i.e., value commitments often sway policy debates and development.

Leaders' *rhetoric* consists of statements and proclamations deliberately designed to create a favorable impression, or to conform to desirable norms. When they offer policy and family rhetoric, policy makers do not necessarily believe in their official press releases, statements, and proclamations. They do believe that such statements are timely in selected situations. Their rhetoric is in service of personal and national interests.

In other words, policy makers use rhetoric to respond to their perceived, everyday realities. Leaders often say that each day seemingly brings a new issue or crisis to which they are expected to respond. This prompts some leaders to view their work as the equivalent of "fire fighting." No sooner is one problem or crisis solved—i.e., one fire extinguished—then another arises. For example, the relationship of policy makers with representatives of the mass media often reflects and reinforces this view of governmental leadership and the strategic use of rhetoric. Rhetoric sounds good. Unfortunately, many of today's rhetorical promises are here today but gone tomorrow. Or, these promises result in lofty proclamations that are shelved quickly and permanently.

By contrast, a policy maker's *ideology* may be more genuine and authentic. Like rhetoric, ideology is expressed in public statements and proclamations. But ideology is different. It represents personal beliefs, values, and commitments. Unlike rhetorical twists that are "here today and gone tomorrow," ideological platforms are more established and enduring. They help form the foundation for permanent improvements in family-related policies and practices. In democratic political systems, political parties can be compared by their ideological platforms, including the extent to which members share beliefs and value commitments and attempt to implement them.

In this perspective, family-supportive ideology is clearly one of the cornerstones for family-centered policies and practices. Advocates and leaders can promote this ideology through education-building and constituency-building activities aimed at governmental leadership and media representatives. These activities have, as one of their primary goals, the challenge of convincing policy makers that governments must accept their responsibilities for strengthening families. *Once family issues are framed as social issues, accountability and responsibility for family well-being must be shared.* Firm ethical commitments, enduring moral responsibilities, and important social accountabilities cement family-centered ideology and action strategies (e.g., Jordan, 1998). Family-related social welfare issues are everyone's issues.

The International Year of the Family was a significant event. It resulted in multiple benefits. Even so, given the crucial responsibilities and significance of families, *every year must be a national and international year of the family.* Family advocates, helping professionals, and policy makers worldwide can work to help governmental leaders (and media representatives) adopt a family-supportive ideology, enabling them to advance family-centered policies and practices. This advocacy is active citizenship at its best (and is emphasized in chapter 9). Grassroots, bottom-up strategies are essential, and they stem from the recognition that family-centered policies and practices will not materialize automatically from top governmental leadership. Family-centered policy makers benefit from this grassroots support because it sends a clear message to other policy makers that they have popular support. It helps them join forces in setting family-centered political agendas.

AGENDA SETTING AND POLICY MAKING

Policy making depends on people's discourses. It also depends on how, when, where, and why governmental leaders frame their individual and collective agendas. Agenda setting begins with a telling question: *If family-centered policies and practices are the solution, what is the need, problem, or aspiration?*

Agenda setting is also called problem setting (e.g., Hennon & Arcus, 1993; Schön & Rein, 1994).[2] Agenda setting is the process of determining needs, wants, rights, and aspirations that policies and practices will address. Agenda setting begins with either, or both, of two questions. What's wrong that needs fixing? What's good and right that needs to be maintained, or strengthened? Policy makers frame and name—and name and frame—individual, family, community, national, and international needs, problems, strengths, and aspirations. They may draw on ideology, or they may offer surface rhetoric. They may view families and family needs as social issues, or they may view needs as personal troubles. To reiterate, language matters when agendas are developed.

Framing and Naming, Naming and Framing

Family-centered policy, practice, and advocacy necessitate identifiable requirements for thinking and talking differently. Discourse (patterned language) is used to reflect and convey thoughts. Formal "knowledge" and "understanding" are also stored in discourses. New ways of thinking and acting require appropriate ways to talk and communicate.

Yesterday's discourse(s) may not facilitate the design and implementation of the family-centered innovations of today and tomorrow. New concepts, including the ones introduced in this book, may be needed. A family-centered policy and practice framework requires that people exercise care in the words they employ to describe families and family-related policies and practices. The words that people use facilitate policy and practice changes.

For example, sometimes policy makers bring familiar social-cognitive frames, and they use conventional language. This framing and naming process involves bringing yesterday's ideas and discourse to today's and tomorrow's needs and aspirations. Neither policy nor practice may change much. At best, this approach to agenda setting brings a reformist orientation.

By contrast, significant change—change that transforms policy and practice—usually stems from a different way of talking, perhaps a new discourse. Why? Because when policy makers talk differently about a need, problem, or aspiration, they "see" or perceive it differently. In short, naming—changes in language and discourse—changes the framing of family-related needs, wants, and problems. In other words, change begins with a way of talking. New ways of talking and communicating pave the way for different cognitions. Different cognitions, in turn, may lead to novel policies and practices as known and familiar needs, wants, aspirations, and policies are "reframed."

For example, the needs of children challenged at school can be framed as "a student problem," one specific to each child. By contrast, one child's problem can be renamed and framed as a family support issue (e.g., Briar-Lawson, Alameda, & Lawson, 1997). At the same time, preconceived notions about a "problem parent" who does not participate in parent-teacher conferences and fails to attend her child's school functions can be changed. Once a child's problem becomes viewed as a family support need, the attributions and solutions change. For example, the parent may need caregiver and employment-related supports and resources. Housing stresses and food insecurities may be at the root of the child's problems at school. Counseling for the child is not the only answer. Improved services, resources, and supports for the family are required.

Similarly, a lack of political participation by adults, once viewed as apathy, can be renamed and reframed. Long-term unemployment, poverty, and the dynamics of social and cultural exclusion often are associated with "apathy." Once this perceived apathy is framed as a policy practice challenge involving poverty alleviation, full employment, and addressing social exclusion, a different agenda will be framed (e.g., Jordan, 1998; Ray, 1998; Sen, 1999). Another example: "At-risk" children and families can be renamed "at promise." In this new frame, "at risk" applies to their environments, not to people (Lawson, Briar-Lawson, & Lawson, 1997).

In brief, there are always alternative ways to name and frame, and frame and name, family-related needs, wants, and aspirations. One way to safeguard individual and family well-being, and to improve the quality of policies and practices, is by checking the frames and names used in policy and practice discourses.

Discourse (a language system of "names") and cognitions (frames) often depend upon the metaphors people use. Two metaphors commonly used by professionals and policy makers are illness/disease and machine. The illness/disease metaphor emphasizes the search for individual, family, and community pathologies. It is deficit oriented.

The machine metaphor emphasizes mechanical and technical-procedural ways of looking at individuals, families, and communities. It conveys images of specialization, especially the assembly line and the factory.

"Systems thinking, "including the idea conveyed in chapter 1 of "family systems" and "family systems theory," derive from this machine metaphor and the view of the world it conveys. Helping professionals, who believe that they know best what individuals, families, and communities want and need, tend to rely upon machine/systems metaphors; illness/disease metaphors; and combinations of the two.

The socioecological metaphor also introduced in chapter 1 emphasizes natural, symbiotic relationships among individuals, families, and communities. It emphasizes individual and family strengths and aspirations. It gives rise to images of families and communities in harmony, of sustainable social and natural environments. For example, Trzcinski (1995) has undertaken cross-cultural studies of families. A key finding from her work supports the use of socioecological metaphors in family-centered policies and practices. Trzcinski found that some cultures view aspects of their natural environment—e.g., corn, trees, and water—as family. These people enjoy symbiotic relationships with these environments because they view them as family related. Clearly, this socioecological metaphor brings a different approach to naming and framing family-related issues than do the other two metaphors.[3]

Families' Voices vs. Professionals' Language

Families' language systems, that is, their discourses, must be honored. Differences between their language systems and that of professionals must be reconciled (e.g., Cowger, 1998; McKnight, 1995). For example, would families describe themselves as clients? Would they see themselves as a "dysfunctional family"? Oftentimes, professionals' language conveys blame and stigma; it is not strength based and family supportive.

Are families' voices and language honored? Look at your community, region, or nation and ask the following questions. Are families positioned to communicate their needs, aspirations, and preferences to policy leaders and helping professionals? What would have to change for families to plead their cases for more responsive or expansive services or resources?

When policy makers and professionals do not achieve their desired outcomes, it is common for them to plead for more, or different, resources. Why not accord families the same opportunities? How, when, where, why, and under what circumstances might they do so? What are the results of ignoring or neglecting families and denying them these opportunities? It appears that there are few such structures and opportunities for families to voice their concerns.

From Voice to Power Sharing

Families must become co-authors in family policy and practice (Briar-Lawson, 1998). For, absent their voices, policies and practices may not respond to families' needs, challenges, and desires. Because families are closest to the needs and barriers that confront them, they have expertise in suggesting the solutions that may best serve them. They have unique knowledge that a policy maker or practitioner cannot have. Policy makers and helping professionals do not "live the lives" of these families. Basic policy and practice must be crafted in ways that give voice to whatever extent possible to families. Moreover, practices must be "tailored" to each family. Rather than being force-fitted into a policy or program that may not really help them, families need to be consulted and given options (e.g., Dunst, Trivette, & Deal, 1994).

There is an emergent literature indicating how policy makers can lead the way in democratizing the policy-making process (e.g., Aaron, Mann, & Taylor, 1994; Reich, 1988a, 1988b). For example, the Luxembourg Committee for the organization of IYF indicated that it was reaching out to families, listening to them, to understand their needs and to actively involve them (Secretariat for the International Year of the Family, 1994).

To summarize, in a family-centered framework, families are partners, co-authors, and co-leaders of policy and practice initiatives. Relationships among policy makers, helping professionals, and families are democratized. Democratization includes three inseparable features:

1. genuine involvement and enfranchisement of families in policies and practices that affect them;
2. nonhierarchical, or less hierarchical, relationships among families, policy makers, and helping professionals; and
3. genuine power sharing as indicated by policy makers' and professionals' responsiveness to families' expressed needs and aspirations as well as preferences for solutions.

In fact, this power sharing is a key feature of genuine empowerment strategies. Democratizing relationships *around* families corresponds to IYF's call for democratizing relationships *within* families (United Nations, 1991a). Ideally, the two are related and advanced simultaneously.

Both inside the family and in the family's relations with outsiders, democratization raises questions about power and authority.

A Word of Caution

In practice, collective family voices will not prevail. Embedded traditions, which may be class based, religious, and patriarchal, may mitigate against democratic participation. For example, women and girls may not have a voice when they are dominated by patriarchy. As family-centered policy, practice, and advocacy builds more democratized institutions and relationships, opportunities will develop to promote equity within and among families. As inclusive voices of individuals in families, especially women, children, and elders, are sought, vulnerable and marginalized individuals and families will be better heard.

Serving as Critical Friends: Promoting Better Policy and Practice Agendas

Policy makers, helping professionals, and family advocates can serve as critical friends for one another, preventing shallow and narrow thinking, ethnocentrism, and unintended patriarchy. Here are the kinds of questions critical friends should ask each other:

- Are present conceptions of needs, problems, and aspirations appropriate, complete, correct, and correctly stated?
- What are current attributions for these needs, problems, and aspirations? In other words, what are their determinants and outcomes? In what ways, and how, can they be changed?
- What are the roles of families in identifying their needs, problems, and aspirations and in framing policies and practices intended to nurture and enhance their well-being?
- What processes are provided to ensure that the voices of the most vulnerable families are heard, especially those that have been marginalized and politically disfranchised?
- What protections and assurances are in place to privilege the voices and perspectives of women, children (especially girls), and elders?

To summarize: The process of agenda setting is the foundation for family-centered policies and practices. Families are priorities to the extent that groups and organizations make them such. In other words, the guiding visions, missions, goals, and objectives for government sectors and departments, private organizations and nongovernmental organizations, and indigenous community agencies should emphasize the well-being of families and family-centered policies and practices. Unfortunately, families and their influence often are not accommodated in most governmental and nongovernmental policies and practices.

However, promising initiatives are emerging. In the United States, for example, a diverse number of initiatives involving parents and families in schools and in school-linked social and health services are developing rapidly (e.g., Dryfoos, 1998; Lawson & Briar-Lawson, 1997; Gerry, 1993; Schor, 1997). Family group conferencing, imported from New Zealand, is gaining popularity as an effective strategy for addressing child abuse and neglect, elder abuse, and adolescent delinquency (Wilcox, Smith, et al., 1991). Similarly, Parents Anonymous in the United States supports mutual aid and assistance, along with shared supports and learning, to address child abuse and neglect.

These emergent initiatives notwithstanding, existing policies and practices often are very specialized. They are sector specific (e.g., education or the environment). The discussion now turns to these sector-specific policies. Policy makers, helping professionals, and family advocates may expect to inherit these kinds of policies. Their challenge is to take these policies and, through agenda setting, turn them into family-supportive and family-centered policies.

CATEGORICAL POLICY FRAMES VERSUS RELATIONAL POLICY FRAMES

Policy initiatives in many nations have followed a predictable pattern. This pattern is understandable once each nation's agenda-setting dynamics are identified. When families are not national and international priorities, and when families are viewed separately and in isolation from other needs and priorities, highly specialized, or categorical policies are developed. Categorical policies often benefit specialized governmental sectors, which gain more of each nation's resources. These other sectors, or categories, include environmental protection, public education, criminal and juvenile justice, health, trade, and economic development.

Similarly, categories of individuals capture policy makers' attention. For example, they focus on children *or* women *or* elders *or* developmentally challenged persons. In other words, rather than starting with families and family systems as integrative, comprehensive, inclusive systems, while considering how other sectors influence them, policy makers have started with more specialized and limited needs and problems. Only later do they consider the impacts upon families—if these impacts are considered at all. This frame is called a *categorical approach* to policies and practices.

In this categorical approach, families are viewed as just another competing priority offered by political interest groups or service sectors. Children and youth often make up one of the other competing categories or sectors. The problem is, even well-intended child-centered policies and practices may erode the capacities of families and compete with a family-centered agenda.

In brief, categorical initiatives have assisted families in some instances, while in others they have not. Sometimes families have been ignored and neglected. Sometimes they have been harmed. This "hit-and-miss" approach must be targeted for change as policy and practice agendas are set. A strategic, explicit focus on families can make a significant difference, as the Family Impact Seminar in the United States documented.

A Relational Approach

In contrast to categorical frames, *a relational approach* to family policies and practices builds from an understanding of the responsibilities, meaning, and significance of families, along with their pervasive influence in each societal culture. Families' relationships with other social institutions and policy categories are prioritized. To reiterate, families influence other social organizations such as schools, and these organizations influence families. To put it another way, relational approaches to policy can build upon the known interdependence among families, other social organizations, and each nation's social, political, and economic functioning.

Table 4.1 introduces differences between categorical and relational approaches to policy development (after Hooper-Briar & Lawson, 1995).

However tempting it may be to conclude quickly that categorical policies are bad and relational, holistic policies are good, or superior, forcing such an easy dichotomy would be a mistake. The world's nations are diverse. They defy sweeping conclusions and broad generalizations. Furthermore, families may benefit from both kinds of policies. And last, but not least, it takes time, learning, and political supports to move from categorical to relational, family-centered policies.

TABLE 4.1. Examples of Possible Differences Between Categorical and Relational Approaches to Families

	CATEGORICAL APPROACH	RELATIONAL APPROACH
Aim(s)	Fix or maintain families, especially the most vulnerable	Support, empower, and liberate all families
Role of families	Clients	Partners, co-authors
Definitional frame	Professional's definitions of needs and problems; positivist policy science	Families' and professionals' views of needs and aspirations; democratized policy development
Delivery systems designs	Stigmatization and "slotting" Rescue work Families alone are targeted	Accommodation of diversity Preventive and developmental work at the same time that crises are addressed Simultaneous attention to families and other problems, needs, sectors
Evaluative criteria, designs	Cost-benefit analysis; experimental cross-sectional designs	Qualitative and quantitative indicators of well-being; participatory, developmental, and longitudinal methodologies
Incentives and rationale	Legal requirements	Moral imperatives
Organizational structures	Vertical	Horizontal
Political orientation	Inegalitarian	Participatory-democratic
Theory of change	Linear, laissez-faire / gradualist	Comprehensive, integrative, family-centered, and community-based
Probable outcomes	Agency-sector gaps increase Many families' needs for supports and services remain unidentified and unachieved	Agency-sector missions and goals become more cohesive and congruent Highest probability that family needs for supports and services are identified and achieved

Mindful of this international diversity and the need for developmental supports, the authors have developed a policy continuum, which encompasses both categorical and relational policies, indicates choices, and signals how today's choice of a categorical policy may lead to tomorrow's preference for a family-centered relational policy.

A FAMILY POLICY CONTINUUM

Agenda setting and policy planning may be facilitated by means of a family policy continuum. An example of such a continuum is presented in figure 4.1.

At the far left end of this continuum is a *family-insensitive framework*. Here, families are neglected or ignored altogether in the policy-making process. At the very least, families are not served or supported, and at worst they are harmed.

A *family-sensitive framework* is next on the continuum. In this framework, families receive "lip service" as policies and practices for another societal sector (education, health) are developed. That is, families are mentioned, or presumed impacts upon them are described in general or vague terms. Certainly this is an improvement upon approaches in which families are ignored and neglected, but, upon close inspection, it is difficult to predict the ways in which families will be assisted and strengthened. Even so, known impacts upon, and functioning of, families have not been systematically assessed in this categorical approach to policies and practices. In practice, family-sensitive approaches may harm families, however unintentionally.

In a *family-focused framework*, families are not merely mentioned; formal outcome and policy statements implicate families, suggesting that

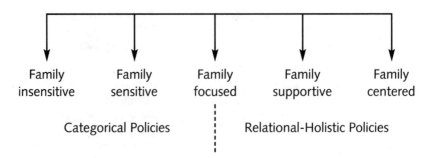

Figure 4.1 A Family Policy Continuum

they have been *considered* and perhaps *accommodated* as policies and practices for another sector are developed. At least information about families and their members is generated.

A family-focused framework marks a transition from categorical to relational thinking and planning. Here, families begin to receive the kind of close attention they merit. Although policies and practices are framed for another sector, deliberations and decisions proceed with two related kinds of assurances for families: (1) that they will not be harmed; and (2) that all foreseeable supports and benefits they may derive are identified and maximized.

A *family-supportive framework* emphasizes the direct and indirect impacts of policies on families. The explicit goal is to support and build capacity in families. For example, family impact analyses, described in the next chapter, guide agenda setting and policy deliberations. The indirect effects of policies on families also are weighed or assessed. For example, the impact of housing development policy on family-to-family informal support networks is weighed. In the same vein, the indirect effects of agricultural policies on family stability and mobility are assessed.

Families become the center of attention in a *family-centered approach*. Family-centered policies place families' well-being as the highest priority. Policies are holistic and family centered to the extent that they are "wrapped around families." Families are recast as the pivotal investment site for all relevant sectors; in fact some of these sectors may be recast, with a "minister for families" replacing separate ministers for housing, health, and income supports. In this approach, families are assigned the highest status over other sectors such as education and health.

In other words, instead of being just another sector or category, families are recognized as a cornerstone institution for civil society—the free, voluntary, and open spaces for individuals and their associations. The primary question that drives policy planning and decisions is this: *What is best for families?* Far from neglecting and ignoring other institutional sectors, in this framework, leaders explore the ways in which other sectors, policies, and practices may be changed or accommodated so that they also become more family focused, family supportive, and family centered.

With a family-centered framework, families are partners, co-authors, and evaluators, instead of merely "clients" or targets. While other policy and practice approaches do not involve families, in this family-centered framework, families are enfranchised as partners in the creation, implementation, and evaluation of policy and practice initiatives. Empowerment strategies aimed at strengthening families and their roles and developing abilities have more "agency." These empowerment strategies are integral to family-centered policies and practices.

Efforts to involve, enfranchise, and empower families are part of a related social development challenge. This challenge is to *democratize* policy making, implementation, and evaluation. Such democratization, in addition to facilitating each nation's development, also impacts family dynamics and well-being. It connects policy and practice exemplars with the IYF's intent to build, in the family, the smallest democracy at the heart of society (United Nations, 1991a).

This policy continuum, comprising family-insensitive, family-sensitive, family-focused, family-supportive, and family-centered frameworks, allows readers to consider families in both categorical and relational policy and practice analytical frames. In brief, the question is not one of categorical *or* relational approaches. Both are needed. However, categorical approaches need to be framed in family-sensitive, -focused, -supportive, and -centered ways.

This family policy continuum is not merely an analytical-evaluative tool, nor is it value neutral. It is prescriptive and normative. The needs and conditions of families compel advocacy for improvements and innovations in family policies and practices. Family policy alternatives promise improvements for families, whether modest or dramatic, directly or indirectly.

To summarize: The family policy continuum can serve as an analytical, evaluative, and prescriptive guide for policy makers and others interested in family well-being. It helps everyone set a pro-family agenda. This agenda may help ensure that each new policy initiative builds from, and is integrated with, the others. If so, this will be a dramatic improvement over prior frameworks, which all too frequently have been characterized as "disjointed incrementalism" (Lindblom, 1990), i.e., where one policy is added to another without any attention to their harmony, impacts, and congruence.

The continuum has two other advantages. First, the alternatives on the continuum (e.g., family insensitive, family sensitive) also can be used to classify the practices of helping professionals. Second, when there are differences between policies and practices, these differences can result in changes that harmonize them, ideally moving either or both toward family-centered policies and practices. To put it a different way, when a

TABLE 4.2. Comparing Policies and Practices to Identify Needs to Harmonize and Synchronize Them

POLICIES	PRACTICES
Family-insensitive health policies	Family-centered health education and promotion
Family-sensitive juvenile justice policies	Family-insensitive, youth-focused rehabilitation practices
Family-focused early childhood policies	Family-sensitive nutrition programs and practices for children in preschools
Family-supportive education policies	Family-insensitive, child-focused, and subject-centered school practices
Family-centered income subsidy policies	Family-focused, household and budget management programs and practices

policy is "out of sync" with a family-centered practice, the practice may stimulate a change in the policy. Or, when a practice is child centered, while the policy is family supportive, the policy can stimulate a change in the practice. Table 4.2 has been constructed to illustrate this relationship between policies and practices. When policies and practices are contradictory and competing, and the tensions are not resolved, neither professionals nor families benefit. Professionals are likely to get caught in some binds until policy environments and practice strategies are aligned, congruent, and mutually supportive in relation to individual and family well-being.

Furthermore, when policies and practices are not coherent, cohesive, and congruent, families also get caught in binds. In fact, families may experience harm. When analytical and planning aids like table 4.2 are employed, harms may be addressed, while benefits are maximized.

One Size Does Not Fit All

For family advocates, professionals, and policy makers, this conceptual foundation provides an important pathway for more informed and effective policies and practices. On the other hand, international diversity serves as an ever-present reminder that one-size-fits-all policies and practices are not automatically desirable or beneficial. What works in one cultural and national context may not work in another. The discourses and frames of reference in one may not translate into another. When policy makers, helping professionals, and advocates engage in blind borrowing of policies, problems are likely to arise, along with unintended, unanticipated, and undesirable side effects.

In the presence of one-size-fits-all approaches, families are vulnerable to blame and maltreatment, to false attributions of deficits and problems. For example, policy is enacted to "fix" families and make them "act right." Knowing more about families' ecologies and also internal family relations can help policy makers, practitioners, and family advocates provide the types of services and resources that are supportive of real, not imagined, families. This way of thinking and talking about families also facilitates understanding of their significance and functioning in diverse cultures and nations. Data gathered from IYF illuminate some of this diversity in thinking, policies, and practices.

HOW NATIONS HAVE APPROACHED POLICY MAKING: A SNAPSHOT

Thus far, the discussion has emphasized how family-centered policy might be framed, developed, analyzed, evaluated, and promoted. The tone has been normative and advocacy oriented. The narrative has been value committed and ideological. Value neutrality is not possible where family-related issues and policies are involved.

On the other hand, important questions remain. For example, how does real-world policy "square" with the preceding advocacy and normative expectations? Although it is impossible to address this important question in detail, it is possible to use some of the data derived from IYF. The discussion turns now to relevant examples.

Despite the limitations of these self-reported data, they are especially interesting and valuable. Keep in mind that every nation's representatives were asked to develop agendas that focused on families. This common focus on families is an uncommon event in the world's history. For this reason alone the data are especially important and instructive. They pave the way for significant improvement and learning in the future.[4]

Boxes 4.3–4.4 capture some of the diverse thinking and practice regarding families. Some examples are categorical. Others appear to be relational and holistic. Some appear to be family focused. Others appear

BOX 4.3

Thailand

A national committee on the family was created for IYF. Accomplished and continuing activities include the following:

- A campaign to strengthen the family
- A focus on the roles of fathers in child development—through seminars and discussions special emphasis has been placed on the roles of fathers as partners in child rearing and in sharing household work
- A series of programs on the family, broadcast on radio and television
- A promotion of family education and family services—the Ministries of Public Health and Education are planning to open up family counseling services in the provinces and communities

Nigeria

Nigeria began its celebration of Family Week as early as 1984. A week has been set aside annually to (a) emphasize the importance of the family in molding the characters of individual members, and consequently the character of the nation; (b) initiate self-examination by family members concerning how they each have been performing their roles and functions within the family to enhance its stability and to curb the lack of discipline in society; and (c) accord due recognition to the family as the world's oldest institution.

Myanmar

In Myanmar, a National Health Committee has been formed to take progressive steps for promoting health and laying down a national family health policy. A National Population Policy was drafted to deal with such issues as education and information, status of women, nutrition, and legal reforms. The government has identified health concerns as a priority issue for families.

Argentina

In Argentina, preparation and observance of IYF was undertaken in concert with many ongoing initiatives and programs for families, particularly with initiatives discharged through the National Youth and Family Council under the direct authority of the Ministry of Health and Social Action. The IYF was seen as an opportunity to strengthen existing programs and schemes, which are developed in close and ongoing consultation with families themselves. (Eleven programs to strengthen families were mentioned in Argentina's plans, including HIV control and prevention.)

Austria

The Austrian National Committee for the Preparation of IYF was established in 1992 under the chairship of the federal Ministry for Environment, Youth, and Family. This committee had representatives from every federal ministry, from the Austrian Cities' Association, the Austrian Communities' Association, and the Advisory Council for Family Policy. Projects for IYF included the recommendations from the advisory committee for a conference on Family Is the Future, the establishment of the Austrian Institute for Family Research, and the formulation of plans for a Family Development Program.

Ecuador

The government of Ecuador designated the Ministry of Social Welfare as the national planning and coordinating body for IYF activities. An Inter-Institutional Committee, chaired by the first lady, was formed to design, execute, and evaluate actions related to IYF. The committee was composed of members from several ministries, including labour and human resources, public health, urban development, and housing, and representatives from the National Institute of the Child and Family, the Episcopal Council, and the UN Children's Fund, as well as NGOs.

Problems identified as having negative impacts on families (both urban and rural) include lack of real alternatives for promoting employment, insufficient care in health and nutrition, and lack of options in the education field. In health, the principal infectious diseases are seen as directly related to poverty, deficient health conditions, insufficient coverage of natal and parental care, and other issues.

Cuba

During the run up to IYF a number of events were organized as part of its celebration. These included the Union of Young Communists 4th Congress, which had two themes—The Young Wife and Family and Society. Problems that arise in the family and social environment were analyzed and solutions proposed. The First International Conference on Protection of the Family and Minors was also organized, and the University of La Habana planned an international workshop on Socioeconomic Conditions and Child Development.

A publication, *From the Ovule to the First Steps,* was being re-edited for distribution by the National Center for Sex Education. Other activities included a hospital project (with UNICEF) called Friend of the Child and Mother, with three such hospitals already in place; a sex education program and aid for parents with physically challenged children; the Ministry of Education bringing together all school activities for family education to create a basic movement that culminated in 1994 in local and national activities; a series of conferences held in 1994 on legal protection of families and minors (developed by the office of Cuba's attorney general together with the National Union of Jurists of Cuba and the Cuban Society of Civil and Family Law); and national level activities centered on attending to minors with behavioral problems and their families. A festival was organized under the motto For World Without End, We Children Want Peace.

BOX 4.4

Examples of Nations Emphasizing Family Rights and Responsibilities

- In Australia, the prime minister agreed to adopt priority areas for action during 1994, including recognizing the rights of families and every family member; also, civil law was being adapted to respond to developments concerning new types of common living arrangements as well as the rights of both spouses.
- In Belgium, there was a seminar on the rights of family members regarding social security.
- In Burundi, the law benefiting women and families was revised.
- In Cameroon, plans were underway to improve the economic situations of families through various projects, such as protection of families through legislation, including revision of the system of family benefits through the Ministry of Labour and Social Welfare and amendment of legal texts relating to minors through the Ministry of Justice.
- In Canada, substantive issues on the public agenda included rights of family members.

Examples of Nations Emphasizing Women's Issues

- In the Syrian Arab Republic, planned activities for IYF included emphasizing family education, in particular the education of women as the pivot of the family, with special attention to rural women; the health and social aspects of life of all family members; organizing training courses for senior personnel; and consolidating the structure of the National Federation for Women.
- In Ireland, family resource centers figure prominently in projects seeking funding, equipment, training in parenting skills, etc. These centers develop the confidence of local people, and experience shows that they can be a catalyst for local development of enterprise and jobs. The Women Grants Scheme was being initiated for self-development, assertiveness, and skill development. This program is especially targeted for women in disadvantaged communities. In a related note, in 1991 the minister for social welfare initiated the ruling that women working part-time should be covered by social insurance, because many women work part-time in order to spend as much time as possible in the household, especially if small children are present.

• In the Republic of Korea, IYF was undertaken in the context of existing programs for families. A family welfare policy is in force for children, women, the elderly, and people with disabilities. Goals included women's welfare projects implemented under the 1989 Mother-Child Welfare Act and the 1961 Prostitution Prevention Act. These mostly consist of counseling procedures to prevent poverty for mothers and children. They include vocational training courses for the underprivileged. The 1987 Equal Employment Act provides equal rights for women in employment, at retirement age, and for child care leaves. A nursery service is supplied for employed mothers at their places of work and on industrial sites.

Examples of Nations Emphasizing Family Welfare

• In the Comoro Islands, priority issues included those related to extreme poverty and interconnected problems in socioeconomic development.
• In El Salvador, the government's aim in establishing a National Office of the Family was to work toward the well-being of the family by promoting, coordinating, and assessing the participation of various sectors of the country in family care programs by focusing efforts on children, adolescents, women, and the elderly. To this end, new national population and juvenile care polices have been drawn up and approved. In addition, proposals for a national plan for women and a policy of care for the elderly are currently under discussion.
• In Ethiopia, post–civil war government programs have concentrated on plans to alleviate the plight of families affected by the impact of conflict, drought, and displacement.

Examples of Nations Emphasizing Housing

• In Turkey, families display a rich variety of differences according to their cultural heritage and economic prospects. Most are nuclear families, especially in urban areas, while a minority are extended. As a result of rapid population growth in this country, many people are migrating into big cities, where they find shelter in what are called *gecekondu,* or "shabby suburbs," among their relatives who

have moved there earlier. As a consequence, a new form of extended family is forming in the larger towns. Five-year development plans are one means by which policies related to families
have surfaced for implementation. The current Sixth Five-Year Development Plan indicates priorities in welfare policies basically related to housing, counseling, and other social service areas.
• In India, the National Housing policy has as its long-term goal the
eradication of housing shortages, improving the general housing
conditions, and providing basic services and amenities.

to be family supportive. A limited number of governments actually involve families in the policy-planning process. Family-centered frameworks appear to be the exception, not the rule.

Once these boxes have been studied, it becomes apparent that policy makers in various nations locate "the family" differently within the
broader array of social issues and society. Needs and wants are dependent upon time, place, and national-cultural context. Different framing
approaches to agenda setting are evident. In some cases, "the family" is
a change agent for other societal changes, while in others it is regarded
as a domain affected by social and economic forces.

In some cases families are seen as embedded within a complex web
of external social forces from which they cannot be extricated. In other
cases, policy planners appear to favor a single problem–single approach
to addressing social issues. Issues such as health and education, or target groups such as women or youth, are often identified as entry points
for strengthening families at the exclusion of other potentially pressing
issues, or of groups such as men.

For example, the best way to improve family life might be seen as bet-
tering the health of family members, with little apparent regard for other
issues such as improving education, promoting gender equality, addressing domestic abuse, or managing family resources more effectively. Also,
power relationships based on gender and generation within families,
and how these influence the "fairness" of access to, or distribution of,
resources, are rarely mentioned in the various national reports.

Alternatively, family may be conceptualized as the equivalent of
women and children. Doing something for families means doing some-

thing for women and children. In a very few cases, governments are apparently engaging families in the policy decision-making process, and listening to what families have to say on how to better their conditions and how to make governments more "family-friendly." This is the challenge of the new century.

It should be noted that family agendas do not always square with the other practices under way in a nation or region.[5] For example, a nation reporting on investments in children's education can at the same time be reluctant to stop their sexual trafficking. Similarly, at the same time that some policy makers, helping professionals, and advocates in the United States are building a Families First agenda, others may be eliminating all income entitlements for poor families. Discrepancies like these are found all over the world. A complete world inventory on practices toward families may be disproportionately filled with more glaring examples of family-hurtful than family-helpful policies. Policy makers, practitioners, and family advocates in general know that each step toward change is often predicated by the last step. Thus, as the social world evolves, people can understand and envision where a nation, community, or family is developmentally, and where it seeks to go. These agendas of nations and policy makers then become anchors for amplifying and further developing helpful family-supportive agendas.

Approaches to Supporting and Strengthening Families

In previous work (e.g., Hennon, Jones, Hooper-Briar, & Kopcanová, 1996), the importance of *supporting and strengthening families* was featured, involving up to two-thirds of the member states of the United Nations. This involves promoting strong marriages and families, family life and parent education, family rehabilitation, and services. There appears to be growing international recognition of the importance of enhancing family life and encouraging families to function well.

Family supports and policies are delivered through various sectors such as health and safety. *Health and safety* also is a major focus for about two-thirds of UN member nations, representing most of the world. Health and safety issues include sanitation, nutrition, traffic accidents, safety in general (including crime), ensuring food security, infant mortality, immunizations, and child, maternal, and elderly health issues.

Families become a lens through which health and safety issues become better understood and addressed. How countries are framing the relationship between health and families is illustrated by the materials abstracted from the reports of Myanmar, Argentina, Austria, and Ecuador.

Myanmar's approach to the promotion of health is another example of how a health agenda becomes fine-tuned as a family support agenda, and of this nation's approach to strengthening families. The material from the reports of the three nations demonstrates that focusing on family needs reveals gaps in services, policies, and resources. Not all these gaps are solely health and safety related. In Ecuador, employment, education, and nutrition were simultaneously identified as needs, along with prenatal and parental care and prevention of infectious diseases. Through the framing focus of families, needs may emerge more clearly (such as pre- and postnatal care), leading to action agendas, new policies, programs, and services.

Family rights/legal protection was cited as a priority among 56 percent of the UN member states. This focus includes the legal problems faced by families, family rights, protection of families, tribunals, wills, reviews by the government of laws concerning families, and legal reforms. These nations' reports shed light on how individual rights and responsibilities are framed in the context of families as well as the wider society. This sampling also provides a way for us to see how the "rights" discourse reflects developmental differences among nations.

Colleagues at the Population Council (Bruce, Lloyd, & Leonard, 1995) also point to this gap. They suggest that a focus on family relationships is the missing link of family policy. These authors write that

> family policy (inasmuch as it exists) is less about the family than it is about the rights and responsibilities of individual family members. More specifically, the emphasis of this policy in most countries has been on the terms of marital formation and dissolution, parental obligations, and children's rights. International policy pronouncements acknowledge that children have "first call" on scarce resources, that women are equals in marriage and the workplace, and that parents have primary responsibility for children—though the boundaries of parents' rights with respect to children are beginning to change. Children's newly defined rights as individuals are placing limits on parents' "rights" to keep their children out of school and to subject them to harmful traditional practices, such as genital mutilation. . . . While acknowledging that well-being and rights are essentially individual, policy must also meet the challenge of encouraging the natural sense

of connection that families can engender. In doing so, policy should not simply foster the well-being of individual family members; it can and should foster the well-being of vital family relationships—in particular, the parent-child link. (p. 97)

Examples of How Individuals' Needs and Rights Are Family Needs

Family policy and supports often involve win-win enfranchisement of all family members. For example, children's rights and needs for schooling—and parents' responsibilities for getting them to school—may be pitted against a parent's right to keep them at home so they can care for other children, or take a job in the informal sector to help support the family. The successful implementation of children's educational policy depends on parents and families having sufficient resources so that children are able to attend school. In other words, when child care needs and inadequate wages are addressed, barriers are removed to parental compliance with children's schooling. When parents are supported, this support also helps promote the children's rights. Children's rights hinge on parents' needs—such as parents not having to endure the sources of stress stemming from child care, caregiving, and worker roles.

Relationships involving family forms outside of traditional marriage also are the focus of rights development. This individual and family rights emphasis is more important in developed nations such as Australia. In these nations, policy plans include protection of nontraditional marriages. Increasingly rights also involve protection for family members as they move into retirement, for women, or for cohabiting partners. Box 4.4 provides examples of rights proclamations.

Women's Needs as Family Needs

Family issues were framed as women's issues in 52 percent of UN member nations (box 4.4). Family-related issues double as women's concerns. Examples of such issues include the development of women, their domestic roles, the political integration of women, and their economic roles.

These illustrations focus on women's training, job preparation, and balancing of family work and employment roles. Giving employed mothers subsidies so that they can stay home and have time with young children is part of an investment in women's combined work and caregiving functions. This focus on women helps to showcase how the concept of families offers a wide-angle lens to pinpoint needed services, supports, and resources, not just for individuals such as women, but also their families.

Youth Development and Family Welfare

Fifty-one percent of nations focused on youth as part of their IYF projects. *Youth concerns* comprise children's and youth's rights, education, health, abuse, nutrition, juvenile delinquency and crime, and special interventions.[6] Nations emphasized growing awareness of the legal protections available to children; creation of therapy and oral rehydration units in medical institutions to better cope with infantile diarrhea; public awareness meetings on youth and AIDS; development of temporary hostels for adolescent girls; shelter programs for children at risk; foster home promotion programs through a state social security fund; and recommendations for public policy based on research concerning day care for children. Box 4.3 reports on how Cuba names and frames concerns about youth. This shows how a child-centered agenda can emerge as well as a family-supportive strategy.

Information campaigns on how to build *family welfare* are clearly one outgrowth of IYF and one major intervention, as seen by the examples in box 4.4. Focusing on families and the need for socioeconomic development is a theme especially seen in poor countries. The focus on families as economic and social development units may not be as clear, however. This is because families are often seen as the victims or beneficiaries of economic forces rather than agents themselves.

Family welfare, cited by 51 percent of UN member states, includes references to social security, standards of living, and the quality of life. It also includes a general reference to enhancing the welfare of families. It is indeed remarkable that, despite world poverty and rising economic insecurity of families, such a concern was cited by only half of the reporting nations. This may be a reflection of the austerity campaign under way as the result of globalization. Box 4.4 emphasizes housing and, by implication, its relationship to family welfare.

To summarize, six substantive considerations—family support/strengthening, health and safety, family rights/legal protection, women, youth, and family welfare—were the most prominent policy foci for nations participating in IYF. The twenty-five most populated nations ranked these concerns in similar ways. In addition, 50 percent of the largest nations emphasized education, housing, and elevating families as an important unit in society. In these nations, *education* was viewed as a prominent family issue. Education meant more than schooling. It meant emphasizing the education of women, in addition to that of children and youth.

Predicting Policy Development Progressions

Data analysis of IYF reports included an attempt to classify their respective policy initiatives according to the level of development of the nation. Although it may not be possible to predict accurately each nation's actual agenda, their respective development plans and intended trajectories may be expected to reflect their respective levels of development.

So, for example, the high-income nations, in which policy makers may assume that basic subsistence needs are being met, can be expected to frame agendas that differ from those of low-income nations, in which basic subsistence and even survival remain important development challenges. The most developed nations may be concerned with rights pertaining to same-sex domestic partners or balancing work and family. Less-developed nations may be focusing on basic minimum subsistence such as shelter and food.

Actual circumstances may confound this type of thinking. For example, living standards, health problems, and individual and family well-being may be as problematic among identifiable populations in high-income nations as they are in developing nations (e.g., Sen, 1999). In fact, the individual and family well-being profiles of some low-income nations often are better than those of selected populations in high-income nations. Poverty and its companions may be as problematic in one nation as another.

It is not surprising, therefore, to observe common problems that are, to some extent, independent of each nation's development status or classification. Previous chapters have outlined some of the causes, correlates, and explanations. This comparative agenda tracking is an area needing future research. In so many ways, IYF data simply do not suffice.

There remains a need for improved family policy research, both national and comparative (e.g., Asay & Hennon, 1999; Mahler, 1999).

Subsequent chapters, like the previous three, will help frame and name some such new-century research agendas.

NOTES

1. Discourse is a recurrent way of using language, i.e., a pattern of speaking and thinking. The discourses of individuals, families, and policy makers both reflect and promote their thoughts, values, and preferences. Hence, if you want to change an individual's or group's thoughts and actions, you need to change their discourse(s).
2. Problem setting conveys to some people deficit-oriented assumptions. Family-centered policies and practices certainly respond to problems, but they also build from strengths, respond to families' aspirations, and promote new, positive visions. With these additional features in mind, agenda setting is a more apt descriptor.
3. Other popular generative metaphors include organism, play, drama, game, and computer-related versions of the machine metaphor.
4. Charles Hennon, Alan Jones, and Katharine Briar-Lawson were responsible for data collection, analysis, and interpretation. Their work was made possible by the generous facilitation provided by the IYF Secretariat.
5. See also Midgley (1997) on other issues regarding self-reports by nations.
6. Here, as throughout, there are simultaneous references where children and youth may be also linked to health and safety agendas.

CHAPTER 5

Analyzing Policy Impacts and Making Strategic Policy Choices for Families and Helping Professions

Hal A. Lawson, Katharine Briar-Lawson, and Charles B. Hennon

Family-centered policies and practices are action strategies for making improvements for families, and for heading people, helping professions, organizations, communities, governments, and nations in new directions. They are informed by scientific findings and thinking, but they are not scientific instruments. They cannot be scientific instruments because policies and practices are not value neutral, or value free (e.g., Schön & Rein, 1994). Family-centered policies are value-committed instruments for maximizing benefits and minimizing harm for families and the professionals who serve them.

Family-centered policies and practices are normative instruments because they are designed to establish new norms and standards. Ideally, family-centered policies "level up" societal and governmental norms and standards. Family well-being improves as new policy "raises the bar."

When family well-being is high, policies are probably family sensitive, family focused, family supportive, and family centered. In other words, policy helps frame the kinds of services, supports, and resources families actually receive. Conversely, when family well-being is low, and when many families evidence need but do not receive services, supports, and resources, then policy silences, gaps, and limitations are implicated. *When family well-being is low, or in decline, family needs signal policy needs, gaps, and silences.*

Helping professionals also feel the effects of these policy silences, gaps, and limitations. For example, helping professionals in many nations lament that they know what a family wants and needs (e.g., flexible income supplements, opportunities to own land for agriculture), but their government's policies do not permit, or enable, professionals to respond effectively to these family needs. In short, policy gaps, silences, and limitations often are at the core of professionals' ineffectiveness, in turn helping to explain low, or declining, levels of job satisfaction. Indeed, some professionals feel trapped by policy silences, gaps, and limitations.

In short, family-centered policy is not merely a paper edict. *Policy describes, and helps explain, what actually happens daily to families and to professionals.* To put it another way, *people's lives and livelihoods are at stake as policies are made, modified, and eliminated.* Difficult choices and tough decisions are involved. For example, new policies often require new financial resources, and these resources tend to be in short supply. When categorical thinking dominates, resources in support of a new family-centered policy may be secured at the expense of a new foreign trade investment or tax relief for a major investor. Furthermore, major policy innovations often are difficult to effect. They take time and require lots of negotiation and compromise. They necessitate lobbying and persuasion. Policy makers and other governmental leaders may be prepared to move only slowly and gradually, considering just one policy at a time.

Therefore, policy makers, helping professionals, and advocates need to think and act strategically. Mindful that it may take years to secure approval for their complete policy package, they need to know where to start in relation to the full range of policy choices related to families. They also need to know how to analyze, and perhaps predict, *policy impacts.* Policy makers, helping professionals, and advocates need to be able to assess past-present impacts and predict the anticipated, future impacts of new policies they are proposing. A growing body of research in social work, family studies, public administration, public health, and other helping disciplines is an invaluable resource. In other words, policies may not be scientific instruments, but scientific findings and reasoning benefit family-centered policy in particular and democratic politics in general (e.g., Brown, 1998).

This chapter emphasizes the importance of analyzing policy impacts on families and making strategic choices in support of their well-being. The impacts of policy on helping professionals are implied throughout. A family impact inventory is presented first. This inventory facilitates evaluation of past/present policies and the potential future impacts associated with new policies. Then key examples of policy alternatives are presented. Some are presented as tensions, i.e., as one alternative or the other. Others are merely introduced. For example, in a growing number of Western industrialized nations, policies in support of *service integration* are being promoted and enacted. Service integration is, in other words, a new policy choice, or alternative. It is defined and described in this chapter so that policy makers, helping professionals, and advocates can understand it, analyze its potential and actual impacts, and make strategic choices.

Finally, choices involving *policy borrowing* are described, along with cautions and limitations. This discussion sets the stage for chapter 6, which addresses the pivotal roles families play in every aspect of family-centered policies and practices; and for chapter 7, which addresses implementation, evaluation, and learning needs.

THE NEED FOR FAMILY IMPACT ANALYSES AND INVENTORIES

Family impact analysis involves analyzing, evaluating, and predicting policy influences, correlates, and effects. Specially designed *family impact policy and practice inventories* may serve as analytical, evaluative, and predictive tools.

In the United States, work has been underway since the mid-1970s to promote family impact analysis (e.g., Spakes, 1988). For example, the National Family Impact Seminar, convened in Washington, D.C., provided tools and findings that enabled policy makers, helping professionals, and advocates to analyze and predict the impacts of policies on families (Spakes, 1988; Ooms & Binder, 1993). Similarly, leaders in the Province of Alberta, Canada, developed family impact assessment tools in conjunction with IYF (Premiers Council, 1994).

An Example of a Family Impact Assessment Inventory

Research reviews and books focused on families are essential guides for the development and use of impact assessment tools. Helping professionals, especially frontline workers, have valuable knowledge about the impacts policies have on them and on the families they serve. Above all, families often are in the best position to determine, assess, and predict the direct and indirect effects on them of existing and proposed policies. Therefore, the impact assessment process and the development of impact assessment tools should include families (United Nations, 1995e).

Table 5.1 presents a list of questions that might make up a family policy impact inventory. Consider this inventory as an example of the kind of tool that is needed in each nation. The questions listed in this

TABLE 5.1. An Example of a Family Impact Analysis Checklist or Inventory

1. Identify the policy issue and describe it briefly. What aspect(s) of family well-being is the policy designed to address?

2. Identify the value commitments and underlying assumptions regarding families, the professionals who serve them, the presenting need or problem, and the existing, or proposed, policy. Are the underlying values and assumptions consistent and coherent, or are they contradictory because of political trade-offs and compromises?

3. Have prior policies tried to address the family need, problem, or want that is being prioritized? What are the lessons associated with this policy history? Why is the new policy an improvement over past policies? Why does the new policy represent a strategic choice, one that is better than other policy alternatives at this time?

4. Does the existing, or proposed, policy (as a solution) match up with the family problem, need, opportunity, or aspiration that stimulated its development? What scientific evidence is available to support the hypothesized, causal connection?

5. What are the effectiveness criteria? Who determined them? How will they be measured and by whom? How frequently will family impacts be evaluated? Will families be involved in these decisions and in the evaluations? Which families? Will frontline helping professionals be involved in these decisions and evaluations? Which professionals? Who decides? Who decides who decides?

6. Brainstorm all of the possible effects of the policy. Start with the policy impacts on different kinds of families and family systems. Include helping professionals, policy makers, and citizen advocates. How might the impacts vary for different families? For different members of families? For example, does a policy for children support families? Does a policy for elders support families? Does a policy that favors able-bodied people discriminate against developmentally challenged individuals and erode the supports for their families?

7. How strong are the relationships between policy intentions and goals and actual impacts? What can be learned about the direct relationships between the policy and its impacts on families? About indirect relationships? About intended versus unintended correlates and consequences?

8. Now that the data have been collected, do the results suggest cause-and-effect relationships? Correlational relationships? What is the magnitude of these relationships? If the predicted or hypothesized impacts have not resulted, is this caused by an implementation problem? An evaluation problem? Or, is the problem one of unwarranted and spurious assumptions that were accepted when the policy was first proposed?

TABLE 5.1. (*Continued*)

9. When policy impacts do not match up with policy goals and intentions, can this discrepancy, or policy gap, be corrected? What corrective actions are indicated? Who should take them? What resource needs accompany them? Or, should the policy be abandoned altogether?

10. To what extent does the existing or proposed policy hinge on major changes, learning, and capacity-building initiatives? Must organizations change? Helping professionals? Families? Has sufficient attention been given to learning and capacity building, especially for professionals and families? Are there sufficient resources in support of technical assistance and capacity building? How are these capacity-building and resource needs determined and evaluated?

11. To what extent are existing and proposed policies operator dependent, path dependent, and context dependent? Do they require a special kind of helping professional, or family (operator dependence)? Do they require a special sequence of events and prerequisites (path dependence)? Will they work in every cultural context, and in every place (context dependence)? Are impact measures and analyses sensitive to the interactions among these three kinds of dependence?

12. What roles, responsibilities, and duties does the policy assume, or prescribe, for families? How were these decisions made and by whom? Were diverse (including gay and lesbian) families represented? Which genders in the family were privileged? Were families policy leaders? How are families' daily experiences evaluated to determine intended versus unintended policy impacts? How are families' and family members' perceptions of their well-being incorporated into well-being indexes and policy accounting systems?

13. Are the policy accountability structures and criteria rule based and compliance based, or are they results oriented? If they are results oriented, how are rule-based and compliance-based systems in government bureaucracies, community agencies, and schools being reformed and transformed?

14. Does the new policy produce ripple effects (also known as domino effects and contagion effects)? Are these effects planned? Are they beneficial? If they are unplanned, and they have negative effects, how can they be controlled, contained, and reversed?

15. What are the implications for new policies and interventions? What corrective actions should be taken to minimize negative impacts, while maximizing intended, predicted, and beneficial impacts?

Source: Katharine Briar-Lawson and Hal Lawson adapted this inventory from the earlier work of Briar-Lawson, D. Fiedler, and P. Willis.

inventory do not exhaust the possibilities, nor do they meet every need. They illustrate both need and possibility. Every such inventory must be tailored to its national and cultural contexts.

Family impact analysis also may attend to the effects of policies on professionals' practices. This focus is justifiable because the services, supports, and resources that professionals employ depend in large part on what their policy and practice environments permit. Alternatively, impact analysis may focus on both families and helping professionals, especially relationships between them. All such analyses may include measures of direct and indirect effects; intended and unintended consequences and correlates; and predicted as well as unanticipated results (Premier's Council, 1994).

Incorporating Scientific Reasoning and Research

In some nations, political interests and ideologies, not research, drive policy development. In fact, policies and the programs they spawn may be promoted in spite of the research. In the United States, for example, school-based drug and alcohol education policies and programs for children and youth have been developed in spite of research that casts doubt on their effectiveness (e.g., Gorman, 1998). Some of this research suggests that some such programs may actually encourage youth to experiment with drugs and alcohol (e.g., Brown, D'Emidio-Caston, & Pollard, 1997). Similarly, American policies related to alcohol use and abuse have fluctuated, not because of research that enables fresh understanding, but because political interests and priorities have changed (e.g., Gorman, 1998; Gusfield, 1996). Jordan (1998) has outlined the same kind of pattern, i.e., one in which ideologies and interests reign over research, in relation to the new politics of welfare in the United States and the United Kingdom. A key challenge for the twenty-first century involves the use of scientific reasoning and research in policy development and encouraging democratic understanding and participation (e.g., Brown, 1998).

When policies are more than symbolic gestures, they command resources. When scarce, precious resources are deployed in support of ill-conceived policies, other policies, which promise to be more effective because of research in support of them, may not receive all of the resources needed to maximize their effectiveness and benefits. There are, then, clear needs for relevant research to be integrated in policy-relevant ways, especially the implications of the research for family-centered policies and practices. Policy, advocacy, and research can be joined in innovative and more effective ways (e.g., Meenaghan & Kilty, 1993; Lawson, Briar-Lawson, et al., 2000).

Research and research reviews serve policy makers, helping professionals, and advocates in much the same way that the rearview mirrors of automobiles help drivers. Research and research reviews show past/present relationships and patterns. In other words, they show policy effects and trajectories. They identify, describe, explain, and perhaps predict findings, relationships, and patterns. They provide policy makers, helping professionals, and advocates with descriptions of current circumstances, including their derivations from the past.

To put it another way, research and research reviews tend to provide "is statements" and "has been statements." Only in their implications may readers find "ought statements," i.e., normative prescriptions for the future. In short, scientific research and research reviews do not tell policy makers, helping professionals, and advocates what to do next, i.e., what they need to consider for family-centered policies and practices. They are, at best, suggestive of new directions.

Strategic, family-centered policy development thus involves the so-called *normative leap* (e.g., Schön & Rein, 1994).[1] After reviewing the relevant research, learning about past/present findings and patterns (what is and has been), and considering their implications, policy makers, helping professionals, and advocates must make value judgments —normative judgments—about what to do next. In this sense, family-centered policies are normative (value-committed) interventions. Policies are social action interventions, attempting to make things different and better, and for heading everyone in new and more informed directions.

Reflect, for a moment, on the analysis in chapter 3. In this chapter, some of the findings and implications from research on underemployment and unemployment were presented. Recall that underemployment and unemployment are associated with individual and family problems and needs, including substance abuse, mental health challenges such as depression, child abuse and neglect, domestic violence, learned hopelessness and even despair, school-related problems for children and youth, and perhaps the social exclusion of families and their members. These needs and problems tend to nest in each other, and they may co-occur (Kessler, Gillis-Light, et al., 1997). Find one and, sooner or later, you are likely to find the others. Furthermore, these needs and problems may be transmitted across several generations of the same family system. In brief, the research shows clear patterns involving individual and family needs. It identifies, describes, explains, and sometimes predicts some of the causes, correlates, and consequences of unemployment and underemployment, especially their impacts on family well-being.

But what should policy makers, helping professionals, and advocates do about unemployment and underemployment? In other words, what are the policy-as-intervention responses? A range of alternatives is possible. For example, categorical policies, which may be family sensitive, family focused, and family supportive, may be proposed. Policies in support of mental health programs, or domestic violence programs, or child abuse and neglect initiatives (e.g., child protection and child welfare), may be proposed, approved, and implemented. Here, policy interventions address the presenting needs or problems, i.e., the "symptoms" or correlates of unemployment and underemployment.

In contrast, family-centered policies may be developed in concert with some of the families who are affected by unemployment and underemployment. They might propose a full and gender-equitable employment policy. They also might propose related policies in support of universal entitlements such as income subsidies and access to health care. In this case, the policy interventions address the root causes of presenting needs and problems. Unemployment and underemployment are framed and named as significant social issues, a framing and naming made possible by research and research reviews and by family perspectives. In fact, the research may signal needs for all such policies, i.e., ones that address the symptoms at the same time that others address the root causes and correlates.

All of these policy alternatives involve normative leaps. To reiterate, every policy, or combination of these policies, represents a social intervention designed to enhance the lives and well-being of families. Moreover, as chapter 4 suggested, each policy alternative is developed in relation to a special way of framing and naming, and naming and framing, what's wrong that needs fixing, and what's right and good, i.e., things that need to be maintained and strengthened.

The key is to include research and research reviews in this framing and naming process. Policy makers, helping professionals, and advocates are strategic when they incorporate and integrate research findings in their front-end planning. The idea is to enhance policy development by ensuring that claims about families' needs and problems are complete, correct, and correctly stated, at the same time striving to prevent wasting precious resources on policies and programs that have little or no probability of working.

Employing Intervention Logic and Methods

Once policies are viewed as social interventions, intervention-related logic and methods can be used for policy planning, implementation, and evaluation. For example, logic models can be employed (Alter & Egan, 1997; Alter & Murty, 1997). Logic models are organizing frameworks. Logic models emphasize the correspondence, or goodness of fit, between needs and problems, goals and objectives, preferred intervention and improvement strategies, evaluation criteria, and the research evidence in support of these correspondence patterns. These models enhance the decision-making logic and planning, in turn enhancing policy planning.

Similarly, intervention planning, monitoring, and evaluation strategies may enhance policy planning and development. For example, current data on low, or declining, family well-being provide a policy baseline measure. These data also compel new policies-as-interventions because they reveal a need or problem. In response, policy makers, helping professionals, and advocates may make the normative leap. They may propose one or more policies, or perhaps a coherent, comprehensive policy package, designed to reverse this decline and improve family well-being.

The initial baseline provides a comparative standard, and policy evaluations in relation to it may improve future policy development. For example, policy evaluations accompanying new family-centered policies may indicate that family well-being stops declining, or begins to improve. Intervention logic suggests that the new policy is having its intended or desired effects. This relationship between policy changes and effectiveness measures, as related to family well-being, is a key contribution to family policy research, and it can be incorporated into future logic models.

On the other hand, these new policies may not have any effect. Even worse, family well-being may continue to decline against the initial baseline. In this case, policy development is also enhanced because these results suggest what doesn't work, i.e., what not to do. In other words, since any good definition includes what a phenomenon is not, the process of eliminating ineffective and inappropriate policy alternatives provides benefits. As each alternative is discarded, policy makers, helping professionals, and advocates generate data and then make new normative judgments in relation to these data and their aspirations for families and their well-being. In this instance, as in others, interventionist logic and scientific reasoning are invaluable components in the policy process. As box 5.1 suggests, this logic can result in generating knowledge at the same

REFLECTIVE TRANSFER FOR KNOWLEDGE GENERATION AND POLICY IMPROVEMENT

Schön and Rein (1994) describe *reflective transfer* carried out by competent policy makers and practitioners. Reflective transfer is "the process by which patterns detected in one situation are carried over as projective models to other situations where they are used to generate new causal inferences." These policy patterns pass validity tests in one situation. When they are transferred, they are subjected to another set of validity tests in the new situation (Schön & Rein, 1994, p. 204). Reflective transfer is not just about importing lessons drawn from other people and places. It also involves exporting knowledge and understanding; and in turn, gaining new knowledge and understanding, which also can be exported. In brief, reflective transfer involves a systematic approach to evaluating, or researching, the direct experiences gained with policy and practice experiments.

Learning and continual quality improvements are embedded in reflective transfer. Policy makers and practitioners are engaged in a kind of design rationality. They make the normative leap, hoping to create improvements. Policy makers, helping professionals, and advocates learn how to read situations and learn from their experiences. They expect situations and experiences to "talk back" to them; and they must be prepared and equipped to make sense of such feedback, learn, and seek improvement. Schön and Rein (1994) provide what they call a ladder of reflection. This ladder begins with concrete operations in which learning and quality improvement are simpler. This ladder culminates in problems and policy and practices that are more complex, uncertain, and abstract.

time that effective, successful policies-as-interventions are transported from one place to another.

Identifying, Analyzing, and Evaluating Implicit Policy Theories

Research and scientific reasoning also are useful in evaluating a policy's key assumptions, which may be called a policy's implicit theories. These assumptions, or theories, are implicit to the extent they are not made public, nor subjected to empirical analysis and confirmation, nor evaluated against ethical codes, moral imperatives, and legal-constitutional standards.

Just as any building is only as strong as its foundation, so too does every policy depend on the supports provided by its foundational assumptions—its implicit policy theory, or theories. Policy makers, helping professionals, and advocates can become more effective as they develop the skills and abilities for identifying these assumptions, or theories. Implicit policy theories need to be made explicit. They must be stated in testable formats. And then they must be subjected to two related kinds of analysis and evaluation, which may not be mutually exclusive.

One kind of analysis and evaluation employs scientific reasoning and intervention logic. It proceeds in relation to the research, and it may be facilitated by logic models. The second kind proceeds in relation to values and value commitments. It involves ethical considerations, moral judgments, and legal-constitutional issues. A recent, high-profile example serves to illustrate the need for, and importance of, both kinds of analyses and evaluations.

Recently, in the United States, a revolutionary policy change was approved and enacted. This change often has been described as welfare reform.[2] Welfare reform commenced when Temporary Assistance to Needy Families (TANF) replaced Aid to Families with Dependent Children (AFDC). In contrast to AFDC's long-term supports for impoverished children and their families, which were provided by the federal government, TANF transferred some of the responsibility for the administration of welfare regulations to each state. At the same time, states were given discretionary authority over the amount of support families were eligible to receive. In response, a number of states enacted time limits for TANF that are shorter than the federal lifetime limits of five years. In effect, states became even more restrictive than the federal government. Families who were raising their children on welfare have been caught squarely between the old AFDC income support approaches and the new TANF employment requirements and restrictions.

How might policy makers, helping professionals, and advocates make sense of TANF and AFDC? One way is by identifying, analyzing, and evaluating their respective, implicit policy theories.

AFDC's major, implicit "policy theory" may be expressed as follows. *If mothers or fathers are provided public assistance, supportive of their role as caregivers, then children's well-being will be safeguarded.* In contrast, TANF offered a different policy theory. *If parents and caregivers are employed, then intergenerational patterns of long-term dependency will end; families will become more self-sufficient; and their well-being will improve.* As suggested by the family impact inventory presented in table 5.1, this dramatic policy change has had ripple, or domino, effects. Some analysts expressed concern that, with TANF, the number of families in the child welfare system would swell, ultimately causing already-troubled systems to fail (e.g., Edelman, 1997).[3] The shift from AFDC to TANF implicated equally dramatic changes at the level of practice. With AFDC, some workers were accustomed to determining eligibility. With TANF, their jobs changed. Under the pressure of TANF's time limits, these workers had to intensify their promotion of employment and fostering of employment-related supports such as job training, transportation assistance, and child care.

What research evidence can be mounted in support of AFDC's policy theory? What evidence supports TANF's policy theory?

If the scientific evidence is incomplete, contradictory, and inconclusive, then value-based evaluations are in order. How can ethical codes, moral imperatives, and legal constitutional issues be brought to bear on these two competing policy theories? For example, is the provision of meaningful employment, not just any job, a legal and constitutional right? Does a mother or father have the right to make the family a workplace, and to receive income supports to stay home with their children? What are the ethical imperatives for professions such as social work? This profession has made firm ethical commitments to fight injustice, oppression, and repression; to address profound inequalities; and to empower poor, vulnerable, and disfranchised individuals and families. How do these value commitments, ethical imperatives, and professional missions help frame the evaluation of these policy theories? What actions, what kinds of normative leaps, do these evaluations compel? Questions like these illustrate how policy makers, helping professionals, and advocates can employ both kinds of policy analysis and evaluation—both scientific and value-based evaluation—in relation to a policy's key theory, or theories.

Policy impacts, learning, development, and improvement are facilitated as data are generated. In other words, policy makers, helping professionals, and advocates may employ action research methods, which facilitate action learning (e.g., Argyris, 1996; Argyris & Schön, 1996; Foldy & Creed, 1999; Lawson, 1999a; Lawson, Briar-Lawson, et al., 2000; Nielson, 1993; Preskill & Torres, 1999). Action research and learning, like scientific reasoning and research, may guide their decisions as they face important policy choices.

KEY POLICY CHOICES AND TENSIONS

Every policy choice is influenced by its surrounding context. Often there is a fine line separating naïveté, ignorance, benign neglect, indifference, and arrogance. For example, every nation faces the challenges of poverty. Seeking solutions to it, rather than neglecting or postponing action, is a major building block of family-centered policies and practices. Anti-poverty strategies may require changes in residual approaches to policy.

Residual vs. Institutional Approaches

In most cases policy makers inherit decision-making agendas that are not ideal. In other words, they are "policy takers" first. Only later are they policy makers. They are like players who enter a game that is already underway, and, for the time being at least, they must play the game and follow others' rules and traditions. Prior planning and decision-making frames are maintained because they enjoy supports and because they are established as policy traditions. In other words, nations and governments have developed ways to think about, and perform, "policy business as usual." Their approaches to policy development, especially to family policy, may follow a familiar, predictable trajectory. This trajectory and the dynamics that serve to maintain it must be understood and appreciated before they can be changed. This may require working with it first, postponing changes until later.

Many policy makers assume that an emergent problem or need requires only short-term responses. Especially when crises develop, people may search for a "quick fix." In other cases, policy makers hope, or believe, that the crisis will dissipate or disappear. It is not surprising, therefore, that short-term, crisis-oriented policy and programmatic supports are sometimes a standard way to address family needs and problems. These supports provide a safe, familiar, and convenient policy path and problem-solving route.

Unfortunately, when policy makers opt for the quick fix, they tend to ignore long-term preventive, proactive investments in social development and families. Instead, problem solving builds conventional and residual programs and services, which may have outlived their usefulness. And because residual programs often are lodged in categorical policies and practices, "add on," quick-fix policies may have unintended consequences, such as eroding the capacities of families to serve as more comprehensive social welfare systems themselves.

Categorical, Crisis-Responsive Policy Traditions vs. Prevention Policies

So, for example, categorical, crisis-responsive family policies may have to be accepted at first. As time, supports, and new developments permit, family-centered policies that encourage and support prevention and early intervention can be fostered.

Family-focused, family-supportive, and family-centered policies that encourage, permit, and support prevention and early intervention are sorely needed in many nations. In some communities in nations such as the United States, more than 90 percent of the funds for services may be reserved for individuals and families evidencing need, many of whom already are in crisis. Because families already are experiencing crises, and many crises have ripple effects, these policies tend to be extremely costly, and they may not be wholly effective. Policies that support early detection and intervention thus save time, money, and lives.

When problems and crises arise, leaders confront choices about stage- or phase-specific intervention and support. For example, what will policy makers do when a growing number of children are victims of abuse and neglect? Do they build orphanages, or do they give families intensive services and income supports to prevent the poverty and institutionalization of homeless and abandoned children? Do they look the other way when children are commodified and then bought and sold? Or, do they invest in both the children and their families?

There are at least two kinds of effectiveness issues here. The first and more important issue concerns the impacts and outcomes for families. The second concerns cost-effectiveness.

It is possible to begin discussions around the idea of a *prevention gap*. A prevention gap index can be derived from examining the proportion of funding allocated to crisis-oriented services and supports as opposed to the funding for preventive and health promotion services, supports, and resources (e.g., Bruner, 1996; Haveman & Wolfe, 1995).

Investing in "front-end" versus "deep-end" services and policies is a choice that nations face as they develop family-centered policies and practices. Once funds are deployed at the "deep end," i.e., for crises, they are difficult to move to the "front end," i.e., for prevention, because such shifts involve major additional expenditures. The absence of a preventive agenda places an increasing number of families in crisis. And once there, they are more costly to serve and support, and difficult to move to the safer "front end." Box 5.2 presents a scenario that indicates how preventive thinking can foster improved policies and practices in support of families.

Policies in support of prevention and early intervention for families also respond to an ethical-moral imperative—namely, that families should not have to experience harm in order to get the help they need. These policies also make helping professionals' jobs easier and improve their effectiveness. Once crises are evident, helping professionals often experience effectiveness crises of their own. They are unable to help families, gain job satisfaction, and enjoy the sense of personal well-being that accompanies job satisfaction.

Selective (Targeting) Strategies vs. Universal Entitlement Programs

In some nations, there are engrained assumptions that strong, healthy families do not require state-initiated policies and practices. Some leaders believe that only the most needy, vulnerable families require such help. From this perspective, the role of policy leaders is to identify and define these vulnerable families and then to "target" them selectively for services, supports, and resources.

Examples include housing initiatives for the poor, substance abuse programs for substance abusers, parent education initiatives for those who have abused their children, and infant and mother food supplement

BOX 5.2

AN EXAMPLE OF "FRONT LOADING"

An Eastern European nation, once a member of the former Soviet Union, has undergone a shift from a planned, or command, economy to a demand or market economy. On any given day over 30 percent of the workforce is jobless. At the same time, inflation is running between 50 and 100 percent. There is no relief in sight. Many corporations, which might have invested in this nation, are taking their economic ventures elsewhere.

In spite of this stagnant economy and its problems, families and community members are remarkably resilient.

The implications associated with each policy decision are enormous. When this nation was part of the Soviet Union, full employment was guaranteed because it was a form of social insurance for families and provided for family supports. In the new market economy, families are without jobs, adequate income, and health care. What are policy leaders in this nation to do?

Policy leaders consider a residual welfare state model, i.e., one where welfare is only for families who hit "rock bottom" poverty. They also consider a child and family allowance. They recognize that, even if they decide on a financial supplement, family size and need may not be factored in, or supported.

A legislative committee and the minister for families and social welfare ultimately decide upon a policy for family allowances, based on family size and need. Because they are concerned about front-end investments, and they are working toward family-centered policies and practices, they recognize that strong families require resources they can deploy to meet their own needs. Family allowances, they conclude, will help offset financial problems among families. Investments in them may help attract foreign investments and encourage families to participate in community economic and social development.

programs for poor families. These programs are, in the main, crisis- and problem-responsive problem-solving approaches, for which families must demonstrate eligibility and/or clear needs.

By contrast, universal entitlements are available to every family. Examples include family allowances, universal access to health care, and mass public schooling. A family-centered approach often promotes proactive, comprehensive policy planning on families' behalf. Family-centered policy and advocacy may result in universal entitlements in support of family well-being.

Presumptive vs. Means-Tested Policies

Many policies are based upon presumptive needs and conditions. Presumptive policies are grounded in the assumption that the needs of individuals and families are known, or have been anticipated. The following examples of presumptive policies clarify their nature and intent.

Universal health care; mass, free, and compulsory public schooling; and universal retirement benefits such as social security in Western Europe, Canada, and the United Kingdom are examples of presumptive policies. They stem from an ethic of social responsibility assumed by government on behalf of citizens.

Some such presumptive policies may eventually result in the adoption of universal programs. Others are more selective and are based on attributes such as age (elder or child) or status (such as family). They are universal in that all who fit the category, regardless of income, receive the grant. They are not based on need.

With means-tested policies and programs, families may have to prove or demonstrate their needs. For example, it may not be enough to say that you are poor. You also must prove beyond a shadow of doubt that you have few or no resources. In fact, you may have to give up some of your resources to qualify as poor. Similarly, it may not be enough that you say you are abused. You need to show proof of hospitalization in order to qualify for aid. These examples illustrate the ways in which policies may force families or family members such as battered women to endure severe hardship in order to qualify for aid while further stigmatizing and eroding their capacity and well-being. They also illustrate how eligibility rules exempt governments from investments in families (e.g., Jordan, 1998).

Current policies related to families may not be so clear-cut. Some policies may be presumptive—for example, ones that provide allowances for universal health care. Every family and family member, regardless of income and socioeconomic status, receives these policy benefits. Moreover, many individuals and families may share the costs. They pay taxes determined in relation to their incomes. Ideally, the higher their incomes, the more taxes they pay. In reality, taxation systems are often regressive because they privilege those with the highest incomes, often providing them special shelters and exemptions.

On the other hand, housing, food supplements, or child care may be means tested. Families often must prove that they deserve and need governmental subsidies. Proving need means being evaluated by a helping professional. These evaluations are tricky. In fact, demonstrations of need may be experienced by families as *moral evaluations* of them and their lifestyles (e.g., Bauman, 1998; Jordan, 1998). In cases like these, being poor is not just an economic hardship; it brings possible stigmas and feelings of declining self- and family-worth.

Serving Families or Caring for Established Organizations

One of the challenges faced by policy makers everywhere is evident in the following two questions: (1) How can governments transcend the limits of bureaucracies and at the same time maintain the benefits? (2) How can leaders and helping professionals avoid the limits of bureaucratic accountability structures and processes, focus on rule-driven, reliable, and predictable performance, and gain more discretion in how they and families improve these results?

Other questions follow. How can governments find better ways to become more family sensitive, family focused, family centered, and family accountable? How can helping professionals comply with organizational rules, yet also share power with families? These related issues stem from a known reality about bureaucratic organizations. Despite their pro-family rhetoric, they often are self-serving and rigid. There are tensions and dilemmas here, and many of these tensions involve the categorical policies and practices of the past. These tensions and dilemmas are sometimes at the center of family-centered policy debates.

Mindful of these tensions and dilemmas and the self-serving character of bureaucracies, this reminder is offered. *Creating and promoting family-centered policies and practices necessitates changes in the ac-*

countability structures and processes of organizations and professions charged with the implementation and evaluation of those policies and practices.

For example, many organizations and professions are shifting from rule-based accountability systems (following proper procedures) to performance-based systems, which means focusing on results and choosing strategies accordingly (e.g., Gardner, 1999). Absent such changes, well-intentioned policies and practices will not be implemented with fidelity, and families will not be as well served. Instead, nations will witness familiar ends-means reversals in which families, rather than being the end or goal, become the means of achieving organizational goals. Professionals force-fit them into existing programs.

There are family-centered policy and practice tools that are designed to tailor services, supports, and resources to each family's wants and needs. For example, flexible funds for special family emergencies or necessities may be used. Other tools involve having families become their own service providers and case managers (Hennon, Brubaker, & Kaplan, 1991; Briar-Lawson & Drews, 1998). If families are empowered, then the role of the helping professional may be less hierarchical, and more that of a facilitator (Alameda, 1996; Briar-Lawson, 2000-b).

Accommodating Policies and Practices to Diverse Families in Local Contexts

Sometimes there is a difference between what families need and want and what policy makers consider, or are prepared to provide. Needs and wants at the village or community level may differ from the capacity of policy makers to hear, or honor, families' needs.

How, for example, can an elected official in a nation's capital, which is hundreds of kilometers away from a tiny mountain village, understand the stresses felt by families encountering cancer-producing toxins in their water because of the polluting activities of a new copper mine? Or, how can a top-level official appreciate the family stress in a rural village, stress that has resulted from mandated changes in agricultural practices because of new import-export policies? In cases like these, appropriate national policies may not have been formulated in response to situations as experienced by families. Perhaps existing policies are off-target, or inflexible. Either way, the result for families is the same. Families do not receive the services, supports, and resources they need, and helping professionals may not be able to help them. The point is, family-centered, national policies need to be sufficiently comprehensive to anticipate the range of family situations, yet sufficiently flexible to allow tailoring of services, supports, and resources to diverse families in local contexts.

For example, a policy to support families in their use of schools can be flexible. In cities, towns, and villages, schools can remain open and serve as helping stations. They may become twenty-four-hour schools, opened around the clock (United Nations, 1993g). Communities can be given funds to design how schools will be used and what services might emanate from them. Schools could be used as a crisis nursery for evening workers without child care, a shelter for the homeless, or as a business incubator site so that more employment can be developed at the local level. Other adult education possibilities abound, including stress management, effective parenting, abuse prevention, and gardening.

The Principle of Subsidiarity and a Key Tension

The principle of subsidiarity is derived from democratic political theory, and it has been promoted by the United Nations in relation to IYF. It recommends seeking solutions to problems at the lowest possible level of a social structure—individuals and families. This principle reinforces the individual's and family's ultimate responsibility for problem definition and solving. Family subsidiarity, i.e., recognizing the responsibilities of families and their members in seeking solutions, offers a unique opportunity for governments and families to communicate. Families may gain a voice in policy development and implementation (United Nations, 1995b).

Subsidiarity also presents a key tension. As Jordan (1998) observes, many governmental policy leaders are able to excuse themselves from national policies, practices, and responsibilities for poor and vulnerable individuals and families by invoking the principle of subsidiarity. That is, they are able to delegate responsibility and authority to local leaders and helping professionals, making the poor and the vulnerable "their problem." Or, poor and vulnerable families are assigned the responsibility to help themselves. Clearly, governments must also act responsibly and prudently, interacting with and learning from local leaders who work closely with families in need. In brief, subsidiarity does not excuse governments from responsibilities. It does imply that they should work closely with families, and that families must uphold their part of the social contract with government.

From Deficit-Based to Strengths-Based Assessments and Policies

Rather than looking only for problems in families and seeing parents as deficient, family-centered legislation, policies, and practices are predicated upon individual, family, and community assets. They aim to promote greater self-sufficiency, rather than dependence. The idea, introduced in chapter 2, is to support families in the duties they perform in economic development, health, education, child welfare, elder care, the prevention of violence and disabilities, and other areas.

Families are the epitome of integrated health, education, counseling, and justice service systems. For family members, education, health, transportation and the like cannot be separated neatly into discrete categories. In the daily lives of family members, these issues and needs, along with those involving food, shelter, and the conditions of their neighborhoods or villages, are interdependent (United Nations, 1992b). Each family is assigned some responsibilities for them. Thus, the design and delivery of services, supports, and resources should silhouette as much as possible the way in which such blending and integration occurs in a family. Otherwise families are treated as fragmented entities, just as service systems themselves are fragmented.

From Categorical Services to Integrated Services

Many high-income nations, like a growing number of middle-income nations, have developed specialized helping professions and equally specialized service systems. These specialized professions and service systems are supported by, and in turn reinforce, categorical policies. In some nations, it may appear that, for every part of the human being and every facet of the family, there is a specialized helping profession (e.g., McKnight, 1995). Many nations have a virtual assembly line of helping professions, mirroring the assembly lines of the industrial societies that spawned these professions.

Each profession has developed its own knowledge base, language system, and preferred intervention strategies. Each has its system of credentials. Professions such as medicine and social work have their own codes of ethics. Each has its own jurisdictional claims, and each controls its own boundaries. In fact, these professions often compete with one another for the privilege and right to help individuals and families (e.g., Lawson, 1998b; Lawson & Barkdull, 2000). For example, the United States is not the only nation in which social workers, counselors, clinical psychologists, and psychiatrists compete for the right to address individual and family mental health needs and marital counseling needs.

When there are so many professions; when individual and family needs and problems are viewed in isolation from others; and when categorical, crisis-oriented policies prevail, public-sector, vulnerable families often get caught in the middle of this assembly line of professions. Some families have as many as fourteen different service providers in their lives (e.g., Hooper-Briar & Lawson, 1994). Providers often do not know each other. They do not work together. Their efforts are not harmonized and synchronized. In fact, families may experience stress because each provider asks them, or requires them, to do something different. No one orchestrates the professions and their services for the family. This is not a success formula for families, or for professionals.

Proposals for *integrated services,* also called *service integration,* have been launched in response (Hooper-Briar & Lawson, 1994; OECD, 1998; Waldfogel, 1997). There is a growing literature about this innovation and the policies that support it (e.g., Gardner, 1999; van Veen, Day, & Walraven, 1998; O'Looney, 1996). Service integration will only be sketched here.

The core idea is to coordinate, harmonize, and synchronize the specialized professions and the services they deliver, thereby removing families from situations in which they are caught in the middle and do not receive help. Service-integration initiatives may be facilitated by policy changes. For example, social and health service policies may become more family focused and family supportive. In the process, these policies may be de-categorized. *Policy de-categorization* involves breaking down the specialized boundaries and perhaps removing rigid rules and eligibility criteria. It may include blending funding streams, thereby enabling frontline professionals to enjoy greater flexibility in the services, supports, and resources they offer to families.

Service integration often is accompanied by proposals for improved communication, service coordination, and collaboration among the various professions. These related activities are described as *interprofessional collaboration.* Because the helping professions have developed in isolation of one another, some may represent the antithesis of collaboration. Most, if not all, may need technical assistance and capacity building. So may the university and college professors who prepare helping professionals. New professional preparation programs in support of this collaboration and service integration are called interprofessional education and training programs; in the community these may be called "cross-training" initiatives (e.g., Knapp & Associates, 1998; Lawson & Hooper-Briar, 1994; Lawson, Petersen, & Briar-Lawson, 2000; McCroskey & Einbinder, 1998). National and international journals now address these related areas. For example, the *Journal of Interprofessional Care* is published four times each year,[4] and there are national and international conferences that focus on service integration, interprofessional collaboration, and one-stop-shopping arrangements such as "full-service community schools" (e.g., Lawson & Briar-Lawson, 1997).

Typically, service integration and interprofessional collaboration result in the formation of new service delivery teams. Team organization and development vary (e.g., Øvretveit, Mathias, & Thompson, 1997). Just as a conductor facilitates the work of a choir or an orchestra, a team facilitator is needed to harmonize and coordinate the work of professionals and families. Often, this facilitator is called the case manager. One member of each team may serve as the lead case manager, or this responsibility may be shared and rotated. For example, the mental health professional may be the lead case manager when the family's presenting problems correspond to this person's expertise, while the social worker may be the lead case manager when child welfare issues are the immediate priority.

Service integration and interprofessional collaboration initiatives often prioritize access to services. Access may be impeded when professionals are located in different agencies and diverse places. For this reason, many proposals require professionals to move to what some consider a convenient place for families. In other words, professionals are relocated. When they are relocated at the same place, i.e., co-located, the idea is to provide a single site for service delivery; a single point of entry into public systems; and a single, perhaps one-time-only assessment of information and needs, which all professionals can share. This co-location arrangement is often called "one-stop shopping" or "one-stop services." Both phrases are code names for integrated services and interprofessional collaboration initiatives in schools, community agencies, neighborhood organizations, religious institutions, and even shopping malls (e.g., Hooper-Briar & Lawson, 1994; Lawson & Briar-Lawson, 1997).

Clearly, these service integration and collaboration initiatives hold promise for families and the professionals who serve them. On the other hand, these bold innovations have presented challenges. Only a few such challenges will be presented here.

For example, one-stop service integration may increase access without improving quality. In other words, if providers were not effective where they were, and the only change is the move to a new place and joining a team, then the quality of service delivery, as experienced by families, will not improve. Moreover, if families were not consulted when the one-stop site was selected, access may not improve at all. For example, some parents have had bad experiences in schools, and they do not experience service providers and educators as "family friendly and supportive." And this observation leads to a final one.

Professionals and their service integration initiatives may become more family sensitive, family focused, and family supportive, but they often do not become family centered. To put it another way, collaboration with families—*family-centered collaboration*—often has not accompanied service integration and interprofessional collaboration (Lawson & Barkdull, in press). It is assumed that professionals are the answer; families provide the questions. Families are not treated as partners, nor are they viewed as experts in what helps and hurts them. In brief, families are still treated as dependent clients needing professional interventions (e.g., Cowger, 1998; McKnight, 1995).

So, even with these promising innovations involving integration and collaboration, families may not have the capacity, or the inclination, to use the help they are offered. More to the point, the help that is offered may not correspond to the services, supports, and resources families need. Family-based resistance and sabotage dynamics may continue. Even worse, families may engage in self-defeating behavior, or end up harming their members because they are so overwhelmed and poorly served by professional helpgivers.

Cohesive, coherent, comprehensive, and responsive service integration and collaboration necessitate family-centered policies and practices. Family policy, legislation, and practice can build on the known realities of diverse family contexts, while building upon the strengths and capacities of families. Some such family-centered approaches will encourage families to support, and advocate for, other families. Others should be directed toward family development. Still others should be oriented toward family preservation. These important directions and differences are presented in the next chapter, which also emphasizes the expertise of families and how it can be used to help themselves, other families, and helping professionals. It will become clear that family-centered practices require the enfranchisement and empowerment of families to serve as active agents of their own development; which, in turn, facilitates integrated social and economic development (Pinderhughes, 1995; United Nations, 1995b).

BORROWING POLICIES AND POLICY LESSONS

Thanks to the Internet, international meetings, and global communications, individuals, families, professions, organizations, and governments of all kinds can learn about what others have tried and done. In the global age, each nation of the world, together with its states and provinces, cities, towns, and villages, plays host to the equivalent of multiple design laboratories, i.e., policy and practice demonstration sites. Box 5.3 presents a case example that illustrates this possibility. Similarly, several of the IYF boxes presented in the previous chapter showed that nations were addressing the same kinds of policy needs and family issues. These clusters of nations might be expected to learn from, even borrow from, one another.

Successes and achievements in one part of the world may help families in another. Limited achievements in one place, disappointing in one sense, may help others chart a different course, which enables an adopting nation or group to avoid problems and increase the probability of success. On the other hand, nations and organizations who engage in

---

BORROWING POLICIES AND LESSONS

BOX 5.3

Three governmental ministers representing health, welfare, and education in a middle-income nation in Asia learned about exciting developments under way in another nation in their region. This other nation had reduced poverty by 30 percent in just seven years. When the three ministers visited this nation, they observed families who had set up small businesses (microenterprises) with small loans from their government. These entrepreneurial families also had formed community-based cooperatives. They offered each other extensive networks of support. The three ministers returned to their country, fresh with optimism, new ideas, and new strategies for addressing the challenges of poverty.

blind, wholesale borrowing of successful policy and practice innovations may learn later that those innovations failed miserably, and even worse, caused harm to families. For example, the wholesale replication of child protection services, based on models from the United States, may cause problems, not solve them. How, then, should policy makers, helping professionals, and advocates approach the prospect of policy borrowing and cross-national and cross-site lesson-drawing? This chapter concludes with a limited, but tailored response to this question.

Technology Transfer

"Technology transfer" is a buzzword that frequently is used to describe cross-national and cross-cultural learning, borrowing, and problem solving. Like all buzzwords, technology transfer is often ill defined. Its diverse meanings complicate cross-national and cross-cultural learning (National Association of Social Workers, 1993).

Frequently, technology transfer refers to plans for exporting and importing large-scale programs, organizations, and policies. Technology transfer also implies that policies and practices can be readily imported and exported once the logistics are finalized. Pierson (1996), for example, suggests that most nation-states engage in *policy taking*—wholesale borrowing from more powerful states—more than *policy making* or "growing their own." As with importing and exporting consumer products, the challenges with technology transfer are often viewed as technical and procedural. Cultural, political, and learning-related factors are given short shrift.

In fact, more precision and cultural sensitivity are warranted. All policies and practices are embedded in particular sociocultural contexts, and they cannot be fully appreciated without referencing these contexts. Furthermore, each policy and practice is constantly evolving, with a life history or "career." When once separate policies and practices are joined and integrated, understanding and duplicating them is even more challenging. It is not surprising that recent work on "technology transfers" is accompanied appropriately by cautions and contingencies (e.g., Baker, 1995).

For example, it is recommended that both the host and the adopting entity give careful consideration to how much they "match up." Are their needs, problems, and circumstances comparable? Similar? Identical? What about their families and family systems? Should family preservation services be identical, despite national and cultural differences?[5]

Policy and practice benchmarking (e.g., Tucker, 1996) is an emergent example of a deliberate transfer-as-learning and improvement process. Its origins are in business and industry (e.g., Americans visiting and studying Japanese industries); so the approach must be tempered and tailored to facilitate family-supportive policy transfers. The basic ideas are sound, however—namely, find others who have successfully addressed the same challenges and needs and learn quickly from them.

Benchmarking begins with the challenge of locating the equivalent of peers who match up on relevant indices (e.g., same form of government, same kind of economy, comparable cultural constituencies, same or similar priorities assigned to families). Once the successful peer(s) have been identified, teams of people visit the site. The visiting team's purpose is to bring back relevant information and strategies that have a high probability of working the same way at home. In short, benchmarking proceeds by intelligent imitation or adaptation of others' successes. While the dangers and limitations of "blind" technology transfer are ever present, ideally, benchmarking is one strategy for agenda setting and problem solving in the relentless pursuit of quality improvements. Benchmark indices are often generated so that comparable data on outcomes among peers can be generated and charted through time. It allows programs and systems in some nations to be "compared" to those in other nations.

Understandably, this "technology transfer" pattern often occurs among nations within similar regions. Regions (and nations composing them) may share identifiable social, cultural, economic, geographic, and political characteristics. Informed transfer of family-centered policies and practices will accommodate national, regional, and local differences. This national, state-provincial, and local accommodation of borrowed exemplars may be encouraged (e.g., Hennon & Jones, in press).

Rose (1993) offers these related hypotheses about *program* transfer (he substitutes "fungible" for transferable and "fungibility" for transferability):

1. The fewer the elements of uniqueness, the more transferable a program.
2. The more substitutable the institutions of program delivery (e.g., schools, community agencies, neighborhood organization), the more transferable the program.
3. The greater the equivalence of resources between governments, the more transferable a program is.

4. The simpler the cause-and-effect structure of a program, the more transferable it is.
5. The smaller the scale of change resulting from the adoption of a program, the more transferable a program.
6. The greater the interdependence between programs undertaken in different jurisdictions, the more transferable the impact of a program.
7. The greater the congruity between the values of policy makers and a program's values, the greater is transferability.

These are testable hypotheses and lessons. They help sensitize policy makers and practitioners to some of the necessary conditions for the transfer of policies and practices from one place to another. As hypotheses, they also offer opportunities for learning and continuous quality improvement. In other words, Rose's hypotheses serve as reminders that policy makers and practitioners do not merely design and implement new approaches once-and-for-all in a specific time and place. Policy and practice involves ongoing learning and continual quality improvement (e.g., Argyris & Schön, 1996; Lawson, 1999a; Senge, Kleiner, et al., 1994).

Lesson-Drawing from Policy and Practice Experiments

Policy makers and practitioners in one cultural national context need to learn from and interact with peers in others. Two related concepts enable them to do so: *lesson-drawing* and *transferability,* which is slightly different from technology transfer. Both are derived from a unified conception of policy and practice, research, and scholarship. In this perspective, the particularities of place, culture, and time weigh heavily in policy and practice comparisons and borrowing. Mindful that place, time, culture, and context are important, an alternative approach, called lesson-drawing (Rose, 1993), has been developed to facilitate cross-nation learning and development.

Richard Rose (1993) describes lesson-drawing as follows: "In the policy process, a lesson can be defined as *a program for action based upon a program or programs undertaken in another city, state, or nation, or by the same organization in its own past*" (Rose, 1993, p. 21, emphasis in original). His approach begins when two or more societies, or societal cultures, confront identical problems and needs. Lesson-drawing involves deliberate decisions by policy makers and practitioners to evaluate and learn from their respective attempts to solve shared problems and meet common needs. It allows them to interact and learn as they address problem setting and problem solving.

In a nutshell, lesson-drawing is a way to document the learning gained through direct experience. As Rose (1993, p. xi) suggests, "The issue is not whether we draw lessons from experience, but whether we do so well or badly." Lesson-drawing involves the search for relevant hypotheses, concepts, principles, and strategies. The process is focused upon key building blocks for effective policy and practices and programs. Its scope and goals are modest in comparison to prior approaches to social development and modernization, approaches in which people tried to export and import large-scale policies, programs, organizations, and even social institutions. Lesson-drawing is more appropriate and valuable because its products—relevant hypotheses, concepts, principles, and strategies—can be accommodated to fit and enrich different societal cultures. This developmental approach enables a progressive and interactive search for solutions to common or similar problems and needs. It allows policy makers and practitioners to proceed deliberately, cautiously, efficiently, and effectively.

Efficiency and effectiveness are improved because success stories reduce the time, energy, and resources needed in the search for solutions. Lesson-drawing involves not only sharing success stories but also identifying negative cases (Lawson, 1999a). These *negative cases,* or instances of family-supportive policies and practices that did not work as intended, are invaluable data sources for family-supportive policy makers and practitioners. Negative cases are especially important when new family-related problems and needs arise. In these instances, finding an appropriate and effective policy and practice is like defining a new concept; ruling out alternatives provides important clarity and precision. Clearly, no one wants negative cases; they have political fallout, and families in need may not be helped. The point is, when lesson-drawing is embedded in policy and practice planning, negative cases are never total failures. Because negative cases instruct policy makers and practitioners on what not to do, and the search for more effective and appropriate family-supportive policies and practices is continual, negative cases may pave the way for future success stories.

Lesson-drawing is a data-driven, developmental approach to deriving the building blocks for appropriate and effective humanizing policies and practices. One by one, or in some combination, these building blocks—

hypotheses, principles, strategies, and concepts—are derived, integrated, and evaluated over time. From the outset, lessons derived from one context are tailored to, and accommodated in, the other cultural-national context(s). In contrast to the cultural imperialism of prior approaches to technology transfer, modernization, and social development, the flexibility of lesson-drawing may preserve and enrich unique societal cultures.

According to Rose (1993), lesson-drawing from experience has two preconditions: shared problems faced by two or more governments who are approaching them differently, and easy access to information about what these other governments are doing. Lesson-drawing is the systemic process of evaluating and deriving relevant information from these policy and practice experiments. Lesson-drawing is normative because it concerns what ought to be done to solve a problem or meet a need. It also is highly contingent; there is no guarantee that a lesson derived from one context will be applicable to another. As Rose (1993, p. 22) suggests, "A lesson is like a jazz number that is more or less based upon chords of a preexisting standard tune. In the process there is both internal selection and unintentional adaptation."

There are five interacting phases in the lesson-drawing process:

1. Searching experience across time, space, and place, to find a strategy or program that appears to "work" in relation to the problem or need
2. Making a model, that is, specifying the relationships between the problems and needs and the programs and strategies
3. Creating the lesson (i.e., the program or strategy) through copying, adaptation, making a hybrid, synthesis, and inspiration
4. Prospective evaluation, involving a pre-implementation review of supportive evidence and gaining a deeper understanding of the context(s) in which it will be implemented
5. Embedding evaluations in the design implementation process so that additional lessons can be derived from it and in-flight adjustments can be made[6]

Skills and abilities related to agenda setting are embedded in all five phases. Expert policy makers and practitioners involved in lesson-drawing find new ways to frame and name existing problems and needs, and create ways to name and frame new ones.

For example, Baker (1995, pp. 342–375) offers a useful way to reframe the opposition of some feminist groups to family-supportive policies. She demonstrates that family poverty is also a women's issue, i.e., that the welfare of a significant number of women is inseparable from the condition of children and families.[7] Finding ways to turn interest group politics centered upon individuals into integrated, comprehensive family-supportive policies is an important contribution of lesson-drawing.

Despite Rose's first phase in lesson-drawing (for historical, cross-cultural analysis), immediate political pressures and family-related crises often intervene in the lives of policy makers and practitioners. Unfortunately, historical analysis is prevented and neglected. When this occurs, negative lessons and cases are likely to result. Halpern's (1995) history of the neighborhood-based initiatives intended to help poor families and individuals in the United States is ripe with negative cases. So is his later work on the history of social services for poor families (Halpern, 1998). Both histories reveal human tendencies to "reinvent the past" and to ignore its negative lessons.

Thus, lesson-drawing, like technology transfer, is highly contingent and not automatic. For example, Baker (1995) spent two years studying family policies in eight industrial societies (Australia, Canada, France, Germany, the Netherlands, Sweden, the United Kingdom, and the United States). Industrialized nations might be expected to share policies and practices, in part because they have the same status as industrialized nations. Nevertheless, Baker found significant differences among them in their approaches to family policy, and specifically in their thinking and approaches to child and family poverty.

A negative lesson, also provided by Baker (1995), is instructive on the importance of timing, i.e., when evaluations and cross-site visits occur. This lesson also emphasizes how important it is that governments "stay the course" and illustrates what happens when they do not. Baker (1995) chronicled a Canadian policy journey that began with the noble aim of erasing child and family poverty. Over time, with changing political actors, circumstances, and resource requirements, this initiative changed course. Poverty was later redefined and, in turn, the government could be excused for offering fewer supports and resources to a smaller number of people. Ultimately, a bitter irony resulted. A policy journey that began in search of effective policy approaches intended to erase child and family poverty actually resulted in practices that exacerbated it (Baker, 1995).

The discussion has come full circle. Effective, strategic policy planning and decision making are essential. Sustainability—staying the course—must be a priority from the outset. Policy makers, helping professionals, and advocates will be more strategic, and enhance sustainability, if they collaborate with families. Family-centered collaboration, and even family-accountable policies and practices, help ensure success. The next chapter addresses these new-century approaches. It picks up where this one leaves off—with families and the professionals who serve them.

NOTES

1. This concept was formulated initially by Herbert Simon.
2. See Jordan (1998) for an analysis of the new politics of welfare, including relationships between the United States and the United Kingdom. The new welfare politics also are associated with the new global economy, as identified and described in chapter 10 of this book.
3. Briar-Lawson (1998), moreover, identified the needs of "double jeopardy families." These families face TANF's time limits at the same time they face another time limit related to child welfare. The Adoption and Safe Families Act (ASFA) requires that a placement decision be made by workers and families within twelve to fifteen months. Thus, a child welfare family may have up to fifteen months with ASFA and up to five years with TANF. These dual stresses imposed by the two requirements may have ripple effects. Family impact analyses in the United States need to anticipate and accommodate double binds like these.
4. This journal may be accessed via its Web page on: http://www.city.ac.uk/barts/jipc.htm.
5. For example, family preservation services were offered to practitioners in Sweden. Swedish practitioners were skeptical and suspicious. Time-limited placement decisions valued by many practitioners in the United States were viewed by Swedish counterparts as potentially hurtful. Swedish practitioners are committed to long-term care agendas, involving prevention, early intervention, and ongoing supports. They were not enamored with crisis-driven, time-limited practices and policies.
6. Lesson-drawing, as a search across the globe, is an example of globalization, which is discussed in chapters 10 and 11.
7. This process is also called the "feminization of poverty."

CHAPTER 6

Families as Experts and Partners in the Development, Implementation, and Evaluation of Family-Centered Policies and Practices

Katharine Briar-Lawson and Hal A. Lawson

The nations making up the world community are diverse. Family-centered policy and practice advocates need to take into account this diversity. They will need to accommodate local, state, and provincial differences. These policy and practice frameworks will need to be culturally responsive and inclusive whenever possible—the exception being when international human rights violations are evident. In turn, they need to promote culturally competent practices by helping professionals. There are, in brief, multiple possibilities for family-centered policies and practices.

As diverse as these policies and practices may be, the mere fact that all such policies and practices are called *family centered* indicates that they are identical in some important respects. All family-centered policies and practices share the following five important features.

First: *Families are considered experts in what helps and hurts them.* They know what they need and want. They also have expertise about their local surroundings. And because they have essential expertise, they often are able to develop policy and practice innovations that are tailored to their local contexts (Briar-Lawson, 2000-b; Briar-Lawson & Wiesen, 2000). In other words, families are innovators. They often create *indigenous inventions*—local, culturally structured and inscribed practices, strategies, and systems improvements. Families' indigenous inventions may be more effective and appropriate than the ones initially envisioned by policy makers, helping professionals, and advocates.

Second: *Families are indispensable, invaluable partners for policy makers, helping professionals, and advocates.* To put it another way, no policy or practice is family centered unless families have been leaders in the development, implementation, and evaluation. Policies and practices are democratized and family centered to the extent that the voices of diverse families and family members are heard, ensuring that all of their needs are met. When families are partners, policies and practices tend to be more comprehensive and flexible. They can be tailored to unique needs and local contexts. When families are partners possessing invaluable, indispensable expertise, policy makers and helping professionals treat them with respect and uphold their dignity. In turn, families are less likely to resist and sabotage helping professionals' interventions.

Third: *Families are not called, or treated as, dependent clients. Helping professionals and policy makers view families as equals, as citizens, with whom they collaborate and whom they empower.* In other words, families, policy makers, helping professionals, and advocates communicate, cooperate, and collaborate effectively. They develop new, democratized working relationships involving the sharing of power and authority. Together they promote *family-centered collaboration* (Lawson & Barkdull, 2000). Family-centered collaboration means that they have developed unity of purpose, including shared goals and accountability for them. Family-centered collaboration complements interprofessional collaboration, facilitates service integration, and promotes broad-based, community collaboration.

Fourth: *Family-centered policies and practices are strengths based and asset based, and they promote family-to-family and community-based systems of care and mutual support.* When policies and practices are family centered, and when families' roles as preventive, comprehensive social welfare systems are appreciated (as described in chapter 2), then policy makers, helping professionals, and advocates will make every effort to maintain and strengthen natural support systems. In other words, professional, governmental, and nongovernmental systems do not erode or replace family-to-family mutual support networks and community-based systems of care (e.g., McKnight, 1997; United Nations, 1994h). Family-centered policies and practices are designed to harmonize and synchronize these systems with families' mutual support networks and their surrounding community-based systems of care.

Fifth: *Family-centered policies and practices promote democratization and gender equity.* That is, family-centered policies and practices equalize power relations in and among families. For example, girls, women, elders, and vulnerable family members have equal voice and equal and developmentally appropriate access to resources. All have strengths, expertise, and aspirations, and each enjoys equal rights in relation to them.

In fact, it is possible to build on families' expertise, assets, and aspirations, providing occupational and educational ladders for family members. The three most important rungs for these ladders are training, financial supports, and new opportunity pathways. Once trained and supported, these family experts can be deployed as paraprofessionals and professionals who help to harmonize and synchronize natural, indigenous family and community systems with professional and governmental systems. To ensure that they are not "aides as maids" (Halpern, 1998), they are provided with opportunities for their continuing advancement (i.e., other rungs on the ladder), including adult education, community college courses, and higher education degrees.

This chapter is structured to describe and explain these five key features of family-centered policies and practices. It emphasizes the importance of family-centered visions, missions, and goals, which structure policy and practice frameworks. All such frameworks are dynamic. They evolve continually in response to data derived from families, advocates, helping professionals, and policy makers. Barriers and barrier-busting strategies also serve as data sources, and they enable learning, development, and continual quality improvement.

Examples from the United States are provided. Similarly, most of the literature that is cited is American. Mindful of this selectivity and its ethnocentrism, readers should view this chapter as an example, i.e., as a kind of agenda-setting tool. It is a point of departure, not a final destination.

DEVELOPING FAMILY-CENTERED VISIONS, MISSIONS, AND DEFINITIONS OF COMPETENT AND OPTIMAL PRACTICES

Family-centered policies and practices must be tailored to fit unique regional, national, state and provincial, and local contexts. They involve a special, dynamic interplay within a guiding vision; specific missions that derive from this vision; and definitions of what it means for professionals to practice competently.

The Importance of a Vision

A *guiding vision* encompasses ideals for families and family wellbeing. Visions may be local, state or provincial, national, and international. A vision at one level may guide a vision at another. So, visions may be incredibly broad and comprehensive. For example, a national vision might promote relationships among families, other societal institutions, and perhaps relationships with the world community. At the local level, visions are the first moment in promoting systems and cross-systems change in support of family-centered policies and practices. Work toward developing a vision may be launched by basic questions like this one: How do we want things to be different and better for families and, in turn, for all of us? This question and other vision-oriented questions like it orient everyone to the future. A vision is basically a plan, or blueprint, to create the future.

The vision, for example, might be improved well-being for all families. This vision might be operationalized to include measurable goals, or effectiveness criteria. For example, a local vision might include the following indices related to family well-being: reductions in family violence, improved access to health care, improvements in family incomes, and the reduction of poverty. When visions like these are developed, and families, policy makers, helping professionals, advocates, governmental leaders, and private sector representatives are all "at the table" participating in the process, broad-based community collaboration is promoted. However different each group, i.e., each community stakeholder, they share the same vision of how things can, and should, be different and better for families.

Anyone, at any level, can convene the initial group that begins work on vision development. A local religious leader may be as important as the prime minister for the nation, or the governor of the state. All have the power to act and convene. Power also is defined, in part, by the collective ability to frame and name an issue, need, or goal. Appropriate language and shared vision are powerful tools. Envisioning an improved state of affairs enables all stakeholders to keep their "eye on the prize" as they learn their way through the ups and downs of collaborative endeavors to improve outcomes and realize the desired vision.

Missions

Missions are responsibilities and obligations that various entities in a societal culture develop. For example, governments at all levels, nongovernmental organizations, public schools, health and social service agencies, neighborhood organizations, and religious institutions develop their respective missions and determine their responsibilities, obligations, and accountabilities in relation to this guiding vision. Each does what it must in order to receive resources and supports, and each supports the others. In other words, missions derive in part from dialogue regarding who will do what, with whom, under what circumstances, when and why; and regarding who is accountable for what, when, and why.

From Competent to Optimal Practices

Competent practice means doing the right things, at the right time, for the right reasons, and with the right results. For example, helping professionals' definitions of competent practice derive from a combination of organizational and professional missions. Family members' competent practice derives from their missions, obligations, and aspirations as comprehensive social welfare institutions.

Competence is the baseline that defines the minimal level of expectation for policy and practice. Novices should perform at this level. *Optimal practices* derive from this baseline of competence. Practices and policies are optimal when they exceed this minimal baseline and transcend basic expectations. Optimal practices typically are designed and performed by experts. These experts help novices move from competent practice to optimal practice. Learning, mentoring, and improvement systems are designed to support the development of basic competence and to promote optimal policies and practices.

A List of Sensitizing Concepts and Questions

Table 6.1 presents a list of concepts and questions that illuminate aspects of this relationship among vision, missions, competence, and optimal policies and practices. This table, like the above text, may convey the impression that vision development is the only starting point; and that the attendant processes of determining missions and defining competent and optimal practices are linear. To the contrary, the developmental process is often nonlinear (Lawson, 1999a). For example, as competent and optimal practices are developed in helping professions, organizational missions may change, in turn illuminating new possibilities and opportunities for a more expansive vision. Or, missions and practices may change simultaneously, in turn promoting changes in a guiding vision. As suggested in chapter 5, when schools and community agencies accept responsibilities for service integration, and when interprofessional collaboration becomes a defining feature of competent practice, their missions change and so may the overall guiding vision.

Thus, there is a dynamic interplay among vision, missions, and

TABLE 6.1. Key Aspects of Systems and Cross-Systems Change

Vision: A blueprint for improvement and change.

- How will families be different and better?

- How will governments be different and better?

- How will organizations, including social and health service agencies, religious institutions, neighborhood organizations, schools, and the police, be different and better?

- How will helping professions be different and better?

- How will the private sector be different and better?

Mission: Determining priorities, goals, and objectives of each participating and contributing entity in relation to vision(s). For example:

- Who and what will make things different and better? Under what conditions, when, and why?

- What is the mission of the state or provincial departments of health or social services? What is the mission of a school, or school system?

- What is social work's mission?

- What is each family's mission?

Competent practice: The minimum acceptable baseline for determining whether each profession and family is doing the right things, at the right times, for the right reasons, and with the right results. For example:

- How are competent, family-centered practices defined, implemented, and evaluated?

  - By governments?

  - By organizations, agencies, and schools?

  - By helping professions such as social work and early childhood education?

  - By families?

Optimal practices: Innovative, successful practices that are well beyond the minimal threshold of competence.

Effectiveness and success criteria, expressed as measurable objectives and outcomes criteria, objectives, and outcomes:

TABLE 6.1. (*Continued*)

- How would you know desired changes if you saw them?
  - Who will assess them? How, when, where, and why?
  - How will evaluation foster learning and continual quality improvements?
  - Are diverse families and their members (e.g., gay and lesbian, youth, aged, women, etc.) co-evaluators?
  - Who decides? Who decides who decides?

Stakeholder assessment: Determining if every key person, family member, and other representatives are involved.

- Who is missing and how will they be recruited and retained?
- Are families present?
- Are the most challenged families viewed as having expertise about what it will take to bring about change and overcome barriers?
- Are representatives from local business, industry, banks, credit associations, and social and health services present?

Action planning and "piecing it out":

- Who will serve as the action team to carry out the change?
- Are all those present willing to share responsibilities for monitoring progress and outcomes?
- Who is responsible for what outcomes, under what circumstances, when, and why?
- When responsibilities are shared, how do different stakeholders communicate and coordinate their respective efforts?
- Have families agreed to become part of the change process?
- Will they be co-developers of it and enfranchised in the process or simply told that they must carry out the action plans?

Necessary conditions for achieving success: The prerequisites and co-requisites for action and improvement.

- Has planning incorporated resource needs, technical assistance, evaluations, and capacity-building?

continued

TABLE 6.1. (*Continued*)

• Have interagency and interprofessional working agreements been formalized?

• Have agreements been struck on how to handle confidentiality issues and share information?

• How will the media be involved, and who will work with media representatives?

Barriers and constraints: Anticipated problems, obstacles, and limitations.

• Has everyone acknowledged that problems and barriers are inevitable? Have agreements been reached on barrier-busting strategies?

• How will learning, knowledge development, and possibly policy change result when barriers are reframed as goals and then removed and prevented?

Work and evaluation plans: Steps and phases for implementation, evaluation, learning, knowledge development, and improvement.

• Have they been formed and adopted, with timelines for all of the action teams?

• Are goals broken down into short-term, achievable objectives?

• Are progress indicators identified?

• Are progress charting procedures identified?

• How will evaluation foster learning and continual quality improvements?

• Are families and their members (e.g., youth, aged, women, etc.) co-evaluators?

Norms: Standards and rules for the quality of mutual treatment and interaction.

• Have norms been adopted on how the group will conduct its business?

• Are there processes and people for norm enforcement?

• When individuals show cultural insensitivity, or gender and racial bias, are follow-up supports available to correct these practices?

---

definitions of competent and optimal practices. Each is guided by, and helps guide, the others. Linear in some ways (and described as step 1 and step 2), the change process also may be nonlinear (described as phase 1 and phase 2). The need for learning, development, technical assistance, and capacity building may be ever present.

Examples from the United States

What might the finished products be? Examples are invaluable. They indicate how visions can result in agreements that facilitate collective action. Table 6.2 presents examples of principles that participants in Dade County, Florida, adopted in support of child-focused, family-centered policies and practices.[1] Table 6.3 includes four components for family-centered policies and practices, components that promote flexibility and tailoring to the needs of unique families.

TABLE 6.2. Core Values and Beliefs for Dade County, Florida's Children and Families

---

We hold to these beliefs about children and families:

- Children's physical and emotional safety must be assured.

- Children should be raised in a stable, nurturing unit most often described as a family, which provides those qualities that are required for safe passage into productive adulthood.

- Families have the right and responsibility to raise their children to be successful adults; the authority to make necessary decisions in the pursuit of that goal; and the responsibility to accept the consequences of their decisions and actions and to teach such responsibility to their children.

- Children and their families have the right to early community support for healthy growth, made available in the neighborhoods where children live.

- Children should participate in decisions concerning their lives. These values suggest primary roles and responsibilities for parents, families, communities, and public agencies.

- *Parents and families* hold the primary responsibility for the health and well being of their children and for providing them with a safe passage into productive childhood and adulthood.

- *Communities* must strengthen and support families so that they can nurture and promote their children's development, adequately and safely.

- *Public agencies* are obliged to offer support in the otherwise private family matters of raising children when families face serious crises, or are unable or unwilling to adequately safeguard their children.

continued

TABLE 6.2. (*Continued*)

Moreover, we believe that:

- Neighborhood and family supports are essential to the growth of healthy children.

- Local communities must take a leadership role in defining the systems of supports for children and their families, with the federal, state, and local government, business, and private agencies all assuming their appropriate responsibilities for the funding of such supports.

- Neighborhoods, religious organizations, friends, family, and local services should be jointly responsible for helping families provide a safe passage for their children to a healthy, productive adulthood.

- Access to such supports should *not* be the sole province of the child protection system but provided *in the community* in which families live, through partnerships of families, neighbors, schools, health services, neighborhood groups, formal and informal support systems, neighborhood development initiatives, public safety activities, as well as crisis and treatment services for families.

- Families and neighborhoods should be supported by all service systems in their responsibilities to raise healthy children; not supplanted by government agencies and court orders unless the safety of their children cannot be maintained in the community.

Florida must formulate policy for children and their families around these basic concepts:

a. Every child must be:

protected from harm;
provided with basic food, clothes, and shelter;
provided with necessary medical services and a basic education; and
provided with the opportunity for cognitive, aesthetic, and emotional
    development.

b. When help is needed, the first obligation is to assist the child in his or her family. If, despite such assistance, the family cannot meet the basic needs of its children, government must assure that their needs are met, regardless of economic status.

c. Local communities are best suited to identify needs, provide accountability, and support a child's sense of identity. Local communities should be given more control in selecting, purchasing, and delivering services to children and families in compliance with statewide standards.

TABLE 6.3. Components of Family Support

Family support is needed by families and their surrounding communities. Families should be able to assess their own capacities, develop a sense of agency, and have their needs for supports and capacity building met.

Family Agency

Drawing on Sen's (1999) work, family agency is the capacity to make changes, to exert some influence and control over the lives and circumstances of members and families. Families with agency may be able to advocate for others. They may be able to step forward to assist with civic work, to advance a new policy. Some of the examples in the book describe families such as the RAINmakers who have agency. As box 6.2 describes, they opened up their own family resource center and child care center. They are advocates for others who are evicted, marginalized, and maltreated. Family agency needs to be nurtured by helping professionals and policy makers. It is a key component of successful foster parenting, and of the Swedish Family Contact program and other initiatives worldwide that pair "ordinary families" with those more "vulnerable."

Family Support

This component broadly supports all families through primary prevention and promotion programs. Families receive basic health care, education, adequate housing, parent education, day care, and the economic means with which to support their healthy growth. Some family support programs involve family resource centers, often operated by families for families. They provide welcoming, non-stigmatizing, family-friendly environments.

Family Development

Family development assists families in addressing early-risk factors that do not require intrusive intervention. Early-risk factors might involve the birth of a special needs child; or the loss of a parent through an industrial accident, necessitating that the other parent receive vocational and employment skills in order to be a provider. Sometimes family development involves enrichment programs that teach parents the skills to parent, to solve adolescent-parent conflicts, and to address marital and gender difficulties.

continued

TABLE 6.3. (*Continued*)

Family Preservation

When a family member is abused (domestic violence, child or elder abuse), there may be a need to preserve the family while the perpetrator receives help or is removed. Family preservation may involve some members leaving the family so that those who remain are intact and safe. Sometimes family preservation involves providing homemaker supports so that a child of a sick parent does not have to go into foster care or an elder does not need to be placed in a nursing home while the caregiver recovers from his or her own risk factors.

ENCOURAGING AND SUPPORTING FAMILIES: FAMILIES AS EXPERT PARTNERS

Some policy makers and helping professionals may find it difficult to view parents, children and youth, elders, and their families as experts and to treat them as partners. They have received training that encourages them to see families and their members as "clients" who depend on professionals to identify and solve their problems (e.g., Cowger, 1998; McKnight, 1995, 1997). If they are to view families as experts and partners, these professionals and policy makers will have to "unlearn" old orientations and behavior and learn new ones. They will need supports. Box 6.1 provides one such example.

Handler (1996, p. 218) identifies three key changes that help account for new orientations by professionals in relation to individuals and families, including the willingness of professionals to adopt an empowerment-oriented approach in which families are expert partners. Professional norms must change as professionals come to believe that former clients are indeed part of the solution to professional practice problems and needs. Second, professionals must believe that this new "parent and family technology" is real and provides lasting benefits. And third, the new cooperative and collaborative relationships develop around mutual interests and resource exchanges. Former clients and professionals value each other and come to realize that they depend on each other; and that sharing power is a win-win solution, not a zero-sum game. Box 6.2 presents a compelling example of how these three features make a difference in forging new partnerships based on appreciation of parents' and families' expertise.

BECOMING MORE FAMILY CENTERED
AND FAMILY SUPPORTIVE

BOX 6.1

A schoolteacher feels overwhelmed by the challenge of educating children. Now she is told that teachers are expected to work with parents because "parent involvement" will increase student achievement, and also to assist parents with their own educational development and use of the school. To reiterate, she is being told (ordered) to do parent involvement.

She never agreed to it, and she wonders about its effectiveness. She probably will be difficult to convince and convert. If there is high turnover among the leadership in the school system and in government, she, like others, may be able to "wait out" the change mandate until it passes. Or, she may conclude that this parent involvement mandate, like other changes in the past, is really "this year's new thing." It is just another passing fancy.

Alternately, if she were provided training, extra help in the classroom, and even had a parent trained to do outreach to the other parents, she might feel motivated to work toward this goal. Tying her salary, evaluations, and promotions to her success with this action agenda will also help her decide whether to make it a priority.

Moreover, the research is helpful. The findings show clear patterns. If she pursues parent involvement and experiences some success, she will find other ways to become more family centered and less child centered. Or, if she does not pursue parent involvement, or does so half-heartedly, she will not experience success and, in all likelihood, she will stay child centered and subject centered.

The meta-messages in the school will influence her orientations and actions. If she goes to meetings and does not hear reports about this new strategy to serve families, and learns little about the opportunities being provided in the school, she will conclude that this was not a serious initiative. In contrast, if her teacher colleagues are engaged seriously in parent outreach and believe that they are more effective as a result, then the change process may accelerate. In effect, there is an emerging "alignment" among policy and practices, and this alignment, in the teachers' minds, is associated with new opportunities for effectiveness and support.

BOX 6.2

THE RAINMAKERS: A SNAPSHOT

The RAINmakers are a group of parent paraprofessionals in Miami Beach, Florida, who have gained national acclaim. The RAINmakers are an important example of how a crisis may become an opportunity (Alameda, 1996; Briar-Lawson, 2000-b; Briar-Lawson & Drews, 1998; Hooper-Briar & Lawson, 1994). Their story is sketched below.

This story begins with a crisis in an elementary school. An increasing number of the children had lice in their hair. When the head lice problem reached epidemic proportions, the school's leaders faced the prospect of having to temporarily close the school.

The school had convened, for multiple purposes, a school-linked consortium, or community collaborative. This consortium consisted of many professionals from the community. Although professionals understood the head lice problem, none of them could address completely the real causes and effective solutions. For example, they recommended lice shampoo, but shampoo distribution did not solve the problem. The crisis continued, and it ballooned into a major school-community challenge.

A family-centered social worker, hired at the school as a family advocate, went to the homes of the families with the most episodes involving head lice. She asked the children's parents if they would be willing to serve as consultants to address the lice crisis. These parents agreed to help.

They then helped the social worker and other professionals understand that the challenge was not merely to get lice shampoo to families. They explained that some of these families lived in one-room apartments that were without running water and electricity. In some of these apartments, as many as eighteen people slept on mattresses, spread out on the floor. These family systems lacked vacuum cleaners and regular access to laundry facilities. These parents helped the professionals understand that these two problems had to be addressed before the lice shampoo would work.

The parents formed a new group. They called themselves "the lice-busters." They took all of their linens to a local laundry facility.

They cut the hair of the children with lice. They fumigated their apartments and cleaned them with battery-operated vacuum cleaners. And then the lice shampoo worked. Together, they had crafted an effective, long-term solution to the lice problem.

Having solved the lice crisis, these parents identified another—children's achievement in school. They explained to the family advocate and others that there was no place for the children to do homework. They asked if they might open a homework club at the school. The professionals agreed to do so. A hundred or more children showed up.

Having solved the lice crisis and opened homework clubs, the parents began other projects. They opened a family resource room at the school, which they supervised and conducted. They formed an outreach team to find and support children and youth that were truant and absent from school.

The parents then named themselves RAINmakers. The acronym RAIN meant Referral and Information Network. The social worker provided them with a training program designed to help them support one another and work with other families and professionals.

The social worker, in cooperation with a social work professor at a nearby university and the principal, developed a way to pay the parents. The parents received small stipends in exchange for their participation and work. For example, the RAINmakers supported other parents, especially new parents and families who moved into the area and did not have other friends and family members to support them. They generated new supports for teachers and for social and health service providers as they began to play key roles as paraprofessional educators and service providers. In short, the RAINmakers brought new energy and effective innovations to the school and to the community.

These parents developed new occupational goals and aspirations at the same time they helped produce benefits for the school and the community. For example, the children's academic achievement, measured by standardized tests, increased significantly. At the same time, absenteeism decreased. Once the worst school in relation to absenteeism, the school became the best in its area.

In 1998, the school received a state award. It was designated as one of the top two schools in its category—a category called "title one" to reflect the high proportion of children eligible for free and reduced lunch programs.

Today the RAINmakers run their own microenterprise program. They are incorporated formally as a nonprofit agency. They run a day care center adjacent to the school, which provides affordable, quality child care. They help welfare recipients get jobs. They work with teachers. They recruit other parents to become future RAINmakers and to intern with them. They have traveled to several parts of the United States to help other schools and communities develop RAINmaker-like programs.

In short, the RAINmakers demonstrate the power of parents and family-to-family networks. And they indicate how parents' aspirations and job development in support of these aspirations enable them to serve as key linking agents, important mediators, between professional systems and family-community systems. Professionals enjoy more job satisfaction and are more effective because these parents and their families are partners, and their expertise is used. Families in the community benefit from friendly supports provided by other parents and families, supports that are more culturally sensitive and culturally competent. Everybody benefits.

Improving the Quality of Treatment and Interaction to Promote Family-Centered Collaboration

The quality of treatment and interaction involving families is pivotal in family-centered policies and practices. For example, improvements in the quality of treatment were essential in the case of the RAINmakers. Norms and rules for the quality of mutual treatment and interaction may be needed to promote healthy interactions and prevent maltreatment and mutual blame dynamics (Lawson & Briar-Lawson, 1997). Every interaction with families sends one or more messages as well as meta-messages. These messages and meta-messages are conveyed explicitly and implicitly, and are responsible for what families perceive, experience, and learn.

For example, families learn whether they are valued, appreciated, trusted, and supported; or if they are despised, blamed, unappreciated, and not trusted. Families may internalize these messages and meta-messages and begin defining themselves accordingly. So, when families are credited for their expertise, members may begin to define themselves as "family experts" (Briar-Lawson, Lawson, et al., 1999). In contrast, when professionals stigmatize and label families as "dysfunctional" and "abnormal," family members may lose sight of their strengths and fall into despair. Furthermore, when patriarchal, classist, racist, ageist, and homophobic policy and practice approaches to families prevail, these approaches may reinforce stress in the home. If families perceive that they are poorly treated, they will not be able to give effective help to their own members and to those who are trying to serve them. Trust will have been ruptured, and partnership and collaboration with helpers outside the family will be impeded.

Families may need to devise their own bill of rights (Hooper-Briar & Lawson, 1994). This "family bill of rights" promotes better and non-discriminatory treatment and interactions, ones that families do not experience as harmful or punishing. All such bills of rights are developed by families, for families. These bills of rights can include such concerns as having their needs understood in terms of their whole family and culture, being treated with respect, and not being blamed or punished.

Table 6.4 presents a family bill of rights. This bill of rights was drafted by families who felt that professionals and politicians were maltreating them. These families represent diverse cultures in South Florida and make up the RAINmakers (Referral and Information Network). The group is made up of parents who serve as informational and referral networks for one another and are a force in a South Florida community (Alameda, 1996; Briar-Lawson, 2000-b). This rights statement was a means to improve professional helping practices in their community.

As the RAINmakers' Family Bill of Rights suggests, families want to be treated as partners, not as clients or as faceless, emotionless supplicants. Furthermore, this bill of rights suggests some of the necessary conditions for helping families become stronger, more vital partners. As expert partners, they may guide others and gain more of a sense of ownership and control over their own lives and destinies.

TABLE 6.4. The RAINmakers' Family Bill of Rights

- All individuals have the right to be treated with kindness, respect, and consideration under all conditions and situations.

- All individuals have the right to be treated with dignity and respect by agencies that work with them to solve economic, health, and education issues. (They should therefore be spoken to in tones that are not demeaning and in language that is worthy of a human being.)

- All persons have the right to have access to second opinions in matters concerning their lives and conditions.

- All persons have the right to representation on the governing boards of the agencies that serve their communities.

- All persons have the right to be given a time frame for when services will be offered. Individuals should not have to wait in clinics or offices all day without lunch, bathroom facilities, or telephones.

- All persons have the right to have service providers who are sensitive to the needs of individuals whether they have legal status or not, because all human beings are entitled to respect.

- All persons have the right to have their cultural background taken into consideration before service providers make plans and recommendations on their behalf.

- All persons have the right to have the family as a unit be the focus of services provided and policies initiated by all agencies.

Bridging Interpersonal Gaps Between Professionals and Families

Policy makers, advocates, and practitioners must ask: *Do our policies and practices reduce the interpersonal gap between the professional and the family?* Bills of rights are one way to close these gaps. There are others.

Paraprofessionals are sometimes deployed to bridge the gap. At other times, policies and practices require that consumers lead or guide in an advisory fashion so that responsive and relevant services are designed and delivered. The growth of self-help and mutual-aid movements involves 25 million people in the United States alone and reflects the profound need for affiliation with persons facing similar challenges (Briar-Lawson, 1998.)

Increasingly in some Western industrialized nations, so-called ombudsmen[2] are being hired to serve as advocates for the families and other "consumers" of services. These mediating persons help to resolve conflict and give families a voice. One such mediator may not infuse the system with sufficient feedback about families' needs, wants, and hurts. Thus family members serving on boards, and as advisors on review and budget committees, all help to create some of the feedback loops that build an organization's capacity to learn and change.

Families as Data Sources

Unless there are built-in feedback mechanisms, how will helping professionals, policy makers, and advocates know if they were inadvertently hurtful to a family? Family members must be asked about their experiences (Briar-Lawson, 2000-b; Briar-Lawson & Wiesen, 2000). How do they experience the teacher, social worker, psychologist, police officer, nurse, and doctor? How do they experience the store clerk? For if they experience maltreatment, and nothing is done to address it, they may not want to cooperate or interact with them in the future. This in turn may affect their well-being, especially if this means fewer services, resources, and supports for the family.

Thus, innovative policies and practices require built-in assessment and evaluative methodologies that promote self-correcting and inventive solutions to problems and stuck points. This challenge then invites all stakeholders, including families, to "learn their ways through" the challenging steps of self-correcting problem solving.

Family Expertise Helps Reframe and Rename Barriers as Goals

Every kind of collaboration—interprofessional, family centered, and community—is fraught with challenges (Lawson & Barkdull, 2000). Multiple forms of collaboration have ripple or domino effects. Changing one thing—for example, deciding that families are expert partners and not clients—changes others—for example, changing the membership of organizational governing and policy-making boards to include families. Multiple changes at multiple levels means that barriers and obstacles

TABLE 6.5. Examples of Barrier-Busting Strategies for Groups and Teams

- The group needs to believe in their power and ingenuity. "There isn't anything we cannot do if we do it together, bringing into our work as many stakeholders as possible." Capacity building and alternative ways to frame and name barriers are prized, along with advocacy.

- Finger-pointing and blaming are avoided. Persistence is an imperative— "There is no such thing as an answer of *no.*" Barriers to "yes" need to be identified and staged, with each attacked successfully. Plan actions as "baby steps."

- The group needs to return constantly to visions, missions, conceptions of competent and optimal practice, and codes of ethics to keep priorities clear and to reaffirm commitments.

- After identifying persons known as barriers, the group needs to engage them as helpers in seeking solutions.

- Assume that there are at least thirty ways to bust a barrier; keep trying until successful. Adopt a "no reject" ethic.

- The group needs to stay strategic instead of fighting one crisis after another; look for root causes in organizational structures and systems. Seek influential and powerful allies who can be deputized to help with advocacy and change.

- Consider legal actions as a last resort.

- Keep a historical perspective, remembering how long the problem or barrier may have existed; use this perspective to develop patience and understanding regarding timetables for change.

- Celebrate each success, no matter how small it may seem.

- Remember that every practice act may be a policy act; consider the policy implications of every breakthrough.

will surface. Each phase, or step, in the change process may reveal new barriers that could discourage actions unless these barriers themselves are seen as the new "subgoals" to be addressed. Agreed-upon barrier-busting strategies are invaluable tools for addressing "stuck points" and, at the same time, promoting innovations that promise more success. Table 6.5 presents examples of barrier-busting strategies (Hooper-Briar & Lawson, 1994).

As the RAINmakers story indicates, sometimes the families who appear to have the most challenges may have invaluable expertise. These families may be a key data source for addressing barriers, improving effectiveness, achieving visions and missions, and enhancing learning and development.

For example, if the goal is to serve homeless families, ensuring that they have decent housing, jobs, and health, then it may be homeless families who can best identify the barriers, the impediments to their goals, and the changes that seem most desirable. They are not only seen as stakeholders because they are beneficiaries of the change, but also are treated as having expertise because they "live" the condition that must be changed. Homeless families may have expertise that no one else has about what needs to be changed. This expertise must be tapped for the change strategy to be maximally effective. Box 6.3 presents another example.

Toward Family-Centered, Consensus-Based Practice

When individuals and families from all walks of life are asked to be part of a change process, they will weigh the benefits and costs to

---

STREET LIFE AND LIVING

A mother and three children have been living in the street, foraging for food and handouts from passersby. Because of tourism and sanitation concerns, a new ordinance is passed requiring all street people to be removed. Any children and youth found in the streets will be jailed. This family and others like them are placed in a deeper crisis and predicament.

In this case such families are defined as a tourism and sanitation / health problem. Their presence is addressed in categorical terms by sectors that may or may not have any reason to protect or invest in families, or to use family-centered policy and goal-oriented solutions to such challenges. Herding people up and forcing them to find other places to live and make a livelihood, while seemingly expedient to some, may do nothing to meet family needs or to develop capacity in the family or community. Just removing these people from the streets

BOX 6.3

may "please" shop owners but will actually solve little. Families' fundamental challenges remain.

A capacity-building approach requires that families in this case be seen as the solution rather than as the problem.[1] Imagine that the ministers for economy and tourism and for health and sanitation reframe the presence of families in the streets as a sign of underdeveloped resources and systems, and thus an important focal point for their policy agendas. "Street families" are seen as somehow falling outside whatever safety nets are available and are now recast as potential economic and social development resources. Such thinking warrants investments in their untapped capacities. Instead of being viewed solely in problematic terms as deterrents to tourism, these families might be seen as key components for new strategies for economic development as well as health and sanitation.

The minister for economy and tourism can generate small start-up loans or microcredit[2] for these families who seek to sell their weavings as microenterprises, perhaps oriented toward the tourist trade, while the minister of health and sanitation helps these families find or build low-cost housing. These strategies are categorical—they address just one need. However, categorical strategies do assist families. Here, these ministers and their implementation staff can build from these categorical initiatives and design social development initiatives that enhance services and resources and thus support these families. This line of action works toward improving the conditions of the families, the merchants, the overall community, and the economy.

[1] In actuality, in this case the problem is more likely defined as a mass of nameless individuals, without regard to the fact that they might have or compose families.

[2] The U.S. Agency for International Development promotes a microcredit program, offering small loans (about U.S.$500) to help people start their own businesses, as a way to lift people from welfare to work. As suggested in one magazine article: "But even advocates offer polite words of caution. . . . There are limits to how well lessons learned in Africa and Asia transfer to U.S. cities: $100 goes a lot further in Dhaka than Detroit, and American entrepreneurs face far more sophisticated competition in the marketplace" (Auster, 1997, p. 40).

themselves, their beliefs, and their other work tasks. They will wonder whether their self-interests, expressed in their success criteria and effectiveness goals, require their commitments and involvement. Self-interest paves the way to engagement and ownership (Lawson & Barkdull, 2000). Each stakeholder or stakeholder group must become a joint owner of the new vision, missions, and goals. And ownership means that they must craft them.

Bricker-Jenkins refers to this process of developing joint ownership and commitments as "consensus-based practice" (Bricker-Jenkins, personal communication, 1995). Consensus-based decision-making and involvement processes have broad applicability. Consensus-based practice can include more facilitating and enfranchising approaches with families.

As in a social worker's interventions for one family, agendas for changing large-scale systems often meet resistance (e.g., Annie E. Casey Foundation, 1995). Consensus-based, family-centered practice has major applicability to collaborative practices among professionals as well as with, and among, families. For example, every potential "collaborator" must own the new initiative. They must want its benefits and be willing to work to realize them.

Many helping professionals and policy makers who share a new vision may lack the skills and resources to carry out what they have been assigned or have agreed to. Families often find themselves in the same situation. Thus, consensus-based, collaborative capacity building is critical to the process. This process often transforms professional development from a narrow, technical, top-down training initiative to a complex change process involving mutual supports and sharing of expertise among professionals and families (Lawson, Briar-Lawson, et al., 1999). Actual learning and organizational development outweigh narrow, technical training.

Honoring Families' Expertise

As the RAINmakers story and their bill of rights suggest, families want to be asked what they think, perceive, and know. They need to be asked about their needs, the challenges they face, and what the solutions might be. It is important to recruit families as part of the solution and for identifying what deterred them from seeking help altogether.

As the RAINmakers story suggests, families are often sources of indigenous inventions. Their ingenuity and home remedies allow them to craft innovative solutions to their problems and ones that professionals, policy makers, and advocates also confront.

Indigenous Invention and Education

The concept of indigenous invention also is related to sustainability, diversity, and successful, effective development (e.g., Bender & Smith, 1997; Escobar, 1995; Goldthorpe, 1996). Derived from studies of innovations in areas such as agriculture, food production, and school reform, the core principle is that local residents, including families, are experts in problems that affect them. Furthermore, the search for solutions must always be pursued in, and accommodated to, local contexts and indigenous cultures. When solutions are tailored to local contexts, they are more culturally responsive and culturally supportive. Mindful of the importance of indigenous invention, planners do not view diverse people and their cultures as "assimilation elements" that need to be "placed" in a melting pot. Planners know that diverse people may resist wholesale assimilation. They resist being placed in the pot, and they refuse to melt and meld. The RAINmakers are again one of many success stories. Many were new immigrants.

On the other hand, it is dangerous to validate automatically all cultural traditions, calling them "indigenous inventions" and culturally congruous. In other words, there is a healthy tension between human development needs, social and health indices, and individual and family rights, on the one hand, and cultural traditions and practices, on the other. When human freedoms are jeopardized and denied, development cannot succeed (Sen, 1999). When human freedom is denied, inequality and inequity are the norm, and both impede social and economic development (Ray, 1998).

Indigenous invention is a developmental asset because it promotes human well-being, social welfare, and sustainability. Grassroots groups, including families, are responsible for these inventions. In chapter 3, the Grameen Bank was described. This bank has helped support women challenged by poverty pioneer the use of microloans to fund cellular phones in their villages. This indigenous invention grew out of their local, expert knowledge about needs and circumstances. Women worked to secure telephones. Their communications by phone became marketing devices for their burgeoning microenterprises.

This invention is especially dramatic within the context. In these poor communities with little access to electronic communications, the cellular telephone has become a critical part of the local economy and social fabric of family networks. Shared, collective access to cellular phones (there are only a few phones in each community) has helped foster the marketing of women's goods (economic development). It also has connected poor women with one another and with other segments of the local, regional, and national economy, serving as a community development support (social development).

Box 6.3 presents an example of potential indigenous innovations among homeless families. It suggests that families have special expertise, which helping professionals and policy makers need in order to craft, implement, and evaluate more effective policies and practices.

Thus, families are key incubators for indigenous inventions. They may craft new innovations. When professionals, policy makers, and advocates collaborate with families, especially the ones that appear to be "hardest to reach and serve," multiple benefits can be realized.

ALIGNMENT, EVALUATION, LEARNING, AND IMPROVEMENT

The alignment of policy proclamations with practices is always difficult. Alignment, in the implementation process, means ensuring fidelity between policy intentions and policy impacts. Many policies are changed during their implementation because there are so many intermediaries. Local place and contexts weigh heavily in adopters' interpretations and implementation orientations. Consequently, policy impacts, i.e., what families and helping professionals actually experience and do, may bear little resemblance to the original plan or envisioned course of action. An array of factors may be responsible for these implementation gaps, including funding, training, staffing, reward structures, and accountability measures.

Alignment may involve the practices of a group of people, at several hierarchical levels and in different places, functioning as a whole instead of going in different directions (after Senge, Kleiner, et al., 1994). Alignment is very important in policy and systems reform. *Alignment indices* are important facilitators for implementation fidelity and for evaluation. They make possible discrepancy analyses, i.e., the difference between what was intended and what actually happened.

Table 6.6 presents examples of alignment indices. The table starts with intraorganizational alignments and includes interorganizational align-

TABLE 6.6. Examples of Alignment Indices

ALIGNMENT IN ONE ORGANIZATION	CROSS-SYSTEM ALIGNMENTS
Families are viewed and treated consistently across all levels and among all departments.	Families are viewed and treated consistently across all organizations and sectors; all are family centered.
Practitioners in the same organization are all family centered and culturally competent.	Practitioners from related systems, which serve the same families, communicate effectively and coordinate their efforts around shared commitments and practices for family-centered work
Practitioners and middle managers are "on the same page."	Practitioners and middle managers in other systems are in harmony within their respective organizations, and they are harmonized across systems as well.
Middle managers are "in sync" with top-level supervisors.	Managers and supervisors are "in sync" within and across systems.
Practices and programs show fidelity to family-centered principles.	Practices and programs across systems are all family centered.
Accountability structures and criteria reflect family-centered principles, policies, and practices.	Accountability structures and criteria are aligned across systems; collaboration in support of shared accountability for family well-being is the norm.
Sector-specific, categorical policies become more family centered.	Cross-sector policy development and policy de-categorization occur to facilitate family-centered practice.

ments. These indices and alignments are very important when professionals and their agencies must collaborate (Hooper-Briar & Lawson, 1994; Lawson & Briar-Lawson, 1997). Many such alignment needs can be anticipated. Other alignment needs appear during implementation, and as a result of evaluations.

For example, new policy can be undercut by the "business-as-usual" practices of persons charged with implementing it. A policy shift toward family-centered and culturally responsive practices may occur in a community social service agency. However, if schools, police, and health and justice systems are not oriented in the same direction—i.e., if they do not share unity of purpose—then there will be alignment problems (Senge, Kleiner, et al., 1994). Helping professionals probably will work at cross-purposes, and families will be caught in the middle.

For example, a health and human service agency has fostered family-centered policies. Social workers, nurses, doctors, and child care providers frame individual need in relation to family support and capacity building. However, the school system remains subject centered or child centered. Families are rarely included in any decision making at the school, and many parents feel unwelcome and maltreated. Families feel they are well treated in one system (the agency), but poorly in the other (the school). These differences signal alignment needs. In short, when alignment problems occur, families may suffer.

Moreover, professionals' jobs may be more difficult. Professionals' efficacy and sense of well-being depend in large part on improvements in families. When systems are not aligned and professionals work at cross-purposes, no one benefits.

Evaluation is especially important. Leaders promoting family-centered policy and practice alternatives need to develop clear plans for assessing the impacts of policies and practices. Both intended and unintended effects must be considered and assessed. Planning for policy and practice learning, development, and continuous improvement must be incorporated into every innovation (Argyris & Schön, 1996; Lawson, 1999a; Preskill & Torres, 1999; Schön & Rein, 1994).

Alignment and policy fidelity may be facilitated by evaluation designs that provide data for learning and improvement. The congruence between policy goals and their implementation effects should be a major focus of evaluation.

Thus, responsive, democratic policies and practices have a cyclical character. New policies are developed in response to emergent needs and aspirations. Then policy implementation and evaluation identify new needs and demands. In turn, these new needs and demands prompt corrective responses. New corrective political interactions, policy changes, and governmental responses follow. The process then begins all over again.

To reiterate, when family-centered policies and practices are involved, families are partners in this process of learning, improving, and correcting policies. This process is better because families' perspectives are valued and incorporated. Even when policy leaders have not involved families in the initial design and agenda-setting process, families can be included in every other phase, especially in policy implementation, evaluation, and learning.

NOTES

1. These examples derive from the collaborative work of Jean Logan, Katharine Briar-Lawson, and their associates in Dade County, Florida.
2. This label was derived from actual experiences and was conceived by women. Sexist interpretations are recognized and not condoned. The authors have an obligation to represent people's language and practices.

CHAPTER 7

Developing Family-Centered Policy and Practice Discourses

Katharine Briar-Lawson and Charles B. Hennon

Discourses are patterns of language use that reflect people's thoughts and values. Discourses are, in other words, practice routines. A key aspect of family-centered policy and practice is changing past/present discourses, which are not family sensitive and family supportive, and helping develop new, family-centered discourses (National Association of Social Workers, 1988, 1993).

This chapter presents some of the possible discourses in specific scenarios that are likely to unfold as policy makers and practitioners struggle to become more family centered in their thinking. Several questions arise in such a discourse: How can policy makers and practitioners charged with a single-system responsibility such as employment or education become more family centered? How can families be positioned as guides? How can economic development, so frequently the overriding concern of elected officials, be tied to investments in families? In what ways can policy leaders become family advocates? What might the discourse sound like as policy makers and practitioners work toward more family-centered and family-supported practices and decision making?

Illustrative dialogues are presented. These dialogues indicate the new discourses that are needed for family-centered policies and practices. Although policy makers focus upon another sector or policy arena, they learn to consider and focus upon families.

An imagined family-centered dialogue is offered, with policy makers and practitioners collaborating in policy creation. These examples of dialogue between policy makers and practitioners are mostly national level ones. The process and related comments may apply equally well to policy making by nongovernmental organizations (NGOs), states, provinces, communities, and other policy-making bodies (e.g., Bruner, 1991, 1997; Council of State Policy and Planning Agencies, 1989).

These and the other dialogues in this book should not be interpreted as suggesting the authors are prescribing "the answer" for similar issues in other nations. All such policy and practice discourses must be sensitive to the requirements of cultural-specific policy and programming (Ghai, 1997; Rural and Appalachian Youth and Families Consortium, 1996). Rather, the dialogues are offered as teaching tools, so readers might benefit from "hearing" how policy dialogue might proceed.

Most policy makers and practitioners will have a categorical charge for which they are responsible—health, transportation, or employment, for example. Making the systems for which they are responsible family centered and supportive may involve a major shift in thinking and orientation.

PROMOTING FAMILY-CENTERED DIALOGUE IN POLICY AND PRACTICE PLANNING

Policy makers, helping professionals, and advocates need to develop skills and abilities to shape policy and practice agendas. They need to be able to promote family-centered discourse through their dialogue with individuals and groups who may need to be persuaded to think, talk, and act differently, in pro-family ways. Four examples indicate how this family-centered discourse can be inserted into planning dialogues.

Family-Centered Economic Development Planning: The First Example

Box 7.1 presents the first policy dialogue. It represents an attempt to connect families to economic development (United Nations, 1992g, 1994c, 1995c). The focus becomes services and resources, such as start-up loans and training to encourage family entrepreneurial activities.[1] Starting this dialogue marks an important educational and capacity-building opportunity. It lays the foundation for future success, even if these policy makers and practitioners do not immediately enact initiatives that would create sweeping changes in economic policy. Moving from a focus only on investments intended to attract big business to including investments in family businesses may be a way to launch a series

BOX 7.1

A POLICY DIALOGUE ABOUT UNEMPLOYMENT

INITIAL DIALOGUE

COMMENTS

Policy maker: "There are 3,000 jobless in one of our provinces, with three companies that are closing to relocate to other areas. Not only are the families of the unemployed suffering, but now there will be more unemployment and problems. We must set up an economic development initiative to replace these companies."

This is a policy maker who sees unemployment as more than an economic issue. It is seen in family terms.

Pro-family policy maker: "We know from other countries and indeed from our own, that many families are small-business entrepreneurs. Those enterprises give both their own family members and others sources of income. If we attract only large corporations, then we will be overlooking the capacity of families to meet community and economic development needs, and some of their own income-generating capacities. Furthermore, some of the companies that have been operating here pay the equivalent of 28 U.S. cents an hour, and that is not a living wage."

The pro-family policy maker is seeking to build on the other policy maker's family sensitivity to promote a family-focused if not family-centered approach. Drawing on experiences in other countries with comparable chal-lenges helps to bolster the strategy.

The focus on families as the investment site is a new concept and one that may not be easily advanced.

Policy maker: "You may be right, but these unemployed people have no money or skills to start up and keep a business going."

A barrier is noted; families are seen as "deficient."

Pro-family policy maker: "Ah, but I think that can be fixed. I know that some nations, some in coop-

A solution is offered. Technology transfer is suggested. Family capacity building is emphasized.

INITIAL DIALOGUE	COMMENTS
eration with the UN, created business incubators and other systems to help families develop the needed skills. We can find funds for venture capital loans to get these businesses going."	Requisite services and resources are indicated. Resource shortfall is acknowledged and alternatives are proposed.
Policy maker: "But where?"	Doubt is expressed. Budget transfer may not be possible.
Pro-family policy maker: "Some can come from the money we would otherwise spend on trying to attract a foreign company."	This policy maker is seeing plans for infrastructure investments, such as roads and utilities, competing with family investments. In some cases these may be essential; in other cases this may be more of a big business investment having little relevance at this time to the needs of families and their businesses.
Policy maker: "So families can be part of a solution to a problem as serious as unemployment?"	A viable alternative is envisioned that builds family capacity, but because it is innovative, doubt still lingers.
Pro-family policy maker: "Precisely! Families must be seen as partners in economic development. We must build their capacity just as we work to make it attractive for TNCs to consider locating here."	The importance of families as creators of economic progress is emphasized as well as reinforcing the need for capacity building.
Policy maker: "What are the pros and cons of this idea? Would we open these opportunities up to the most needy families or the ones with the most promise as entrepreneurs? Would this be open to all families regardless of their backgrounds?"	Some probing questions concerning the consequences of doing things differently are raised. These questions must be carefully answered. For example, will this investment be an entitlement or one that will selectively target just some families?

INITIAL DIALOGUE	COMMENTS
Pro-family policy maker: "On the con side, families are risky investments because many small businesses fail, especially if they lack sufficient marketing know-how or fiscal resources and skills. In fact, we will need to project how many families will default on their loans, and the impact of this on our budget. We also will need to develop safeguards to ensure funds are being used for enterprise development.	The pro-family policy maker begins to develop a "balance sheet" of potential problems and benefits of such an innovative policy. More careful planning will be required as the outlines of the policy start to take shape.
On the pro side, we might look at family enterprises as more than just revenue generation and income supports. Family enterprises contribute to the needs of the community and beyond. Families without income sources often lack ways to feel valued and needed, people become depressed, and often marginalized. Such lack of industriousness may lead to addictions, abuse, and stress-related health problems and even crime.	Reviewing the pros and cons of a proposed action versus inaction helps to advance the decision to proceed. Pointing out that one way or another the government and nation pay for the absence of jobs helps in sharpening the point of the approach being advocated.
Families with growing and stable enterprises are not going to relocate. This will help ease some of our overcrowding in the cities and the other problems we are experiencing with migration. TNCs are mobile, often have few ties to the community, and may relocate at any time. And besides, family businesses often make it through bad economic times precisely because	Note that a systematic family impact analysis is not being conducted here. This policy maker is speaking from knowledge of how programs like this have worked elsewhere. Any policy and its implementations will have to be tailored to the local context. For example, will the program be reviving an entrepreneuring spirit, or having to create one? Will family entrepreneurs be

INITIAL DIALOGUE	COMMENTS
they are family businesses. Families will often sacrifice short-term gains for longer-term ones, including having something to pass on to their kids."	scorned, or will they be seen as pillars of the community, helping all through job creation? The pro-family policy maker is concerned about sustainability. The policy orientation is one of early intervention versus a crisis or more remedial approach.
Policy maker: "What you are saying in effect is that we have a choice among investing to attract big corporations, which may or may not provide the kind of economic stability we want; investing in income supports such as welfare; or promoting more economic initiatives in which families and communities will hopefully grow their own jobs. Is this correct?"	These policy makers are beginning to understand alternatives and the costs/benefits of each. Understanding that, in the long run, the costs of not investing in families so greatly outweigh the costs of such investment may accelerate family-supportive thinking and solutions.
Pro-family policy maker: "It isn't either/or. Perhaps some large corporations will be attracted because the type of stability and auxiliary businesses that they want are here. We might need to provide some incentives. And there will always be families requiring income supports due to disability, family size, and insufficient wage structures that don't meet minimal subsistence needs of families. Some people are unable to work outside the home because of caregiving burdens. On the other hand, countries investing in labor market and employment strategies that are tied	This person is showing a realistic understanding of what is involved. Multiple services and resources will be required for economic enhancement, whatever the strategy taken.

INITIAL DIALOGUE	COMMENTS
to local initiatives tend to have fewer dollars going into welfare and income supports.	
I believe these countries also experience more livelihood development, more employment, and higher standards of living. We can investigate all of this and see what other strategies, including those to attract large corporations, are most feasible. Perhaps the best approach is eclectic, innovatively weaving the best of several approaches together in something entirely new that has not been tried before.	The pro-family policy maker is seeking win-win outcomes so that families' needs and capacity building are not pitted against infrastructure building in communities. In this way, policy makers can believe that they have partially "won." They will also then have an easier time "selling" this win-win approach to others who also may champion one approach versus another, rather than a little of both. Not seeing family investment strategies in win-lose terms (at the expense of larger-scale economic development projects) is part of a diversified policy strategy.
Investing in family development is a form of community and social development requiring new roles for the government and policy makers and practitioners like us. The government might need to help with marketing these new products, and help with creating favorable trade climates.	
But I believe our families can draw on ancestral talents to produce textiles far more appealing than the garments they have been producing for that one corporation that is relocating. Other products and support services can be created	This policy maker believes that the best social welfare program is a good job that preserves families and local cultures. This person recognizes the necessity of social safety nets but seeks ways that the talents of families can be productively tapped.

INITIAL DIALOGUE	COMMENTS
by family businesses. Some might provide marketing services and transportation, or computer and other know-how."	This stems from a concern that solely offering income assistance rather than productive employment will backfire as policy makers may at some point strip families of such assistance. This policy maker is thinking about both the short- and long-run sustainability of policy decisions so that they become settled courses of action rather than vulnerable to the preferences of succeeding generations of government officials. The investments in families double as cultural preservation initiatives. Linking small businesses to a system that might help market their goods and services may help improve these new businesses' chances of survival and success.
Policy maker: "So how do you propose that we proceed? Should we set up a type of family enterprises organization? Should we try this in one part of the province, the whole province, several? You said something about incubators also. Should we give funds to banks so that they can make high-risk loans? Should we start by creating a committee to look into this?"	Ways to proceed are being explored. The benefits of a family-centered strategy are perhaps starting to be recognized. Both policy makers are beginning to explore the family-supportive services and resources that may be required, such as loans and training. There is concern over whether to develop a series of pilots or immediately move to a larger, perhaps national, strategy.
Pro-family policy maker: "Perhaps our first step is to look at how other nations are dealing with their development issues as businesses relocate. We can find out	The lessons learned by others are a resource that policy makers can tap.

INITIAL DIALOGUE	COMMENTS
what the possibilities are, from in-dustrial to developing nations.	
I have read where the goal to be-come more self-reliant can be turned into a community economic development initiative, creating partnerships among families. This moves the agenda out of a national- or provincial-level coor-dinating function, to one closer to families and communities.	The pro-family policy maker is showing how economic and social development becomes fused with family investments. This is relational thinking.
At the national level, we will still be responsible for setting policy frameworks and funding. We will need an advisory board of families, union leaders, local bankers and politicians, teachers, clerics, and people already running businesses to help in guiding us. We want to be sure that they understand our goal is a more diversified partner-ship for economic development. This group can then work with local advisory committees to set goals attracting new business as well as growing jobs and liveli-hoods out of the talents and skills that exist. If necessary, that is, if families see the need, we might also set up business incubators and other training mechanisms for family entrepreneurs who need skills and even certification to move into certain jobs. We can bring our higher education institu-tions into the discussions as well."	Here the pro-family policy maker is trying to move more in the direc-tion of family-centered practice, with families as co-designers. In this way the process will become more democratized, at least in the sense that some families may help design local policy and programs.

INITIAL DIALOGUE	COMMENTS
Policy maker: "I'm going to ask again. How will we fund all of this? We have rising debts, and all of our service sectors are not reaching their goals of educating all our children, universal immunization and prenatal care, and the like. They also need money."	Budget allocations of any type, especially taking funds from one program (more crisis oriented perhaps) to give to another (more preventive oriented perhaps) is a political issue with consequences for one's career, one's employer, and one's nation.
Pro-family policy maker: "If you look at what we are spending for jails, more police, and dealing with health problems, I think you will agree that we are spending a lot of money on preventable calamities. Many of these might have been avoided had families already been investment sites and partners in economic development."	The pro-family policy maker is trying to show that the nation is already paying for the costs of family poverty and unemployment. Investments in families' earning power and creative productivity would then become more preserving and protective investments. Giving communities and thus families the funds that would be spent in dealing with problems after they happen could help to create employment through family businesses. This helps in moving from the deep-end, remedial, crisis sector of the funding and policy continuum to the front end in a family promotive and preventive strategy.
Policy maker: "I can't agree with what you are suggesting. We cannot close down the jails or police forces. We have to keep our anti-dysentery program intact. What do you mean that families are investment sites?"	Both policy makers are exploring the fiscal benefits and costs of family investments as preventive and promotive approaches versus what they are now spending in remedial services such as prisons.
Pro-family policy maker: "We should think of families as comprehensive and preventive social service systems providing cradle-	This is a "bottom-up" rather than "top-down" goal-setting orientation, where localized groups help set goals and plan accordingly. The

INITIAL DIALOGUE	COMMENTS
to-grave services to their members. If we invest in them and help with employment needs, they will be better off. The best social welfare program for a family may be a good job or jobs. What we can do is look at how to set goals with communities and families so that instead of the explosion in costs for jails and the like, we can look to communities to do more planning for the kinds of places where families want to live. We will attempt to limit the growth in jails while investing in livelihood development. Because the strategy I'm suggesting involves loans that are revolving and repayable, there will be less drain on our nation's finances. What I am proposing is a sustainable investment strategy, resulting in more long-term stability and better use of governmental investments."	overall policy planning process, however, is still top down. Giving both families and communities the chance to own the options of moving forward or just doing nothing helps to build a sense of ownership in the proposal that will emerge. Neither policy maker may have to act at all. Inaction is one choice and course of action.

of regional pilot or demonstration projects. In this way the effectiveness of the approach can be tested, evaluated as it is in progress. If results are favorable, policy makers and practitioners may decide to "scale up" (Melaville & Blank, 1991; Melaville, Blank, & Asayesh, 1993). That is, they may build from a local success to a state- or province-wide, even national, initiative (L. B. Schorr, 1989; A. Schorr, 1997).

Health: The Second Example

As professional health care systems develop more complexity, families may see their own roles and responsibilities diminishing, as well as the place of traditional home and community remedies (United Nations,

1994h). Building a stronger health system while also building family capacity adds resources to the overall health and wellness planning process. The next scenario, presented in box 7.2, identifies some of the challenges of launching an outreach strategy that may temporarily increase costs and demands for hospitalization or other professional health care. Once mutual-aid and outreach networks are established, there may be a decrease in catastrophic medical problems and an increase in more home-based and preventive health care. Policies and programs to train, encourage, and provide necessary resources to families, seen as chief health care providers, can enable families to be frontline health promoters (United Nations, 1994h).

The dialogue indicates that when policy makers and practitioners recognize that families do the bulk of health care, diverse problem-solving choices appear (United Nations 1994h). Health promotion, education, and preventive approaches, which build on families' capacities and strengths, are one choice. Another choice is seeing catastrophic medical and remedial health solutions as all that exist. Policy makers and practitioners grapple, in an environment of restrictive budgets, with ways they can afford the programs and policies they seek and that families need. The more preventive-oriented approaches may potentially offer more budget-neutral finance options. The program developed, like all programs, should be forecasted by family impact analysis and assessed through program evaluation.[2]

Many different aspects of family and community life can and should be considered, both the negative and positive outcomes. Among the possible things to consider would be the influence of such proposed programs on family dynamics, including interpersonal relations, food choices, resource allocations, and health outcomes. Transformative learning (Hennon, in press) could also be assessed. Have the participants in the program become empowered? Have they acquired new skills and enhanced self-esteem? Have they gained new knowledge and capacity that helps them initiate other programs? Are they prepared to find better ways to improve the quality of life (Family Resource Coalition, 1996; Grace Hill, 1995)?

Social Services: The Third Example

Families are key personal problem solvers; they counsel one another all the time (United Nations 1991a). In many cases they are also the

A POLICY DIALOGUE ABOUT HEALTH

BOX 7.2

DIALOGUE

COMMENTS

Policy maker: "Our health care costs are the fastest rising expenditure in the country's budget. I have charted the projected trends for the next ten years. I'm afraid we are going to have a fiscal crisis from which we will never recover."

This policy maker shows how cost analyses done in isolation of the people and families they reflect may create limited policy choices. Cost-cutting will often be seen as the solution and may be done without regard for its human and thus family impact. Nevertheless, charting trends and projections is fundamental for establishing the costs that will be absorbed if new courses of action are not pursued. The crisis becomes an opportunity for innovative action.

Pro-family policy maker: "Most of the expenditures are costs that might be prevented if we could motivate people to adopt more healthy behaviors and wellness lifestyles. I think families should be the place to start. They decide on what food to serve and can do a lot to help reinforce changes in behavior that can be more promotive of health and the prevention of illness. Of course we will have to deal with how this can dovetail with folk beliefs and home remedies. And we have to do something about all the advertising done by the tobacco and rum industries. Giving free samples of cigarettes to people and having ads everywhere promoting drinking is just making things worse.

The pro-family policy maker attempts to move what began as a "family-insensitive" approach to one that is more "family sensitive." This is done by pointing out that families and their members can be viewed not just as patients, but as agents of their own health and wellness. Like the pro-family policy maker in box 7.1, the perspective put forth is that families are resources in a prevention and investment strategy, not drains on the economy.

The importance of thinking about individuals embedded in a family context, and how behavior and life changes are thus influenced, is recognized.

DIALOGUE	COMMENTS
Just imagine the benefits if we could mount a campaign seeking to reduce dependence on nicotine and alcohol. While we are at it, just think how great it would be if we could cut down, even eliminate, some of the pesticides and other agricultural chemicals currently being used. They create health problems for agriculture workers, and the residue on the produce is not healthy. And just think of what our country would be like if every family could have its own garden plot, even those in our cramped cities.	Their fiscal crisis is prompting them to move to more of an early intervention if not prevention agenda.
Dream about a program for training, from among the families in each community, a cadre of health promotion specialists and agriculture advisers. We could use their help in achieving goals of clean water, more naturally grown food, more in-home health care as well as use of outreach programs from the clinics so that diabetics and others would not have to be hospitalized. They could also be helpful in promoting the advantages of breast-feeding, and setting up "postpartum" support groups.	Rather than a top-down directive such as requiring shorter hospital stays or cutting off funding for some services, they are exploring if an effective campaign for wellness can be mounted in partnership with families and communities. Families are depicted in innovative roles such as outreach and supports for one another.
Every neighborhood might have the equivalent of a health care advocate trained to offer support and to mediate between the clinics and families, while promoting more in-home services.	"Costs" related to current practices are compared to what might be possible with a change in policy.

DIALOGUE	COMMENTS
You know that as we have analyzed hospital usage, it is often for illnesses and emergencies that are related to poverty, addictions, crimes, or the lack of more preventive and promotive health care. All these can be addressed by families, probably better than any other way. We could help in building family capacity in this area by policies that encourage the creation of networks among families."	A family impact analysis should be completed to assess the "costs" as well as benefits that families might experience. This information can help inform future dialogue and help plot the course of action to be taken.
Policy maker: "If we deployed local citizens in a health promotion campaign, they might find more people who have illnesses and catastrophic medical crises that need attention. This will cost even more, and we do not have the money."	This policy maker is correct about increased cost. Many times when there is accelerated outreach to families, unmet needs are discovered. So in the beginning of a program, there may be a great demand for health care help. Only when this backlog of needs is addressed can the impact of the investment be more clearly seen. Policy makers and practitioners must prepare for an initial increase before demand levels off, as the benefits of promotive, preventive, and early intervention strategies take hold.
Pro-family policy maker: "That may be true for a year or so as people who need medical attention get helped. If we were to provide incentives to communities to invest in local jobs for health care promotion and in-home health care aides, as well as education and incentives for more family care, we might be able to shift some of the	The policy makers and practitioners are exploring ways to give the medically needy more assistance by helping families become more of a source for caretaking and health promotion, as a substitute for expensive hospital-based medical care and costs.

DIALOGUE	COMMENTS
predictable financial outlays that we know will double in five years anyway and reprogram these into communities. In this way we are converting money that would be spent on undesirable outcomes into earlier intervention. It is only this way that we can reverse the syndrome of waiting until a crisis, thus resulting in costly hospital-based care and enduring catastrophic health problems. At this point, medical treatments are required that could have been prevented.	
What if we had a universal health promotion policy while selectively targeting communities and families with the most severe medical needs and catastrophic health problems? In this way we could maximize our resources.	The pro-family policy maker delineates a universal health promotion agenda and the targeting of the most needy patients for in-home care. To implement this course of action, there perhaps would have to be eligibility screening. The most medically needy, as defined by the program, would be targeted.
Health and wellness as a promotive agenda is not that costly. The training and supervision of family health advocates as well as agriculture advisors serving as outreach workers, along with home health aides or family members themselves to provide in-home care, might divert patients from costly hospital, inpatient, medical care episodes. This might be a cost-effective way to proceed. We might even find that the savings just from	Building the capacity of communities and families is seen as a way to provide localized, predictable, and lower-cost care. The impacts on families as well as on others such as those in the medical profession should be investigated. Any program initiated should be evaluated as to cost and positive and negative consequences.

DIALOGUE	COMMENTS
the reduced use of hospital care benefit not only patients, but the family members and others trained to do more in-home care. Patients will not only have help in their homes but earlier medical attention and in-home care rather than in hospitals. This will benefit the patients and their families both medically and also in terms of the wages that now will go to family members and others who do this community home health care work. This expenditure shift might not add any new costs to the system in the long run."	

source of the stressors that lead members to seek help. Yet often, through professional counseling or education, family members learn what they wish they had known earlier—to prevent or better manage stress, anger, and harms to themselves and others. Thus social service partnerships with families constitute both prevention and enhancement of families. Policy makers and practitioners (and families) can conceive of families as frontline practitioners for others in their social support networks, their communities, and workplaces (e.g., Apple, Berstein, et al., 1997).

The dialogue presented in box 7.3 illustrates that sound family policy and its tailoring to fit specific contexts does not negate the need for clear standards about human rights. The United Nations covenants provide ample evidence of the zero-tolerance for abuse and harm that can be adopted worldwide (United Nations, 1988a, 1988b; United Nations World Conference on Human Rights Preparatory Committee, 1993; Wronka, 1998). In effect, these rights become inalienable. While policy makers and practitioners may wish to offer less punishment-based and more family strengths–oriented approaches, there are some non-negotiable protections and standards that have been agreed to worldwide (Van Soest, 1997).

BOX 7.3

A SOCIAL SERVICE POLICY DIALOGUE

DIALOGUE	COMMENTS

Policy maker: "We need to accelerate services available in this community to address domestic violence and neglect. We must have laws that ensure minimum levels of protection against being harmed in the home by family members. We have too many violent families."

This policy maker reflects a frustration and even blame syndrome toward families. With such frustrations, it is hard to instead see families as both the focus and the agents of change in violence reduction and prevention.

Pro-family policy maker: "I see many choices here. First we should remember that families do more policing of one another than law enforcement agencies will ever be able to do. Ensuring all people's safety is our first job. Second, families that are terrorized by an abuser may have several members at risk, and therefore they are unable to protect one another as they all are victims. A father, depressed over finances and drinking heavily, may be prone to victimize a child and a spouse. Sometimes the spouse may be unable to seek help for fear of harm both to herself and her child. Neither spouse may know how to effectively communicate or to negotiate their needs, or deal with their anger. The way they have been interacting as a family may only make things worst.

This policy maker recognizes that families are systems that may create violence when functioning is impaired. Some might see this as misplaced blame, seeing instead the genesis of violence in the culture, socioeconomic conditions, or gender role socialization and family power politics. Differing views of the "cause" will lead to differing views as to the solution. Naming and framing are important aspects of the problem-setting processes. Naming this as domestic violence and framing it as a legal issue lends credence to specific languaging and approaches.

Thus, it is important that some "targets" of our program become trained as key service providers

The pro-family policy maker underscores how much violence prevention families already do. Thus the

DIALOGUE	COMMENTS
and protectors as well as being protected themselves. A mother who does not want the father jailed, but instead rehabilitated, may require assistance and resources—for example, training in assertion skills so that she and her children remain protected. We can provide restraining orders, but the family must partner with us in this process. Job training as well is needed to ensure that she can become more economically secure and independent."	strategy that can evolve is one that builds on this capacity. This would be a strengths-based rather than a deficit approach, focusing on assistance and resources rather than services alone.

The pro-family policy maker and practitioner reflects a family systems perspective on the ways in which an adult in pain may pass this pain onto other vulnerable family members. Likewise, this perspective is reflected in the understanding that family strategies for dealing with daily life as well as abuse (or other problems) can often be detrimental, perpetuating the harm.

More of a resource and support approach as well as service-based approach starts to emerge.

This pro-family policy maker is not just pitting victims against abusers, but is suggesting ways that a person, in this case a mother, can be a protector and have more backing her up so that she and her children are not financially tied to an abusive family situation. This leads to a plan for education, law enforcement, and more shelters to ensure that children and mothers are protected and have safe havens. |
| *Policy maker:* "How can we prepare families to be frontline providers of services when some members are victims from their own childhood and thus continue the cycle of violence?" | The cycle of violence is seen as unavoidable and thus must be dealt with by laws and punishment. How can "the problem" be a solution? Doubt is expressed due to the use of a framework more "deficit" |

INITIAL DIALOGUE	COMMENTS
	oriented and invasive (i.e., laws and punishment) in approach.
Pro-family policy maker: "Many victims, including those adults who were victimized as children, require support groups. It may be much less expensive to feature in every neighborhood special classes on anger management, conflict mediation, and stress reduction while promulgating policies of zero tolerance for abuse of any one. We can give families incentives to attend these classes through small stipends. Maybe a business or civic group will underwrite this. The libraries, schools, churches and temples, or even work sites can be used. "Lunch and Learn" sessions might be one possibility. These classes can encourage and facilitate support groups to become like teams of protection aids for one another.	"Talking through" the issues allows this policy maker to start thinking of other possibilities. Providing services and resources that whole families or some members can access creates a more complex and holistic intervention. This thinking also reinforces seeing families as partners in solutions, not just as the problems to be fixed. Education as a component of preventive intervention is recognized.
And, another idea: We will offer families respite for their children and for themselves. We can pair them up with a mentor or support family who is also prepared to be a respite and counseling resource. This would be a community-wide, universal program offered as an entitlement, with every family who is interested in having access to these resources and services. These support families will need training and stipends. Perhaps we can get a grant for that."	As this dialogue proceeds, alternative funding sources are suggested, and other resources, such as shelters and other options for safety, respite, and support services, are named.

DIALOGUE	COMMENTS
Policy maker: "This sounds interesting."	
Pro-family policy maker: "Of course, this would be volitional on all accounts. The program based on my vision is innovative but it does not replace the need for protection experts addressing domestic violence at all levels. Nor does it reduce the need for police to be well trained in order to be key interventionists with restraining orders, arrest, and incarceration if need be.	The pro-family policy maker is both victim centered and family focused. Moreover, the solutions are diverse, involving the simultaneous building of a professional backup system, such as care for abuse victims, incarceration for perpetrators, safe networks of homes, and options for those needing complete protection.
Partnering up like this gives the professional community more capacity to draw on, including families to do their own self-policing, self-protection, and self-referrals as well as to get help in alternate pathways before the violence runs the risk of escalation."	The pro-family policy maker sees promise in partnerships among professions and families. Building the capacity of families to devise their own safety strategies when abuse and violence threatens is seen as a smart investment. A big challenge will be that of finding less stigmatizing ways to teach and help families. The pro-family policy maker is also concerned with proceeding beyond punishment-policing models to ones that change behavior with anger management and conflict mediation skills. The role of police and law enforcement is not negated, just not seen as the only solution to domestic violence.
Policy maker: "In this community, many of our homes are more dangerous places to be than even the most crime-ridden areas of town.	If families are the problem, how can they be the solution? This is a common way to think, one we believe must be overcome.

DIALOGUE	COMMENTS
How do we enlist the help of families when they are already under siege with abuse patterns?"	
Pro-family policy maker: "We have learned from other nations, such as Sweden, that our first job is to enforce and promulgate enforcement standards to ensure a zero tolerance for violence. Secondly, we need to consider the requirement that beating another family member is simply not to be tolerated. In effect, this level of safety becomes the norm that we strive to achieve.	This policy maker sees policy change as culture changing—creating a safer culture in the family and society.
Laws that make it illegal for a family member to hit another member may not be politically supportable in our community. Thus, we may have to try the norm enforcement, teaching, and capacity-building approach.	This policy maker is sensitive to cultural norms.
We also may want to have trained practitioners in all helping fields who can recognize the signs of abuse and promote helpseeking through many different avenues. This includes teachers and health care providers, employers, the police, and social service workers.	Additional resources and services to support families are recognized. These will need to be budgeted and practitioners trained.
We need to offer more aid to families themselves to reduce the excessive reliance on police and courts. We also need to build shelters for children and families who are escaping an abuser.	The building of more shelters would be a remedial, crisis-driven remedy to the defined problem.

DIALOGUE	COMMENTS
But think what it would be like if our schools provided classes in parenting, anger management, and conflict mediation to every student, making this a universal program. In this way we would be trying prevention rather than sending abusers to jail or anger management and parenting classes after the damage has been done."	Prevention or early intervention are suggested as alternatives to crisis or remedial services.

In this scenario, policy makers and practitioners in one community struggle to build family-centered approaches that are not in conflict with individual rights of protection. One way to achieve family preservation is through ensuring that a child, elder, or a victim of spousal abuse or domestic violence is protected, and that protection dovetails with initiatives to effect change in the behaviors of the known perpetrator.

This scenario depicts an attempt to balance in win-win ways the integrity of the family unit with the protection of the victim, and to create families as safe social spaces and their homes as safe places (United Nations, 1993c). What makes family-centered policy so paradoxical, and at the same time somewhat complicated, is that those who are seen as the problem are enlisted to be part of the solution (Alameda, 1996; Briar-Lawson, 2000-b). Policy makers and practitioners can come under attack if they err too far on the side of one group versus another, such as victims versus perpetrators, or children versus parents. Thus, policy and practice that is family centered attempts to build win-win strategies and does not give power to the dichotomies that do not have to exist and may turn out to be false. Finally, this example shows policy makers and practitioners moving away from a punishment approach toward one attempting to create incentives, from an approach that is stigmatizing to one that is a capacity-building and family-development strategy.

Law Enforcement and Policing: The Fourth Example

Box 7.4 presents the case of two policy makers discussing crime and drug trafficking. They are seeking ways to enlist more help from families

BOX 7.4

A POLICY DIALOGUE ON LAW ENFORCEMENT

DIALOGUE	COMMENTS

Policy maker: "Our community is at a new level of crime and victimization due to rising unemployment and drug trafficking. We must find new ways to give some sanctity back to the neighborhoods. There will never be enough police no matter how much we rely on getting more money to hire more police."

Here there is a sense of crisis. While perhaps not apparent to this policy maker, such crisis worry can be an opportunity for proactive approaches to supporting and building families. The recognition that professionals alone will not solve the problems of the day is important. This policy maker is problem focused, not family focused. The drug and crime problems are not yet reframed as family challenges and family-based solutions.

Pro-family policy maker: "Families are the first line of defense in our community. They know who the drug traffickers are, the growers and the users. They know who may be carrying guns. Families are often terrified to leave their homes. We must form citizen councils for crime abatement that begin with families finding other ways to produce income for themselves. All the interdiction in the world will not solve the crime problems if people or even whole families depend on the illegal drug industry for their income.

The pro-family policy maker moves from a problem to a family investment strategy. Thus, enlisting families can build on their strengths. Moreover, by recognizing that families know the drug networks, this policy maker affirms their unique expertise, lacking among the police. Using such expertise can multiply the by-products of direct investments in families. For example, families can help to motivate others (perhaps their kin) to turn to drug-free livelihoods. They may be the best at developing these alternative livelihoods because they can use themselves as examples.

Ask any family. They will tell you they are scared. They would like to get their members out of the drug business. They think they

The pro-family policy maker presents an understanding of how economics, drugs, and family incomes are interdependent. Given this

DIALOGUE	COMMENTS
cannot afford to, because there is no other livelihood. Thus we must enlist these families as we supply new livelihoods options for them. We can also create new neighborhood roles, including those involving community developers, crime patrols, and safety leaders. This means investing in the very families who may now be part of the problem. In fact, it may also mean offering extensive ongoing support groups for sobriety and drug-free behaviors."	framing of the issue, a major investment in families is needed to stop drug cultivation. Families require new intergenerational livelihoods. Moreover, the drug problem is now seen as an occupational development challenge. This is common. A government minister charged with responsibilities in one sector (drug interdictions) may find that the solutions lie within other sectors over which he or she has no responsibility or jurisdiction. In this case the minister concerned with drug trafficking will have to convince three other ministers—of labor, of families, and of justice—to collaborate to promote this comprehensive strategy.
Policy maker: "This sounds like an enormous undertaking. We do not have people trained in community development and mobilization of this sort."	
Pro-family policy maker: "We may want to reach out to a team of families and police who will be trained together in skills to build the necessary supports, step by step, to regain a sense of control and safety in our neighborhoods. Families are the experts. They will tell you how overwhelmed their neighborhood is and some of the barriers to this plan. They will adapt it to local needs. Our citizens are the stakeholders. Families	The pro-family policy maker now moves into family-centered dialogue, suggesting that families themselves can design what may work best for them. This policy maker sees families as experts because they live with their situation daily. To plan without them is to leave out important data for designing an effective strategy. Furthermore, this approach assumes that those seen as part of the "problem" can be helped to be

DIALOGUE	COMMENTS
want safe streets and homes. They are motivated. We just need to capitalize on this."	part of the solution. Without them there may not be as effective a solution. Moreover, enormous challenges can be pieced out in small steps so that little by little a grand social change schema may rely on small victories and their diffusion and replication. Additionally, the dialogue shows how family-focused thinking seeks ways to use incentives that are meaningful to elicit new responses from people. A drug interdiction campaign without providing other sources of income and livelihood is a limited strategy.

in their community (United Nations, 1992b). These policy makers and practitioners focus on the persons who were originally seen as the problem; at the same time, they enlist help from others. This proactive strategy creates alternatives to "getting tough." The plan is to eliminate barriers to helpseeking and helpgiving, providing help to families with a more broad-based policy approach.

There are several major transitions here. The first is moving from a single-sector to a multisectoral strategy. This is accompanied by the design of a more comprehensive family-centered strategy. The next is to get all the other ministers to function collaboratively to put this initiative in place. Job training and job creation are required. So is formal education. Training for community development, neighborhood patrols, and family-to-family support networks also are key pieces in this puzzle.

SOME SUMMARY PRINCIPLES

The following themes were interwoven in these four examples. In each case, the processes of naming and framing, and reframing and renaming, were essential. They were key aspects of agenda setting, as is outlined in the following.

Framing and Naming

- Framing the problems or policy concern in new ways so families are seen as resources, partners in the solution if not the key, and as investment sites
- Framing the work with families as capacity building through services and resources supportive of families
- Attempting to use a no-blame approach whenever possible so that families, even if defined as the problem, are also seen as one source of the solution

Prevention

- Moving from remedial to preventive solutions, from selective and targeted approaches to universal ones

Cost-Effectiveness

- Finding budget-neutral ways to fund these investments

Alignment

- Achieving cohesion in values and policy frameworks as an essential feature of noncontradictory approaches to families, and for more effective and efficient use of support strategies

Cohesion and Collaboration

- Functioning collaboratively as policy makers—like families themselves—to create comprehensive family-focused and family-centered strategies

FAMILIES AS POLICY COLLABORATORS

Imagine a scenario in which families are represented in the design, planning, and evaluation process (e.g., Alameda, 1996; Briar-Lawson, 1998; Briar-Lawson, 2000-b; Briar-Lawson & Wiesen, 2000). They are working with pro-family policy makers and practitioners, and they also have the opportunity to say what options they would like for addressing their needs, wants, and aspirations. If asked what changes and new policies and practices they would like to see in services (whether delivered through schools, social agencies, health, employment, or law enforcement), they might lay out some of the following concerns.

Resource Gaps

- Lack of access due to transportation, the times that services are available, or long waits, which impede helpseeking
- Lack of guaranteed supports when life-threatening situations are present, like family violence or serious illness
- Lack of help to address caregiver stress and burnout

Maltreatment, Cultural and Family Harms

- There is a lack of courteous and engaging (i.e., not disinterested) treatment, making helpseeking demeaning and distressing.
- There is an obsessive preoccupation with bureaucratic rules, leaving little flexibility to make services more tailored to diverse families and their situations.
- When problems occur, families often feel blamed and punished as if they are criminals or "bad" or incompetent people.
- Their own opinion or perspective is often not solicited or respected and does not shape the service plan.
- Many decisions may affect the entire family, but rarely are they made with a family impact in mind.

Taking these findings to heart, two policy makers have convened a planning meeting with representatives for families nominated from each community. Box 7.5 has been constructed to show how new designs result from the enriched naming and framing that occurs when families are viewed as policy and practice partners. A new kind of service system results.

Next Steps

Back in central office, these ministers gather to report their findings to the prime minister and other ministers. This has been the first in a series of meetings undertaken to determine the best ways to better serve local needs and to build the infrastructure within, and between, communities. What the ministers propose is a series of redeployed staff who

A POLICY DIALOGUE ON FAMILY VIOLENCE

BOX 7.5

DIALOGUE

COMMENTS

Minister of families and social welfare: "We are gathered here today to imagine together the best way to ensure that families who are stressed have more access to services so that their stress does not become a source of family violence."

That the challenge is placed before a collaborative group including families sets this problem solving apart from the other scenarios presented. This is but one beginning example of the process of family-supportive policy making. Because family violence is the focus, police and child protection services might be the topics of discussion in a professional-only dialogue.

Minister of finance: "Our goal is not to just remove children or elders from their families, but to help to keep families intact whenever possible, especially if that is what the victims desire. We want to invest more in prevention than in punishment, changing family behaviors rather than splitting up families."

Preserving families while changing the way the total family interacts may be new, perhaps resisted, ideas for families and professionals. In this part of the dialogue, these ideas are being presented "down" to families, rather than "up" from families. Thus the problem as defined by families, and their solutions, is not yet known.

Father once charged with abuse: "It is humiliating to have an investigation, to be thrown in jail, and then to have my family say that I hurt them but not so very badly that they want me in jail. I have had a very hard time with the death of my brother, my job ending, and my diabetes. I am not a criminal. I want help to make it possible for people like me to be understood when we are in pain."

Police intervention is seen as isolating the "perpetrator" and "protecting" the family. This man suggests that his needs were not understood by his family or "the system." While protection may be necessary, helping the entire family function more adequately is also required.

Minister of families and social welfare: "I hear several principles

The concepts and language of the father are reframed in terms of

DIALOGUE	COMMENT
that we may want to address in our policies and services. One, finding a better balance between protecting members when they are at risk and dividing up families. Two, getting services to family members as they experience stress and pain before they take it out on others. Three, even with abusers, there may be deep feelings and sensitivities that need to be addressed rather than criminalizing them once and for all."	possible policy. One family's experience becomes data for inducing broader principles that might be integrated into policy. These "principles" are more likely "working hypotheses" to be tested against the experiences of other families. As more family-generated data are acquired, further refinements to the basic principles and concepts of a policy can be made. Family impact analysis is a different data-gathering process, not to be confused with this process.
Minister of finance: "What other ideas would you like to share?"	
Father who is a farmer: "Our family is caught between the need to keep the farm going and the need to find work in the city. This keeps us divided most of the year and we do not have good transportation services. Our children are often left alone, sometimes for days when one of us must go care for our own parents who are ill. We are then suspected of neglecting our children. Caring for our parents and trying to make a living are stressful enough. We are doing the best that we can. We don't need to be hassled over our kids. Why aren't these social workers concerned about me and our parents instead?	Here and below violence and protection issues become ones of isolation, or a caregiving crisis at home, with parents away and frail grandparents who cannot adequately provide for their own needs. Rather than focus on abuse and neglect, the needs of caregivers become the focus. This happens because families themselves are present.
We have to take time off from work and go care for our parents.	This man details what is the reality for many others—families dealing

DIALOGUE	COMMENTS
I get threatened with losing my job by my boss all the time. What am I supposed to do? Not be a good son? But I have to feed my family too? I, perhaps I should say families, need to be able to have a job so that family members can all live and work in the same community. I hardly get to see my wife and youngest son who are living on the farm. Getting time off from work when you need it is important also. I work hard, I'm not a slacker, but I get treated like one."	with many issues and demands at the same time, all important and all interrelated. Being in over demand is a stressor. This person also points out feeling unsupported, perhaps even blamed. A single-sector approach is not enough to help his and similar families.
Minister of finance: "So we need greater employment opportunities, in-home support for children when parents must care for elders, and, for those working in the city, better transportation so that returns home can be accelerated. Flextime or other ways to balance the demands of work and family also look like a key issue."	The ministers are beginning to see that the professional policy maker cannot be as informed about what is needed without the perspectives of family members themselves. Moreover, the way in which the helping systems for families are categorically divided up makes it almost impossible for services to be cohesive and coordinated. In fact, they may begin seeing that some of what they do is anti-family. These diverse ministers are extremely hard pressed now to reconfigure how they talk and think about families; even the violence issue has been reframed for them. They will need to focus, among other things, on caregiver stress and to reconfigure their own work as more "family like" and collaborative rather than segmented and separate. A care giver investment strategy rather
Grandmother raising three grandchildren upon the death of her daughter: "I have no place to turn for my own relief. I am frail and cannot do much lifting. These three children take a lot out of me. I have no one to turn to. I cannot get around very well. If something were to happen to me, there would be no place for these children to go. I am alone, way out of the village."	

DIALOGUE	COMMENTS
	than a violence intervention approach alone becomes possible.
Minister of families and social welfare: "Again it sounds as if there is a need for more accessible services, even ifwe delivered them to your home rather than expecting you to be able to get out yourself. We wouldhave never known of your needs if we had not discovered you through your church."	It is important to notice that what began as a discussion of family violence has turned to many other, interrelated issues. This realization is facilitated with relational, systems-based thinking. Otherwise, there might be a temptation to "keep the discussion on track," not appreciating the interconnections among many different aspects of family life.
An abused mother: "I have been sitting here listening to all these other stories and wishing that there were more mothers like me here to tell you all what it is like to be abused and to also see your children hurt and bruised. In our terror, we call the police and there is no response. They say it is just a family problem. We go to hospital and are told that there are no places for us to get help. We need shelters and money when we flee our homes to protect our children and ourselves. We must have these guaranteed to us. Otherwise the need to stay will be too great. Even if we are attacked and injured, our husbands nonetheless bring home paychecks that we and our kids need to survive. What are you going to do to guarantee that when we leave there will be adequate protections to help us and our children get on our feet?"	Caregiver abuse and economic dependency crises are now introduced, adding a critical dimension to the discussion. This suggests how the remedial approach can still be fused with guarantees and entitlements. Otherwise, women and children may be forced to remain in abusive homes. This perspective is a new one for these ministers. They were unaware of some of the reasons an abused parent might remain in an abusive situation, perhaps blaming the person for not getting out. Previously, these ministers were not certain that having a dialogue with family members would add to their policy plans. Now, they reveal increasing enthusiasm for the perspectives that are shared and for their own learning.

DIALOGUE	COMMENTS
Minister of families and social welfare: "She is right. We have many injured and maimed women and children, some killed, because we do not provide guaranteed protection or provide for their other needs. Perhaps what we need is a special demogrant for abused women. This would allow for relocation to new housing if necessary, not just a temporary shelter. This would also provide income supports until work can be found. This is a calamitous if not life-threatening time in a family's life, and it needs to be a top priority. It needs to be part of our caregiver investment strategy. Thus when the caregiver is at risk, a more remedial approach is needed that ensures not just protection but income guarantees. It is clear that many of the concerns you have expressed cross many of our service sectors—law enforcement, health, social services and respite care, employment, transportation, and so forth."	The dialogue is shifting from services to also include the need for new resources that would be entitlements. Caregiver investment is another possible policy initiative. This minister starts to see the relationships between these issues—caregiving, stress, protection from abuse, employment, etc.
Minister of finance: "After this meeting we will see if we can better integrate service systems to best meet your needs at the local level. We certainly need to have minimal standards in all areas that ensure swift responses to abused spouses, children, and elders. We will also want to ensure that local	The ministers are increasingly realizing that the way in which their social service delivery systems are organized may not promote much collaboration or the ability to do more comprehensive planning and policy development. Representatives from many of the service sectors that are necessary

DIALOGUE	COMMENTS
needs, identified jointly by families and community officials, are addressed and in such a way that we build more prevention into our programs. We need to find a balance between the dilemma of specialization and more holistic, comprehensive, and generalist approaches."	to build a comprehensive approach are not at this meeting. There is still much work to do, dialoguing with other ministers as well as, hopefully, more families as a comprehensive, responsive policy takes shape.

are comprehensive, cross-systems leaders both at the administrative and community level. They also are determined that middle managers in these systems, often supervisors, have access to others who are able to cross the boundaries of various systems (like education, social services, and health) and to mobilize at their level the changes necessary for these systems to be more family and community responsive.

Families are sought as consultants at all levels—top-level policy arenas, middle-level management, and line level where direct practice is provided. In the process, local problems and needs impact thinking and policy at the top, at the same time that policy impacts move downward to frontline practitioners and families. In other words, policy and practice are linked and enriched. They have a more immediate "up and down the chain" response rather than being seen by top-level bureaucrats and policy makers as central office problems with no resolution. The prime minister offers to go with all the ministers to various communities and seek ideas from families concerning this plan, and to get other ideas as well so that the infrastructure improvements begin with her own cabinet and systems.

As a new prime minister, she has vowed to reform the way services are delivered and government is experienced so that families can be a priority concern. She had been active in the International Year of the Family and now seeks to promote, during her leadership, some of the next steps in family strengthening to which her predecessors also have pledged (United Nations, 1995a). She sees all her policy decisions as opportunities to bring about better outcomes for families and communities, and many of the decisions that she and the ministers undertake are ones that could be used to enfranchise families as collaborators in these "high-level policy choices" (Briar-Lawson, 1998).

SELECTED LESSONS LEARNED

This chapter presented some of the various dilemmas that ensue as people move to using policies and programs as family-strengthening and enfranchising tools. Sectoral and specialty approaches make it more feasible to focus on specialized outcomes, such as health, crime, and so forth. When families are the focus, and indeed when they are more than informants but policy design collaborators, categorical thinking, planning, and programming become problematic. Families are understood as dealing simultaneously with a variety of issues and living in specific contexts that may limit their options.

But holistic approaches to policy and practice are complicated by the fact that family and human needs, while not fitting neatly in a categorical box, are still "serviced" by sectors that often resist changing their claim on specific domains (Center for Study of Social Policy, 1989). Experience shows that many single-sector issues, such as child abuse or elder abuse, become compounded when they are accompanied by co-occurring needs such as substance use and underemployment. Similarly, some health issues are tied to income, employment, and transportation concerns (United Nations, 1995a, 1995e). When the many needs and desires of families drive policy and planning, their interrelatedness will be outside the conventional lines or boundaries of thinking. When families' voices drive policy and planning, their language will not be in "neat," discrete, service sector terms. This is often hard for bureaucracies and those they employ. The shift to cross-boundary thinking may be perceived in traditional bureaucracies as a form of rule violation. There may even be sanctions for such thinking and acting. For example, a mid-level manager in education who attempts to build a collaborative and tries to influence a mid-level manager in mental health may be chastised because she did not go through proper channels.

In the scenario, the prime minister and her ministers use cross-national networks to learn their way through some of the inevitable implementation problems and barriers, and will chart their progress in "baby steps" rather than giant leaps (United Nations, 1995e). Progress can be slow, especially when it requires many people, including families, to think and act in new ways.

Requisites for such integrative and comprehensive approaches, which prioritize holistic family enhancement and family outcomes over discrete categories such as number of immunizations, number of "drug busts," and number of children in school, include the following:

1. family-centered policy statements to which all agree;
2. interagency agreements that require collaboration, cross-agency staff development and training;
3. hiring, promotion, and reward structures that treat family-centered practices as a priority; and
4. training and educational programs that increase skills in working with and enfranchising families.

Moving to family-centered practices and collaboration among service providers involves major transitions that may take several years to develop. It is possibly hard for leaders at all levels to envision such internal change taking so long, and being so impeded by other, more categorical and individualistic ways of thinking. Yet decades of socialization into compartmentalized thinking and deficit orientations make this journey into the territory of family enfranchisement and family-centered practice and policy making a transformational move (Annie E. Casey Foundation, 1995).

NOTES

1. See Hennon, Jones, et al., 1996, for more information on this concept and process.
2. See Hennon & Arcus, 1993, and Hennon, 2000, for more information on program evaluations.

CHAPTER 8

Introducing Policy-Practice Skills for Family-Centered Change Agents

Katharine Briar-Lawson

There are two adages that help to guide the next two chapters. First, the very minds that created many of the problems facing the world's families as the twenty-first century begins are *not the ones* to solve them. Second, the dominant stakeholders who seek fewer investments in welfare states and more protections for free markets *are not likely* to initiate a family investment agenda.

Advocates and helping professionals must harness the rhetoric about the importance of families. If they do, they can become solution based in their own neighborhoods, communities, networks, and organizations. Or perhaps they will address demise syndromes beyond their own workplace, neighborhood, and network and team with a community thousands of miles away.

Just as families connect individuals to society, so too will family-centered advocates, helping professionals, and policy makers be the connective links that redress family harms with tools, perspectives, and action agendas. These two chapters attempt to reaffirm and build the growing cadre of advocates, professional helpers, and policy makers who draw the line in the sand, step forward, and work to nurture and advance the capacities and sustainability of the world's families.

Policy makers, helping professionals, and advocates around the world are struggling to build strong democracies, healthier economies, better services for citizens, and stronger families (e.g., United Nations, 1995a, 1995e). But they cannot do this work alone. Above all, they cannot do this work in isolation from families and family advocates.

Many citizens around the world are capable of being family advocates. They often perform family advocacy roles daily for their own and other families. These family advocates are exemplars; their achievements indicate that the idea of family advocacy as a key part of citizenship is feasible and desirable. In fact, many advocates are family-centered change agents. They understand the change process, and they possess important skills and abilities. They know that policy influences practice and that every practice act is a kind of policy statement. They are, in short, effective policy practitioners.

This chapter builds from their experiences and achievements. It identifies and describes strategies for citizen family advocates. It describes the process of change in relation to policy-practice skills and abilities required for change agents. These family advocates and change agents can be very important and effective policy practitioners.

The question is, how can an ordinary citizen who sees a need make a difference? Other questions follow. How can localized work on behalf of families serve as a model for other locations? How does concern about one's own family double as concern about others? How can citizens step forward and work to strengthen families? How can families be policy practitioners?

A person does not have to be elected or appointed to high-level government offices and positions to enhance outcomes for families (Haynes & Mickelson, 1999). Much of the work one does can serve as a form of "policy pilot." When a pilot is successful, it can be transformational in its own right. Anyone can see a community need or problem, or one that affects just a family or two, and decide to do something about it. Because this pilot may be applicable to other families and even other communities, this work then serves as a pilot for what could be policy for an entire community or region (Alameda, 1996; Naples, 1998; Schorr, 1997; Welch & Briar, 1991; Wilkinson & Quarter, 1996).

Even though individuals and families are capable of making such impacts and contributions, poverty, deep deprivation, starvation, and gender repression keep millions around the world from exercising these skills in citizen- and family-based change. Multinational corporations, dictatorships, special interest groups, and policy leaders are often hostile to the poor; to indigenous groups; and to racial, sexual, and religious minorities. Some may be impeded from taking action. Others may be enslaved and lack the freedom to undertake action (Bales, 1999). It is thus all the more compelling that family advocates who care about poverty, oppression, and repression, persons with time, energy, and freedom from dire needs and repression, step forward as change agents (Haynes & Mickelson, 1999). They can work locally, regionally, nationally, and internationally.

THINK GLOBALLY, ACT LOCALLY

The environmental protection slogan "Think globally; act locally" helps in imagining how localized work can be part of a support and investment strategy for the world's families. While making a contribution in the local neighborhood, people can connect their work to a world mosaic. This is how social movements get started and mobilized—when many people, in their own locales, step forward wherever and whenever possible to make a difference. However different they are, they are joined in an effort to stop the pain and hurtfulness in families, communities, nations, and thus the world.

Local mobilization and capacity building, like family-centered policy practice, is one way to reverse the process of family decline and harm experienced all over the planet. Stepping out to help others is a human and community act. Staying silent and not going the extra distance is not as social or civil, and the consequences may eventually prove hurtful to those who remain silent, as they too may be caused anguish either directly or indirectly.

BUILDING ECOLOGIES OF FAMILY TRUST,
ASSETS, AND SOCIAL-CULTURAL CAPITAL

This chapter incorporates Fukuyama's work (1995) regarding trust, spontaneous sociability, and the consequent foundations for social and economic activities (see also Putnam, 1993). Here, the family is connected to a social and ecological support framework provided by their surrounding community. The social work activist Jane Addams once argued that people should strive to make communities like healthy families. The proverb "it takes a village to raise a child" helps convey rich ecological imagery. Mirroring the investments in human capital—the untapped and often underdeveloped human potential—the intent is to build family capital, which starts with individual human capital, but constitutes a whole (family capital) that is greater than the sum of each part (human capital). Family capital, in turn, builds community capital and its related assets (Kretzmann & McKnight, 1993).

Family capital and community capital start with interdependent, cohesive, and purposeful actions that improve conditions for oneself and others. Like the work of family members to help another family member in time of need or to advance their development, the work of policy practitioners involves similar investments, but perhaps on behalf of strangers.

Trust, Families, and Community Building

Fukuyama (1995) argues that the key to healthy economic exchanges involves trust. People do not purchase goods from a shopkeeper whose products are not trusted. The social trust that builds in families, even unevenly, may not spill over to the community or workplaces. Without social trust there may be an inadequate foundation for "family asset" and "family capital building." Communities rise and fall, in part, upon the social capital that families help build (Putnam, 1993).

Trust is a critical ingredient in the asset- and capacity-building process. The employer who believes that local community members will test positively for drugs will not recruit them to fill the jobs that are vacant. The neighbor who is fearful of the theft of her purse will venture out less and less. The employer who believes that men are abusing drugs out of boredom, and believes they will perform well once they have meaningful work, may reach out, even offer support groups for those with severe problems. The neighbor who initiates a block watch turns her fears into action and in turn makes it possible for children and elders to have safer streets (Barnes, 1997; Ife, 1995).

The well-being of the world's families requires starting at home to build and advance the community social supports, resources, and services that families require. Hospitals, nongovernmental organizations (NGOs), social service agencies, and many civic associations, including clubs, are often initiated by citizen drives to address well-being and to advance the civic side of community life (Feldman, Stall, & Wright, 1998; Putnam, 1993). Thus, what Fukuyama described as spontaneous sociability and Durkheim (1964)[1] described as organic solidarity become the foundation for collaborative initiatives to build community and improved outcomes in health, social services, schools, safety, law enforcement, housing, and jobs.

Unfortunately, some of this capacity building has included tendencies to blame families. In other words, this spontaneous sociability may castigate families, rather than build family capacity. Castigation and blame are "right on schedule" if there are no alternatives, such as the Swedish Contact Family Model involving stronger families helping more vulnerable families. Rescuing family members and replacing the family with state-run or voluntary organizations, such as orphanages, may be more costly and less effective (e.g., Bruner, 1997).

Sometimes civic energy results in mobilizations that improve outcomes in one's community, especially when such action is inspired by anger over an injustice (e.g., Alameda, 1996; Briar-Lawson, 2000-b; Naples, 1998). Or, stepping forward may result from one's sense of conscience, which sees silence and nonaction as complicity. Other motivations stem from personal self-interest—to feel safe walking home at night or to be sure that there are adequate bus systems. Regardless of the reasons, the impulse to act for the betterment of others as well as oneself is a social act of citizens. Without such civic commitment and courage, the world would be without grassroots reforms and demands for democratized practices, as well as laws to protect individuals and to enhance each nation's civil society.

Citizen activists are critical to societal change. Work undertaken by citizens in east St. Louis through the Grace Hill Settlement House fosters neighborhood colleges, barter, and economic development initiatives. The RAINmakers (cited in chapter 6) were recent immigrants who were poorly treated in a community. They wanted to create more effective outcomes for families. As seen from the RAINmakers' bill of rights and the Dade County norms, many have the capacity to help mobilize others for collective improvement. Many can develop shared commitments to making life better for others. They can be involved in determining visions, missions, and competent practice as well as in writing bills of rights. Anyone who has worked to build an effective, healthy, and strong family probably has skills that are transferable. Many skills for building healthy families can be scaled up and transferred to the challenges of building healthy and responsive communities.

Grassroots policy developed in local efforts may in turn be the guide for improvements in regions or even nations. As the boundaries of nation-states become less relevant, it is ever more important that local citizen activists and practitioners see themselves as part of a world force of change agents (Ife, 1995).

ENVISIONING BETTER OUTCOMES AND ACTING STRATEGICALLY

As discussed in earlier chapters, resistance to change is often greater than change agents anticipate. Thus, finding ways to make change safe and "win-win" for all affected is one tenet of reform efforts. Another facet in building effective change strategies is using energy appropriately. Each change agent must weigh the pros and cons of where to place his or her energy and time. Simultaneously, many people use a felt need, problem, or crisis to shift into a problem-solving process. Often in times of need, crisis is opportunity. Because crises tend to disorganize people and social systems, crises may produce conditions that foster the examination and advancement of new ideas. Thus, *people may view a crisis as an opportunity.* It is the opportunity to imagine a new and better set of outcomes for others, and for themselves.

Just as a crisis opens the self and others to new possibilities, simply imagining or having a vision for how things might be different and better in the future may help fuel a change agenda. Having and sharing a vision for better outcomes may allow oneself and others to "keep their eye on the prize," a new and better future. It is hard to give up a vision if it is relatively feasible and possible to achieve.

This visioning process replaces negative thoughts with more positive solution-focused strategies. In a sense, people catapult themselves into an imaginary, desired state; "try it on"; decide that it is the preferred state; and then backtrack to figure out all the ways that they might begin to get there.

NEW ROLES AND RESPONSIBILITIES FOR FAMILIES

There are countless examples of families setting out every day to bring about change for themselves and others like them. The hordes of families on the move in search of better living and working conditions, immigrants and refugees, are all imagining a state that is better, desirable, and necessary (United Nations, 1994d). Initiating change is a common feature of family life.

Families as Change Agents and Policy Practitioners

If families are nothing else, they share the capacity to be, and become, change agents. They often change behaviors and the life courses of individuals. They may change living situations as they move. They may change the infrastructure on which they depend as they move in and out of various livelihoods. Families as change agents in service of their own interests and well-being may be just one step away from being policy practitioners (United Nations, 1995c).

Families are also the world's foremost policy makers. In fact, families do more policy making than any other institution. Family policies include rules, norms, and contracts among family members, and agreed-upon courses of action for the family. How does this same policy-making skill and initiative get taken outside the family to address issues that shape, and thus harm or protect, family functioning among others?

The concepts of framing, naming, and reframing are again helpful, and so is the idea of agenda setting, or family agenda-setting (see chapter 4). Reframing involves taking what often is seen as an individual's problem, need, or even deficit, and turning it into an opportunity for new family actions and policies. A problem- and deficit-based blame and castigation approach is replaced by an approach that promotes resources and services supportive of families (Briar-Lawson, Alameda, & Lawson, 1997).

Moreover, reframing involves looking socially and ecologically, not just at the individual in the family, but at the individual and family as part of many other social ecologies (after Hartman & Laird, 1983). In many cases these other concentric ecologies also must be strengthened (United Nations, 1993a).

Reframing is, in a public- and media-relevant way, often critical in the policy-practice process. It is not uncommon for policy makers, the media, and citizens alike to see a problem (like youth crime) and immediately blame and punish the youth (see United Nations, 1992b). Instead, these concerns can be reframed as ones of insufficient or ineffective services, resources, and support for the youth and family (Hooper-Briar & Lawson, 1994). Once reframed, these needs lead to new alternatives (e.g., how can the community be more helpful to the youth and family?).

In many cultures, problems and needs are often taken to the family for the first step in resolution. The Maori in New Zealand, for example, show how the process of reframing a child's issue as a family-systems and family problem-solving opportunity may be key to case planning, building stronger families, making changes in undesired behavior, and in honoring family strengths to initiate change (Wilcox, Smith, et al., 1991). As a result, the Maori family group conference is now public policy in New Zealand. This family group conference approach also has been adopted, or is under review for adoption, as a new policy approach in several states in the United States, in Canadian provinces, and in the United Kingdom. A key lesson learned from this approach is that, until such time as the family's culture, its members, its problem-solving skills, and its resilience are taken into account, formal, external, public sector interventions may be blunted and thus become wasteful. In some cases families may experience outside interventions as hurtful (Alameda, 1996; Lawson, Briar-Lawson, et al., 1999).

This is not to say that state intervention is not appropriate. Nor does this book legitimate harmful practices such as child and elder abuse and neglect and domestic violence, which require outside intervention to protect the safety and security of family members, especially women, elders, and children. The point is, families' capacities to help themselves and each other should not be replaced or eroded by the helping of others.

Moving from Vision to Action

Advocates may also need to take a long view about the change process. The questions to be asked include the following.

Am I indeed expecting major change immediately? Will I give up after the first or second or third setback? How resilient am I in this process? Have I considered the time it may take to see the agenda through so that others can carry it on if I get called to spend my time differently (with my family, my job, my own self-care)? This kind of self-assessment is critical. It helps set boundaries and identify progress markers. It allows change agents to know when "enough is enough."

In many cases, change efforts are something like a sporting event. The first team launches an initiative. Then replacements take over. Thus, when the goal is scored (i.e., a goal is achieved), a different set of players may be on the field at the time, doing the work. Civil and human rights movements are examples of this. For example, Martin Luther King Jr. had a dream. Others on his team have been carrying on his work. Nelson Mandela has symbolized a dream for South Africa in particular and Africa in general, and he has led the struggle to realize it. Others now work to implement his vision.

Sometimes changes occur in waves. Other changes will be discrete, marked by particular times and places. Others occur gradually and incrementally, e.g., getting public transportation for a community or putting up a traffic light so that children are safe. Relapse and regression tend to be steady companions of change. Change thus requires constant boosters, reminders, supports, reinforcements, and capacity building. Change also entails learning, and learning is a form of change. But change for the sake of change is not the aim. Change in the service of improvement in the lives of individuals and families is the aim. An envisioned, more desirable way of doing things becomes reality—this idealized vision ultimately may become what *really happens* (Ife, 1995).

Shared Goal Setting and Multiple Means for Goal Achievement

Many change initiatives break down not because the goals and vision are flawed, but because the means to their achievement become hotly debated and divisive. Many goals are notable because they are humane; they seem like the right thing to do. For example, most people do not want to see harm done to others or see preventable tragedies occur. In brief, they care about others, and their ethic of care is what makes one human, striving for a better world. Such honorable values reside in the many millions of families worldwide. Thus, as seen from the RAIN-makers example earlier, actions for change often originate from families, perhaps on the behalf of other families (Alameda, 1996; Briar-Lawson, 2000-b).

Many families want to be part of a solution, but they may be overwhelmed or simply cannot see how they might find the time, or feel safe enough, to participate. Finding ways to tap their interest and willingness to help, while also recognizing their boundaries, is key. The scenarios presented in boxes 8.1 and 8.2 illustrate some of these change principles. Attempts to build win-win strategies are illustrated in the other scenarios. In other words, conflicts over power do not have to create winners and losers, resulting in declining participation by the losers.

In the first scenario, Lev and his partner, who live in a developing nation, set out to turn discomfort into action (box 8.1). The story about Lev demonstrates how reframing in a nonblaming way makes it possible for one concerned citizen to mobilize a wider net of help, from the school, community council, his partner, and from the families of these vulnerable children. Lev and John use reframing as a key tool to see the issues in broader terms—as part of a family, community, and even national systems concern. Only when they reframed the issues, from parent and family blame to the absence of resources, could Lev and John get beyond the children and families to also bring in the school and community council to do some of the problem solving.

BOX 8.1

LEV AND JOHN

Lev passes through a neighborhood every day on his way to work at a factory. In this neighborhood are many children without supervision and playing in the street. He is concerned that they will be injured or are at risk of child abductions. He first thinks about wanting to protect just the children and sees this as a children's issue. Then he looks at the homes in which they live and realizes that their families are struggling with poverty and housing problems. Many homes lack complete roofs. Elders are often out on the streets, trying to gather food, he thinks. He wonders where the other adults are. It appears older children are the only ones left to tend to the younger children. There is a school nearby, but on some days Lev sees that there are few children there. Lev thinks it is because children go with their parents to work, or perhaps because there is no one at home to see that they go to school. Or maybe these families just don't care. It must be hard, Lev thinks, to both manage work lives and get the children to school some distance away. Virtually no one here has a car, as far as Lev can tell.

In his mind and heart, Lev wants to rescue the children. While this is his first inclination, he nonetheless begins to think about these children's families and then their community. He reframes what he has seen. He now understands the children are at risk because of the lack of neighborhood or family infrastructure to protect and support these children, or to help them get to school. He sees them lacking requisite resources and services. There seems to Lev to be little in the way of governmental support for these families and probably no communication. While he sees that the school might be positioned to be a resource, the school apparently has not prepared staff to do outreach to these children and their families. On the way home from work, Lev starts to imagine a set of scenarios that might help the families of this neighborhood. He realizes, though, that he really does not understand these families and their situations. He is just thinking all this up. So he sets his imagined solutions aside, and decides to ask his partner, who works in the vicinity and knows these families better, to further explain their situation.

His partner John says that these families are attached to the mines and factories in a neighboring village. There is one bus a day that transports them to and from work. The bus cannot accommodate children. Meanwhile, there is no bus route that children can take to get to school. Because the children have slipped so far behind in their reading and writing, they no longer feel comfortable going to school. So they stay home where they are assigned tasks by their parents and other relatives.

John senses that most families are not happy with this arrangement, but this is all that is possible. He has heard that many of these families hope they can earn enough in the mines that they can move to be either closer to their jobs and a new school, or closer to their children's current school. Meanwhile, he says that the children are not in fact without supervision, as several elders actually stay at home along with older children to supervise.

Lev wonders if it is really fair that his own children have a bus and school that is very accessible, and that he does not have the same problems getting to his workplace. He is tempted to go to a member of the community council to solve the transportation and school problems, but first decides to have his brother arrange some meetings with families to see what they would like if the government or others were to offer some assistance.

On a nonwork day, Lev and John meet with representatives from several of the families. There they learn that families have been relocating recently in this affordable neighborhood following the opening of the mines and some factories. They have come from many different parts of this country as well as others. There is a rich mixture of religious and other cultural practices, and several languages are spoken. They see these mine and factory jobs as providing opportunities for a better life. Some have been displaced from their original homes by changes in land usage such as urban renewal; other have chosen to move in search of better jobs. All these families are seeking to rebuild their lives and, more than anything else, create a more stable existence, permanent residence, and opportunity for their children. In this new neighborhood, without a great deal of economic or political clout, and as newcomers, they are not sure there is much they can do at present other than try to get by the best they can.

Lev wonders what has been done to support the families through tough times. After he and his partner and several of the families have discussed their situations, he encourages the families to consider devising a plan to seek more help from the local school and the community council. He suggests that the school might help the children with their discomfort in returning because they are behind and are embarrassed. Teachers might also do outreach to the families and the children. And the school might become more child centered and family supportive rather than subject centered and academically focused. The community council might be lobbied to reexamine the bus patterns both for the children going to school and for the workers going to the mines and factories.

Lev and John talk more with several family representatives, and from this it is agreed that a wider meeting of families will take place. John agrees to ask the local principal and some teachers to come to this meeting. Lev agrees to contact the community council to try to alter the bus routes.

After the meeting, during which they were surprised to hear of all the troubles faced by these families and of their sensitivities and desires for the children, several teachers agree to work in the neighborhood to bring the children up in their reading and writing levels. The principal did not attend, but the teachers say they will talk to him and encourage his cooperation and support. A year later, 50 percent of the children are working up to their grade level. Almost all children are attending school and are making progress. While no new bus routes have been put in place, there have been two buses running daily to ease the transportation needs of the parents.

Safety remains a big concern in the mine. This is now being brought before the community council by Lev and John, as the workers and their families fear reprisals from the company if they raise this issue.

None of these problems would have been brought forward had not Lev, with his partner John, reached out, serving as a bridge between newly relocated families and the organizations that are to serve them. Unsure of their place in this community, feeling generally vulnerable, these families were not comfortable about speaking out on their own behalf until encouraged to do so by others who believed in them and their needs. Good things started happening once people took an interest and starting seeing personal troubles as social issues, and started advocating for families rather than blaming them.

Once they reframed issues, they could identify a wider array of change targets. This takes the onus and burdens off the "problem persons." Enlarging the action arena also enriches the kind and type of solutions that might be mobilized (Ife, 1995). Had Lev solely blamed the parents, he might have become so frustrated that he would have found an alternative route to go to work so as not to be confronted with children in need. Instead, seeing the children each day served as an early, continual warning that more had to be done. Lev's discomfort guides his problem solving. His discomfort is used beneficially; it is not a cause of harm, avoidance, blame, and rejection.

Sharing the Agenda

When policy makers are left with most of the responsibilities to problem solve, they are hard pressed to keep pace with unmet needs. Often citizens and lobbyists with the most power and funds reach policy makers and thereby turn their attention to issues that may not necessarily be "family serving." This pattern has been discovered around the world as issues of commerce, trade, and transnational corporations (TNCs) dominate much of the public policy agenda (Nader, 1993). Families may not fare well, and their needs may not be addressed, if money and power interests define the agenda. As stated earlier, the persons and groups who are able to name and frame the issues, and control the discourse, have the power.

Around the world, corporate profit-making agendas or loan repayment concerns of the World Bank and the International Monetary Fund

BOX 8.2

JANA

Jana works on the evening shift at a plant in an industrialized nation. She learns about the impending layoffs at a nearby plant where her sister works. She is very concerned that similar layoffs will occur at her plant. She begins to discuss her fears with her family and her sister's family. Already they talk about trying to move both families in together to save money and other resources. Jana wonders about the dependence she and others have on these two companies. She feels like a helpless victim, and thinks that this condition puts her and her family as well as others in jeopardy. While there are few places to turn, she holds a small meeting before work with others who are also feeling restless and worried. They discuss alternatives to this dependent role. They consider moving, trying to attract new business, and starting their own businesses.

Jana introduces the notion of a barter system, where even if money is in jeopardy, they at least can create their own interdependent resource exchange. This would protect the few funds they have and make it possible to explore collectives and cooperatives, including trying to pool resources to produce their own goods should the firm leave. This action in a sense "buys them time" until other jobs are found.

Jana is worried about her role as the leader and the fact that she is now under great demand to stay as the leader. This leadership role is untimely given the added responsibilities she has at home with two families under one roof.

Recognizing that they can write their own policies, she offers some norms to the group who has adopted and share her concerns. One is that no one become disproportionately burdened by the leadership roles. She believes these roles can be rotated and that as many people as possible should have access to the roles they want. This dividing up of tasks, similar to what has been working well in the expanded family life at Jana's home, also serves to protect her, in that the group's work is not seen as Jana's agenda. If this were the case, she might get caught in win-lose dynamics. This sometimes occurs with others who feel powerless, or see power as a commodity to be sought. Jana does not want to legitimate win-lose competition for roles. This is because she holds to the goal of betterment for all. She keeps her focus not only on the vision, but on the way she wants to feel in the process. If she feels threatened by others, then she will, as will others, reduce involvement, and under those conditions she might even move. She sees the sharing of responsibilities as an empowering process.

Jana does help set up a barter system so that those who donate time and resources to another can draw on them as needed for reciprocal help. Child and elder care, aid with transportation, crop cultivation, weeding, tools, books, meal preparation, hair cutting, clothes washing, and home cleaning are all resources and services now being exchanged.

What began as a source of deep personal trouble and family worry for Jana and her sister, became a public concern of the wider community and of co-workers. Her willingness to step forward, to talk through with others the problem-solving options, was critical to this change process. Such initiating steps could have been undertaken by any member of any of the families affected.

Rather than try to solve problems in isolation from this larger group, Jana and others found that by collectivizing their concerns, they were able to promote more supports for one another and their families, and to organize plans for several collectives and cooperatives. Two of these were in place even before Jana's layoff and plant closure occurred. Despite these setbacks, she and others feel more empowered and self-sustaining.

Jana saw much of her role as that of building a team to forward the problem solving, rather than just she and a few other colleagues taking up the challenge alone. This made her feel less burdened, and it also built in a comfort level, ensuring an inclusive, rather than exclusive, strategy. When it came to meeting with the local mayor, Jana did not attend. But she worked hard to be sure that her ideas were among those presented.

may claim much of the attention of elected officials. This is not to say that policy makers are not charged to some degree with, or concerned about, the responsibility for addressing human well-being. Nonetheless, if family and human well-being were the first priority, citizens would experience very different actions, investments, and priorities emanating from the world's governments (Gil, 1998a, 1998b).

Communities may only be as strong as their weakest link. This adage is a key reminder that if the needs of neighbors are ignored, or those with deep suffering are disregarded, their pain may be taken out on those they love and on others in the community. To take the extra step is to simultaneously invest in one's own well-being by caring about others. This win-win proposition makes it all the more compelling that more family advocates move into the policy-practice arena. Clearly, one can step out as Lev and John did in a leadership and spearheading role, or act and encourage others to take this role on while playing a supporting one.

The concept of teaming builds upon this. It derives in a sense from what it means to be a healthy family and community, and becomes one of the building blocks for developing an action system for change.

Teaming

A team is a group organized to accomplish a shared goal. When someone recruits and mobilizes others, this person is essentially teaming with them on shared agendas and visions. This teaming ability is one that is learned early in families, but often not practiced in the wider domain of citizen activism. Consequently, the skills that have been fostered are underdeveloped and underutilized, as is the sense of agency and efficacy. Citizen movements are being built to encourage individuals and families to team up. Once they do, they may use bartering systems to exchange care, skills, and talents in nonmonetary exchange networks, providing an alternative, or supplement, to the fee-for-goods-and-services, market economy (Cahn, 1997; Cahn & Rowe, 1992).

Each culture has terms and conditions about proper collective behavior and patriotic duty. Sometimes these are religiously determined, as are roles in the civic problem-solving sphere. In some cases there may be severe sanctions for speaking out and trying to solve certain kinds of problems. Severe recrimination and even life-threatening consequences may accompany some of the teaming activities. Thus when moving into policy-practice roles, one must weigh carefully the calculated risks to self, loved ones, and those others for whom one is advocating.

Yet there are families on the move, engaging in strategic social action. For example, some are demonstrating against TNCs. Others oppose religious oppression, or challenge dictators or other tyrannical governments. Still others are risking and losing their lives as they migrate in search of a better environment for their families.

Currently, there are some 26 million such families in throngs around the globe (Henderson, 1996). Many families are taking life-threatening risks. Others are dying (e.g., in Rwanda and Zaire). These escalating death rates are agonizing reminders of the need for funds in support of family-centered action and improvement strategies.

Similarly, protests have been mounted in Ecuador for more welfare support instead of an austerity campaign to ensure repayment on this nation's loans and national debt. These protests have been echoed in France, and strikes have been threatened. Women in Turkey have rallied and protested against governmental controls over their dress and work habits. Union members have resisted daily, around the globe, practices that result in structural unemployment and job loss (Shore, 1987). Throughout history, individuals and families have taken to the streets, the roads, the seas, and other byways of the planet to act on behalf of themselves and others when needs and rights are threatened. They form teams and act more effectively as teams.

Teaming often becomes something of a protection, as people find like-minded friends, neighbors, co-workers, and acquaintances who will make time to work on issues of concern. All over the world, groups of citizens, entire families, are participating in policy practice. They are working on improved housing, sanitation, jobs, transportation, health care, and social supports to assist other members of their communities (Naples, 1998). Some work through their religious association; others through work groups; still others as members of a neighborhood or other association (schools, family resource centers, sports clubs, civic or professional associations).

Box 8.1 provided one approach to change. Box 8.2 presents a different scenario. Here, one person's and family's pain is shared by others. Only through teaming are others gathered to share a new vision, implement action steps, and realize potential benefits.

Advocacy and Protection

Advocacy roles are well within the reach of family members. For example, parents advocate for their children. Children advocate for one her. Elders advocate for other elders and their families, crossing intergenerational lines. Sometimes advocacy centers on the needs of a person or family. The work of families has always involved advocacy for their members, or those like them. Sometimes advocacy expands to include others in similar circumstances (Andrae & Beckman, 1996).

Advocacy for others is a natural extension of what one does for one's own interest. This advocacy can take various forms. It can begin with a simple needs assessment (Dunst, Trivette, & Deal, 1994).

Ask others what it is they need to be more successful, what would make family life more effective and smoother, what might help individuals feel more supported or develop more effectively. Then information from such a needs assessment can be presented to interested leaders. Sometimes this information is generated from a simple set of questions; sometimes it is generated from an itemized list of needs and the consequences of unmet needs. However it is obtained, this information needs to be presented to other stakeholders, including the policy officials who are in position to address these needs. Stakeholders may also include others who will be negatively affected if positive change is not made.

Often the media will want to feature these findings and improvements, especially if they constitute a success story, a compelling human interest discovery. Often the individuals and families most in need are the ones whose voices are not heard (Alameda, 1996). Their lives involve the daily struggles of just trying to stay alive.

Similarly, families most in need may be embarrassed to plead their case because they are made to feel like they are the problem or that they are failures in some way. Feeling stigmatized, they are reluctant to expose their sense of "deviance" or "shortcomings." This unfortunate response to conditions that are often not of their own making serves to suppress the very information that advocates, practitioners, and policy makers need to be more responsive. It is often necessary to form a chain of advocates to assist and empower the families who evidence the most needs.

Most compelling for policy makers are the costs of nonaction (Bruner, 1997). For example, if 30 percent of young children die before the age of five because of preventable disease, then sanitation and medicine may be a less costly investment than the costs associated with preventable deaths, or with long and painful hospitalizations. The labor of public health workers, days lost from jobs to help a sick child, and the lack of a healthy workforce all involve costs that must be factored into the equation. The fact that children and their families remain unprotected and tragically neglected, when anti-dysentery and child-saving techniques abound worldwide, becomes a human rights issue. But to generate improved supports and resources may require a strategy giving the power to speak out to victims as well as those who worry that they too are at risk (Ife, 1995). See box 8.3 for a story that illustrates how a grassroots initiative has positive benefits.

MOBILIZING AND ACTING ON THE FINDINGS FROM FAMILY IMPACT ANALYSES

There are major gaps in policy, and families organize and mobilize to address them. In addition to these gaps, many policies are family insensitive,

---

A CIRCLE OF PARENTS

Yoko and Naoko are two mothers who have lost their children to dysentery. They meet weekly to document the needs and to strategize for ways that they could get help. They turned to the churches and governmental officials, especially in public health. Both groups were concerned that if needs were addressed only in this one community, it would not be fair. Other communities had similar needs. Neither the churches nor the government have money for a broad-based program.

The circle of parents learned about new measures to prevent dysentery, including improved sanitation. In their home community, they worked on some of these sanitation techniques and set their goal as no more children dying of dysentery. The circle then formed a help group to ensure that a family not having access to clean water had someone to turn to. They also sought special support from a church mission so that drugs that could help were made available. Once this had been accomplished, the circle charted the impact of their reforms and the benefits of these donated medicines.

Because of their success and the publicity it generated, the work started by this circle of parents became a family and community policy-practice project. Rather than having to perpetuate this work through their own volunteering and the assistance of the church mission, the

BOX 8.3

circle now sought to make it part of a regular regional public health initiative. This is the point where they found reluctance, and had to encourage policy makers to see the low costs and great benefits of such efforts.

After a year, only one child had died, compared to thirty in the previous year. Families are feeling empowered. The sense of grief, loss, and despair persisted. However, the families believed that they were turning their deep sorrows and pain into action.

Their goal becomes making these low-cost medicines and sterilization strategies a policy entitlement rather than a program organized by families themselves. To do this, help is sought from the church and from the public health officials. A meeting is convened with the local official whose election in part depends on support from many of the families affected. These families seek a three-year plan to phase in a village project, and if successful, to have it expanded to other villages in the region and then nationally. There is some concern raised at the meeting about the costs of going regional or nationwide.

As theirs is a poor nation, with most new resources going to interest on international loans, policy makers are rightly concerned about the commitment they are being asked to make. They agreed to a new education program, however, that would reach out and educate all families with children in school about how to sterilize water, prepare foods, and sanitize their homes and neighborhoods. An action committee appointed by the village leaders saw this development as a beginning step. They wanted more, however. They also needed and wanted medicines. Over a three-year period they worked to show the economic benefits. They used cost accounting, including days lost from work. They showed that the current costs of inaction were more costly than the medicines.

Employers then helped the village organization advance a strategy that would be endorsed by employers. Several times an employers' representative came to meetings to help with problem solving. Eventually, the families of the village were successful in their multifaceted work. They were able to reduce the high rates of child mortality.

i.e., they have been instituted without any regard for their impact on families. A critical policy skill is the ability to act on the findings from family impact analyses (see chapter 5). Ideally, all agencies and organizations would have the requirement that no new policy gets set in place that has a negative impact on families. Yet many do, and some are deliberate. When hurtful policies are in place, they require impact statements so that the negative aspects can be corrected. Currently, some Western industrialized nations such as the United States and the United Kingdom are engaging in a get-tough, anti-welfare, go-to-work approach to poor people, refugees, and immigrants (Jordan, 1998). Yet, as argued throughout this book, if there are not enough jobs, people's lives many not be better off. In fact, some costs will go up as the social, emotional, and health tolls increase. Tracing such impacts is essential for positive change to occur (Briar, 1988).

Some policies have an explicit family focus, and thus the impact analysis should be an obvious and routine expectation. Other policies have an implicit family impact, such as cutting off aid to people with serious disabilities or addictions. This also requires impact analyses. With such safeguards in place, it would be harder for policy makers to pass policy as expeditiously as they might like. Thus for some, impact analysis seems like a burdensome requirement.

Impact analysis is often a requisite before a decision is reached, before a law is enacted. Most often, to gauge impact, the proposed law or bill will need to be discussed and assessed at local levels with families of diverse backgrounds. Only in this way will the widest understanding of consequence be evident. While in many cases impacts are too difficult to gauge, key questions and concerns can be generated, serving as a new platform for action. Box 8.4 offers an example of how a grassroots group of concerned families initiated a needs assessment.

Consumers' Investments and Boycotts as Strategic Policy Change Tools

Consumer and investor boycotts have been effective through history. Consumers who mobilize as active agents in their purchase of—or refusals to purchase—products, goods, and services are powerful policy and practice change catalysts. Civil rights strategies in the United States and in South Africa are two visible examples. There are others.

Increasingly, globalized production involves the exploitation of labor-

BOX 8.4

ACTING ON THE FINDINGS FROM IMPACT ANALYSIS

In an urban community of an industrialized nation, a racetrack is being proposed for the west side of town. Families are not contacted about it because it is seen as revenue generating and as the work of the gambling commission. The racetrack is simply not seen as a family issue. Nonetheless, several families read about it in the newspaper and decide to meet. Roger knows that power is the ability to convene a group and to enfranchise one another to take action; he hosts a meeting at his home. Ten people come. They are concerned about racetrack activities interfering with children's safe access to schools, and recreational access to their one park. They are also concerned about the displacement of several blocks of homes, currently occupied by lower-income families, in order to build a portion of the track. Housing is expensive, and low-income families have difficulty finding adequate and affordable housing; this group is concerned that there will be more homelessness. Few, if any, of these issues were discussed in the planning of the racing track. Some perhaps even saw it as a good thing to limit homes in disrepair. After all, those charged with such responsibilities are not necessarily experts in family policy or in human development. They framed the racetrack as an economic venture devoid of potentially hurtful consequences to families in the area.

Roger's meeting reveals that grave concerns are shared. Some worry about the consequences of increased traffic flow into their neighborhoods, about the pollution and the noise. Others worry about displacement from their homes, with more than five blocks potentially affected. Still others are concerned that the racetrack divides them from their children's school so that in order to get to the school they will have to walk over the new highway. Some families believe that this may destroy not only their sense of community but the children's sense that the school is indeed family and neighborhood friendly. After-school and evening activities may all be constrained by the increased access barriers.

While some of these concerns may or may not be founded, the group decides to research what has happened with other racetracks in their country. They go to the chief policy maker's office and ask that a study committee be formed to examine the family and neighborhood costs and benefits of this proposed racetrack. While this proposal is initially met with some resistance, it becomes increasingly win-win for all to slow down the timetable and to reexamine, as well as to better predict, consequences. The racetrack commissioner and elected officials all agree to this study committee. The study committee also has a small travel fund so members can visit another racetrack to determine the family and neighborhood consequences and the various ways in which the negative impacts were mitigated or prevented.

What began as a felt concern among a few neighbors is now elevated to a commissioned committee study, a precursor to any formal decision making.

ers, especially women and children. This exploitation invites consumer advocacy and action to redress illegal, harmful practices and exploitation. Warranties can be required for products, ensuring that their production did not occur at the expense of sweatshop labor, especially that involving women and children. World consumer leagues may prove to be a pivotal stronghold in requiring more democratized and accountable corporate practices.[2] The growing student anti-sweatshop movement in the United States is a powerful example of how consumers can advance human and worker rights worldwide.

POLICY REVIEW AND CORRECTION PROCESS

The policy review and correction process is somewhat universal. Just as families make rules and policies and often change them later to accommodate different members' situations, so too must policy makers. Thus, the policy implementation and correction process offers a critical opportunity for families and citizen advocates to disclose unintended impacts and consequences. Sometimes a policy will go into effect with a clause attached requiring that once enacted, impacts need to be documented and the entire legislation reviewed in a year or two. Even when this clause is not attached, it is expected that there will be unforeseen consequences that require mediation. Sometimes at the outset of the policy deliberation process, even families cannot predict the impacts. But several years into the implementation process, their lived experiences are vital to the self-corrective responsibilities (Bruner, 1994). These responsibilities are too important to be left to policy makers alone. Furthermore, policy makers may have moved on to other agendas. This is a family-dependent and practitioner-based feedback loop.

Data-Driven Policy Practice

Most of the cases cited in this chapter, like the cases in previous chapters, signal a clear pattern. Many policies are reactive and crisis oriented, not proactive and preventive. No matter how hard people try, families will not receive all that they need and want until they are viewed as worthy social investments (e.g., Midgley, 1997, 1999). When they are viewed as social investments, policies may become more proactive and preventive (Gil, 1998a, 1998b).

Sometimes it is hard, even impossible, to grasp all the dimensions of a challenge. A crisis may erupt, such as the preventable death of a child or elder, and the community will organize to address this death, not realizing that many more have died of the same tragic, preventable conditions. Gaining access to the dimensions of a problem takes on a power of its own. Data can become important for mobilizing the media and organizing others to care. Rather than seeing the incident as an isolated tragedy, others may begin to see that it is indicative of a need or pattern. In instances like these, the data sometimes speak for themselves and thus compel the need for systems change. As offered in the scenario above, the data gathered on the number of children dying of dysentery helped to mobilize the churches and the employers in the area.

Family-supportive and family-centered policies and practices may be facilitated by appropriately designed data sets and systems (Adams & Nelson, 1995). For example, family and gender counts would result in even more deliberate actions and activities by all community stakeholders and eventually by policy makers. The following are some examples of what might be helpful family and gender count data.

A Check List

Identify and assess the condition of the number of families who

- are poor;
- are without sanitation or decent housing;

- experience violence (spouse, child, or elder abuse);
- face environmental hazards—toxic wastes, lead paint, etc.;
- are without transportation;
- suffer because of insufficient medical care or without immunizations for their members;
- lack enough food, in which one or more members are hungry part of the time;
- are challenged by unwanted, unplanned pregnancies;
- lack access to prenatal care;
- have HIV-positive or AIDS-infected members;
- have experienced the death of a child or a mother during the birth process; and
- have low-birth-weight babies.

For gender-related needs, the data might include the number of hours devoted to

- cleaning;
- caregiving in the home, employment outside the home;
- purchasing, mending, and cleaning clothing;
- meal preparation and food gathering;
- household maintenance tasks;
- furnishing the home;
- transporting oneself and others, including commuting to work outside the home;
- discretionary time to relax and rest; and
- sleeping.

These lists help to reveal differences in the level of analysis and, in turn, the policy-practice strategies that are needed when the entire family, or gendered roles in the family, is the focus. In other words, focusing on children, a benefit in one sense, also is a problem. The focus on children deflects attention away from others in the family and from entire families. Multiple, family-related "counts" are needed. In addition to "Kids Count," leaders need "Families Count" and "Elders Count" and "Women Count" indexes and impact analyses.

Asset Mapping

Part of family advocacy also involves mapping assets. As the scenario involving Yoko and Naoko evolved, depicting their advocacy to acquire medicines, they found that they had to turn to churches, the media, and even their employers to get help. Naoko and Yoko arrived at these out-reach ideas because they had done an asset map. Asset mapping is look-ing at all the resources within one's family and action team, as well as those in the wider community that can be tapped, deputized, or con-verted to be part of the solution (Kretzmann & McKnight, 1993).

LOOKING AHEAD: TOWARD NEW POLICY-PRACTICE SKILLS FOR HELPING PROFESSIONALS

This discussion of policy-practice skills continues in the next chapter. Because change often requires collaboration among all the stakeholders —helping professionals, policy makers, advocates, and other citizens— the next chapter addresses some of the strategies and roles for bringing together everyday citizens as family advocates to team with profession-als. Many citizen advocates and families help to inspire practitioners to move beyond their job descriptions and to advance more proactive poli-cies and practices for families (Naples, 1998). Thus, helping profession-als need additional policy-practice skills. These other skills are exam-ined in the next chapter, and they are framed against the backdrop of democracies.

NOTES

1. As Hal Lawson (personal communication, February 2000) observes, Durkheim wrote with an optimistic eye toward the possibilities for spe-cialized professions and occupations in the division of labor. He did not see specialization as the opposite of progress. On the other hand, Durkheim's overall work was functionalist—preserving of the status quo. Clearly, this is not the position of the authors. Thus, organic solidar-ity is being imported from Durkheim in service of family-centered policy practice.
2. See, for example, Students Against Sweatshops and World Child Labor (http://home.sprintmail.com/~jeffnkari/USAS/; http://www.umich.edu/~sole/usas/about/index.html; gcough@uniteunion.org).

CHAPTER 9

Promoting New Alliances Among Families, Family Advocates, and Helping Professionals

Katharine Briar-Lawson

This chapter builds on some of the action strategies and policy-practice skills that were identified in the previous chapter. The aim of this chapter is to encourage and offer support for family-centered helping professionals who take risks on behalf of families (Hartman & Laird, 1983; Zlotnik, 1998). These family-centered professionals are special leaders. They are innovators and advocates. They refuse to be limited by their job descriptions and formal roles, and they often stretch their responsibilities in response to family needs. As they do, they pioneer new policy practices. Through their efforts and achievements they change organizational structures, cultures, and policies (Haynes & Mickelson, 1999).

Because they work with families and because their effectiveness depends on them, helping professionals are the natural allies for families and family advocates. When they form effective alliances, they become the most likely source of energy and expertise for reform (e.g., Family Resource Coalition, 1990, 1995). This chapter builds on chapter 8, by providing additional policy-practice skills. To put it another way, it provides some "tips and tools" and practice guidelines for family-centered helping professionals. These tips, tools, and practice guidelines are framed in response to questions like the following: How can professionals work on behalf of families? How can professionals escape some of the limitations of their job descriptions, stepping forward and working to strengthen families? How can professionals ally with families to better work to provide them with the types of services, resources, and supports they require so they can flourish?

PROFESSIONALS AS POLICY-PRACTICE PIONEERS

Professionals, like families, can become grassroots policy pioneers (Jansson, 1998). Because they operate from organizational and institutional power and resource bases that are very different from those of families, professionals are able to mobilize resources that families themselves would not be able to access. On the other hand, some practitioners may fear reprisals because of rigid bureaucratic mandates and accompanying supervisory/accountability structures. Policy-practice learning and continual quality improvement structures and organizations, described in chapter 5, foster some of the alliances and innovations described here.

Many of the change strategies discussed next build upon those discussed in the preceding chapter. They are as critical to families themselves as they are to frontline practitioners. These practitioner-based change strategies, combined with the work of family advocates who serve as grassroots policy practitioners, can maximize the effectiveness of community level policy reform (Naples, 1998). Many change strategies are culturally conditioned; they must be adapted to local norms, customs, and practices (Barroso, 1994; Ife, 1995).

Practitioners, like families, can have a change repertoire that is vast and untapped. Most practitioners are not expected to be change agents. Their job descriptions may lack expectations for creating change. Nonetheless, many reforms begin with family advocates and frontline practitioners who are the closest to, and most knowledgeable about, unmet needs. Once these two are allied, they can advance practice missions for change.

AGENDA SETTING IN FRONTLINE PRACTICE: CHANGING THE FRAMES AND THE NAMES

Practitioners can begin their advocacy by reframing individual issues and needs in family terms. To return to a key principle, the discourse needs to change. It must become more family centered (Adams & Nelson, 1995). Thus, professionals might start by introducing themselves and their commitments to persons they are serving in the following way.

There may be others who also understand your circumstances and can give a good perspective on it. It is important to understand their perspectives and roles so that solutions that are devised are the most helpful and build from the supports you already have. Whether it is immediate family members or friends who function like family, it is possible that when we see your situation from everyone's standpoint, we may be able to be more helpful in the solutions that are designed. Moreover, because those close to you may also share your concerns or also be affected, we all may benefit from their ideas about the best way to proceed.

An introduction like this allows the individual and his or her challenges to be addressed from a "family systems" context. Solutions and changes also need to take this family system into account so that it can be used and built on as a resource, rather than supplanted (Hartman & Laird, 1983). Thus, a teacher may reframe a child's absence from school differently. Instead of viewing the child's absence as a family deficit, this teacher views it as a sign of family need for support, resource, and services (Briar-Lawson, Alameda, & Lawson, 1997). This teacher can then hold back with any problem solving until the solutions can be crafted with families as expert partners (Apple, Berstein, et al., 1997).

Practitioners are increasingly learning that, when they have findings from home visits, from families' definition of the problems, needs, barriers, and solutions, their practice is sharply improved (Lawson & Briar-Lawson, 1997). Home visits provide experiences that develop more ecologically based understanding and empathy. Practitioners also gain more data, which they can use to improve their practice. The data and perspectives that come from home-based family interviews, including seeing and experiencing the ecology of the individual and family, may create immediate shortcuts—and remedy flawed approaches.

Deferring to the views of the family and redefining the individual's needs in family systems terms provides other benefits as well (Wilcox, Smith, et al., 1991). This process allows for better understanding of family strengths, needs, and capacity (Kinney, Strand, et al., 1994). Such perspective building also provides a more sound basis to determine the barriers and facilitators to promoting various courses of action. For example, if a nurse learns that an elder's isolation from services is worsened by the overwhelmed adult child's struggle to keep two jobs, then she may build family supports rather than blame and punish the adult child. Or, if a teacher learns that a family's child care barriers keep her student from attending school, she may see the issue as the absence of a child care service, rather than a child or parent's poor attitude toward school. Because of this, she may be more likely to help find some child care supports. She may even advocate for a new child care center in the school, a center that enables her student to attend.

While family-centered practices are not always the preferred method of problem solving (especially when abuse has occurred and members are at risk of reprisals from the abuser), they may offer an expanded set of family-based solutions. As professionals become more involved in the lives of families, family members may diminish their roles and even abdicate the good work that could be done (Kretzmann & McKnight, 1993). They may feel that professionals know best; they may be relieved to have others do the work; and they may learn very quickly that they are either not valued or even blamed in the course of the nonfamily-oriented problem solving.

Many professions were created with the goal of lightening the load, if not replacing the functions of families. Family "relieving work" has inadvertently become family supplanting (McKnight, 1995, 1997; Kretzmann & McKnight, 1993). Box 9.1 offers an illustration of capacity building, rather than family supplanting.

The scenario in box 9.1 shows how justice professionals can redefine adolescent issues in family terms. Once reengaged as helpers for their sons, the families redouble their efforts to interest them in a plan that includes "perfect" school attendance and after-school plans. Feeling support from the detention center, these families are now able to work with a probation officer who will do follow-up with the youths. These youth, in essence, are on "school probation," but they are not on the traditional, youth-centered probation plan. This new plan is expanded to include the parents (Wilcox, Smith, et al., 1991). Their role in promoting access to work for their sons is emphasized. In this way, parents can assist their sons with learning more about business practices, hard work, and responsibility, while helping them reap the positive consequences if their school attendance and performance improve. This is a new strategy for the detention center and the probation officer.

In this example, none of the policies for the justice agency necessarily call for this family-centered practice. The officials involved are being held accountable only for the offenses and recidivism of these youth. Nonetheless, as an effectiveness tool, family mobilization offers more problem-solving options for what might otherwise be more narrow, "offense-specific" interventions (Wilcox, Smith, et al., 1991).

To continue with this example: Back at the station with other police officers, Ron finds that there is not much support for this more

FAMILY CAPACITY BUILDING

BOX 9.1

Ron is a local police officer. He encounters five youth who are known for vagrancy, theft, and truancy from school. He detains them, placing them in a detention facility. Here they are removed from the streets, have good food, and a bed. While relocated off the streets, these youth nonetheless are skidding one step further into the criminal justice system. It is here at the detention facility that they learn more skills for a life of crime and also are introduced to new kinds of drugs.

Their parents had been talking and trying to devise plans to help move these youth into more productive roles involving the sale of family-farm crops and other goods. These work roles and the wages earned were to be used as rewards for the youth returning to school. Now that the youth have been placed in a detention facility, they are all the more adrift from their family support strategies. They nonetheless will have another chance because of a teacher at the detention center, Elena, who works valiantly to reconnect youth with their family supports. She learns that in this case, each of these five young people wants to finish school and to have a good-paying job. Even though lured by the drugs and "easy" money others talk about in the detention facility, they are still amenable to the supports from their parents and from her.

Elena in turn has elicited the support of a social work supervisor who agrees that it is a good idea to bring the parents to the detention center for a meeting to plan more intensive supports for them and for their adolescent sons. Here the focus is on supporting the parents so that they can become more involved in the "rehabilitation" of their adolescent sons. By this time, however, two parents were very angry and wanted to have nothing to do with their sons. They were feeling like failures and were prepared to redirect their attention to their other children.

Once reconnected to the other parents and the hopeful and supportive teacher and social worker, they too agreed to give it another chance.

comprehensive practice. For the probation and the detention center staff to become family inclusive or family centered in its practices and policies, there would have to be a major shift in policies and programming. Thus, Ron, Elena, and the social worker present their work at a case staffing. They argue that family-centered practices may be expanded ways to address offenses and recidivism. Further, they argue that the offenses of the youth are symptoms of issues that lie deeper in their impoverished and job-poor communities. These have to do with hopelessness, beliefs that school will not lead anywhere, and the absence of rewarding job opportunities (Watts, 1984). The idea that these youth in cooperation with their parents might create their own microenterprise, and have this be contingent on school attendance, allows for a more strengths-based intervention strategy that simultaneously addresses some of the related problems. In the United States, there is a growing research base that supports this family-centered practice (e.g., Kumpfer, 1999; Adams & Nelson, 1995).

This case staffing encourages several others among the police and detention facility to consider doing more family-centered work. It is agreed that a team will continue to test this strategy and meet weekly to discuss progress. They will report on their success three months later. At that time several families co-present their experiences. Once reviewed, the director of the detention center and the police chief agree that expanded policies for more family-centered practice might be adopted, if only on a trial basis.

POLICY ASSESSMENT

Practitioners can advance a form of policy assessment, which reframes the needs of the individual and family in policy terms. For example, consider the Ghotos family. They lack electricity and water. They have three children with severe malnutrition. A teacher visits their village and seeks to encourage the children back into school, but the barriers are enormous. Rather than seeing the children as simply needing educational intervention, the teacher sees the barriers to their schooling as policy issues.

Refusing to be part of the "cover-up" of these needs, she determines that all services that might have been available were provided. Then she forms a work group of other teachers who believe that more should be done with the children and families they serve so that their basic needs are met. This leads to a meeting with policy makers who hear the detailed stories of need and also receive a report, an impact statement, on the consequences of children's arrested education. As a result, these policy makers make a tentative pledge to do more about poverty in the village and to advocate more aggressively for income supports so that families can thrive. Teachers pledge to monitor the outcomes of these policy promises; they see themselves as the vital link between the children and families and the policy responsiveness in the nation's capital.

Such policy practice on the part of the teachers is strategic. They realize that they could do all the home visits that were required, but if the essential needs of children and families are not addressed, neither they nor the children and families will be successful in achieving the educational goals to which all had subscribed. Stepping out like this, going beyond one's job description to address related issues, to advocate for more policy responsiveness, is in part what it means to be an effective practitioner (Ife, 1995).

Some of the skills that these teachers employ are familiar ones. They involve framing, naming, and reframing and renaming. These teachers in essence reframe the schooling issue as service, support, and resource issues for both children and their families (Briar-Lawson, Alameda, & Lawson, 1997).

In turn, they take this policy-practice tool to policy makers who could address and prevent situations like this (Jansson, 1998). In the course of their work, they also generate public concern about the families who are too poor and resource-needy to send their children to school. They offer to provide in-home schooling in the form of teacher aides who take tools and materials to the families and the children. They view outreach to these children and families as a temporary solution.

These teachers have learned that they are early-warning systems for children, their families, and even communities at risk (Van Veen, Day, & Walraven, 1998). They also have learned that their job descriptions have expanded. More than simply teaching a group of students—as important as this is—their jobs have expanded to include advocacy and outreach, as well as innovative in-home schooling strategies. Had the policy makers chosen not to act, they as teachers would have had to devise some other method to advance their policy agenda.

HOLDING A PRESS CONFERENCE

In a community in an industrialized nation, three social workers discovered serious problems involving child labor. They saw repeated signs of employer abuses of children. Children were hired to do heavy machinery work. They were forced to work long hours. Ultimately, one was injured. The social workers discover that child labor is extensive in this community.

At the local hospital the medical social worker interviewed the injured child. She learned about the child labor practices, and evidenced the consequences of the child labor violations. She and several other social workers formed a tracking group to estimate how many child labor violations they had seen in the last six months. They then gathered a wider group of professionals and citizens around the issue of child labor. This also included the local ecumenical church council.

In the first meetings they determined that the public needed and had a right to know that these abuses were ongoing. They also contacted the public officials whose job it was to oversee child labor and child labor violations. Determining that there were loopholes in current laws, these social workers and the broadened group of advocates decided to issue a press release and to hold a press conference. At the press conference they planned to kick off a year-long child labor protection campaign. They wanted to influence politicians and to stimulate new legislation, which would prevent some of the causalities and crises that they had been seeing (United Nations, 1995c).

To develop their press release, they issued a short statement about some of the problems that they were seeing and the fact that a campaign would be launched. In their press release they specified the day and time for the press conference at which they would unveil their plan of action. They made sure that they had press coverage by personally contacting the print and electronic media representatives so that the reporters who covered human interest stories and school services and employment would be deployed to cover their press conference.

By this time, other associations and professionals had joined in; police, nurses, teachers, student groups, and labor unions were also assisting with the campaign. The press conference was kicked off by the local mayor. The mayor had agreed to give more leadership to the issues, now that they were presented to him. He also had his aides gather data to assist in estimating the numbers of children working below child labor standards. At the press conference, a leader of a local manufacturing group spoke, saying that these infractions would stop. This representative believed that infractions would stop voluntarily and that new enforcement or legislation was not needed. The press conference also became a work session in which subcommittees formed around action agendas to address several facets of the problem.

Rather than the group splitting up, into those who believed legislation was needed and those who believed voluntary compliance was sufficient, the group decided to pursue as many strategies as possible. They sought to keep a win-win approach to the agenda so that the group would not break down into warring factions. They realized that the group would work better if everyone kept their focus on their vision: that no children be exploited in labor situations. They recognized there were many ways to address the goal. Being as inclusive as possible allowed for many different approaches to be seen as potential options in a trial-and-error process. The group also rotated leadership so that as many volunteers as possible acquired new skills, a sense of efficacy, and opportunities to develop themselves while working on behalf of children and their families. In their efforts to be more than child centered, the group reached out to families and saw child labor violations as symptomatic of deeper issues, especially those challenging families with marginal incomes. They turned to the employer community to find ways to increase jobs for adults through shorter workweeks, eliminating the use of overtime, and other mechanisms. They also worked to ensure that other labor violations did not persist, such as punishment for union organizing.

Seeking Media Coverage for an Issue

There are many ways to get media coverage for issues. When topics appear newsworthy, they may generate sufficient media contacts and interest. In this case, little outreach is necessary. Because there are so many competing issues, however, family advocates and practitioners may seek multiple ways to ensure that there is (continuing) media coverage, especially if they believe that the public has a right to know about an emerging situation or development. As discussed earlier, practitioners and advocates will often invite the media to meetings. Or all along they may seek press coverage by launching a campaign for action. If a report or study is completed, it can be shared with the media. It is also sound practice to seek an appointment with the editors of electronic and print media. In this way an issue can be positioned to be a media concern. Asking the media to address a problem themselves, such as tips and tools on how to parent or where to turn for school scholarships, becomes a form of advocacy that requires media commitment to an agenda beyond assessments of whether it is newsworthy.

Responding to an issue that already has enjoyed some coverage, or choosing to write to question the lack of coverage on an issue, helps bring it to light and to give it more public airing than it might have had. Sometimes, especially when issues become high profile, there many be a flurry of letters to the editor. The collective impact of many such letters can powerfully influence policy makers (Jansson, 1998).

Letters to the Editor, Guest Editorials, Circulating Our Own Writing, Using the Internet

There are many ways to both share ideas and mobilize others to join in a cause. In more democratized countries, there is access to newspapers through letters to the editor, where one voices concerns. These are generally short pieces that may be edited for length and even content. While these letters may not generate action, they at least begin to create discourse and connections among others who may share in a cause. Published letters are often read by policy makers and their staff. Those letters that cite data may exert a powerful impact, especially when referencing formal research, which may be of the public discourse.

When writing a letter to the editor, advocates and practitioners are essentially stating a position on an issue, along with the reasons for that position. Justifications are important, but not enough. Action strategies need to be included, especially the actions that should be taken and ones that should not be used.

Guest editorials are longer. These editorials may explain an agenda, need, opportunity, or plan, providing richer detail. Writing editorials that give the human side (of families suffering, communities in need, a personal experience), helps readers personalize the issue and even envision the people behind the story.

Some guest editorials are invited by publishers. Or a person may call or visit the newspaper editor or write a letter describing the guest editorial and how the topic might be treated. This kind of writing has multiple uses. The same content may also be used for a policy brief, or as an organizing (slate) plan that can be used at a press conference.

Mahatma Gandhi, the famous leader from India, was an exemplar in communicating ideas through "fliers" and routine publications that could give up-to-date information about local needs and solutions. Many action groups use newsletters to keep collaborators informed, to report their discoveries and action steps. Now the electronic superhighway, such as the Internet, makes it possible to communicate and organize among those with shared commitments, concerns, and passions (Johnson, 1999; Schwartz, 1996; Yaffe, 1998).

PETITIONING

A petition may be useful to get an issue before voters or policy makers. Here is an example of the use of petitions.

A drive is under way to increase the sales tax by 0.5 percent so that teachers, child welfare workers, and public health nurses will have more funds for children and family issues. To get the initiative on the ballot for the next election, the organizers must get a certain percentage of voters to sign a petition. The organizers have three months to collect signatures and to ensure that they have public support. Going to places where people gather becomes the joint strategy of citizens and practitioners. Shopping malls, movie houses, pubs, and sporting events are the most popular places to collect signatures. Some people stand on street corners and ask for signatures as well.

Getting the initiative on the ballot is just half the job. Finding popular support for what could be a very fragile initiative is the next step. Worried that businesses are likely to fight this initiative, it is decided that a business task force should be working with and educating the business sector. The organizers map out all the sectors of the community so that the pockets of resistance can be identified—for example, other special interest groups and those against any type of tax increase. Each group that might be in opposition can then be seen as a target for mobilization. Having a large and diverse enough network of supporters is seen as critical, as they may be able to take on the organizing of these various sectors and neutralize others that might become a problem.

DEVELOPING A POLICY BRIEF ON THE COSTS OF FAILURE AND THE BENEFITS OF SOCIAL INVESTMENTS

Much of the process of change, especially involving family supports, goes beyond person-to-person organizing. It also is critical that the costs and benefits of proposed actions are documented (Bruner, 1997; Ife, 1995; Midgley, 1997, 1999). Policy briefs can include action agendas as well as impact statements, which assess the costs of doing nothing, the costs of failure, and benefits of action.

Adding up the costs versus the benefits may make the initiative seem not only like the right next move, but also less costly. Drawing a trend line that reflects current fiscal and human costs as well as projections in the future may also move others to action.

For example, a group of community residents seeks to have all children and elders immunized so that no more will die of diphtheria, flu, and other preventable disease. The costs of the immunization are, they think, relatively similar to the costs of hospital care. These residents, along with a group of public health nurses, school teachers, and a team of parents whose children and elders had long-term diseases, such as polio, gathered to look at the costs and benefits and to place their assessment before their elected officials (Bruner, 1997).

These teams expanded to several communities so that this issue was seen as a multicommunity event rather than an isolated, local concern. Public health nurses and teachers gathered the families of children and elders. They helped to document the long-term health care costs; the number of days the children were out of school or elders were in the hospital; and the hours of employment missed by adults due to caregiving.

This group picked the high-cost infections that would "tell the story for them." Using examples of the children and elders themselves as well as the cost analysis, the group delineated that the cost of immunizations would be less than the cost of the days in hospital and absenteeism from work. In several cases, children and elders had died; their stories were also gathered and recorded. The cost analysis, examples, and stories were then taken to the elected officials as well as to administrators in the public health and educational systems. More funds for immunizations were included when the national budgets were developed. Several newspaper articles also covered the story, highlighting the human side of costs, including the deaths that had occurred.

RECRUITING INDIVIDUALS, FAMILIES, AND GROUPS EXPERIENCING THE SAME CHALLENGES AND NEEDS

Most practitioners are in prime positions to help mobilize others, especially families, who have been affected by the same challenges, barriers, and needs (Adams & Nelson, 1995). All too often they are not supported in their organizing, which is seen as a threat to systems seeking control among frontline staff. Thus many self-help groups grow out of rage, shame, and a sense of violated rights; frustration is turned into collective action (Grace Hill, 1995; Natoli, 1997).

Parents of children murdered and mothers against drunk driving are just two of the examples. Victims and supporters find each other and seek media coverage so that others can be recruited and their story told. This is done in the hope of preventing others from suffering. They also watch the newspapers and related media for public interest stories or news coverage as a way to identify and recruit others into their cause. Many practitioners gather the members of groups who share the same concerns. If their job descriptions do not allow them to do the gathering of their "clients, patients, parents of students," they can send out fliers or otherwise inform people by word of mouth of the existence of a support group or an action being undertaken. They can do this as private citizens if not as helping professionals.

For example, Jane is a welfare worker who is aware of the number of teen mothers on her "caseload." In her community there is a big push to deny young mothers income benefits and to encourage them to stay in school. Jane knows that many teen moms have had problems in school. Many have low grades. Many have had abusive experiences in their families and with their partners. Many see motherhood as a career, i.e., as the only available role for themselves and a "way out." At the same time, their child's father may view drug dealing as the only way to make enough money.

Jane is aware of the formation of an action group of teen mothers. This action group is fighting income reductions. The group members also hope to expose the reasons behind their pregnancies. They intend to show that dropping benefits will hurt them and their babies. For example, their children may have to be placed in foster care. This movement of teen mothers falls outside of the job descriptions of Jane and her co-workers. But Jane and her co-workers help to distribute the fliers about the meeting. They also go to the meeting, after work hours, as citizen advocates to play a supportive role. They are able to give advice about how to gain access to some of the policy makers that ought to be hearing from these young women directly.

USING PUBLIC FORUMS AND CONFERENCES TO FEATURE CONCERNS AND PROMOTE EFFECTIVE ACTION

The appeal to the public and to policy makers for change can often be fostered through the use of a public forum, such as a conference. This may enable many who have perspectives on a problem to share findings from their work as well as design even more strategic approaches (United Nations, 1995e). The exchange of ideas among persons who share similar commitments and interest creates new reinforcers for their work. Having the press cover the conference and feature several of the findings also helps to alert the public and policy makers that issues are being analyzed and even potentially addressed. Asking public officials who are otherwise inaccessible to be lead speakers on panels, where they can learn about the key issues from others, helps to educate and influence them.

ISSUE TRACKING

Corporations and, increasingly, public officials engage in what is called issue tracking. This involves the scanning of the external environment to determine the extent to which issues may become policy concerns of the public and private sector. Issue tracking becomes a form of early-warning system, alerting potential stakeholders that there are trends and concerns requiring action in the public and private sector. Issue tracking is also a tool for practitioners and citizen advocates. It becomes the basis for getting attention as trend lines are drawn and the implications of inaction are mapped (United Nations, 1995e).

PRIVATE SECTOR POLICY MAKING

Professionals working for corporations, such as social workers, psychologists, dietitians, health professionals, family support staff, personnel managers, or attorneys, may be called upon to initiate new codes of conduct, new ways of doing business, to promote new approaches to holistic employee health and wellness. Increasingly in the industrialized nations, many of these practitioners have had to show that what is good for the employee is also good for the employer by linking proposals for change to the bottom line, that is, profits.

Thus, *family advocacy needs are not merely public sector issues. Family advocacy must target the private sector as well* (United Nations, 1993d). Private sector policies regarding the health and well-being of workers, their families, and their communities are key to policy practice and family advocacy. Those who work within corporate and labor policy-making environments can mobilize to advance improved outcomes for families and their members (Schön, 1983).

Sometimes this work will involve direct support for the policies of a union or a professional organization. In other cases, it will involve the creation of a program or service, such as a child or elder care center at the workplace (United Nations, 1993d). Sometimes impact statements on the harms caused by practices such as excessive or irregular work hours may be tools for change inside the business, corporation, or union (United Nations, 1993d).

TESTIFYING

Every day individuals take positions on issues that concern them. In essence, when they take a position, they are testifying. They testify before colleagues, friends, and family. They develop discourses intended to persuade others.

Of course, the formal process of testifying involves making presentations before a group of elected officials. Testifying necessitates developing formal, logical arguments. It means using data for advocacy. Upon closer inspection, testifying involves developing and telling a compelling story, one that is persuasive because of the data it emphasizes, the needs it identifies, and the successes that it communicates.

People often testify for several reasons. Two reasons are especially important.

The first is to attempt to influence the decision about a policy proposal, a legislative item, a budget, or a perceived policy shortcoming. The second reason is to gain wider public interest and support for a position so that testimony also functions as a communications strategy to reach the broader public. This works because the media often keeps track of testimony and selectively seeks more in-depth perspectives. As the media converges on an issue, it may take on more momentum as others become involved and interested. There may be letters to the editor or featured guest editorials about the issue. Radio and television stations may also provide editorials. And commonly, shortwave radio broadcasts focus on specific topics or are addressed to specific interest groups.

For those who cannot testify but want to be heard, there are numerous ways to reach elected officials. Elected officials often find it remarkable that so little interest is generated about issues. Officials are often left to formulate their own positions, often following the position of political parties they represent or the lobbyists who petition them. Personal contacts, letters, phone calls, and e-mails on opinions and actions send a message about how important a concern is, or how controversial the official's own position is (Schwartz, 1996).

SEEKING LEGAL ACTION

When human and family rights and needs go unaddressed by elected officials, and when they are in violation of their own laws, or with nationally ratified laws, then court action may be required. Usually the courts are used when all other means have been exhausted or when they appear to be the most direct route to rectifying a situation. Sometimes activists will seek a legal injunction to stop an action, such as the termination of benefits. Tribunals in many nations also address and monitor possible violations not just of national laws but international ones. For example, these may involve international human rights ratified by the nation (Rights & Humanity, 1987).

SUMMARIZING FAMILY-CENTERED POLICY-PRACTICE SKILLS AND ABILITIES

The following list of skills serves as an introductory policy-practice inventory. It is suggestive of the kinds of change agent roles that can accompany family-centered practice.

Agenda Setting and Analysis

- Naming and framing
- Reframing and promoting new discourses
- Creating public concern (kid counts, family counts, and elder counts)
- Promoting and using family impact analyses
- Calling for a study committee
- Developing a policy brief with cost-of-failure, benefit-of-success data, along with expenditure shift strategies

Appealing to the Public

- Holding a press conference
- Issuing a press release

- Writing letters to editor, op-ed columns
- Developing relations with the media: e.g., seeking media coverage for an issue, an action step, a conference

Mobilizing People for Collective Action

- "Deputizing" and mobilizing others for action
- Using the Internet to persuade, organize, and mobilize others
- Promoting shared leadership among as many individuals and families as possible to build a movement
- Working with local organizations to mobilize them and the families they represent

Developing an Action System

- Convening a problem-solving group
- Convening a collaborative team, or several teams
- Building innovative coalitions and alliances
- Developing interagency working agreements, interpersonal working agreements (contracts)
- Turning a work or a task group into a problem-solving and policy-oriented change group

Collective Advocacy with Public Officials and the General Public

- Testifying before governmental officials and private sector leaders
- Holding a conference
- Meeting with representatives of various levels of a hierarchy to put them on notice regarding an issue, ways they can help, what should change
- Proposing a legislative initiative
- Lobbying

Grassroots Change in Laws

- Knowing human rights and using this knowledge to frame needs as legal issues
- Initiating legal action to address rights violations and needs related to family well-being

SUMMARY: A NEW KIND OF PROFESSIONAL

A new vision for a different kind of professional is implied in the preceding discussion and previous chapter. This is a vision for a social trustee/ civic professional (Lawson, 2000). The roles of citizen and professional are inseparable in this vision. This new professional builds social trust networks and, in turn, is trusted by individuals and families. This new professional knows the value of citizen engagement and civil society.

Service, support, and resource strategies are developed for other citizens; power and authority differences are minimized. Democratic relationships are prized. For the social trustee/civic professional, the needs, wants, and well-being of families are the center of their work. These new professionals model a "whatever it takes" attitude. They eschew self-serving specialization and emphasize multiple forms of collaboration, especially family-centered collaboration. They are uncompromising and relentless advocates for the persons they serve, and their strategies are grounded in the new realities and challenges associated with globalization, which are identified in the next two chapters. These new-century helping professionals are family-centered policy practitioners.

CHAPTER 10

Introducing Globalization's Challenges and Opportunities and Analyzing Economic Globalization and Liberalization

Hal A. Lawson

A great transformation in human history is under way. The industrial age is giving way to a global age. *Globalization* is a relatively new concept, and it is used with increasing frequency to describe this transformation. Although some consensus has developed about this transformation and the process of globalization, diverse perspectives remain. Analysts everywhere continue to wrestle with globalization's defining features, correlates, influences, and effects. Little wonder: Globalization is a multifaceted, comprehensive process. It poses the ultimate, interdisciplinary challenge, and its challenges for family-centered policies and practices are even more formidable.

Globalization's analysts must cross disciplinary boundaries. In addition, they must describe and explain globalization and this historic transformation at the same time they experience them. Each analyst brings a particular standpoint, or scholarly gaze. Each gaze reflects the influences of a discipline, gender, national identity, cultural affiliation(s), and ideology. Place, time, context, and recent events influence every analysis. Selectivity and silence are inevitable and unavoidable.

Nevertheless, family-centered policy makers, helping professionals, and citizen advocates confront ever-increasing needs to understand globalization's challenges and opportunities, especially as they pertain to the well-being of individuals and families. Social and economic development agendas at all levels of government must take into account globalization's multiple influences. Development planners, policy makers, helping professionals, and advocates must facilitate effective and appropriate responses to its social welfare challenges and opportunities. New conceptual frameworks for innovative, effective, and appropriate policies and practices are needed, and they must focus on improvements in the well-being of individuals and families. For example, in these new frameworks, issues involving well-being are inseparable from others involving species survival, national and international social justice, individual and family rights, and environmental protection.

Globalization and its companion processes, opportunities, and challenges illuminate the limitations of the nation-state (and nationalism). Paradoxically, they also signal new-century, social welfare opportunities for nation-states, regional alliances among them, and international governing bodies. Foremost among these social welfare opportunities are ones related to family-centered policies and practices. Complexity, novelty, uncertainty, and stress are ever present. Schön's (1971) forecast, with its double meanings, is appropriate: *The global age means the end of the stable state.* National governments lose stability, and perhaps some of their legitimacy, at the same time that surrounding national and international contexts are destabilized. With the loss of the stable state, there is a growing need for local, national, regional, and international systems that offer rapid responses, effective learning, adaptability, and continual improvement. These systems span several levels, including individual, group, organizational, societal, and international. Each level is influenced by the others.

Bold claims like these derive from a particular standpoint in relation to globalization, the great transformation it promotes, and the threats and opportunities it poses for family-centered policy makers, helping professionals, and advocates. The aim of this chapter is to share this standpoint. The focus is on globalization, together with its companion processes and some of their consequences for families, along with policies and practices in support of them. Six basic questions structure the ensuing analysis:

- What exactly is globalization, and what causes it?
- What analytical tools are needed to analyze it?
- What influences and effects does it have, and where would one look for them?
- Will globalization result in a standardized, homogenized, and uniform world, or does it increase the degree and kind of diversity?
- Are individuals, families, groups, organizations, communities, nations, regional alliances, and international governing bodies powerless as they confront globalization?

• How might policy makers, helping professionals, and advocates frame new-century policy and practice agendas in response to globalization's challenges and opportunities?

Each question merits a separate chapter and collectively an entire book. This chapter and the one that follows merely explore the questions. Both chapters are framed by relational analysis. Together, these two chapters illustrate globalization's complexity.

Both chapters introduce an enormous range of new ideas. Relationships among these ideas are highlighted. Emergent national and international patterns are identified. The discussion in both chapters is condensed. Indeed, it may be helpful to treat each chapter as several condensed into one. With these qualifications in mind, readers new to the concept of globalization may wish to proceed slowly and gradually.

This chapter provides an introduction to globalization. It focuses on economic globalization, the political changes that accompany it (liberalization), and some of their antecedents, correlates, and consequences. It concludes with a call for more effective and appropriate political structures and processes.

The next chapter picks up where this one leaves off. It focuses more on the social, cultural, geographic, and psychological aspects of globalization. It emphasizes the importance of international people flows and cultural flows, and it concludes with a new conceptual framework for family-centered policies and practices.

INTRODUCING GLOBALIZATION

Globalization is easier to understand if new ideas are introduced gradually throughout the chapter. Globalization invites various definitions, in part because it is not a single process, and it develops unevenly. For example, some analysts equate globalization with economic globalization, which was introduced in chapter 3. Although these two concepts are related, they are not synonyms. Economic globalization is just one facet, albeit a significant one, of the more comprehensive, multifaceted process of globalization.

Globalization also encompasses political, geographic, social, cultural, and psychological facets, or components. These five components often are intertwined, adding to globalization's complexity. Like chameleons, these five components and their economic counterpart often appear to take on different forms and appearances during different times and in different places. It matters where one looks, when one looks, how one looks, and who looks.

A good place to start is with the relations among economic globalization and its companion social, cultural, geographic, and political processes. In this perspective, *globalization refers to the process of standardizing social institutions, economic policies and markets, and governments and governmental policies; homogenizing people and their cultures; and substituting uniformity for diversity in policies and practices.* In this view of globalization, universal norms, standards, and practices replace particularistic ones. Globalization thus may connote "internationalization" (e.g., Geyer, Ingebritsen, & Moses, 2000). Here, globalization may connote a future world devoid of diversity and empty of the rich meaning diversity provides. Paradoxically, globalization also may connote humanitarian ideals, especially progressive movement toward "one world" and even "world community." It may invite the generative metaphor of "the world family."

When this second connotation is introduced, globalization's psychological facet follows. Increasingly, *each individual has a global consciousness and awareness* (Robertson, 1992, 1995). *This new global awareness is associated with new cognitive frames and knowledge claims about the present and its relation to the future* (e.g., Geyer, Ingebritsen, & Moses, 2000).

Held (1997) adds another psychological change: *growing awareness of interdependence.* Some of this awareness is beneficial, and some individuals and families experience it positively. Others experience it differently.

Giddens (1994), for example, suggests that global awareness may be experienced negatively as part of what he calls "the new heuristics of fear" (p. 20). *Each person, every family, with this awareness and the new heuristics of fear knows about global problems, which humanity has created, and which now affect everyone, everywhere.* For example, they are aware of the collective threats posed by global problems such as species extinction, environmental destruction, global warming, and nuclear weapons. Because so many of these problems and threats are enormous, complex, and seemingly outside any one person's or family's control, they may be experienced negatively. People often fear them. Identities, meaning-making systems, preferences and lifestyles, and action strategies may change as a consequence.

For example, the heuristics of fear may compel people to join international social movements (e.g., environmental protection movements, peace promotion and anti-war movements) that are organized to address global problems and meet global needs. The heuristics of fear compel them to mobilize for action. In contrast, individuals, families, and national leaders who are unable to cope with the heuristics of fear may try to hide from their awareness.[1] Like ostriches that stick their heads in the ground when they sense threats and danger, these people may seek refuge in local affiliations and selfish orientations. For example, they may decide that they owe allegiance only to the lowest common denominator —themselves and their families.[2] Or, they may use their religion and/or their ethnicity to disconnect themselves from global awareness and responsibilities (Huntington, 1993; Kennedy, 1993). Indeed, their religion and ethnicity may encourage them, albeit indirectly, to blame "outsiders," even encouraging conflicts.

These psychological changes and others accompany globalization. Identities, meaning-making systems, lifestyles, and life politics are constructed and reconstructed in relation to new awareness about time, space, and place relationships. In turn, cultures may change as individual, family, and group meaning-making systems and identities change (e.g., Friedman, 1995; Hermans & Kempen, 1998; Pieterse, 1995). As cultures change, other changes may follow, including social, political, and economic. Globalization is associated with such *ripple effects* (where one change initiative triggers others, which, over time, cause still others, including changes in the original initiative).[3] Globalization is also associated with *multiplier effects* (increasing the intensity and magnitude of a change initiative, including unanticipated and unintended consequences). Little wonder that globalization connotes rapid, complex, and dramatic change.

Interdependence and Space-Time Compression

Globalization is reflected and fueled by twin developments: (1) incredible advances in communications media, computer systems, and information management technologies; and, (2) revolutionary, worldwide systems of finance, monetary exchange, and trade. Individually and in combination, they compress space and time.

With globalization, *individuals, families, groups, organizations, communities, and governments become aware that they make up interdependent, "overlapping communities of fate"* (Held, 1997, p. 261). Perceived interdependence is a part of a new worldview. *Globalization changes space-time-place relations.* Some local events and phenomena have global implications, and some events and phenomena elsewhere in the world impact local issues. Space and time are compressed. Local and global changes interact rapidly, at unprecedented speed, and multiplier and ripple effects often accompany them.

For example, thanks to the new, global communications media, the Gulf War was not a distant event bracketed by time, place, and information delays. Individuals and families with access to the cable television network CNN, and its affiliates, experienced some of the war as it happened. They were taken to Kuwait and Iraq, live and in living color, to view with fascination and horror the release of "smart bombs" and their devastating effects. There was no denying the war; it could not be turned into a remote, distant event. To the contrary, its violence, devastation, and death were visible to everyone with access to a television. Everyone with access to a television was able to view immediately some of its effects on the soldiers, innocent bystanders, and their families. Suddenly the world became a smaller place. Space and time were compressed.

Another example: At the time of this writing, national and international concern lingers about the threatened collapse of some national economies in Asia. When the crisis was current, it had ripple effects. It demonstrated the interdependence and mutual fragility of stock markets around the world. With this impending crisis (which also was viewed by some investors as a golden opportunity), economic and political leaders and citizens alike depended on the communications media for instant information. All looked for key "decision signals" (Held, 1997) that they could use to inform their rapid-response systems. Indeed, *this international search for economic and political decision signals, along with new policies and practices, is another feature of globalization.* Enabled by rapid communications, computer technologies, and an expanding number of global networks, *globalization also promotes new cognitive structures, approaches, and rules for framing problems, forming solutions, making decisions, and learning from them.*

What's New Is Also Old

Although the concept, globalization, is new, the process is not. As Robertson (1992) has demonstrated, globalization actually began in the fifteenth century. The standardization of weights and measures, the development of standardized and uniform time (Greenwich mean time), the science of map mapping and navigation, the progressive development of an international language for communication (primarily English), and the establishment of world trade were early contributors to globalization. In Robertson's (1992) view, the world is now in the fifth phase of globalization—the uncertainty phase, which began in the late 1960s.[4]

Although the processes and changes associated with globalization have a long history, the sudden surge of interest in it is real, and it probably will increase. For example, globalization discourse is becoming commonplace, and it may feed on itself. That is, the increasing use of globalization in everyday and scholarly discourse also acts to promote and disseminate it. Globalization's growing popularity is also attributable to the dawning of the twenty-first century and the various representations of its meaning and significance, especially by the mass media. The twentieth century was characterized as one involving rapid and dramatic change, in turn, heightening awareness of the interdependence between national priorities and international events and affairs and the futility of isolationism. At the same time, many of these media depictions foreshadowed a twenty-first-century global world ripe with uncertainty, technological innovations, novelty, complexity, opportunity, and vexing national and international problems associated with the heuristics of fear.

Resistance: Modernization, Development, and the Americanization Thesis

Globalization, especially economic globalization, is associated with social and economic development. It is associated with modernization, i.e., the process of replacing traditional practices and institutions with "modern" ones. Some associate it with colonialism, i.e., claims to ownership and subsequent exploitation of a nation or community by another, more powerful one. Others associate globalization with imperialism, i.e., forcing the logic and meaning systems associated with capitalism and modernism on nations, communities, and cultures that are oriented differently. Still others associate globalization with all of them—modernization, colonialism, and imperialism (e.g., Goldthorpe, 1996; Hoogvelt, 1997; McMichael, 1996).

Globalization may mean "Westernization," i.e., the promotion of lifestyles exhibited by people in the high-income nations of the global north (e.g., Hoogvelt, 1997). For others, narrower interests dominate. For them, globalization means "Americanization." For example, Barber (1996) references the American fast-food chain McDonald's, along with the lifestyles and economic structures associated with it. He suggests that the pervasive presence of these fast-food restaurants signals broad-scale Americanization in pursuit of "McWorld." In the same vein, Mc-Michael (1996) traces the undesirable effects of the widespread consumption of hamburgers, especially in the United States, on development in South America. Here, development is associated with a range of problems, including deforestation, the destabilization of forest dwellers, problems in rural communities, misguided agricultural policies, misplaced priorities regarding imports and exports, and the substitution of beef production for subsistence farming (cereals, corn, and beans).

These alternative conceptions and interpretations are important for two reasons. They suggest that *globalization involves power relations, vested interests, and economic relationships.* They also suggest that *globalization involves contests for control.* As with all contests for control, individuals, families, groups, organizations, communities, and nations are not passive and powerless. They may offer resistance, and, indeed, some do.

For example, some nations, notably those associated with fundamentalist Islamic religions, may have national development agendas that Western analysts, such as Hoogvelt (1997), have characterized as both anti-globalization and anti-development. Even if they are, these agendas have been framed in relation to a growing awareness about globalization and leaders' perceptions of the threats and dangers it poses.

That the global age is not welcomed universally also has been evidenced in acts of resistance. If sabotage and terrorism are increasing, the growth in these activities may be inseparable from perpetrators' perceptions that they are striking back against the forces of globalization, modernization, Americanization, Westernization, colonialism, and cultural imperialism. For example, Barber (1996) suggests that Americanization, which promotes "McWorld," triggers tribalism and cultural resistance ("jihad"), including terrorism.[5]

Another example: At the time of this writing, demonstrators in Seattle, Washington (USA), have voiced their concern, displeasure, and resistance to the World Trade Organization. They have resisted aspects of economic globalization.

Globalization is thus a powerful sensitizing concept. It provides a way of looking at the world. Confronted with so many meanings and ideas, it is important to identify and clarify the analytical framework and conceptual tools used to analyze and describe globalization.

RELATIONAL ANALYSIS AND DIALECTICAL THINKING, DISCOURSE, AND PLANNING

Because globalization means international interdependence, and living in overlapping communities of fate, it compels relational analysis. Relational analysis was introduced initially in chapter 1, and it has appeared regularly in subsequent chapters. To reiterate, relational analysis emphasizes interdependent patterns and relationships. It focuses on power relations and contests for cultural authority and control. This relational frame also harbors another important conceptual tool—dialectical analysis.

Dialectical Thinking, Discourse, and Planning

Globalization requires nondichotomous thinking, planning, and action strategies. For example, with globalization, the question is not individuals or families; it is both. It is not national or international priorities; it is both. It is not local need versus national need; it is both. It is not policy versus practice; it is both (Lawson, under review-a). Globalization's economic, political, social, cultural, and psychological components cannot be separated and dichotomized. Their relationships are crucial to an understanding of globalization and its companion processes and changes.

Relational, nondichotomous, integrative thinking is required. To be sure, there are tensions, but these tensions are especially important. For example, tensions exist between individuals and families; and between national and international policies and practices. These tensions will not vanish. In fact, they are healthy tensions because they help prevent dichotomous thinking, policies, and practices. Few things in life are mutually exclusive, as family-related issues demonstrate. In short, these never-ending tensions help lay the foundation for more comprehensive policies and practices, ones that can be viewed in "win-win" rather than "win-lose" terms.

This nondichotomous view of the world, with its emphasis on enduring tensions, interdependence, and relationships, has a formal name. It is called *dialectical analysis,* henceforth called dialectical thinking, discourse, and analysis. As with globalization, what appears to be new also may be old and even familiar.

For example, although professionals in social work, community psychology, health promotion and education, and family and consumer sciences may not use this formal language, dialectical thinking, discourse, and planning often are implicit in their literatures and practices. Dialectical thinking, discourse, and planning are close relations of systems analysis, especially its emphasis on overlapping levels of analysis. Box 10.1 has been constructed to introduce globalization's multiple facets; to answer partially the question about where to look for its correlates and effects; and to emphasize dialectical relationships among these various levels.[6]

Dialectics also are embedded in multimodal intervention and improvement strategies. If they are to be optimized, these complex practice strategies must be anchored in dialectical thinking, discourse, and planning and surrounded by a relational analytical frame. This fresh combination promises new knowledge and understanding, skills and abilities, values and sensitivities. They are among the practical necessities for the global age.

As awareness grows about the global causes, correlates, and indices of individual, family, and community needs, professionals who lack understanding and analytical abilities will find it increasingly difficult to be effective. In fact, future definitions of professional ineffectiveness, even malpractice, may develop in relation to this new combination. To put it another way, policy and practice problems may be expected to stem from the failure to understand, and address effectively and appropriately, the relationship between globalization's challenges and opportunities and the well-being of individuals and families. New conceptual frameworks and the innovative policies and practices they may spawn are among ethical and moral imperatives.

Emergent Ethical and Moral Challenges and Problems

Globalization is facilitated by scientific understanding and, in turn, technological innovations. It presents important technological challenges, problems, and opportunities. However, its most important challenges are ethical and moral problems. Although science and technology may inform some of the planning and decision making, they cannot provide all of the answers. Recognizing the limits, in addition to the benefits, of science and technology is a key challenge in the global age (e.g.,

BOX 10.1

TRACKING THE MULTIPLE FACETS
AND EFFECTS OF GLOBALIZATION

Globalization is a multifaceted process that requires multilevel analysis. The perspective provided by analyses of any one nation-state may be as misleading as it is revealing. Tracking indications of globalization starts close to home—with the psychological orientations of individuals and their implications for families.

Globalization's impacts on *psychological states* are not well understood. It is clear, however, that globalization influences people's identities, meaning-making systems, and commitments. It has an impact on factors that people perceive as normal, natural, or inevitable. For example, job security is weighed against the ever-looming threat of plant closings or relocation. Continuing employment insecurities may become normalized, and wage compression and benefit reductions may be viewed as inevitable (e.g., Hoogvelt, 1997; Ray, 1998). Nationalism is a key psychological construct. Does it grow, wane, or vary?

In turn, individual psychological states impact on *indices of well-being in families and family systems.* For example, what is the tolerance for alternative family forms? What are the sources of stress and insecurities? How has family well-being changed over time? Why?

At the next level is *organizational analysis.* Both public and private organizations may be assessed for increasing homogeneity, standardization, and uniformity. The predicted pattern with globalization, for example, is that schools and school systems in one nation will be patterned after those deemed successful in a comparable nation. Social and health service agencies in one state, province, or nation will be patterned after those in another.

Governmental analysis follows suit. Governments that share aspirations and confront the same or comparable problems will learn from each other and pattern themselves after each other. With globalization, it is predicted that a growing number of governments will exhibit uniformity, homogeneity, and standardized practices and policies.

Analysis of the *economic sector* is one of the first requirements. Economic analysis includes levels, kinds, and sectors of employment and unemployment; indebtedness, especially to the International Monetary Fund and the World Bank; import-export balances; growth in the formal and informal sectors; and the extent to which indigenous agriculture, craft industries, and small businesses are vibrant or dying.

In the *political sector,* the issues revolve around the establishment and support of democratic structures and the accompanying demise of tyranny and nepotism; and the effects of structural adjustment policies, or their equivalent, on social welfare policies and local, governmental capacities for self-determination.

In the *cultural sector,* analyses of globalization's effects must include the tensions between local cultural and ethnic-religious traditions and the homogenization of meaning systems, lifestyles, and identities—especially as part of a global consumer culture. The effects of a global "infotainment industry—film, television, and computer-assisted technologies—are especially important (Barber, 1996).

In the *social institutional sector,* issues begin with the well-being of individuals and families and the institutions that serve them. The development and homogenization of the global city (Eade, 1997; Sassen, 1991) is another part of this social institutional challenge. Social demographics and social geographies are especially important. Place and context matter. So do national and international people flows involving immigration, migration, and refugees. How do cities change and why? How are rural communities and frontier villages changing and why?

After examining each of these four sectors in a nation-state, *cross-sector analyses* are needed. For example, how do reductions in health care track into reductions in income supports, child supports, transportation assistance, employment development programs, schooling subsidies, and food assistance? Such growing cross-sector interdependence in each nation-state often clashes with sector-specific, categorical governmental structures and policies.

Tracking the effects of globalization only begins with the nation-state and the immense challenges associated with it (Pierson, 1996). After examining globalization within a nation-state, *inter-nation and regional analyses* are required. Comparisons are needed between stand-alone nation-states and those in the growing number of regional alliances such as the European Union.

Finally, *worldwide* economic, political, cultural, geographic, and social changes need to be analyzed as people and their representatives interact and learn. Here, twin needs emerge: (1) International monitoring and integrated data systems; and (2) new regional and global governance systems.

Thus, tracking globalization and finding appropriate indices is reminiscent of Rudyard Kipling's tale of eleven blind men trying to understand an elephant. These blind men deluded themselves into believing that the part of the elephant that each experienced defined the elephant—and Kipling's elephant was standing still. In contrast, the globalization elephant is moving rapidly, and it continues to grow and foster change.

Brown, 1998). The stakes are high. Human dignity, freedom, well-being, and survival are involved, and they involve important tensions and difficult choices (e.g., Mohan, 1992; Stoesz, Guzzetta, & Lusk, 1999).

The case of world hunger, malnutrition, and food-related deaths provides an important example. Each year insufficient and inappropriate food affects the well-being and productivity of at least 840 million persons, including countless families and at least 200 million children. Presently, at least, it appears that there is sufficient food to feed the world's population. The main problem is with its distribution, transportation, and utilization (Bender & Smith, 1997). Food waste is a special problem. Food preferences are another, implicating changes in agriculture, trade, and subsistence farming. Will individuals and families who enjoy food securities care about those who do not? Will those who have food and resources sacrifice for those who lack? Will governments intervene? Who decides? Who decides who decides?

These questions implicate ethics (right conduct) and morals (e.g., ideals about justice and virtue). With these questions, it is impossible to separate the roles of family member, citizen, helping professional, policy maker, and family advocate. They require dialectical thinking and discourses that address the tensions among personal, family, local, national, regional, and international needs.

Refer now to box 10.2. The narrative has been constructed to illuminate ethical-moral choices (including some moral dilemmas); to show that individuals live in interdependent, overlapping communities of fate; and to introduce the pervasive effects of economic globalization.

The narrative in box 10.2 is just one of countless case studies that can be constructed. The box offers this important implication. As the relational, dialectical perspectives for globalization increase in popularity, individuals and families in the high-income nations may find it difficult to hide from, and excuse themselves from, the consequences of individual and family lifestyles. They must confront daily the heuristics of fear. When people live in overlapping communities of fate, individual and family choices and changes in one place and context often have both multiplier effects and ripple effects. These bold claims set the stage for an introductory overview of economic globalization.

BOX 10.2

TRACKING THE CORRELATES AND EFFECTS OF CONSUMER AND LIFESTYLE CHOICES

The majority of consumers live in the global north. They are the targets of a huge marketing, promotions, and sales industry, which typically has an international reach. Highly mobile and flexible production systems produce the goods and services they sell. Consumers, marketeers, and industrialists alike benefit from the labor of persons in the south, people who are denied equal privilege. Roughly four-fifths of the world's 5 billion people have no access to consumer credit. Many produce consumer goods and services that they cannot afford to consume and use. Many lack discretionary money, and they usually lack insurance policies that protect them against possible perilous futures.

Against this context, consider the ripple effects associated with three examples: (1) the burgeoning use of paper products, such as napkins, newspapers, toilet paper, and magazines; (2) diets high in meat products, especially beef and, more particularly, hamburgers; and (3) eating with chopsticks, using charcoal for cookouts, and relying on wood chips for cooking fuel. These three examples were chosen to implicate diverse people in different parts of the world, to avoid indicting any one culture. As it turns out, these three examples have similar, even identical, ripple effects, albeit not in the same nation(s).

For example, this freedom of choice is a major cause of deforestation. In British Columbia alone, the Mitsubishi plant converts stands of aspen trees into seven to eight million pairs of chopsticks each day, while in Chile, old-growth forests are being devastated to produce wood chips (McMichael, 1996, p. 152). Forests are disappearing to produce pulp for paper in several parts of the world, including Canada and the United States. Moreover, cattle require grazing lands, not forests. The beef industry is associated with deforestation in many South American nations, including Brazil and Argentina. As beef production escalates, the production of essential grains and cereals often declines. With these declines, reliance grows on grain imports, notably from the United States and Canada. Everywhere, the beef industry also means increased water consumption and perhaps air pollution (see Robbins, 1992).

In short, consumer choice as a lifestyle preference is a cause of deforestation. In turn, deforestation is correlated with global warming (the "greenhouse effect"), the loss of arable land, reductions in food production, and the dislocation of people.

The chain of effects continues. It is not uncommon to find overgrazing by cattle raised for the world hamburger industry, massive erosion of arable soil, and ill-advised agricultural production methods. The net result is the loss of arable land, the loss of agricultural employment, and the decline of subsistence farming.

The chain of effects only begins here. Population dynamics, basic family income, power relations in the family system, and governmental policies regarding farmers, agriculture, and social insurance are involved.

For example, in developing, low-income nations of the global south, rural families often face taxes imposed to support the people in urban areas, land rents, and profound insecurities related to income, housing, and food. Parents must produce more children to meet the demands of basic living (e.g., Dasgupta, 1995; Ray, 1998). In these contexts, population growth and child labor are rational strategies selected by individuals and families because they are essential to survival.

Children's work on the land and in the home frees adults to do other chores and have other jobs (e.g., in the wood chips industry or in the cattle industry). Moreover, children are family assets. In developing nations that lack personal insurance and social security systems, children and youth are the equivalent of personal insurance and social security policies for their parents and other family system members (Ray, 1998). Income- and subsistence-producing children and youth safeguard the future of parents, elders, and other adults in the family.

In many cultures, men are assigned—or take—the role of "breadwinners," or providers. Power, status, and privilege among children in the family system derive from this tradition. Boys are viewed as more valuable than girls. Parents assume that male children are more likely than female children to provide resources and income when parents become unable to support themselves and their children. Because male children are viewed as insurance policies, as economic assets, parents invest in their development. Inequitable access to food, education, and privilege in both family systems and cultural systems thus has an economic calculus. There is an underlying rationale to patriarchy and to population growth in these family systems (e.g., Riley, 1997).

Access to social and health services and to public education also are involved. For example, when access to health care is low, and when infant mortality rates and premature death rates are high, parents are encouraged to have more children.[1] Their future and the family's well-being hinge on more helping hands for labor. So, population growth is part of an understandable, rational decision-making chain, especially in rural communities of developing nations (Ray, 1998).

But the chain of effects does not end here. Children and youth who labor do not attend school. Absent schooling and the job-related training it may provide, these children are destined to remain in poverty, and, in all likelihood, they will contribute to the population problem. For example, levels of education, especially for girls and women, impact upon birth rates. The more schooling girls and women have, the less likely they are to have too many children, too early.

As the effects of poverty compound and well-being declines, at least one member of the family probably will travel to a city to seek work. Profound social demographic changes follow. A growing number of people move from rural communities to cities (called rural-urban flows), and rapid urbanization is the predictable result (Bradshaw & Wallace, 1996).

The chain continues. Unfortunately, cities are unable to keep pace with the demands for employment and housing. Industrialization is uneven, and there are not enough jobs for the growing number of people seeking them. Everyone, employers and employees alike, is aware of growing competition for an insufficient number of jobs in the formal economy. Because of pervasive employment and economic insecurities, wages and benefits are compressed, even reduced. Unions become less effective and popular, if they were present in the first place. Because of these pervasive employment insecurities, a growing number of persons must seek employment and the resources it provides in the informal sector of the economy where "sweatshop" labor is commonplace, health and social benefits are not provided, and both working and living conditions may be deplorable.

Women and children often are forced into the informal sector to support their families. As in rural contexts, when children and youth are working, they are not in school. Here too, poverty begets poverty. Similarly, absent social security, personal insurance, and income entitlements and supports, individuals and families daily confront profound vulnerability and economic insecurity. Here, too, children are economic assets, and population growth continues.

There are more ripple effects. Fragmented and disconnected families foster lower levels of well-being among all of their members, and their children suffer the most. Prostitution and the sexual exploitation of children may be commonplace. Crime and delinquency may increase. Problematic by any definition, they are nevertheless rational responses to circumstance and need.

Moreover, children who suffer harm often pass along their pain once they become parents. Intergenerational needs related to poverty and suffering are increasingly common. Helping professionals are affected, too. The greater the human suffering and the more plentiful the social and physical environmental needs, the more difficult become helping professionals' jobs and working conditions.

The chain continues. The world's burgeoning population threatens the carrying capacity of the planet. With the growing loss of arable land and a growing population, more and more people, especially women and children are starving, and others are suffering. Global warming affects everyone and will impact landmass and species survival. Species continue to disappear daily, and not without profound costs. For example, the resins from trees and plants hold promise to cure diseases such as AIDS (McMichael, 1996). Many valuable ecosystems for animal, plant, and human survival already are lost forever, and many others are threatened. Water tables in many parts of the world are falling, and the quality of the water that remains is suspect in many parts of the world. Every individual and family in the world community is being affected, and a more challenging future is expected.

In short, consumer choice as freedom is not automatically compatible with individual and family well-being, environmental sustainability, and even survival. Profound human rights issues are implicated in the global age. So are issues of social, economic, and environmental justice. The heuristics of fear imply both challenges and opportunities related to the global condition and family well-being.

[1]As Ray (1998) observes, widows are especially vulnerable to risk and lack of supports in some cultures, especially older women who no longer have the capacity to bear children.

THE GLOBAL ECONOMY, ECONOMIC
GLOBALIZATION, AND LIBERALIZATION

To reiterate, globalization is more comprehensive than economic globalization. The two are not synonyms. Economic globalization is the subordinate concept. Economic globalization (a continuous process) and the global economy (the focus and the result) are, however, key driving forces for the superordinate concept, globalization. Economic globalization refers to the process by which capitalism, in effect, "goes global." Capitalism may be defined simply as "a competitive market system in which goods and labor power are commodified" (Giddens, 1994, p. 11). To put it another way, industrial capitalism often was associated with the nation-state. Global capitalism changes this frame to an international one, along with the accompanying competitive game.

Economic globalization—global capitalism—usually is accompanied by the descriptor *liberalization* (e.g., United Nations Conference on Trade and Development [UNCTD], 1996a, 1996b). Liberalization connotes free trade and eliminating governmental constraints and restraints on the economy. It also refers to a convergent set of governmental policies and practices, which will be identified soon. For example, liberalization encompasses the restructuring of the welfare state (e.g., the devolution of responsibilities to local governments and the privatization of services).

When liberalization and economic globalization are joined, their union emphasizes the intersections between economic processes and political processes and decisions. In other words, issues regarding economic globalization and liberalization are ones of *political economy* (e.g., Barber, 1996; Hoogvelt, 1997). They involve the exercise of governmental power and authority in the never-ending quest for legitimacy (politics). They also involve the allocation and distribution of resources, in relation to markets and key indicators such as per capita income and gross national (gross domestic) product (economics).

In classical liberal democratic theory, *the polity controls the economy*. Government of, for, and by the people controls the economy. The economy serves the people and the common good. This classical relationship helps introduce economic globalization and liberalization, especially a new and recurrent problem associated with them. *In a growing number of nations, the economy now appears to control the polity.* In other words, there has been an inversion of ends and means. Instead of markets serving governments, individuals, and families, i.e., where markets are means and improved well-being and social welfare are ends or goals, governments, individuals, and families serve markets. When means and ends are inverted, the political economy changes dramatically. Democracy is threatened, in turn imperiling individual and family well-being (e.g., Barber, 1996; A. Goldsmith, 1996; Greider, 1997; Nader, 1993).

The economy escapes local, national, and international controls. Absent national governmental controls and international legal restraints and regulations, global capitalism can be characterized as being on a "runaway course." Corporate capitalist leaders look for hospitable sites around the world, ones that will maximize profit. They move production facilities, and in some cases, corporate headquarters, to these more hospitable sites. These relocation projects are important in their own right, but it is equally important that relocation means "for the time being." Once it is out of control, runaway capitalism becomes nomadic. It is not rooted automatically in local places, nor is it focused on aims related to individual and family well-being.

Although some analysts and advocates detest and resist capitalism under any circumstances, in the global age there is increasing doubt about the viability of alternatives (e.g., Fukuyama, 1995). The collapse of the former Soviet Union meant the loss of an alternative. Similarly, China is incorporating policies associated with capitalism, e.g., ones that permit property ownership through a system of home mortgages.

The moderate (or middle ground) position is that it is not feasible to present an alternative to capitalism. In this view, capitalism, per se, is not the problem. Runaway, nomadic capitalism is the root problem, and it implicates three others.

One problem lies in the absence of controls, indeed the relinquishment of responsibility, by governments. Another lies in the absence of international governing bodies and authorities (e.g., Held, 1997) that reign in, and temper, capitalism, ensuring that it does not threaten species survival, destroy environments, and erode individual and family well-being. A third problem stems from the system of international relations. This problem includes a long history of war and conflicts over scarce resources and the desire for political control. In this third problem frame, the dialectic between competition and cooperation is lost. Global competition reigns as cooperation wanes. Absent international concords and controls, nations must play at a high-stakes, zero-sum game, in which there are clear winners and losers. One nation's gain often means another's losses, or at least willing sacrifices. Family well-being is among the high stakes in this game.

Economic Globalization and Liberalization as a Kind of International Game

This new economic game occurs within nations and among them. Indeed, there is a dialectical relationship among national and international rules and regulations, and among the key players. Communities, states, and provinces within nations compete with each other. For example, economic developers in London, England, compete with developers in Glasgow, Scotland. At the same time, these developers are competing with developers of other nations, and of regional blocs and alliances among them, such as the European Union. To reiterate, these competitions have gamelike features, and a growing number of players, including policy makers and leaders of transnational corporations (TNCs), know the rules, strategies, and rewards. Policies and practices become more standardized as more players learn the rules and learn one anothers' successful strategies.

Both policy makers and TNC leaders know that profits will be maximized when enticements are provided. For example, when trade policies are liberalized (a key component in liberalization), and when governmental leaders reduce, or remove, taxes and tariffs, production costs also are reduced and profits grow.

Another key strategy is to address labor costs. Labor costs, including salaries and benefits, make up most of the production costs. Raw materials costs and transportation costs are close behind. These materials and transportation costs do not vary significantly from place to place. By contrast, labor costs do vary significantly. To return to a point made in earlier chapters, labor costs are higher in the global north than they are in nations in the global south.

Another strategy (and goal) is the ability to attract and retain foreign direct investment (FDI) (e.g., Woodward, 1996). This strategy is especially important to the low- and middle-income nations of the world. Investors are attracted to the extent that nations and their governments offer political, social, and cultural infrastructures, which support economic growth and development. Investors also look for increases in savings rates by individuals and families (Ray, 1998). Foreign direct investment requires high-performance, high-efficiency governments and supportive infrastructures. To borrow a common business phrase, these national governments must demonstrate that they are "lean and mean." They must rid themselves of what leaders may define as "unnecessary" or "too expensive" obligations.

For example, they must privatize services, which has identifiable effects on families (e.g., Hennon & Jones, in press). They must place caps on spending (e.g., capitated services and managed care); reduce, or eliminate, social welfare programs; and delegate some responsibilities and problems to local authorities. *Privatization, devolution, welfare state restructuring,* and *capitated spending* are four key, related components in political liberalization. As governments liberalize, the polity and the nation are more hospitable to FDI and economic growth. The nation gains comparative advantage in the international, global economic game. *The polity changes in service of the economy.*

Strategies for playing the international economic game derive from these realities and others. To return to a point made in earlier chapters, nations around the world offer to TNCs, businesses, and corporations competing claims about the quality of their workforces. They claim that product quality depends on workers' quality and qualifications. To reiterate, workforce quality is described as *human capital,* and leaders make corresponding claims about the quality of their workers because of their investments in human capital development (Ray, 1998). Universal schooling is the most important engine for human capital development, especially as production relies on technological development and workers' technological literacy. Universal health care is another human capital development strategy. Health care is a human capital investment because players know that unhealthy workers do not work to their capacity, and absenteeism, due to health problems, cuts productivity. Thus, each nation's claims in this economic game focus on human capital investments.[7]

For example, even though their labor costs may be higher, leaders in nations in the global north claim higher human capital than their competitors in the global south. These leaders attempt to persuade private sector leaders that their higher human capital compensates for their higher labor costs.

Worker quality and qualifications are co-determined by production technologies and requirements. Once players in this economic game qualify equally, or comparably, in this important respect, the competition focuses on labor costs. For, once production quality is ensured, reduced labor costs become the key to profit maximization for TNCs, other corporations, and businesses. TNCs have thus moved to nations offering the lowest costs, the highest production quality, and enticements such as tax relief and ready access to land, resources, and inexpensive electricity.

These nations' gains have been other nations' losses. Losing carries severe consequences, including the loss of jobs and revenues. To put it another way, as capitalism goes global, and TNCs move, jobs move with them, and job loss often is permanent. Individuals, families, communities, states and provinces, and entire nations are affected.

So, in the global north, the "developed" nations also are intensifying their recruitment and retention of TNCs. Their primary strategy is to develop cost-containment policies, which look very much like those in the developing nations. In short, liberalization is a global tendency.

Once the economic game is presented and understood, international patterns are easier to identify and understand. In fact, a new language is developing, and it is replacing the other language and classification system (e.g., first-world, second-world, and third-world nations; industrial, industrializing, and postindustrial; high income, medium income, and low income).

Core Economies, Flexible Production, and Commodity Chains

One way to identify high-income nations is by evaluating their consumption patterns and lifestyle preferences. These nations have well-developed commercial advertising and marketing systems, systems designed to persuade and convince individuals, groups, and families (consumers) to purchase their products. In these high-consumption nations, a growing number of advertising and marketing systems try to persuade consumers that their respective products are associated with particular identities and lifestyles. For example, the American sporting goods manufacturer Nike promotes an image with its marketing slogan "Just do it!" Nike uses this marketing image to sell athletic shoes and clothing (e.g., Korzeniewicz, 1994; Maguire, 1999). Countless other companies and businesses do the same thing.

In this emergent framework, analysts (e.g., Gereffi & Korzeniewicz, 1994) make distinctions among three kinds of economies and nations. The *core economies* control production and capital and do most of the consuming. The *peripheral economies* produce the goods and products, which line workers typically cannot afford. The *mediating economies* link the core and peripheral economies in the chain through transportation and component part production.

The core economies are the high-income and consumption nations. They host the corporate headquarters of TNCs and many of the world's financial institutions. A growing number of cities in the core economies are defined by these corporate headquarters, financial institutions, and accompanying service industries (e.g., advertising and marketing, hotels, restaurants, mass media).

Production is flexible for two reasons. It occurs rather rapidly in response to demand, thus reducing needs (and costs) to stockpile products. Flexible production also enables quick changes in response to market changes, especially the development of new micromarkets (market niches) that marketing and promotion units help to create. More to the point, component parts are manufactured in diverse parts of the world. New product assembly plants are developed to connect them, and they serve as convergence sites for international trade. When assembly does not require high levels of education and training, but rather an assembly-line-oriented "work discipline," product assembly typically is located in low-income and middle-income nations of the developing world. Developing nations actively recruit such plants through enticements.

A growing number of these nations offer to TNCs and foreign investors special production sites called *export processing zones* (e.g., McMichael, 1996; Woodward, 1996). These sites are located conveniently for transportation needs (e.g., along the U.S.-Mexico border). In addition to inexpensive, low-skilled labor, governments offer TNCs various enticements and incentives, including tax privileges, lower costs for water and power, and facility development.

An example further illuminates the dynamics of commodity chains and flexible production. It also involves Nike. A pair of Nike athletic shoes with a retail cost of approximately $70.00 in the United States may have a production cost of less than $1.75 because the shoes are made in a peripheral economy, which offers lower labor costs (Maguire, 1999, p. 134). Moreover, Nike's footwear company subcontracts all of its goods production (some $4 billion worth). Nike itself employs about 9,000 people, while some 75,000 are involved in subcontracted production (Hoogvelt, 1997, p. 127).

In the peripheral economies, especially in export processing zones, wages may stay compressed. Fierce competition for these jobs compresses wages (e.g., Ray, 1998). Wages also stay compressed because women and even children may be the primary production workers.

In short, the peripheral economies produce products and consumer goods that the people in the core economies consume. In simple terms, profits are differences between the money made on the sale and the acquisition, production, transportation, and marketing costs. Patterns of interdependence are built among core and peripheral economies as commodity (product) chains are built.

Commodity chains and flexible production are associated with a system of international relations, one that heightens differences among nations and economies. These differences include inequalities between players, among players, and between players and nonplayers, i.e., nations who are left out of the game and these chains. As nations who are left out try to gain entry, they pattern themselves after some of the players. In this way, economic globalization and liberalization are driving forces behind the broader process of globalization—including homogenization, standardization, and uniformity in economic development, government structures and policies, and strategies designed to improve each nation's comparative advantage in the quest for TNCs and FDI.

Specific examples help. In the next section, a basic composite of these features is outlined. National context matters; this composite is biased toward high-income nations of the global north. Therefore, this composite is more of an analytical aid than a perfect summary of how economic globalization and liberalization look, or unfold, in each nation, especially in the low-income, developing nations with, or striving to attain, status as a peripheral economy. On the other hand, this composite illuminates some of the costs, correlates, and consequences of living in a core economy, a high-income nation.

A Brief, Simplified Composite

- In the high-income nations (or core economies), a growing number of local businesses, industries, banks, and other lending institutions find it difficult to compete with national competitors and transnational corporations (TNCs). Local entities are compelled to freeze costs (including wages); reduce the number of employees; or close their doors.
- In all nations, but especially in the high-income nations, large production corporations, whether self-contained or as components of TNCs, threaten to move elsewhere. This strategy is designed to re-

ceive concessions from workers (e.g., limits and reductions on benefits and wages) and from governments (e.g., tax reductions, land
allocations, environmental protection policies are not enforced
strictly). As concessions are made, local revenues often decline in
many communities (e.g., Heying, 1997).

- Some corporations and TNCs in the high-income nations simply
close their doors and move production facilities elsewhere in the nation or to a different nation, typically one in the developing world
where labor and production costs are reduced dramatically. One
nation's gain is another's loss. Structural unemployment may be reduced in the developing nation, but at the same time it probably increases in the nation vacated by the TNCs.

- At the same time that production facilities close and move (called
deindustrialization), a growing number of businesses, small and
medium industries, and banks sell out to national competitors and
TNCs. Increasingly, the private sector does not represent local residents and their interests. This process is called *delocalization,* and
it is associated with the erosion of elite leadership, charitable giving, and investments in local communities (e.g., Heying, 1997).
Together, deindustrialization and delocalization have devastating
effects, especially in the cities of the high-income nations of the
global north.

- Even in the high-income nations of the global north, families face
economic pressures because salaries and benefits are compressed.
Social and health benefit programs are reduced and "capped," and
individuals and families are required to pay more for them (e.g.,
Blau, 1999). Both parents in nuclear families may feel compelled to
work.[8]

- As local small businesses and banks experience stress and insecurity, and some even decline and collapse, fewer jobs are available,
real wages and spending power decline, and there are fewer investment dollars to promote goodwill, help the needy, and solicit the
support of local citizens.

- As economic globalization restructures national economies, it
changes the characteristics of their workforces. Formal sector employment declines, and the jobs that are available in it also change.
Low-skilled jobs are lost, or they are subject to outcontracting and
outsourcing.

- In the high-income nations, men who lack formal education, knowledge, skills, and abilities for high-demand, high-tech jobs may be

viewed as redundant and too costly. New technologies such as robotics substitute for their labor. In nations, cultures, and family systems where men's roles and identities have been formed in relation to their provider, or "breadwinner," functions, the loss of meaningful work brings ripple effects. Especially as women and even children assume these roles and responsibilities, men's identities and self-esteem can be expected to change. Gender relations in the family also change. Beneficial in one sense because of the gender equity they promise, these changes also have ripple effects. Formerly employed men now face unemployment and underemployment, both chronic and structural. The stresses on men, women, and their family system also tend to mount, including increases in substance abuse and domestic violence.

- Unions and other workers' associations lose some of their bargaining power (e.g., Western, 1997). In addition to psychological insecurity, the economic threat of plant closings and relocation loom as an ever-present possibility and constraint.
- Both public and private organizations rely increasingly on outcontracting and outsourcing, i.e., hiring out selected kinds of work and services (e.g., custodial jobs, building maintenance, delivery services), to cut costs, increase profits, or both. Contracting businesses and companies often employ "temps," i.e., workers whose jobs are part of the informal economy and for whom they often do not provide social and health benefits.
- At the same time, technological innovations in agriculture and in industry make many low-skilled jobs and workers redundant. Technological innovation may contribute to structural unemployment, especially in the high-income nations.
- Workers in deindustrialized cities who lack education levels, knowledge, and skills for "high-tech, increasing-demand jobs" thus confront structural unemployment. Many are men who face the choice of unemployment or jobs in the informal economy with underemployment. Gender roles in the family often change as women become "breadwinners" through employment in the formal sector or, for a growing number of vulnerable families, in the informal sector.
- Family members may begin to lose hope for a better future (e.g., Fine & Weis, 1998; Watts, 1984; Wilson, 1997), while others turn to crime and the shadow economy of large cities (Jordan, 1998).
- In nations of all sizes and kinds, a growing number of agricultural workers, faced with the loss of jobs and family farms, either migrate

to cities in search of work (called rural-urban flows and described in box 10.2), or seek employment in the informal sector of the agricultural sector.[9] Many who migrate to cities also will end up underemployed, in informal sector jobs. Urban growth, especially in the developing nations, cascades.

- Rural-urban flows also increase in developing nations as deforestation, the loss of arable land, agricultural taxes, and import substitutions result in the loss of subsistence farming, other indigenous agriculture, and local craft industries (e.g., Ray, 1998).

- Increasing rural-urban flows are related to structural unemployment in the formal economies of cities. A growing number of people, especially women and children, seek and gain employment in the informal sector (e.g., Ray, 1998; Sanyal, 1996).

- Intra-nation rural-urban flows are accompanied by inter-nation migrations of individuals and families (e.g., Martin & Widgren, 1996). For example, foreign workers are recruited into service industries and low-skilled jobs that citizens will not perform, or these workers move to new countries through family system and friendship networks. The informal sector grows. Many families are often divided, as one or more members travel to another nation in pursuit of employment.

- For those who remain in rural areas, the downsizing of the workforce through rural-urban flows results in work intensification and stress. The amount of work that needs to be done remains the same, absent technological innovation. This means that fewer people must perform the same amount of work, and that children often are forced to labor and women's work and responsibilities may increase significantly (Ray, 1998, p. 361). Stress and insecurity grow in rural families.

- Government spending also is reduced through outsourcing and outcontracting; there are changes in entitlement programs, and caps on health care costs (e.g., capitated services and managed care).

- Welfare state downsizing and restructuring in high-income nations is matched by comparable and identical initiatives in the low- and middle-income nations. In these latter nations, changes also are required by international aid and loan packages, and they include firm rules for how governments may spend their funds. These policies, procedures, and firm spending rules and priorities are called structural adjustment policies and programs. They are described briefly in box 10.3.

BOX 10.3

STRUCTURAL ADJUSTMENT POLICIES: A SKETCH

Structural adjustment policies (SAPs) often accompany foreign aid and international loan packages (e.g., Bello, 1996; Hoy, 1998; Ray, 1998). Structural adjustment policies are policy and change mandates that nations must meet in order to receive funding. As the adjective "structural" suggests, recipient nations must make permanent changes in their spending patterns and their governmental infrastructures. In other words, they must change their spending priorities and establish improved systems for planning, management, and evaluation. For example, a nation's spending priorities must change so that debts on loans can be repaid. Improvements in governmental performance and overall economic efficiency also are targeted because these improvements attract foreign investors.

Structural adjustment policies are intended to promote modernization, industrialization, political democracy, and economic development—simultaneously. For example, SAPS require developing nations to promote democratic political systems; to comply with human rights platforms; to end unjust and inequitable systems of nepotism and political patronage; to reduce social welfare expenditures; to invest in public goods such as dams, irrigation systems, and public utility companies, or to privatize them; and, all in all, to comply with the mandates of leaders in the first world who control the purse strings. Like the development agenda that harbors them, these SAPs have their proponents and their critics. To wit: While proponents claim that SAPs promote democratization, critics assail the reductions and terminations of social welfare benefits to the needy and the poor.

- As governments of all kinds reduce, or devolve, social welfare and health benefit programs, local, regional, national, and international nongovernmental agencies are asked, compelled, or volunteer to "take up the slack." Despite noble intentions, good work, and exciting achievements, the absence of resources, selective service delivery, cultural insensitivity, and overwhelming individual, family, and community needs make it clear that they are not an effective substitute for active, effective governments.

- Governments of all varieties learn and improve in relation to one another as they seek to improve their comparative advantage, address common needs, and solve common problems (e.g., Massey, 1997). *Policy taking* becomes as popular as *policy making*. In the process, the government structures and policies of comparable nations, like their economies, appear to become more homogenized (e.g., Ham, 1997; Massey, 1997; Pierson, 1996).
- Many governments emphasize the importance of human capital development, but, at the same time, they privatize services and add fees for services, and some may even add direct and indirect fees for public schooling. Privatization, capitation, and fees-for-services place special hardships on vulnerable families and the professionals who serve them.
- The scarce economic resources of many low-income nations must be dedicated to debt relief and repayment.[10]
- In high-, medium-, and low-income nations, generous social welfare programs, and some universal health programs, are reduced and eliminated to gain funds that can be reallocated for economic development. In the calculus of economic globalization and liberalization, investments in these programs are dysfunctional, and so are their accompanying tax, spend, and redistribution strategies (e.g., Hoogvelt, 1997; Jordan, 1998; Walby, 1999). As these programs (and social safety nets generally) are dismantled, in the end the *competition state* replaces the *welfare state* (Pierson, 1996, p. 206; see also Dunleavy, 1997).
- In the high-income nations, appreciation and empathy for the plight of the most vulnerable individuals and families, especially the long-term unemployed, declines. Liberalization is manifested in the restructuring of the welfare state, and a new welfare ideology is promoted (e.g., Jordan, 1998). In this new ideology, individual and family self-sufficiency through any kind of employment is a top priority.[11] It assumes that individual and family dependence on governmental social welfare benefits interferes with self-sufficiency.
- As social welfare investments decline, investments in governmental surveillance, policing, and prison systems often go up (e.g., Jordan, 1998).
- In some cases, politicians promise that social welfare benefits and other public sector programs that protect and enhance individual and family well-being will be restored and enhanced once govern-

BOX 10.4

TRICKLE-DOWN THEORY: A SKETCH

Economic determinism guides the thinking of some political leaders, business and corporate executives, and policy makers. They assume that, if the private sector profits, then so will governments. In turn, these leaders also assume that profits in the private sector will have economic ripple effects for the public sector. Their policy theory goes something like this: *If TNCs and other corporations are recruited and retained and they make profits, and if foreign investments increase, then profit flows will enhance governmental revenues; in turn, these benefits will "trickle down" to individuals and families.* To reiterate, in this line of thinking about the political economy, significant social welfare investments and economic investments in the other public sector programs and services are postponed until such time as the economic development agenda provides the "ripple effects." Once these ripple benefits accrue, leaders can focus on the other sectors, distributing these benefits from the top—i.e., facilitating their "trickling down" to people and communities in need.

So-called trickle-down theory has become the dominant way to think about economic development. For example, it gained dominance during the years of Ronald Reagan's presidency in the United States and Margaret Thatcher's term as prime minister of Great Britain. It remains dominant today in many parts of the world. As Ray (1998) observes, this trickle-down theory may be attractive to some, but evidence in support of it is lacking.

mental revenues are enhanced because private sector profits increase. (See box 10.4.)

- Governments also reinvest former social welfare funds in enterprises and development projects that will attract businesses and foreign investors and keep existing ones. In essence, *while the risks of these investments are collectivized, the opportunities for profits remain privatized.*
- Governments that cannot compete alone form regional alliances, such as the European Union, and forge regional trade agreements.

As these alliances are formed, the power of individual governments declines, and both social welfare and economic policies are the purview of the regional alliance (e.g., Walby, 1999).

Clearly, this composite list of changes is incomplete and selective. Aspects of it apply more to some nations than to others. But it does set a context for analyzing economic globalization and liberalization, along with their correlates and impacts.

Thus, economic globalization and liberalization are multifaceted, comprehensive, and paradoxical. Multiplier effects and ripple effects are associated with them. They are driving forces behind the broader, comprehensive process of globalization, which is described in greater detail in the next chapter. A fitting way to close this one is to explore key implications, which derive from the preceding analysis of economic globalization, liberalization, and commodity chains.

A SELECTIVE ASSESSMENT

Clearly, *globalization and liberalization promote standardizing and homogenizing tendencies both within nations and among them.* Governments in localities, states, and provinces within nations begin to resemble one another in many ways. Some ways are obvious, others are subtle, and still others are in flux. Governments also can resist these homogenizing and standardizing tendencies (e.g., Geyer, Ingebritsen, & Moses, 2000). The same can be said of businesses, financial institutions, and corporations.

International patterning and mutual learning also are commonplace. They bear witness to the pervasive effects of economic globalization and liberalization as states and provinces, nations, and regional alliances play the global political economic game.

There are clear winners and losers (UNDP, 1999). And, for the time being at least, some players must accept the consolation of the equivalent of a tie; their economic indicators are about the same. Other would-be players may be satisfied with their progress.

Encouragement is offered to continue playing. For example, the following strong endorsement is included in the first conclusion of the United Nations Conference on Trade and Development: "globalization has fostered greater interdependence and cross-border linkages between the countries of the world. Countries that seek to delink, and opt instead for isolationism, risk paying a high price in future economic growth" (UNCTD, 1996a, p. 9). Moreover: "while most of the developing nations will gain from the globalization process, some will benefit more than others, and a number of countries with initial conditions that make them less suited to take advantage of globalization will lose out and become more marginalized in relation to other countries" (UNCTD, 1996a, p. 9). The implication is clear: Becoming a player and playing well and effectively means addressing these "initial conditions" that serve to disadvantage some nations. Liberalization, including restructuring the welfare state and increasing investments in human capital, are key strategies for addressing them. As aspiring nations implement these strategies, they contribute to the growing homogenization and standardization of governments and economies, with governments changing in service of economic globalization.

Competitive game theory, with its ideas of winning, losing, and no net gain ("draws" and "ties") suggests that *economic globalization and liberalization are associated with the production of a comprehensive, interlocking system of relations.* For example, economists can scan the world as one system and assess the impact of globalization and liberalization on the reduction of absolute poverty. Indeed, some have. They have spanned the globe and analyzed changes in the mean score (numerical average) for poverty. Their twin conclusions are that *absolute poverty has declined already, and it is likely to decline some more* (UNCTD, 1996a, p. 10).

But what are the effects of globalization and liberalization on *relative poverty,* i.e., poverty within each nation? And, beyond economic averages, what are the effects on life quality, especially the life quality of families living in poverty? Has the quality of their lives changed? Similarly, what are the effects on individuals and families who have not experienced poverty's challenges? What is the significance of commodity chains and the relations they structure? Answers to these questions highlight the relevance of what it means to individuals and families when their nations are players, winners, and losers. There are important opportunities for research here.

One way to approach this question is to look at the division of labor, the conditions of work, and the distribution of opportunity for employment. Analyses must consider this important finding: *Economic globalization, liberalization, and commodity chains help produce an international division of labor* (e.g., Hoogvelt, 1997, p. 47). In other words, where many products are concerned, the world has become a factory system (e.g., McMichael, 1996). As production facilities move from the high-income nations to the low- and middle-income nations, individuals and families experience the consequences.

Some individuals and families in the low-income and middle-income nations who gain employment in the formal sector are, in one sense, winners.[12] Although line workers' wages in the new production facilities may be deplorably low compared to what line workers in the high-income nations once received for the same work, in the low- and medium-income nations these wages represent a significant improvement for line workers and their families. Their national profile also looks better. Per capita income tends to go up, while relative poverty levels tend to go down (e.g., UNCTD, 1996b). The future may hold more of the same. As Hoogvelt (1997, p. 240) points out, the continuing transfer of production facilities and jobs (because of inexpensive labor) is likely to result in work for some 1.3 billion people in the low- and middle-income nations over the next generation.

Not everyone benefits. New jobs for workers in the developing nations usually occur at the expense of workers and their jobs in the high-income nations. Moreover, national averages (mean scores) for individual and family incomes deflect attention away from the lower extremes, the second and third standard deviations, of the poor in each nation. Only those individuals and families associated with the new production facilities, i.e., management and labor, benefit immediately. The long-term unemployed individuals and families challenged by persistent poverty may not benefit in the slightest. Management and investors often benefit disproportionately, as evidenced in growing income gaps in each nation.

Meanwhile, working families in high-income nations who lost their jobs, along with some of the middle managers victimized by downsizing and relocation, are the losers (e.g., Blau, 1999; Fine & Weis, 1998; Wilson, 1997). *Nations permit corporations and businesses to move from one nation to another, but most workers cannot move with their companies* (Jordan, 1998). In the globalization-liberalization logic, allowing workers and their families to move, and supporting their moves, would be counterproductive. After all, corporations and TNCs move to reduce labor costs and increase profit. Why move workers and their high salaries unless they are absolutely essential?

Because the corporate headquarters for the world factories typically remain in the high-income nations—especially the accounting functions and sales, promotion, and advertising functions—*managers and executives in these TNCs are among the winners.*[13] As in the low- and medium-income nations, the gaps between the wealthy and the poor are rising, and for good reason (e.g., Reich, 1993; Thurow, 1996).

Millions of workers in the high-income nations tend to be affected. To reiterate, the looming threats of company and business relocation, closing, and corporate takeovers produce an ever-present cloud of employment insecurity (e.g., Blau, 1999; Hoogvelt, 1997; Jordan, 1998). Just one layoff may result in lasting insecurity. Even when the worker gets a new job, the effects of the initial unemployment remain. Workers tend to invest themselves less in their new jobs, in part because they are ever-wary about their future, and they may not be as productive (e.g., Darity & Goldsmith, 1996).[14]

Remember, the relocation of TNCs brings pervasive deindustrialization and delocalization, and both are continuing. When comparable production-oriented jobs in the formal sector are not created to replace those lost from TNC movements, structural unemployment increases. Moreover, when official unemployment levels remain low at the same time that a growing number of industrial jobs are lost forever—and structural unemployment grows—something else is going on. Pushed into some kind of employment because social welfare benefits have declined, and perhaps seeking to avoid the stigmas of unemployment, a growing number of individuals and their families pursue and *gain employment in the informal sector of the economy. Or, families endure hardships associated with unemployment.* In comparison to their previous jobs, workers are paid less, have fewer or no benefits, and are effectively underemployed. In turn, the well-being of their families may decline.

Place matters. Some people, in some places, are affected negatively more than others. For example, in the United States, Wilson (1997) chronicles the harms experienced by African Americans in cities when work disappears. Similarly, Fine and Weis (1998) describe the erosion of hope, the harms and stresses experienced by women, and growing intercultural and interracial tensions that have accompanied deindustrialization in Newark, New Jersey, and Buffalo, New York. The implication is that these cities, as well as their families, are on downward spirals.

Furthermore, *wages and benefits become compressed.* Weighed against the rate of inflation, they even decline. This trend describes what has happened to middle- and low-income working families in the United

States since the early 1970s (Reich, 1993; Ray, 1998), and it transcends this nation's boundaries. Jordan's (1998) analysis indicates national and international patterns:

> The Scandinavian countries—and especially Sweden—have suffered a relative decline in their prosperity, and a rapid growth in unemployment and social assistance claims (especially in Finland). The Continental European countries now suffer from high and persistent unemployment, and rising contribution rates for social benefits and services. The Anglo-Saxon countries have the highest rates of poverty and inequality, and insecurity of employment, along with evidence of rising social conflict (such as rising expenditure on criminal enforcement). Furthermore, even the success of the "tiger" economies of South East Asia, with their rapid growth of incomes and their dramatic expansion of manufacturing and share in world trade, is now called into question. . . . [M]uch of this success was founded on the availability of artificially cheap capital, rather than some novel and enduring solution to the problems of sustainable development and social stability. (Jordan, 1998, p. 11)

In short, *the incomes and benefits of many workers and their families in the high-income nations go down at the same time that the incomes (and perhaps the benefits) of many workers and their families in a few low- and some middle-income nations increase.* Some economic theorists (e.g., Thurow, 1996) see an international pattern in these tendencies in support of a theory. Price factor equalization theory predicts that incomes among selected classes of individuals and families will converge over time and standards of living will be more comparable. "Leveling up" for *some* workers and their families in the low- and middle-income nations also means "leveling down" for *some* of their counterparts in the high-income nations. For those nations who neither win nor lose, the temporary result of the game is no difference, a draw or a tie.

Economic globalization, liberalization, and commodity chains produce variable, paradoxical results like these. They produce processes and results that can be interpreted as a race to the top, a race to the bottom, or a dialectical relationship between them.

On the other hand, there is less ambiguity about one of their effects. *Economic globalization, liberalization, and commodity chains reinforce and produce a system of social and economic relations, especially subsystems of inequalities.* Inequalities exist among nations; within nations;

among states, provinces, regions, and localities within nations; among individuals and families; and within family systems. These levels interact, and they affect individual and family well-being.

It is unreasonable to hold economic globalization and liberalization solely accountable for these inequalities. They predated discourse and planning for economic globalization and liberalization. For example, inequalities were antecedents of the capitalist, industrial revolution. In fact, one of the revolution's effects was to exacerbate inequalities. The modern welfare state, which is being restructured now and may be in decline, arose as a kind of class compromise in response to these inequalities (e.g., Giddens, 1994; Jordan, 1998). The welfare state's social safety nets ensured that individuals and families would not suffer irreparably from unemployment, which was viewed as a temporary condition. Because individual and family hardships were alleviated, or reduced, individuals and families did not revolt and cause upheavals. The welfare state thus helped safeguard social and political stability by providing benefits to families.[15]

Economic globalization and liberalization thus may not be solely responsible and accountable for inequalities, but they appear to be inseparable from the restructuring of the welfare state and the progressive dismantling of social safety nets for individuals and families. They also are responsible for increasing structural unemployment and for the swelling number of individuals and families employed in the informal sector of the economy.[16] Reductions in the social safety net usually translate into lowered well-being for the most vulnerable individuals and families. *In all of these ways, economic globalization and liberalization do not benefit many of the world's families, including many in the high-income nations.* To the contrary, they exact profound human costs.

This assessment flies in the face of the rationale for economic globalization and liberalization. *They have proceeded, in part, because of the promise that they would help address inequality problems, especially ones associated with poverty* (e.g., Jordan, 1998; UNCTD, 1996a, 1996b). At least in the short term, this amazing promise has not been kept. Indeed, questions remain about whether it was realistic and achievable to begin with. *Some nations, especially ones saddled by heavy debt, limitations in political infrastructures, and evaluated by outsider investors as being low in human capital, cannot qualify as true players in the global economic game.* And, absent major external assistance and massive, internal changes, they are destined to remain on the outside looking in (e.g., Barber, 1996; UNDP, 1999; Woodward, 1996). Once these inequalities are taken into account, de facto trade patterns and economic opportunities can be evaluated against broad claims that the benefits of economic globalization and liberalization have been, and will be, distributed equitably and generously.

In fact, trading patterns and attendant economic opportunities are not distributed either generously or equitably. For example, Hoogvelt (1997, pp. 74–75), like Woodward (1996), has analyzed the relevant data. Their conclusions are much the same. To quote Hoogvelt (1997):

> the record of world trade can neither be summoned to testify to "the increasing interconnectedness which characterizes our world economy," nor to evidence "the deepening and widening penetration of the core by the periphery." Rather, it stands as evidence of a modestly thickening network of economic exchanges within the core, a significant redistribution of trade participation within the core, the graduation of a small number of peripheral nations with a comparatively small population base to "core" status, but above all to a declining economic interaction between the core and the periphery, both relative to aggregate world trade and relative to total populations participating in the thickening network. (p. 75)

This conclusion also affects analyses of absolute and relative poverty. Once inter-nation variability is considered, and the search involves "have-not" nations, a different picture emerges. *Relative poverty in some nations of the world, indeed the entire region making up sub-Saharan Africa, actually has increased as economic globalization and trade liberalization have advanced* (e.g., Woodward, 1996). It takes little imagination to wonder about the tolls exacted on families.

Opportunities for poverty alleviation and the improvement of individual and family well-being, unevenly distributed prior to economic globalization and liberalization, remain so. At least sixty nations have not improved since 1988, and many are worse off than before (UNDP, 1999). On the other hand, *opportunities have improved in some nations in Asia that are international players* (e.g., Korea, Taiwan).[17]

Social inequalities among individuals and families in different nations are inseparable from economic inequalities. Consumption patterns, lifestyle choices, identities, and well-being hinge on economic resources. *Workers and their families in the formal economies of the low-income nations may be better off than before, and better off than individuals and families who are unemployed or employed in the informal econ-*

omy, but they are not as well off as workers in the high-income nations. It is ironic, but revealing, that *many production workers in the low-income nations cannot afford to purchase the products they assemble for consumption in the first world* (e.g., McMichael, 1996). In the global age, these differences usher in new, international issues involving equity and social justice (e.g., Jordan, 1998).

Data systems for the global age may need to be revised accordingly (e.g., Halstead & Cobb, 1996). Data used in national systems about social and economic differences and inequalities (social stratification) are no less important, but they miss an important part of the story. *Comparative international data systems for family well-being are needed, systems that assess the number of families that enjoy an acceptable standard of living threshold and that are sensitive to the differential purchasing power of the same amount of money in different nations, as well as in various parts of each nation.*

Data systems like these will respond to needs for valid, accurate, and comprehensive information about the effects of economic globalization, liberalization, and commodity chains. Evaluations of their impacts, with an eye toward family-centered policies and practices, will improve when these data are gathered, organized, and made more accessible.

REINING IN GLOBAL CAPITALISM: CONTOURS OF THE NEW POLITICAL ECONOMY

Some issues simply cannot wait. Indeed, some problematic patterns are already clear. They are part of the new heuristics of fear involving problems that humanity has created for itself. The time has arrived to address them.

Global capitalism is nomadic and on a runaway course for at least three reasons. The first set of reasons stems from the actions of the nation-state in the name of liberalization. Global capitalism is nomadic and on a runaway course because national policies have not only allowed this, but enabled the process (e.g., Langmore, 1998). To reiterate, leaders in many nations have enabled an inversion in the political economy; the polity serves the economy. With this inversion, the imagination and creativity of policy makers are crippled. They must remain riveted on the needs of the economy, in the here and now. They lose what Mills (1969) called the "sociological (social) imagination"—the capacity to assess the limitations of today's world and to imagine and work toward a better tomorrow.

The implication is clear: Governments must act in new, more appropriate, and more effective ways. And they will be encouraged to do so if their citizenry will not permit anything less.

On the other hand, economic globalization is immensely challenging. What can governments effectively do? This question is linked to the second set of reasons. Each nation-state is, in some respects, limited. As Giddens (1990, p. 65) observed, in the global age, the nation-state is "too small for the big problems of life and too big for the small problems of life."

When the nation-state is too small, as it is in the face of some aspects of economic globalization, a third set of reasons enters the picture. New international, governmental entities are needed. These entities must be larger than the nation-state and larger and more comprehensive than regional alliances such as the European Union. In other words, democratic, international governance and governing bodies are needed that steward global welfare, including the well-being of individuals and families (UNDP, 1999). These international bodies depend on a new brand of citizenship among the world's people. They must be oriented simultaneously toward local needs, national priorities, and international, global welfare. They must be able to engage easily in dialectical thinking, discourse, and planning. With this perspective in mind, proponents of a new international citizenry and international governance advocate a new world ethic (e.g., Kung, 1991; Mohan, 1992), world citizenship in pursuit of species interests and survival (e.g., Boulding, 1988), and cosmopolitan localism (e.g., Held, 1997).

Knowing that such world citizenship must be voluntary—it cannot be forced—proponents emphasize needs for a new concept of civil society. Civil society refers to the free spheres of human association and activity. In the past, it has been a national concept. Today, civil society may build from its national arms and develop an international reach. Krut (1997), for example, emphasizes the importance of a new kind of nongovernmental organization, the international civil society organization (CSO). She provides examples of the global reach and political effectiveness of CSOs in addressing transnational issues (e.g., policies and practices associated with the American fast-food chain McDonald's; human rights successes) and local issues (helping 263 families of the Sei Balumai people of Indonesia's North Sumatra Province). In brief, international governance means people and structures working from the bottom up.

Bottom-up efforts and structures may not be enough. Top-down governing bodies also are needed, ones that are closely harmonized and synchronized with nation-states. These international bodies must build on the strengths of the nation-state and address its weaknesses—i.e., when it is either too big, or too small. David Held (1996, 1997), a political scientist, has envisioned international, democratic governance, and key examples from his work are instructive to policy makers, helping professionals, and advocates (see also Weiss, Forsythe, & Coate, 1994). These examples are provided in conclusion.

For Held (1996, 1997), cosmopolitan democracy is the top side of bottom-up cosmopolitan localism. His orientation is forward looking, but he is careful to specify the general conditions for which cosmopolitan democracy is suitable. These are the conditions associated with economic globalization in particular and globalization in general. In other words, cosmopolitan democracy is not a retreat from globalization; it is an attempt to gain some control, especially to reign in runaway capitalism. It is an attempt to maintain a principle of autonomy, while at the same time recognizing what is enmeshed, or entrenched, in regional and global networks as well as in national and local politics (Held, 1996, p. 358). To put it another way, when individuals, families, and nations are part of overlapping, interdependent communities of fate, autonomy cannot be isolated, nor is isolationism appropriate. The implication is, *cosmopolitan democracy requires dialectical thinking, discourse, and planning.*

It also depends on the willingness of individuals, families, policy makers, and world leaders to accept the following general conditions:

- Continuing development of regional, international, and global flows of resources and networks of interaction
- Recognition by growing numbers of peoples of increasing interconnectedness of political communities in diverse domains, including the social, cultural, economic, and environmental
- Development of an understanding of overlapping "collective fortunes," which require collective democratic solutions—locally, nationally, regionally, and globally
- Enhanced entrenchment of democratic rights and obligations in the making and enforcement of national, regional, and international law
- Transfer of increasing proportions of a nation's military coercive capacity to transnational agencies and institutions with the ultimate aim of demilitarization and the transcendence of states' war systems (Held, 1996, p. 359)

To reiterate, if these general conditions and the assumptions they embody are unacceptable, then Held's proposal for cosmopolitan democracy may not be appropriate.

How might cosmopolitan democracy be developed, and what are some of its specific features? Held identifies both short- and long-term measures (Held, 1996, pp. 358–359). Table 10.1 presents many of these

TABLE 10.1. An Adaptation of Held's Model for Cosmopolitan Democracy

SHORT-TERM REFORMS	LONG-TERM CHANGES
Reform the leading UN governing institutions (e.g., Security Council), giving low- and medium-income nations a significant voice and decision-making capacities.	Develop a new charter of rights and obligations locked into different domains of political, social, and economic power.
Convene an international constitutional convention.	Create a global parliament (with limited revenue-raising capacity), one connected to regions, nations, and localities.
Create a new, international legal system, including a Human Rights Court, a Family Rights Court, and an Environmental Protection Court; and ensure compulsory jurisdiction before the International Court.	Develop and extend an interconnected, global legal system, one that embraces elements of criminal and civil law.
Establish an international police force that is effective and accountable.	Shift progressively and permanently a growing portion of each nation-state's military coercive capability to regional and global institutions, with the ultimate aim of demilitarization and transcending states' war systems.
Enhance nonstate, nonmarket solutions through family-centered national and transnational civil societies; invest in family supports and family-centered community development.	Create and support a diverse array of self-regulating associations and groups in civil society; and support and strengthen families so that they and members can participate effectively.
Provide resources and supports to the most vulnerable nations and people, enabling them to articulate and defend their interests.	Develop a multisectoral economy, emphasizing plural patterns of ownership and possession; encourage land reform and support new ownership in rural communities.

features. Some of these features have been adapted, and others have been added (e.g., the Family Rights Court).

Perhaps the most compelling aspect of the powerful combination of cosmopolitan localism, CSOs, and cosmopolitan democracy is that they provide a sense of hope and agency for everyday people, families, policy makers, helping professionals, and advocates. Together they provide an important answer to an equally important question, which was raised at the outset.

People and governments are not powerless to confront globalization. They can be active agents. The question is one of political will, and political will depends in turn on personal, family, professional, and national ethics and morals. *Political will involves a sense of mutual obligation and responsibility to address the problems that humanity has created for itself in the global age; and an ethic of caring to steward and support the vulnerable, the unequal, and the less fortunate in a world compressed by globalization and its companions.* Other challenges related to political will are presented in the next chapter. These challenges represent new opportunities for family-centered policies and practices.

NOTES

1. I appreciate Michael A. Lawson's reminder about this ever-present temptation to retreat and hide.
2. Banfield (1967) called this retreat "amoral familialism." He linked this limited, selfish orientation to the problems of what he called "backward societies." Comparable concerns are being raised today in the United States about the retreat of citizens from civic life and national affairs and their preoccupation with themselves and their families (e.g., Putnam, 1995).
3. Readers from health-related fields may reference these latter effects as "social contagion effects." Another synonym is "domino effects."
4. The other phases are, in historical order: (1) the *germinal phase* (early fifteenth century until the mid-eighteenth century; (2) the *incipient phase* (from the mid-1700s until the 1870s); (3) the *take-off phase* (mid-1870s to the mid-1920s); and (4) the *struggle for hegemony phase,* involving disputes, wars, and the establishment of the principle of national sovereignty, and the crystallization of the third world (Robertson, 1992, pp. 58–59).
5. Barber later apologized for implicating Arab nations and Muslim people with this label, "jihad." Terrorism-as-resistance to "Americanized development" is not limited to fundamentalist Islamic groups.
6. This box is like an ideal-typical model. It enables readers to look for pat-

terns and, in turn, to act differently in relation to these patterns. These patterns are oversimplified and slightly exaggerated.

7. There are different interpretations of the human capital concept and policies in support of it. One interpretation is narrow, and it links human capital development with improvements in public schools. U.S. President Bill Clinton emphasizes this narrow view. The broader conception includes schooling, but is not limited to it. It includes health care, nutrition programs, population controls, and many other initiatives.

8. There are ripple effects. For example, the provision of more employment opportunities for women and the increasing number of women who want and deserve meaningful careers is another contributing factor. In the United States, movement of women into the labor force has been accompanied by a decline in their volunteer activities (Putnam, 1995, 2000).

9. Urban growth is limited in the high-income nations. In contrast, it is increasing dramatically in middle- and low-income nations. Data are presented in the next chapter.

10. In fact, they are caught in *debt traps* in much the same way that poverty traps many families. For example, at the beginning of the 1990s outstanding debt in low-income nations stood at about 1 trillion U.S. dollars, which is the equivalent of one-third of the combined GNPs of all of the developing nations (Hoogvelt, 1997, p. 50).

11. To return to chapter 3, the distinction between meaningful work and commodified labor is conspicuous in its absence.

12. Deplorable working conditions and exploitative management-worker relationships in export processing zones (EPZs) must be considered, too (Woodward, 1996). Women often are recruited because, where patriarchy and poverty are commonplace, employers believe that women are, in comparison to men, easier to control. Child labor is used in some EPZs. Families are affected in all such cases. It is hard to declare these people "winners" under these exploitative circumstances.

13. At least they are winners to the extent that they are not targeted for downsizing. With economic globalization, line workers are not the only ones challenged by employment insecurities.

14. The health-employment-unemployment relationship is tricky, however. For example, Mastekaasa (1996) uses data from Norway to analyze how initial health problems may help explain a person's inability to secure and keep a job. Workers may be laid off because they are less productive than others, and here, too, health problems may be involved. Employment insecurity is a cause of some health problems. Being laid off also may cause health problems. There are important opportunities for research and for innovative, family-centered policies and practices here.

15. On the other hand, industrial capitalism, industrialization, and the work ethic are associated with patriarchy; with moral exclusion related to the deserving poor (temporarily unemployed) and undeserving poor (chronically unemployed); and with factory-oriented work organization and work discipline (called "Fordism" because of the influence of Henry Ford on assembly line production technology). The welfare state did little to buffer these significant changes (Bauman, 1998; Giddens, 1994; Hoogvelt, 1997).

16. In Van Soest's (1997) framework, these effects, along with employment insecurity, unemployment, and underemployment, implicate institutional violence.

17. It is intriguing and revealing that successful union activities in these "tiger economies" have resulted in another set of moves to nations (e.g., Malaysia, Indonesia, and Thailand), that offer fewer labor challenges and lower-cost production (Hoogvelt, 1997, pp. 209–210).

CHAPTER 11

Globalization, Flows of Culture and People, and New-Century Frameworks for Family-Centered Policies, Practices, and Development

Hal A. Lawson

Economic globalization, liberalization, and commodity chain effects are part of an international game. They may be driving forces behind the more comprehensive, multifaceted process of globalization. Clearly, they have standardizing and homogenizing effects. To return to the questions posed at the beginning of chapter 10, do these effects predict even more pervasive sameness and uniformity? As globalization progresses, will cultural diversity gradually disappear? Are indigenous ways of living destined to be "erased"? Are people powerless to protect their religious and cultural traditions and to resist globalization?

This chapter picks up where the previous one left off by addressing questions like these. It presents globalization's other facets, especially its cultural, social geographic, and psychological dimensions. These other facets are related to economic globalization, but they also merit separate analysis. Once these companion processes are presented, it becomes more apparent that economic globalization is not a synonym for globalization. Like these other processes, it is a subordinate facet of globalization.

GLOBALIZATION'S OTHER COMPANIONS

Will cultural diversity disappear? Lively debates continue in response to this question. The homogenizers view globalization's destiny as international sameness and the progressive loss of diversity. They view globalization through the lens provided by modernization. By contrast, the heterogenizers use a postmodern lens. They look for, and find, resistance to globalization, including the promotion of growing diversity.

Dialectical thinking, discourse, and planning help here. The case will be made that there is a never-ending tension between the global and the local, i.e., between the homogenizing forces of modernization and the diversifying forces of postmodernism. Globalization's companion processes illustrate dialectical interplays, and they implicate future changes in planning, policies, and practices.

Glocalization

Globalization is not a one-sided, all-powerful, and uncontested process. National governments, local cultures, practices, and contexts, especially religious traditions, continue to exert powerful influences on people, practices, social institutions, and policies. In brief, local influences interact dialectically with global forces.

Glocalization is a new sensitizing construct derived from the combination of two processes—namely, localization and globalization. It is an important companion of globalization.

Glocalization describes the never-ending tensions, the dynamic interplay, between global and local forces (e.g., Eade, 1997; Pieterse, 1995; Robertson, 1995; Smith & Guarnizo, 1999). It depicts the dialectical relationships between the global and the local; and among global, local, and regional forces and influences. Each penetrates the others. Their interpenetration is simultaneous and continuous, and people are active agents in this glocalization. Furthermore, glocalization emphasizes *social geography,* i.e., the importance of particular places, at particular times, in relation to social, cultural, political, economic, and psychological interactions and changes (e.g., Friedman, 1995; Hermans & Kempen, 1998).[1]

So, it is not the global, the regional, *or* the local; it is all three in continuous tension. In other words, dichotomies are inappropriate and misleading. In the global age, dichotomous frames (e.g., national versus international; Occident [west] versus Orient [east]; modern versus postmodern; culture as place-bound versus culture as "moving" and "mobile") no longer work.

Individuals and families are moving in unprecedented numbers and at an unprecedented rate. People movements and shifting social geographies are key features of the new global age. What do these movements mean? What do they portend for the future? Globalization's other companions help address these questions.

The Deterritorialization of People and Their Culture(s)

Another companion concept, *deterritorialization,* illuminates patterns, enhances understanding, and signals the attendant challenges and opportunities for family-centered policies and practices. Deterritorialization may be introduced by emphasizing an important feature of globalization—the unprecedented flows of people, both individuals and families. These national and international people flows are significant in their own right. Box 11.1 presents information about movements within nations. Box 11.2 presents information about the international flow of people.

When people move, they take their cultures and cultural practices with them. Culture is deterritorialized as individuals and families move (e.g., Hermans & Kempen, 1998; Pieterse, 1995); so, oftentimes, is citizenship (e.g., Mahler, 1999). For example, Riley (1997) cites studies of culturally diverse, immigrant families whose special practices and traditions for family-based patriarchy moved with them when they came to the United Kingdom.

To put it another way, culture has been treated as a place-bound concept. Analysts have assumed that culture is something that is confined, or largely limited to, a given space or territory. Deterritorialization thus refers to growing relaxation of place-related boundaries and constraints on cultures. It emphasizes that when people move, they take their cultures with them, even when the host nation may be promoting other values, norms, and practices. In this sense, as culture is deterritorialized, it develops many faces, and these faces change over time and in different contexts. Culture is both local and translocal.

Culture is deterritorialized in another way. With globalization, time-space compression also affects cultures and cultural practices. In fact, cultures and cultural practices are disseminated quickly and effectively. The mass media and computer-related technologies also are involved in these cultural flows.

For example, the popular American TV music channel MTV is now available in the majority of the world's nations. It disseminates cultures, identities, affiliations, and lifestyles, not just music. It is part of a vast, growing, international information and entertainment ("infotainment") industry (Barber, 1996), an industry that is a defining feature of globalization. This industry facilitates cultural flows. For the time being, it is dominated by American cultural values and lifestyle pursuits. In

THE FLOW OF INDIVIDUALS AND FAMILIES WITHIN NATIONS

BOX 11.1

Rural-urban flow patterns within each nation reflect and fuel the process of globalization. Although flows are two-way and may change over time, especially as policies change, the dominant flow pattern is from rural areas to urban areas. These flows are associated with the economic insecurities of individuals and families, land reforms, agricultural policies, new technologies that make labor redundant, and taxes imposed on farmers (e.g., Ray, 1998). Along with population growth, these people flows are associated with rapid urbanization. With globalization, rapidly growing cities tend to exhibit a homogenized "city face" (e.g., Eade, 1997; Sassen, 1991).

Intra-nation flows, the circumstances that surround them, and their causes, correlates, and consequences have important impacts on the well-being of individuals and families. In short, people flows in many nations are changing their social geographies. Place matters. Family-centered helping policies and practices must be sensitive to families' surrounding social geographies. For example, poor migrant families and refugees often suffer as they move, and their challenges may continue, even worsen, after they move. Settlements may be temporary, and new places may bring perpetual destabilization.

Intra-nation people flows thus are important. The following examples will illuminate some of these dynamics, especially in the developing nations:

- In Brazil, 28 million small farm owners were displaced between 1960 and 1980 (McMichael, 1996, p. 72).
- In Central America, at least half of the rural population is now landless (McMichael, 1996, p. 101).
- During the 1980s alone, some 300–400 million people in the developing nations were involved in internal migrations (McMichael, 1996, p. 188).
- Fueled by the North American Free Trade Agreement (NAFTA), Mexico established the *maquiladora,* an export production zone located along its borders with the United States. Mexican workers, many of them women, assemble components that are often made

in another nation. At least 500,000 workers are employed here, and at least 70 percent of them have moved from rural areas (McMichael, 1996, pp. 180–181).

• According to data from the World Bank, in the period between 1980 and 1993, the average rate of urban growth in forty-five low-income nations was 3.9 percent each year, a rate nearly twice that of overall population growth; in the sixty-three middle-income nations, urban growth each year was 2.8 percent, while overall population growth was 1.7 percent (Ray, 1998, p. 38).

• Led by Tokyo, Japan, with a projected population of some 26 million people, by the year 2010 the world will have at least twenty-six *megacities* with populations exceeding 10 million people. Twenty-two of the twenty-six will be located in developing and low-income nations. Another thirty-three cities will contain between 5 and 10 million people, and twenty-seven of them will be in developing and low-income nations (Bradshaw & Wallace, 1996, pp. 165–167).

• 20 million or more individuals (and their families) have had to abandon their homes and flee to seek safety and security. Because they have remained inside their national borders, they do not meet the classification criteria for the status of "refugee." Therefore, they fall outside the purview of the international laws and organizations that might assist them (Crossette, 2000). This kind of intranational people flow destabilizes individuals and families, and predictably, their well-being will decline.

• In the high-income nations, individuals and families with economic resources may flee the cities in pursuit of "fortress communities," i.e., walled-in and socially enclosed communities served by private schools and private health and social service providers. A "private club mentality" is evident (Jordan, 1998). For example, some 30 percent of Americans now live in walled-in communities (Putnam, 1995, 2000).

other words, selective aspects of "American culture" are deterritorialized through MTV and the infotainment industry. This deterritorialization is an important social, cultural, and psychological companion of globalization.

Culture is also deterritorialized when it is marketed and promoted

GLOBAL FLOWS OF PEOPLE

BOX 11.2

Documenting the international flows of individuals and families is complicated. Some nations don't assess these flows. Others lack the infrastructure for valid record keeping, strict border controls, or both. Nations that keep records often have different accounting procedures. Furthermore, some individuals and families (e.g., refugees, so-called illegal aliens) enter nations without immigration permits, and they do not want to be noticed and counted. Another limitation: Record keeping usually emphasizes individuals, not families.

So, these limited data probably underrepresent international migration patterns, and they provide even less information about families. Border relationships also need to be investigated. For example, it is hard to know how many people are turned back, but it is known that health and environmental problems are associated with border crossing and border relationships (e.g., Kamel, 1997). Mindful of these limitations and others, here are key indicators of international people flows, as presented by Martin and Widgren (1996):

- At least 125 million people (individuals and families) live outside their nation of birth or citizenship.
- This number is predicted to increase by 2–4 million each year.
- In 1995 at least 15 million people were classified as refugees, and another 12 million people were known to be in transition. At least half of these 27 million displaced people were in developing nations of Africa and western Asia, and most of them were women and children.
- In oil-producing nations of the Middle East, the majority of the workers are foreigners, and overall, in the Middle East, there are some 2.8 million imported workers, including at least 17,000 Vietnamese (see also McMichael, 1996, p. 187).
- In South Africa, at least one of every seven workers is a foreigner.
- The high-income nations host some 60 million recent immigrants and refugees.
- Seven of the wealthiest nations (Germany, France, United Kingdom, United States, Italy, Japan, and Canada) have about one-third of the world's migrant population; and there are at least

20 million immigrants from other world zones in Europe (Mc-Michael, 1996, p. 187).

- Approximately 1.25 million Mexicans were granted legal immigration permits into the United States between 1990 and 1993 (Bradshaw & Wallace, 1996, p. 167), and the number of both legal and undocumented immigrants continues to increase.
- In Germany, migrants account for all of the net new population growth, while in the United States they account for one-third of population growth.

Furthermore, according to McMichael (1996),

- at least 3.5 million Muslims, representing Arab and North African cultures, now reside in France after they were recruited to work in industry and construction; they make up about one-quarter of the total immigrant population;
- in Germany, there are at least 1,000 mosques for Turkish workers;
- hundreds of thousands of Indonesians harvest rubber and copra in Malaysia; and
- Japan provides work for at least 700,000 Koreans.

Because family-focused accounting systems are not employed, comprehensive data about families are not readily available. Inferences must be made.

Although the data will not be reported here, it is possible to derive clues about family-related global flows in nations that offer family reunification policies (Lahav, 1997). Clues also can be derived from the data sets of nations, which permit immigration based on marriage, or the intent to marry (e.g., Martin & Widgren, 1996).

There is another way to make inferences about the global flows related to families and family systems. Martin & Widgren (1996, p. 10) reference an important relationship between demographic data and economic data, using Colombia, Mexico, Bangladesh, Jordan, Portugal, and Turkey as examples. Using U.S. dollars as the currency equivalent, they present estimates of the amount of money earned in a foreign nation that was returned to the people in the home nation. For example, each year an estimated 400 million dollars earned in another nation is returned to Colombia. In Bangladesh, the figure is 900 million; in Jordan, it is 1 billion; and, in Portugal, it approximates 4 billion dollars annually. It seems safe to infer that these wage transfers subsidize families and family systems. Similarly, in the United States, interest is growing in the increasing number of "nomad dads" who live elsewhere and who spend more time on the road than at home, usually as a consequence of their jobs in the new global economy (e.g., Heying, 1997).

Thus, it is evident that global and national people flows are responsible for a new social geography of families and their homes. This social geography involves two related concepts: the *faraway bedroom community* (Martin & Widgren, 1996) and the *divided, international family system* (after Bruce, 1989).

as part of part of the global economy. The mass media promote multiple choices and pathways, and so do businesses. Children and youth are marketing targets. So are women, especially in the high-income nations. Commercial micromarketing of identities-as-lifestyles includes clothing, jewelry, and other appearance-related identity-makers such as body sculptures and tattoos. To return to an example cited in chapter 10, Nike's popular advertising slogan, "Just do it!" conveys a broad image involving identity and lifestyle. Micromarketing and promotion of cultures and lifestyles via the Web and the media are only in their infancy, but already the possibilities for promoting both cultural diversity and homogeneity are seemingly endless. While now primarily resources for business and industry, they also may serve as new opportunities for microenterprises (small businesses) for individuals and families in the future.[2]

Glocalization Plus Deterritorialization Equals Hybridization

Cultures thus are deterritorialized via the infotainment industry and as people move and interact. As people communicate, interact, mix, marry, and procreate, cultures penetrate and interpenetrate. Global forces interact with local people, influences, cultures, and contexts (glocalization).

Some analysts see special developments in this powerful combination of glocalization and deterritorialization. They suggest that, as people and cultures move, diversity in identities, lifestyles, and cultural practices grows. Hybrid subcultures, lifestyles, and identities develop. Analysts refer to this "glocalized and deterritorialized diversity" as *hybridization* or, referencing long-standing cultural mixtures in New Orleans, Louisiana (USA), *creolization* (e.g., Friedman, 1995; Hermans & Kempen, 1998; Pieterse, 1995; Robertson, 1995).

Examples include Thai boxing by Moroccan girls in Amsterdam; Asian rap in London; Irish bagels; Mexican girls in Greek clothing performing Greek folk dances; and Chinese tacos (Pieterse, 1995). Similarly, new cults and cult-systems arise from combinations of existing ones.

This hybridization also is evident in the construction and transformation of individual and group identities and lifestyles. The same clothing items and body sculptures mean different things in diverse places. For example, Michael Jordan's clothing line has multiple meanings and purposes in the world's micromarkets. Air Jordan shoes may signify an aspirant athlete in Savannah, Georgia, or a skinhead in Dresden, Germany. Global and local influences interact, producing both variety and homogeneity. Glocalization, deterritorialization, and hybridization thus constitute a powerful formula for diversity.[3] They serve to introduce another set of companion ideas.

Intercultural Contact Zones: New "Scapes" for Action and Advocacy

Both people flows and cultural flows are very important facets of globalization. So are the interactions among people and their cultures. Special interest resides in the contact zones between and among cultures and people, both within and among nations. Understanding is growing about the importance of *cultural flows* in the special intercultural and international contact zones (e.g., Appadurai, 1990; Hannerz, 1992; Hermans & Kempen, 1998).

These contact zones are called "scapes" because they are associated with parts of the world, i.e., different social geographic "landscapes." These scapes are sites for cultural ebbs and flows. They are sites for intercultural transactions, communication, and learning through space and time. In the past, analysts (e.g., Appadurai, 1990; Hermans & Kempen 1998, p. 1117) have identified five such scapes, or intercultural contact zones:

- *Technoscapes*—These scapes are related to the global configuration of technology, both mechanical and informational: e.g., new sociotechnical systems and infrastructures in support thereof and new information management systems.
- *Ethnoscapes*—These scapes are related to people flows: e.g., immigrants, tourists, refugees, guest workers, exiles, and other moving groups.
- *Mediascapes*—These are the scapes associated with the infotainment industry: e.g., newspapers, films, television, computer and netware systems.
- *Finanscapes*—These scapes are associated with systems of finance: e.g., currency markets, stock exchanges, commodity speculations, and loan opportunities, including ones available to community co-operatives and to the poor (e.g., the Grameen Bank).
- *Ideoscapes*—These are the scapes associated with secular ideologies: e.g., ideologies associated with socialism, communism, capitalism, individualism.

For some analysts, these five scapes are associated with the top-down homogenizing and standardizing forces of globalization.

These five scapes and others also can be approached from a grass-roots, bottom-up approach. In other words, scapes may be viewed as opportunities for grassroots advocacy, political and social mobilization, and sites for collective action. To return to the last part of chapter 10, these scapes can be organizing and action zones for translocal civil society organizations (CSOs).

Once scapes are viewed as action and advocacy zones, individuals, families, groups, and organizations can use the Internet and the infotainment industry (mediascapes) to achieve collective goals. In other words: *Every international social movement is a potential scape, or contact zone.* These social movements often are bottom-up, grassroots responses to globalization's challenges and problems, especially runaway capitalism that does not heed human rights agendas and is unresponsive to individual and family well-being. Already many social movements have their own Web sites. Many have electronic newsletters and bulletin boards, "listservs," and chat circles. At the same time, advocates are learning how to use the media to their own advantage (e.g., Schwartz, 1996).

In this view, scapes are potential policy and practice innovation sites. They are simultaneously local, national, regional, and international. Diverse people in separate parts of the world may take advantage of the opportunities associated with globalization's Internet and infotainment industry to mobilize locally, nationally, and internationally for collective action to enhance family well-being and international social welfare.

Some scholars (e.g., Johnson, 1999) call this grassroots organizing and mobilization for collective action "globalization from below," or "transnationalism from below" (Smith & Guarnizo, 1999). It is a kind of globalization because it unites diverse people in common causes. It helps coordinate, integrate, and synchronize their efforts. It aligns, as needed, agendas and efforts that otherwise might be contradictory, competing, and less effective.

On the other hand, it may not be desirable or beneficial to link these grassroots efforts with the idea of globalization. After all, globalization has negative connotations, and grassroots organizers are not interested in homogenizing and standardizing the world. Instead, they invoke the environmental slogan "Think globally, act locally." They are mindful of local diversity and needs to protect and enhance it at the same time they promote this kind of collective action. This slogan is suggestive of cosmopolitan localism. It connotes glocalization and hybridization—in short, the preservation of diversity and the value of local, indigenous innovations.

Connotations of diversity and pluralism like these are important with scapes. As with effective community planning, organization, and mobilization strategies, divergent viewpoints are not eradicated. Divergent viewpoints and different strategies are strengths or assets. Healthy tensions and new choices derive from this diversity. "Globalization from below" is thus a dialectical process. It also requires strengths-based or asset-based development and mobilization strategies.

The point is, policy leaders, helping professionals, and citizen advocates can employ the same "globalization from below" social movement strategy to advance comprehensive, holistic improvement agendas in relation to important scapes. Here, then, are additional scapes for cultural flows, collective action, and perhaps international social movements:

- *Genderscapes*—These scapes address gender relations, especially patriarchy and women's issues: e.g., national and international social movements for the rights of girls and women; feminization processes, including the feminization of poverty (e.g., Standing, 1989); and future movements for the changing identities, responsibilities, and commitments of men.

- *Ecoscapes*—These scapes address environmental protection, enforcement, and justice issues: e.g., regional and international environmental rights, protection, surveillance, and planning networks and organizations.
- *Polityscapes*—These scapes address macroconcerns such as the development of international governments and governing authorities as well as policy innovations at the national government level: e.g., the growing number of mechanisms for rapid learning, response, and improvement systems in governments at all levels—local, state, provincial, national, and regional. Polityscapes also include contact zones for political mobilization, agenda setting, and advocacy, including the promotion of new family rights and the support of family-centered political candidates.
- *Legalscapes*—These scapes address legal issues regarding individual and family rights and the protection of basic freedoms: e.g., freedom to organize and freedoms from social, cultural, political, and economic exclusion as well as from oppression and repression.
- *Eduscapes*—These scapes address opportunities, structures, and changes related to schooling in particular and the broader process of education, especially as they relate to the promotion of individual and family well-being and the reduction of inequality, poverty, and population problems.
- *Developmentscapes*—These scapes address specific plans and larger issues, both national and international, concerning social and economic development: e.g., plans for alleviating poverty, providing full, equitable employment, and building social infrastructures that support local village and community development.
- *Urbanscapes*—These scapes address special issues concerning the world's cities, especially their effects on the well-being of individuals and families: e.g., urban planning for the informal sector, transportation needs, and housing needs.
- *Identityscapes*—These scapes are concerned with the promotion of identities and diverse lifestyles, as well as securing social supports from others for them: e.g., social supports and action strategies for diverse lifestyles, sexual preferences, and persons who feel socially excluded.

- *Healthscapes*—These scapes are concerned with important issues regarding health and mental health promotion and education, especially disease prevention and cures: e.g., AIDS prevention organizations and other organizations and networks that focus on specific diseases,[4] and mutual aid and assistance groups that address mental health issues via the Web.
- *Childscapes,* or perhaps, *youthscapes*—These scapes are concerned with the well-being of children and youth: e.g., child labor, risk-protective factor indices, access to health and mental health services, anti-delinquency and crime prevention programs.[5]
- *Elderscapes,* or perhaps, *agingscapes*—These scapes are concerned with the well-being of elderly people and the process of aging: e.g., health-enhancing activities, intergenerational family supports, volunteer and community service programs, special needs for services.
- *Religioscapes*—These scapes are concerned with the promotion and analysis of formal religions, schools of thought regarding spirituality, and counter views such as agnosticism and atheism.
- *Knowledgescapes*—These scapes are associated with the helping professions and disciplines, especially their respective research agendas, knowledge bases, policy preferences, and practice exemplars: e.g., national and international associations and publications that promote and interweave local and national knowledge and practices with their international counterparts.

Each of these scapes, important in its own right, also may interact with one or more others. So, for example, social movements might combine women's rights with environmental issues and health-related needs. To reiterate, *every advocacy and special interest group can create its own scape(s) to facilitate collective action. Scapes are, in short, policy and practice tools for the new century.*

Every scape identified here affects families and, in turn, families influence them. The implication is clear: *familyscapes* also are essential.[6] Familyscapes are intercultural contact zones that address the well-being of the families in every context—local, state/provincial, national, regional, and international. Although separate scapes for children and youth and elders also might be structured, as suggested earlier, they also belong in familyscapes.

Indeed, familyscapes encourage family-centered, relational approaches as substitutes for categorical policies and practices for elders as well as for children and youth. Familyscapes also are sites for the communication and hybridization of family-centered policies and practices.

Family-centered policy makers, helping professionals, and advocates may start work on familyscapes now, in their local communities, states and provinces, and nations.

Familyscapes, like the other scapes, are sites for collective action. To return to the conclusions in chapter 10, familyscapes and other scapes are sites for cosmopolitan localism, civil society organizations, and cosmopolitan democracy. They allow people to address the problems created by aspects of globalization through globalization's opportunities and technologies. As formidable as economic globalization and political liberalization are, people are able to confront them and transform them in pursuit of improvements in individual and family well-being.

Globalization's technological advances, time-space compression, and intercultural contact zones enable the development of bottom-up, grassroots, rapid communication, response, and mobilization systems in support of individual and family well-being, species protection, and environmental preservation. Here, too, it is clear that people are not powerless; they are able to challenge and change the course of human history. Indeed, this agency, this transformational capacity, is what Roudometof and Robertson (1995) imply when they describe new possibilities, in the global age, for the "reinvention of tradition." Familyscapes, like other scapes, are new traditions that policy makers, helping professionals, and advocates can invent and reinvent. A growing number of families who are literally "on the move" may be among the first to benefit from these new-century familyscapes.

MOVEMENTS OF FAMILIES WITHIN AND ACROSS BORDERS: THE NEW SOCIAL GEOGRAPHY FOR POLICIES AND PRACTICES

Global flows of individuals and families, both national and international, are a defining feature of globalization. That they are moving in unprecedented numbers and at an unprecedented rate is clear. But the crucial question remains: *Why do they move?* Responses to this question will help guide the development of new-century, family-centered policies and practices. Relational analysis and dialectical thinking are needed because this question involves the interplay of psychological, cultural, social, geographic, political, and economic factors at several levels—local, national, regional, and international.

When individuals and families move, recruitment, attraction, and selection processes are involved, individually and in combination. Gender, especially family-based gender relations as proscribed and inscribed by cultural and religious traditions, also weighs heavily in these movements (e.g., Riley, 1997); so does the socioeconomic status of the family. Place, time, and local context must be considered. In a nutshell, the analysis of people flows is complicated.

Martin and Widgren (1996, p. 8) provide a good place to begin. They emphasize the interplay among three kinds of factors: *pull factors, push factors,* and *network factors.* They help explain global flows. In addition, a fourth factor is introduced—*keep factors.*

Pull Factors

Needs for family reunification serve to introduce pull factors. When families are divided because one or more members move, and they wish to become reunited, family reunification is a pull factor. Family needs "pull" people, causing them to move.

Other pull factors are economic, and they involve employment, including active recruitment and demand structures. For example, imported, low-cost labor for the services and agriculture in the formal economy is a structurally embedded demand factor, which pulls prospective workers. When citizens in the home nation will not perform this work, the recruitment of guest workers and immigrants is a viable solution (Martin & Widgren, 1996).

Similarly, in the "high-tech" fields, demand for new kinds of specialists (e.g., in computer systems design and networking, information management systems) often exceeds domestic supply. In fact, nations often compete with one another for brilliant scientists, inventors, and engineers (e.g., Barber, 1996; McMichael, 1996). These workers are pulled. Many kinds of people with special talents also are in high demand, and they are recruited and pulled. Professional athletes are an obvious and important example. Imported athletes now make up a significant number of the players on European football (soccer) teams and American baseball teams (Maguire, 1999).

In some cases, trade policies and immigration policies result in intriguing relationships between pull factors and the next category, push factors. These policies also are associated with the deterritorialization of culture, and they signal the need for international governing bodies to coordinate labor and production. For example, Germany restricts the import of Polish apples to protect its own apple industry. At the same time, it permits Polish apple workers to enter Germany to harvest its apples. Polish workers are both pushed and pulled to move to Germany to get jobs (Martin & Widgren, 1996, p. 13). So, national and international import-export policies influence push-pull dynamics. When jobs are lost or reduced in one nation, the same kinds of jobs may be available in others. Individuals and families move as they are pushed and pulled simultaneously.

Push Factors

Push factors refer to local and national constraints, changing circumstances, social problems, and barriers related to employment and social and cultural exclusion. These push factors compel individuals and families to look elsewhere and then move.

Push factors implicate migrants and refugees, along with the various causes and correlates of their movement. For example, individuals and families move—if and when they can—when they are denied basic human rights. They move when they are persecuted for their religion, culture, gender, and sexual preferences, and when they are denied access to health care, schooling, and other basic services. They often flee from political upheavals, civil strife, genocide, war, epidemics involving infectious diseases, and famine. These and other causes and correlates may interact. Individually and collectively, they cause individuals and families to move.

Structural unemployment, introduced in chapter 3, also is associated with push factors. Absent employment prospects in the home nation, individuals and families move elsewhere. Population dynamics also can be considered push factors, especially when population growth is combined with structural unemployment. For example, population growth in Mexico, Turkey, and the Philippines is associated with structural unemployment and, in turn, migration. Each year some 500,000 to 1 million, net, new employment opportunities must be developed for a burgeoning population of youth ready to enter the workforce. In China and El Salvador, job supply cannot keep up with population demand; in these nations 20–40 percent of the population is always unemployed or underemployed (Martin & Widgren, 1996).

Population growth and structural unemployment do not operate in isolation, however. They interact with the forces of globalization, especially subsistence insecurities and job opportunities, and national policies involving taxation, social welfare benefits, and landownership and use related to agriculture (e.g., Goldthorpe, 1996; McMichael, 1996; Ray, 1998).

Network Factors

Network factors involve people relationships, especially family relationships. In fact, family-related connections are associated with awareness of opportunity structures and processes. For example, a Turkish worker employed in Germany learns of opportunities for others in his family system to gain employment if they are willing to move to Germany. He contacts family members in Turkey and works in Germany to enable their immigration and employment.

Women are especially adept at networking, as demonstrated by the powerful recruitment performed by Mexican women in the United States, and the access to immigration permits and social and health services they facilitate (Riley, 1997). In brief, families are employment recruiters and facilitators in the global arena, and women appear to be especially important. Like families, friendship networks also facilitate awareness and movement.

There is another kind of network, and it has insidious effects on individuals and families. A "shadow economy" operates in many parts of the world (e.g., Jordan, 1998), including the United States. For example, labor smugglers subsidize the migration of both individuals and their families in exchange for a percentage of each person's wages (e.g., Martin & Widgren, 1996). Migrants' employment is often "hidden" in the informal economy. It may involve crime, delinquency, the sexual exploitation of children, and prostitution. In all cases, these contractual arrangements may become permanent. The smuggler has the upper hand because the immigrant and her/his family are classified as illegal immigrants, and they confront the ever-present prospect of detection and deportation. In brief, this labor smuggling industry is a modern-day form of indentured servitude, and it is illegal and immoral. Even worse, labor smuggling is allegedly producing modern-day forms of slavery involving women and children. Practices like these signal a need for the kinds of action and advocacy scapes identified earlier.

Keep Factors

The sensitizing construct of "keep factors" appears to be an original contribution. It refers to the reasons, forces, and circumstances that compel some families and family members to remain where they are. This construct derives from dialectical thinking, discourse, and analysis. It is grounded in two important assumptions:

1. Understanding of who moves (one family member, some members, or the entire family), when, how, where, and why is incomplete without an understanding of who stays, including who is left behind.
2. Over time and with changing circumstances, keep factors may turn into pull factors and network factors.

Keep factors call attention to the importance of gender and its social construction in ethnic, cultural, and national contexts. Gender refers to the differential roles and responsibilities of men and women and the varying power they enjoy (e.g., Riley, 1997). As indicated in chapters 2 and 3, discussions of gender are associated with patriarchy. More specifically, the gender-patriarchy relationship emphasizes the interplay between the differential roles and responsibilities of men and women, especially differences in the power and authority each enjoys (e.g., Riley, 1997, 1999).

Patriarchy may be an important keep factor. Reflect briefly on how patriarchy, manifested as the inability of women to pursue and gain employment, "keeps" them home. For example, if a woman's husband moves to gain employment in a patriarchal nation that effectively disallows her employment, and the woman is unwilling to give up her job because of the meaning it holds for her and the power it gives her, institutionalized patriarchy becomes and is a keep factor. It serves to divide families.

Similarly, in comparison to an unemployed man, an unemployed woman in a low-income nation may be denied equal opportunities to migrate to a middle-income nation to secure employment.

Cultural differences, especially ones involving language, lifestyles, and religion, also are keep factors; they are associated with divided family systems. Over time, cultural preferences, which acted initially as keep factors, may become pull and push factors. For example, consider the case of a Vietnamese father who migrates to an oil-rich nation in the Middle East to secure employment, and in search of a better life for his family. The family stays behind, but they make plans to reunite members once the family's "scout" is employed and more secure. Unfortunately, the father is greeted with harsh realities. These realities may include the dynamics of social and cultural exclusion and religious discrimination. He feels pushed out and is pulled back home.

Keep factors also are inseparable from population dynamics, profound poverty, and their relationship. In this perspective, members and entire families may move, but when they do, they leave others behind. In brief, keep factors emphasize the dynamics of abandonment, especially abandoning infants, children, and elders. Where poverty is concerned, abandonment dynamics are inseparable from economic hardship. Abandonment is also associated with increases in family size that outstrip income and subsistence supports.

Population dynamics are very important, and they are related to population control policies and gender relations. The hardships imposed by poverty interact with population dynamics. Any explanation of abandonment and the premature death of children must weigh their joint influences.

For example, Riley (1997) describes the tragic effects of extreme poverty and population dynamics in remote villages in Brazil. In contrast to mothers elsewhere in Brazil and in the world who demonstrate their nurturing orientations and behaviors in caring for the feeding and health of their children, mothers in these villages demonstrate their caring by their "death watches." They remain by the sides of their children, watching them die because of food shortages and the lack of health care.

Gender relations as structured by cultural traditions also play important roles. In China, as in other nations such as India and Ghana, male children are viewed as more prestigious and important than females. In this system of gender relations and cultural traditions, males carry on the family name, and they are among the family's economic assets. Males are treated as economic assets because they are viewed as employable, and their future incomes will support the family, both in the short term and in the long term, i.e., when parents become elders. Elder support is crucial in some of these nations because elders lack retirement and social insurance programs.

By contrast, when these patriarchal relations are evident, women may be treated as economic assets in just one sense—their abilities to bear male children (the tangible assets). Otherwise, they may be viewed as resource drains, especially when a future dowry is involved, or when economic hardship means that an older woman (e.g., a widow) is just another mouth to feed (e.g., Ray, 1998). People flows and population dynamics must be framed against this system of gender and cultural relations.

As Riley (1997) observes, China's strict population control policy limits the number of children women may have. Urban women are permitted to have just one child, while rural women may have two. The pressure on families, especially women, to bear males is enormous. Ultrasound technologies, which identify the sex of the fetus, are used with increasing frequency, and abortions are on the rise. Families also resort to extreme measures. It is suspected that some family members kill infant girls (Riley, 1997). A growing number of families have opted for the less extreme strategy of abandonment. Families may move, but they leave infant girls behind. Orphanages must assume responsibility for them. Where these infants are concerned, being a female is a keep factor.

However, the practice of abandoning infant girls in particular and children in general is not limited to China. Abandoned infants and children are evident nearly everywhere in the world. They are separated from their families as their families move. Although some of these children may be unwanted, their abandonment is not always the result of being unwanted. Many are abandoned because of poverty and population pressures, which make it impossible to support every family member. The point is, powerful keep factors involving gender relations, cultural traditions, and poverty's hardships often interact in powerful ways to divide families, which in turn influences the well-being of infants and children.

Two final observations are required on the subject of global flows. Some people take their social and economic status with them, while others must leave them behind. For example, McMichael (1996, p. 187) references a gynecologist from Romania who must make a living selling apples in the streets of Geneva, Switzerland, and Polish engineers who pick grapes in Swiss vineyards because they can earn in five weeks what would take five months at home. Both national immigration policies and trade policies weigh heavily in these patterns. Many workers are guest workers who are not permitted to stay.

In contrast, some people are permitted and encouraged to bring their credentials and skills with them. Some are immediately viewed as equals, i.e., the equivalent of citizens even if they lack formal citizenship papers. Others face immediate social, political, economic, and cultural barriers, stratification systems, eligibility requirements, and even exclusion dynamics.

Similarly, McMichael (1996, pp. 186–187) references literature that differentiates between rich nomads (privileged foreign nationals) and poor nomads ("boat people on a planetary scale"). In both cases, easing immigrant and refugee transitions is a key challenge for both national and international policy makers. Nationalism can be both a facilitator and a constraint.

Nationalism is interesting and important for another set of reasons. Individuals and families who move across borders often have identity, commitment, and affiliation challenges. For example, is the Iraqi who works in the Netherlands an Iraqi, a Dutch citizen, or both? Pieterse (1995, p. 49) is among the analysts who call attention to new orientations such as "long-distance patriotism" and "absentee nationalism." And, what should analysts make of foreign athletes representing, even dominating, the home team and the national team (Maguire, 1999)? What does "home" mean in the global age? Nations may be "imagined communities" (Anderson, 1994), but nationalism is real in its consequences. Nationalism continues to provide identities and communal bonds.

As people move, as cultures mix and match, if the local place is foreign, and if national commitments are far away, how will people live and work together effectively? How will they mobilize for the collective? Why should they care and become involved when they lack any commitments and feel no obligations to others in their community, or to the nation that supports them? How will policy makers, helping professionals, and advocates work with families whose bonds are distant, not local? How will democracy work?

This increasingly unstable context, with its challenges related to identity, commitments, cultural diversity, and "home," compels individuals and families to seek stability, security, and continuity. Where will they find them? According to Huntington (1993) individuals and families will find stability, security, and identity- and commitment-related continuity in their religion, ethnicity, and cultural traditions. Religion and ethnicity, individually and in combination, will substitute for nationalism in the global world. Conflicts and wars, like the dynamics of social, cultural, and economic exclusion, will derive from differences in religion, cultural traditions, and ethnicity (Huntington, 1993; Kennedy, 1993). These differences, together with their links to social norms and values, pose ever-important challenges for policy and practice.

Clearly, Robertson (1992) labeled the current phase of globalization "the uncertain phase" for good reason: *The needs and challenges associated with migration, immigration, and refugees are key concerns for family-centered policies and practices at every level—local, national, regional, and international.* These needs and challenges also support claims made in the last chapter about needs for cosmopolitan democracy and world citizenship.

A BRIEF SYNOPSIS AND TWO SETS OF IMPLICATIONS

To recapitulate: Globalization involves people flows and cultural flows. Increasingly, culture is deterritorialized. Local orientations and responses to globalization, i.e., glocalization and hybridization, are associated with social, cultural, psychological, and geographic changes. These changes may have multiplier and ripple effects. Perhaps most importantly, both cultural flows and people flows have profound effects on families and their well-being. In turn, individuals, families, and family dynamics (especially gender relations) affect both kinds of flows. Pull, push, network, and keep factors are also family matters. Furthermore, families' migration, immigration, and fleeing patterns present important challenges and opportunities. Thus, globalization and its companions present new challenges and opportunities for family-centered policies and practices. Two sets of implications illustrate this claim.

The New Polyculturalism and Today's Multiculturalism

Cultural flows and people flows, along with glocalization, deterritorialization, hybridization, and new intercultural contact zones (scapes), have resulted in growing diversity, one that is new in many ways. This diversity is the new polyculturalism of the global age (Pieterse, 1995), and it has important implications.

This polyculturalism, with its infinite number of hybrids, is fundamentally different from dominant assumptions about multiculturalism, including ones promoted by helping professions. Multiculturalism and multicultural practices have been framed by nationalism and attendant assumptions about national and cultural territoriality and boundaries. So, to be culturally compatible, congruent, and appropriate is to consider cultural diversity and treat it sensitively from a national, institutional perspective. Most of these strategies support cultural assimilation. Some culturally responsive practices promote some cultural accommodation. For example, when mainstream institutions such as schools endeavor to become culturally responsive, they bend their rules, practices, and languages, and even change them in response to multicultural challenges. Even so, culturally responsive practice usually is framed by national interests.

In contrast, polyculturalism is both a national and an international concept. It is related to multiculturalism and multicultural policy and practice, but it also is broader and even more challenging. The most formidable challenges are practices that are institutionalized in one place, even though they are in violation of international rights and national laws. These practices move with individuals and families when they move. Female genital mutilation (FGM), a traditional practice among some families in diverse cultures of the world, provides a compelling example (e.g., Khadja, 1999). When families move, this practice often moves with them into nations such as the United States, Canada, and the United Kingdom where it is illegal. The fact that it is illegal does not guarantee that the practice will stop. In fact, it often doesn't. The familiar multicultural strategies of the helping professions are of little use here. Female genital mutilation is just one of many new-century challenges that polyculturalism will bring.

Family-Centered Immigration Policies

A second set of implications concerns family-centered policies that respond to national and global people flows. These flows of immigrants and migrants may be greeted with some resentment in relation to the jobs they occupy and the diverse cultures and lifestyles they represent. For example, anti-immigration legislation is being promoted in Denmark, while in Sweden anti-immigration sentiment is linked to the actions of neo-Nazis.[7] The Ku Klux Klan continues to protest in the United States.

Arguably, resistance, resentment, and social exclusion dynamics are experienced more frequently and intensely by the immigrant poor. If social exclusion, poverty and its correlates, and pervasive inequality are the key to successful, effective social and economic development agendas (e.g., Mohan, 1992; Ray, 1998; Sen, 1999; Stoesz, Guzzetta, & Lusk, 1999), then the needs of these individuals and families must be addressed.

In the same vein, Martin & Widgren (1996) suggest that immigrants, migrants, and refugees pose internal and external policy challenges. Building on their suggestions, four critical family-sensitive, family-focused, and family-centered policy needs are evident.

One internal challenge is to enable immigrants and their families, especially culturally diverse and poor families, to be accepted quickly and appropriately as equal, productive members of society—if not as full, voting citizens, then at least enjoying equal status and rights (after Martin & Widgren, 1996). This policy challenge implies, for example, that parents and children should be viewed as worthy social investments because they have the potential to become leaders in the future.

A second challenge derives from the first. It involves full, equitable access to social and health services, to public education, and to other governmental entitlements that are associated with citizen status and agreed-upon standards for individual and family well-being.

The third policy challenge is both internal (national) and external (international). It involves appropriate and responsive family unification policies (Lahav, 1997). Presently families are caught in double binds between international legal and human rights facilitators and constraints and prohibitions imposed by national governments. Once again, the need for international governance, cosmopolitan democracy, is evident.

The fourth policy challenge may help address the third regarding family reunification. Following Martin & Widgren (1996), the challenge is to strike an appropriate, effective balance amid clear and important tensions. A balance needs to be struck among these related needs: (1) to import labor, especially relatively unskilled workers who are culturally diverse; (2) to respect and honor human rights charters that permit and encourage immigration and migration; (3) to respond to the needs of the growing number of persons in the developing, low-income nations who want and need to move in order to maintain and improve individual and family well-being; and (4) to take into account the employment needs of the domestic labor force, especially culturally diverse families in poverty who are harmed by social, political, and economic exclusion.

GLOBALIZATION'S CHALLENGES AND OPPORTUNITIES: NEW FRAMEWORKS FOR SOCIAL WELFARE POLICIES AND PRACTICES AND FOR FAMILY-CENTERED POLICIES AND PRACTICES

Globalization poses new challenges at the same time that it provides fresh opportunities for social welfare in general and family-centered policies and practices in particular. New frameworks are in response to, and in anticipation of, the global age, including its heuristics of fear. These new frameworks must be framed by relational analysis, and they must incorporate dialectical thinking, discourse, and planning.

National frameworks are perhaps more important than ever before. As Langmore (1998) has suggested, national governments are not powerless in the face of globalization. To the contrary, their policies, especially trade liberalization, import-export decisions, and structural adjustment policies, by whatever name, have enabled the cascading effects of a runaway, or nomad, form of capitalism—as economic globalization. However, the nation-state may be either too big or too small. Local governments are very important, and so are international ones. In short, in the global age, policies and practices must be multifaceted. They must be local, national, regional, and international—simultaneously.

Moreover, new frameworks for policies and practices need to take into account profound national and international diversity—hence the plural, *frameworks,* not a one-size-fits-all framework. These frameworks also must respond to present-day political realities. In most nations, social welfare is a collection of categorical sectors, policies, practices, and, in turn, specialized helping professions. Here, families are a competing category, even though they are related to, and inseparable from, the others.

At the same time, however, it is important that the past not dictate the future. Family-centered policies and practices are sorely needed around the world. They must become both national and international priorities. Normative, futuristic frameworks thus constitute important contributions. They create healthy tensions, dialectical interplays, between conventional social welfare and futuristic family-centered policy and practice frameworks. Figures 11.1 and 11.2 have been constructed with needs for both frameworks in mind.

Figure 11.1 provides an exploratory frame for new-century social welfare agendas. The dialectical relationship between national and international priorities is at the center of this new-century agenda. Chief among

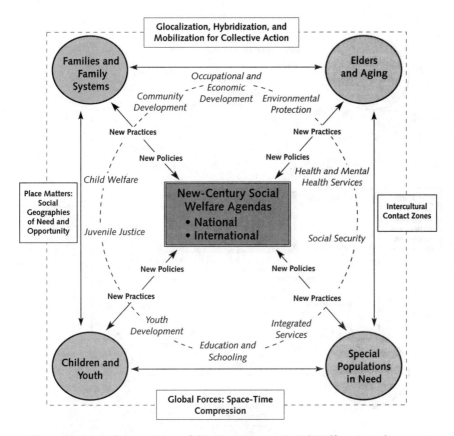

Figure 11.1 A Preliminary Map of the New-Century Social Welfare Agenda

these priorities must be the well-being of the world's families and family systems. Improved well-being depends on the abilities of advocates, helping professionals, and policy makers to address profound structural inequalities, which exist among nations, within nations, and within families and family systems.

The other portion highlights the dialectical relationships among globalization and glocalization, and it emphasizes the heart of the new-century social and economic development agenda—namely, local mobilization for appropriate, effective, and efficient collective action. Place, time, and context matter, and intercultural contact zones that mediate between the global and the local.

Families and family systems are essential, but in a dialectical frame

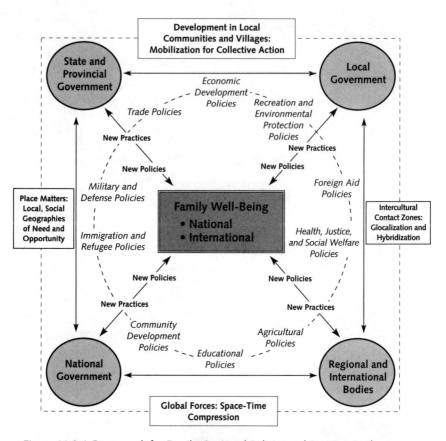

Figure 11.2 A Framework for Family-Centered Policies and Practices in the Global Age

they are not exclusive of foci on children and youth, elders and aging, and special populations (e.g., persons with developmental challenges, vulnerable women, migrants and refugees suffering from social exclusion dynamics). Amid so much complexity and change, new practices will be invented, in turn leading to policy changes; and at the same time, family-centered policy changes will result in new practices. This dialectical relationship between policies and practices, which constitutes a new definition of policy practice, also is depicted in figure 11.1.

Relational and family-centered policies and practices do not signal the end of categorical policies and practices, or the end of specialized governmental service sectors such as child welfare and juvenile justice. Here, too, dialectical thinking, discourse, and planning modes are essential. With these modes, healthy tensions become apparent. Discourse and planning focused on these tensions promotes policy innovation, learning, and continuous improvement.

Figure 11.2 presents a futuristic framework for family-centered policies and practices. In 11.2, families and their well-being are the centerpiece for both national and international policy. Note that the outer ring continues to frame the global-local interplay *and* that the content of the boxes has changed. For example, local community action is an important focus, especially in relation to interplay between intercultural scapes and local needs.

The four circles in the next ring identify dialectical interactions among various kinds and levels of government. Relationships among these levels highlight the need for coordination, synchronization, and alignment, along with possibilities for mutually beneficial policy learning and innovation.

Specific kinds of policies are identified in the next ring. They provide opportunities for family-centered policies and practices. The implication is that policies can be family sensitive and, perhaps, family focused. In other words, the policy continuum, which was introduced in chapter 4, can be applied to each policy sector. Ripple effects may be important. For example, if immigration policies become more family focused, this may facilitate an initial discussion on how trade policies can become family sensitive.

Thus, globalization and its companion processes expand and change the frames for social welfare policy and for family-centered policy. Mindful of globalization's ripple effects, the frameworks for social development and economic development also expand and change.

FROM NEW POLICY FRAMEWORKS
TO EXPANDED DEVELOPMENT AGENDAS

New frameworks for family-centered policies and practices are one cornerstone of the global age's new cosmopolitan democracies. New frameworks for development planning are another cornerstone.

In the global age, the definition of development changes somewhat. It builds on the foundation provided by others (e.g., Mohan, 1992; Ostrom, 1990; Roseland, 1998; Ray, 1998; Sen, 1999; Stoesz, Guzzetta, & Lusk, 1999; United Nations, 1994a, 1995c; UNDP, 1998). *Development refers to the ability of individuals and families, localities, states and provinces, nations, regional alliances, and international coalitions to organize and mobilize effectively to facilitate appropriate, efficient, and sustainable collective action in service of individual and family well-being and environmental preservation.* Moreover, *development, orchestrated and synchronized at all levels, is a plan that defines the future, provides hope, and enables people everywhere to address the heuristics of fear.* In other words, development is a plan for ensuring that the future is not merely a replication of the past. *More than merely forecasting the future, development involves creating more desirable futures.*

In principle, development is not done to these people and governmental entities. That is, development planning is embedded in, and informed by, democratic politics and practices.

All are involved in an interactive planning and decision-making process, which spans every level, starting with individuals and families and encompassing international governing bodies. It is not possible, in this book, to outline new development frameworks. It is possible and appropriate to present key sensitizing principles for development because they connect it with globalization.

These principles are sensitizing in at least three ways. They sensitize policy makers, helping professionals, and advocates to the importance of development agendas and their relationships to family-centered policy and practices. In addition, they highlight important development foci for strategic advocacy and action. Third, policy makers, helping professionals, and advocates can use these principles to initiate *developmentscapes,* i.e., intercultural contact zones for collective action.

Thirty such principles, which serve as examples, follow. Some are merely listed. A brief, explanatory note or an example or two accompany some principles. They are numbered for convenience; a rank order is not implied. Nor does this numbering sequence suggest that development is a linear process. To the contrary, development unfolds in multiple, interactive, and iterative phases. In the global age, development is a premier example of complex change, and it involves evaluation-related learning from implementation successes, limitations, and failures.

1. Like globalization, development encompasses psychological, geographic, social, cultural, economic, and political changes, and it requires relational analysis and dialectical thinking, discourse, and planning.

2. Social development and economic development cannot be separated; they must be coordinated, integrated, and synchronized (e.g., UNDP, 1998; Stoesz, Guzzetta, & Lusk, 1999; Woodward, 1996).

3. Each nation has the power and authority to structure its development agenda and to influence its future livelihood (e.g., Langmore, 1998; Norberg-Hodge, 1996; Ray, 1998).

4. National development planning must proceed in concert with regional alliances and, in turn, with new international governing bodies and authorities (e.g., Held, 1997; Langmore, 1998; Mohan, 1992; Ray, 1998; Woodward, 1996).

5. Development planning at all levels—local, provincial-state, national, regional, and international—must focus on structural inequality among nations, within nations, among states and provinces, within local communities, and within families (e.g., Hoogvelt, 1997; Ray, 1998; Sen, 1999).

6. Environmental planning, protection, and sustainability must become integral to new-century development agendas (e.g., Dahl, 1996; Daly, 1996; Roseland, 1998).

7. Because the planet's environmental carrying capacity already has been exceeded, and because human well-being and survival hinge on environmental restoration and preservation, development planning must include firm, fair, and equitable limits to growth (e.g., Clayton & Radcliffe, 1996; Daly, 1996).

8. Because development cannot be growth intensive in every nation, international development planning must focus on an equitable redistribution of opportunities for low-income and some middle-income nations to become involved in sustainable, economic development.

Woodward (1996) refers to this international economic restructuring as a "ladder effect." In order for some nations to move in (become players) and move up (experience economic growth), other nations must be willing to make space for them, i.e., to accommodate and facilitate their entry into the global economic system. To return to an example cited earlier, Germany's trade policies regarding apples must be restructured to encourage Poland to enjoy enhanced apple production. If so, Polish apple workers and their families can stay home, and Poland reaps some of the benefits of its apple industry. Germany must make sacrifices in support of international development.

Where food production is concerned, some such national sacrifices and compromises may be minimized. Once an international commitment is made to "feed the world," renewable, sustainable agricultural markets may open for more nations. In this scenario, Poland's gain does not result in Germany's loss. For example, less than 1 percent of the arable land in sub-Saharan Africa is used for agricultural production (Bender & Smith, 1997). Similarly, agricultural production is a development opportunity in the Ukraine (e.g., Jordan, 1998); it may pull urban dwellers back into rural areas.

9. Lifestyles and consumption patterns among wealthy persons in all nations must be scaled down in recognition of global needs and the adverse impacts of some lifestyles on scarce environmental resources, air and water quality, global warming, and individual and family well-being.[8]

10. The high-income nations have internal development challenges that parallel those in many low-income and middle-income nations (e.g., Sen, 1999).

For example, when the well-being of African Americans clustered in high-poverty communities in New York City is compared to comparable measures of individuals in developing nations such as Bangladesh, it becomes clear that, on average, individuals in the developing nations are better off than African Americans (Sen, 1999).[9]

In brief, development planners must look inward as well as outward. National development planning in the high-income nations must address the needs of three categories of people and their surrounding communities. The first category is indigenous people—for example, in Canada and in the United States, First Nation (Native American) people on reservations. The second category is populations of poor and vulnerable people who are clustered in a nation's cities. The third category, also clustered geographically, includes immigrants, migrants, and refugees. Clearly, these categories are not mutually exclusive. In cities, for example, all three categories of people may face the challenges of persistent poverty, long-term unemployment, housing and food insecurities, and underemployment in the informal sector of the economy and in household economies.

11. The specialized preparation of helping professionals (e.g., social workers) for community organization and practice must be reframed as

part of national and international development planning (e.g., Shuman, 1994; Stoesz, Guzzetta, & Lusk, 1999), in turn, providing opportunities to promote, implement, and evaluate family-centered policies and practices.

12. Development planning must focus on poverty, including its antecedents, correlates, consequences, and ripple effects (e.g., Bauman, 1998; Ray, 1998; Sen, 1999).

Ray's (1998) pioneering work on development economics must be referenced here. Assailing poverty as "the worst curse there is" (p. 267), and claiming that the poor in low-income nations are "twice cursed" because they face poverty's challenges in a nation without sufficient resources, Ray outlines a new, expanded economic development agenda that focuses on poverty:

> We move on, therefore, to arguments that *link* the incidence of poverty to mechanisms that drive its creation. It is also important to understand the informal mechanisms that spontaneously arise to cope with poverty. These mechanisms tell us something about what causes poverty, as well as the wider effects that poverty has on the economic system, and they are fundamental to the creation of appropriate policies. (1998, p. 267)

Moreover:

> The fundamental feature of poverty is that it affects the access of poor to markets, and this change in access has repercussions for the entire economy. Practically all markets are affected: the ability to obtain credit, to sell labor, to rent land for cultivation. (p. 267)

Ray, like Sen (1999), thus proposes a new frame and calculus for economic development: "Economic development should not be restricted to a small minority. This means, in particular, that development is also the removal of poverty and under-nutrition; it is an increase in life expectancy; it is access to sanitation, clean drinking water, and health services; it is the reduction of infant mortality; it is increased access to knowledge and schooling, and literacy in particular. There is an entire multitude of yardsticks" (pp. 8–9). Relational thinking and analysis are implicit here.

Effective development, for Ray, includes access to credit, including innovative loan policies promoted by the Grameen Bank. It means encouraging microenterprises. Community cooperatives provide another important strategy (e.g., Wilkinson & Quarter, 1996). In lieu of looking exclusively at needs and problems, this approach to development entails looking for assets and understanding the microdynamics of families. For example, this asset-vulnerability approach focuses on the strategic decisions made by families in poverty every day. Anti-poverty strategies thus must be grounded in families' microecologies, and they must build from these family strengths (e.g., Moser, 1998) while weighing the influences of the social and structural characteristics of their villages, communities, and cities and their personal-family support networks (e.g., Edin & Lein, 1997).

13. Development necessitates eliminating social exclusion dynamics and promoting individual and family freedom and equality (e.g., Gil, 1998a; Isham, Kaufmann, & Pritchett, 1997; Ray, 1998; Sen, 1999).

If individuals and families are expected to organize and mobilize effectively for collective action, and work toward an agreed-upon conception of the common good, they must enjoy conditional equality and fundamental freedoms (freedoms to, freedoms from). Conditional equality means freedom to act, but it also means freedom from oppression, repression, moral exclusion,[10] and discrimination based on religion, race, gender, ethnicity, abilities, age, and sexual preferences. *In this perspective, codes of ethics in fields such as social work, which prevent oppression, repression, unjust discrimination, and social exclusion, are essential components in new-century development frameworks, policies, and practices.*

14. Development planning must take into account civil society, voluntary actions in it by individuals and families, and the powerful enabling potential and actions of nongovernmental organizations of all kinds, including international CSOs (e.g., Fisher, 1998; Krut, 1997).

15. Development planning must focus on policies and strategies for providing conditional equality for immigrants and refugees. Even if individuals and families are not granted citizenship in a particular nation, they must be granted the privileges associated with citizenship, including a voice in matters that affect them, access to public schooling, social services, health benefits, and opportunities, as well as developmental pathways for adults and children to become future leaders (e.g., Booth, Crouter, & Lanvale, 1997; Lahav, 1997).

16. Development planning must incorporate strategies that build multiple social trust networks, which are culturally responsive and inclusive.

A growing number of development proposals and planning guides emphasize the concept of social capital. It connotes a monocultural version of social trust affiliation networks, including norms of reciprocity and mutual aid and assistance (e.g., Putnam, 1993, 1995, 2000). Social capital is associated with melting pot theory and cultural assimilation. It is often linked to the idea of a civil society.

In the global age, with its polyculturalism, social capital may not be as useful as some advocates have suggested. As Jordan (1998) suggests, many friendship, family, and community networks are like clubs, which recruit insiders and keep them in, while keeping outsiders out. One network's social capital is not necessarily another's.

Polyculturalism emphasizes that there are multiple, diverse networks and that these networks are cultural, not just social (e.g., Bourdieu, 1986; Boulding, 1993). Conventional ideas about social capital and civil society often have been framed by dichotomies, and they have not accommodated women's lived experiences and identities, which emphasize connections, not dichotomies (e.g., Hirschmann, 1998). Moreover, with polyculturalism, cultural accommodation is as important as cultural assimilation, and both policies and practices must be culturally responsive. Therefore, in lieu of the singular, monocultural concept of social capital, the plural concept of *social-cultural capital* (Lawson, Briar-Lawson, & Lawson, 1997) and its companion concepts of community competence, civic culture, civic infrastructure, and social organization is proposed (e.g., Lawson, under review-b; Newton, 1997; Potapchuk, Crocker, & Schechter, 1997).[11] They are more suitable for the global age.

17. Development planning necessitates taking into account and trying to change social norms, religious beliefs, and cultural traditions (e.g., Ray, 1998; Riley, 1997), and thus it is vulnerable to allegations of colonialism and imperialism.

18. Development planning must focus on patriarchy, especially women's special needs, their rights, and their special talents related to social and economic development (e.g., Berger, 1989; Braidotti, Charkiewicz, & Wireinga, 1994; Chen, 1989; Jiggins, 1989; Grown & Sebstad, 1989; Harrington, 1999; Ibrahim, 1989; Lind & Farmelo, 1996;

Pietilä & Vickers, 1996; Ridgeway, 1997; Riley, 1997; Staggenborg, 1998).

19. Local and national histories influence every development agenda, and so do people's social memories, place, time, and recent events (e.g., Ray, 1998).

20. Effective development planning is predicated on understanding past/present development trajectories, including how and why they are promoted and perpetuated; and, in turn, strategic, targeted intervention and improvement strategies on key people, sites, and processes (e.g., Bauman, 1998; Hoogvelt, 1997; Ray, 1998).

21. Development planning necessitates building strong, efficient, and effective governmental infrastructures, which are responsive to economic requirements; and which keep the economy under control without compromising, or sacrificing, social welfare, education, and health benefit programs, which are essential to individuals' and families' freedom, dignity, well-being, and survival (e.g., Woodward, 1996).

22. Development planning necessitates addressing the complex relationships among poverty, population, and rural-urban flows, especially in middle- and low-income nations; and rural poverty must be a special priority (McMichael, 1996; Ray, 1998).

Ray's (1998) work is especially insightful. He pinpoints foci for many strategic interventions. For example, he proposes income subsidies that equalize wages between rural and urban workers (because rural workers and families migrate to pursue higher wages in cities). He also proposes social insurance policies (comparable to social security in the U.S.) for individuals and families (because families have children to allow successful aging, which promotes favoritism for boys and perpetuates patriarchy and discrimination against girls and women).

23. High-income nations and international monetary authorities such as the World Bank and the International Monetary Fund must help the low-income and middle-income nations of the developing world meet their needs and challenges; aid, loan, debt, and foreign investment policies are crucial development resources (e.g., Hoy, 1998; Bradshaw & Wallace, 1996; Woodward, 1996).

Today the World Bank's top priority is eliminating poverty. Other promising proposals are being developed, and they require compromise and sacrifice. For example, the proposed Tobin Tax levy taxes all international trade transactions; in turn, these funds would be redistributed to nations in need (Langmore, 1998). Proposals for debt relief include key compromises that serve the international common good. For example, in exchange for debt relief and forgiveness, developing nations agree to protect, preserve, and enhance fragile environments (e.g., rain forests) that are essential to human well-being and survival (McMichael, 1996, p. 253).

24. Every nation must focus strategically on the needs and challenges of individuals and families in the informal sector of their economy (e.g., Nuralamin, 1996; Sanyal, 1996).

25. Development planning in every nation must focus strategically on creating full employment, which necessitates expanding definitions of meaningful work and monetarizing activities that promote and safeguard individual and family well-being (e.g., Bauman, 1998; Giddens, 1994, 1995; Peck, 1996; UNDP, 1998).

26. Development planning in every nation must focus strategically on providing wages and benefits for work performed in households, especially by women, and specifically by women and men with full-time caregiving responsibilities.

27. Development planning in every nation must include investments in human capital development, beginning with schooling and the broader process of education (e.g., Spring, 1998), but also including the provision of health and mental care and social services and encompassing family support and community development strategies.

28. Policy makers, helping professionals, advocates, and other leaders in every nation must begin to envision the postwelfare state and its surrounding world of the future, a future in which societies need not construct and maintain artificial scarcities (e.g., unemployment), along with the status differences, inequalities, and well-being problems that these scarcities produce (e.g., Bauman, 1998; Giddens, 1994, 1995; Leonard, 1997).

29. Development planning must include investments in low-income nations, especially their most vulnerable individuals, families, and communities, as safeguards for national and international security, including the prevention of wars and conflict and of crime and delinquency[12] (e.g.,

Bolderson & Roberts, 1997; Cassen, Wignaraja, & Kingdon, 1997; Hoogvelt, 1997; Kennedy, 1993; Mohan, 1992; Van Soest, 1997).

30. Development planning in every nation and in regional alliances must include strategic investments in families, especially vulnerable families, and family well-being must become a key goal and evaluation criterion in all development agendas (e.g., Cass & Cappo, 1995; Hennon, Jones, et al., 1998; Hooper-Briar & Lawson, 1995; Mason, Skolnick, & Sugeraman, 1998; Midgley, 1997, 1999).

A FINAL NOTE

Thus, globalization has multiple facets—psychological, social, cultural, geographic, religious, economic, and political. Economic globalization is an important driving force, but it does not act in isolation. In fact, it interacts with other processes and facets, e.g., the massive movement of the world's people and families, the deterritorialization of cultures, glocalization, and the development of new intercultural contact zones ("scapes"). Individual and family well-being and, in turn, the status of their villages and communities, states and provinces, nations, and regional alliances, often swing in the balance of globalization's multiple facets, correlates, and consequences. For these reasons and others, Featherstone and Lash (1995) have claimed that the global human condition is the new problematic for social theory.

Clearly, the global human condition, and especially the well-being of the world's families, is also the key problematic for the helping professions of the twenty-first century. There is work to be done.

Today, national interests frame the knowledge bases and theories of the helping professions. In contrast, the idea of knowledgescapes for action compels an international frame, one that includes relational analysis and dialectical thinking, discourse, and planning. Such a global, international frame will facilitate more expansive macrotheorizing and enriched valid meso- and microtheories and practices.

Social work provides a ready example. One of the first courses for M.S.W. students is typically Human Behavior in the Social Environment (HBSE). Add a global frame, one that focuses on the global human condition and incorporates globalization and its companions, and HBSE's limitations become evident. In contrast, consider an alternative like this: Developing Individual and Family Well-Being in Global Contexts. This title expands a national frame to an international one. It promotes international social welfare, but not at the expense of national needs and interests. It emphasizes globalization and promotes relational analysis and dialectical thinking, discourse, and planning. Today's HBSE content and understanding may be reframed against this global, international frame. Some of this HBSE content can be incorporated, other parts can be accommodated, and still other parts, which may appear to be overly narrow, psychobehavioral, ethnocentric, and even anachronistic, may need to be discarded.

Social work is not alone in confronting needs like these. Proposals for interprofessional education and training programs, which provide a common denominator of preparation for all of the helping professions, also need to focus on the global condition, especially the well-being of the world's families. Like one's native language, this global understanding will be nothing to brag about when it is possessed and used, but it will be a source of embarrassment and even malpractice when professionals lack it (after Mills, 1969).

This same claim can be made about family-centered policies and practices framed against globalization's challenges and opportunities. They are essential components of specialized, effective professional education and practice. And they are centerpieces for interprofessional education and practice. Toward this end, the last chapter presents key change propositions for family-centered policies and practices. They strengthen both preparation and practice. And, they summarize and integrate some of this book's most important findings and their implications.

NOTES

1. Helping professionals' intervention strategies and policy makers' planning increasingly take into account social geographic parameters. For example, they plot special needs regarding child welfare and juvenile justice in identifiable geographic areas, perhaps using postal codes. Computer-assisted technologies involving geographic information surveys (GIS mapping) are invaluable tools for family-centered policies and practices.
2. For example, Mele (1996) describes the effects of globalization on property values, neighborhood development, and small business opportunities on the lower east side of New York City. In economic decline at one point, local cultures and lifestyles became marketable and profitable with globalization. Real estate developers quickly capitalized. The more residents resisted, the more they contributed to it. Once again, glocalization produces paradoxical and contradictory processes, consequences, and correlates (e.g., higher property values and gentrified neighborhoods on the heels of outmigrations and property devaluation.

3. Is this diversity one of degree or kind? In other words, is this manufactured, commodified diversity produced by global capitalism, i.e., a diversity of degree? If not, it is a diversity of kind. Who knows?

4. The case of AIDS in sub-Saharan Africa is a compelling, tragic example. Some 6,000 adults die each day from AIDS. An estimated 10 million or more children are orphans (Masland & Nordland, 2000). This is a modern day Holocaust, one deserving immediate mobilization for collective action.

5. See Maguire (1999, pp. 136–137) for an important example of how growing awareness of the widespread use of child labor in the production of soccer balls in Pakistan has been met by international resistance, forcing the World Federation of Sporting Goods Industry to condemn child labor and to promote enforcement through selective purchasing from companies, which have abandoned this heinous practice.

6. Katharine Briar-Lawson immediately envisioned the need for *familyscapes* and is starting work on them. She may be contacted at kbl@csc.albany.edu.

7. Articles about each appeared in volume 8145 (1999) of *The Economist*, pp. 54–55.

8. A shift in social norms is involved, too. Identity and moral worth must be separated from market-driven ideas about consumption abilities and patterns (Bauman, 1998).

9. Comparisons like these are important. The Human Development Index (HDI), developed and promoted by the United Nations (1998), facilitates such comparisons. The HDI is a composite of three basic components: (1) *longevity* (derived from life expectancy indicators); (2) *knowledge* (derived from a combination of adult literacy and mean years of schooling); and (3) *standard of living* (derived from purchasing power, with adjustments based upon per capita gross national product and local cost of living). For Van Soest (1997), declining well-being is one kind of cultural and structural violence.

10. See Opotow (1990) for a comprehensive list of practices associated with moral exclusion. Moreover, see Bauman (1998) for a different kind of moral exclusion, one related to consumerism, rooted in the work ethic and related to patriarchy.

11. In the same vein, Rawls (1996) has changed his approach to social justice to accommodate cultural pluralism.

12. Hoogvelt (1997) is one of many analysts who view the dismantling of the welfare state as the beginning of the police state. There is a choice. Invest in individuals and families, or invest precious resources in state-operated surveillance, compliance, regulation, and enforcement systems (Jordan, 1998).

CHAPTER 12

New-Century Investment Strategies and Social Action Agendas for the World's Families

Hal A. Lawson and Katharine Briar-Lawson

The dawning of a new millennium may mark a historic turning point for the world's families, along with the policy makers, helping professionals, and advocates who serve them. Groups, organizations, nations, and regional alliances among nations, which have never before joined forces, may do so now to advocate and gain support for family-centered policies and practices.

These new-century policies and practices will be integrative and comprehensive. They will promote and safeguard the rights of women, children, refugees, elders, and indigenous people. They will help to ensure environmental protection and sustainability. They will address patriarchy. They will incorporate needs related to gender-equitable, full, and meaningful employment. They will respond effectively to the multiple challenges posed by globalization, capitalizing on the attendant opportunities. In brief, these new-century policies and practices will help to address these key priorities and others, all of which influence family well-being. Each new family-centered policy, every new family-centered practice, is a small but important step toward a national and an international family investment agenda. Every crisis presents a new opportunity for policy and practice improvement and change.

Families merit "first call" on resources. They need to be centerpieces in local, state and provincial, national, and international discourses. Once families and their well-being become the centerpieces for national and international policy and practice, the limitations of narrow, categorical thinking and approaches become evident. Because families are arguably the most important social institution in every nation, and because families influence, and are influenced by, every policy and practice sector, family-centered policies and practices are by their very nature broad, integrative, and comprehensive.

As this book has illustrated, these needs for sufficient breadth, coherence, comprehensiveness, integration, and effectiveness may seem daunting. Furthermore, as the authors of this book have learned, when the analytical frame moves from national needs to international priorities, what was initially a daunting challenge may become an overwhelming one.

The world's diversity and complexity compel a profound sense of humility. In turn, humility breeds caution and suspicion about generalizations regarding the world's families. International analysis may result in policy and practice paralysis.

On the other hand, silence is the voice of complicity. Silence, justified by international complexity, reinforces the status quo. It excuses people from all walks of life from using their knowledge and understanding, acting strategically, and improving family well-being and its correlates.

The dawning of a new millennium is not an occasion for either silence or complicity. It is a time for advocacy and strategic action.

Incredible international diversity notwithstanding, this book has identified and emphasized universal needs and thus commonalties. This book draws to a close with a composite summary of action agendas in response to these needs. They do not exhaust the list of possibilities associated with this book. They are merely examples.

These action agendas are presented below as testable propositions. They are stated in a "when this, then that" action framework. When propositions are stated in such an action framework, they predict the intended consequences of each action, especially the benefits.

In other words, each proposition represents a testable, microchange theory. Together, they form the foundation for a family-centered theory for policy and practice.[1] To put it another way, these propositions pave the way for a family-centered theory of action (e.g., Argyris, 1996; Lawson, 1998a).

In turn, this new, family-centered theory of action compels a new world ethic (Henderson, 2000; Kung, 1991; Mohan, 1992). This new ethic builds from the idea of world citizenship. It integrates now-separate identities, roles, and responsibilities—e.g., family member, citizen, student, policy maker, advocate, and helping professional (Lawson, in press). Last, but not least, this ethic promotes a worldwide Familywatch, which is described in the conclusion to this chapter.

FAMILY-CENTERED CHANGE PROPOSITIONS
FOR STRATEGIC ACTION

To enhance clarity and promote integrative thinking, the following change propositions are grouped under convenient headings. To provide readers the equivalent of a meaningful summary, the most important chapters for each proposition are listed in parentheses.

Individuals and Families

- When individuals and their families are treated as interdependent investment sites, both will benefit, and their well-being will improve. (chapters 1, 2, 4, 5)
- When individuals are treated as separate entities and segregated from their family systems—as members define them—social supports and welfare investments will be less effective and both individual and family well-being will be impeded. (1, 2, 3)
- When the needs of women, children, and elders are framed as family issues, and democratized, and family-centered policies and practices are developed in response, individual and family well-being will improve. (1, 2, 3)

Democratized Families

- When patriarchal policies and practices are perpetuated in the family and in the wider society, the health and well-being of women and girls will decline. (1, 2, 3)
- When patriarchal policies and practices persist, the potential contributions of girls and women to social and economic development agendas will be curtailed or eliminated, and these agendas will be less effective. (1, 2, 3, 10, 11)
- When patriarchal policies and practices persist, and when women and girls are not given the opportunity to voice personal and family issues and needs, helping professionals will be less effective. (1, 2, 3, 11)
- When women are not given the opportunity to voice individual and family needs, and their de facto needs are not addressed, these unmet needs will affect the next generation of the family. (1, 2, 3, 11)

- When patriarchal policies and practices persist, civil society institutions will not be strengthened, and social-cultural capital networks will not be improved. (1, 2, 3, 10, 11)
- When family relations, both internal and external, are democratized and gender equitable, social capital will be developed, civil society will be promoted, and democratic participation will improve. (1, 2, 3, 10, 11)
- When food distribution and consumption, education, health, and employment are democratized and gender equitable, individual and family challenges involving abuse and health problems will be reduced, and social and economic development will be facilitated. (1, 2, 3, 11)
- When girls and women are provided equitable access to, and strong supports for, education and schooling, family well-being will improve, local and national development agendas will be more effective, and reproductive policies will be more effective. (2, 3, 11)

Poverty, Inequality, and Exclusion

- When local, state and provincial, national, and regional social and economic development agendas fail to address poverty and its companions, development will be less effective and individual and family well-being will continue to decline. (3, 4, 5, 10, 11)
- When development agendas effectively address individual and family poverty, democracy will be strengthened; the economy will improve; children's school performances will improve; elders will fare better; and family well-being will be enhanced. (1, 2, 3, 5, 10, 11)
- When occupational and economic development resources and opportunities are inequitably distributed; when full, gender-equitable employment is not provided; and when the special needs of high-poverty families and their communities are not addressed, development agendas will be less effective and more governmental funding will be allocated for surveillance, monitoring, policing, and justice systems. (1, 2, 3, 6, 10, 11)
- When poverty and its companions are not addressed, growing numbers of individuals and families will migrate to cities; the informal sectors of the economy will grow; the families in migration will increase; and the harms associated with poverty will increase in number and intensify in effect. (10, 11)

Social and Economic Development

- When policy leaders view families as the centerpieces of their national development agendas, social and economic development initiatives will be integrated; development will become more sustainable; and family well-being will improve. (3, 10, 11)
- When families are viewed as sites for small business development, they will claim and secure a greater share of governmental economic investment funds. (2, 3)
- When families are treated as investment sites for economic development, they will generate more of the world's small businesses. (3, 10, 11)
- When governments support family-centered small businesses and cooperatives, family well-being will improve, and social and economic development agendas will be more effective. (3, 10, 11)
- When families and their communities receive strategic social investments, economic and social development agendas will be more sustainable and effective. (3, 10, 11)
- When family-centered social and economic investments increase, the efficiency and effectiveness of the welfare state will increase, and family well-being will improve. (2, 3, 10, 11)
- When education, housing, health, criminal justice, income supports, and social insurance become family centered, and as families are viewed as strategic social investments instead of resource drains, social and economic development initiatives will be more efficient, effective, and sustainable; and family well-being will improve. (2, 3, 7, 10, 11)
- When immigration and employment policies are family centered, and when families are permitted and encouraged to reunite in a new nation, individual and family well-being will improve and community development initiatives will be more effective. (11)
- When immigration and employment policies are family centered and culturally competent, culturally diverse immigrant families will play important leadership roles in supporting other families, promoting community development, and facilitating education, mutual assistance, and health care. (11)
- When international cooperation in service of family well-being is the norm, high-income nations (core economies) will make sacrifices that "make room" for low-income nations, inter-nation in-

equalities will be reduced, and family well-being will improve. (1, 10, 11)

- When international cooperation for family well-being is the norm, fragile natural environments will be protected and preserved; and the quality of the air people breathe and the water they drink will improve. (1, 10, 11)

Welfare State Policies and Functions

- When families are treated as the most important social and economic investment sites, welfare state functions will be inseparable from social and economic development, and development outcomes will improve as family well-being improves. (2, 3)
- When families are viewed as investment sites, market and welfare state resources will become interdependent, and human, family, community, and development outcomes will improve. (2, 3)
- When family-based caregiving is recognized as work and supported with wages and benefits, the state's social welfare system will become more efficient and effective, the GNP will improve, and individual and family well-being will be enhanced. (2, 3)
- When governmental health and social welfare policies provide universal income entitlements to families, especially families employed in the informal sector and the household sectors of the economy, individual and family well-being will improve. (2, 3, 10, 11)
- When informal sector jobs and family caregiving are brought into conformity with human rights legislation and fair, humane labor standards, individual and intergenerational family well-being will improve. (3, 10)
- When gaps grow between "have" and "have-not" families, overall well-being may decline, citizens will become more segregated and unequal, and delinquency, crime, and health and longevity problems will rise. (1, 2, 4, 5, 10, 11)
- When local, state and provincial, and national policies are family insensitive and categorical, family well-being will decline, poverty may grow, and social and economic development agendas will not be effective or sustainable. (1, 3, 4, 5, 10, 11)
- When family well-being is ignored and neglected and when services and policies are crisis oriented, there will be increasing needs for nursing homes, prisons, juvenile corrections facilities, orphanages and foster care facilities, and homeless shelters. (2, 3, 10, 11)

- When families become the focal point for service integration and policy and practice coherence, service outcomes will be enhanced, helping professionals' job satisfaction will increase, and family well-being will improve. (4, 5)
- When families and their well-being are a focal point for policy integration between the market and welfare state, tensions between the market and welfare state investments will be reduced, and precise human and family development goals will head the list of national and international development priorities. (10, 11)
- As the world's collective responsibilities for families are understood, families and nations in need of resources will receive aid in support of family-centered social and economic development, poverty and inequality will be reduced, and family well-being will improve. (1, 2, 3, 10, 11)

Helping Professionals and Families

- When professionals view families as experts in what helps and hurts them, and treat them as partners in service delivery, professionals' job satisfaction and effectiveness will improve, and so will family well-being. (6, 7, 8)
- When professionals stop viewing families as clients and begin addressing families' co-occurring needs, families will be more responsive to professional assistance and resistance to change will be reduced. (4, 5, 6, 7, 8, 9)
- When professionals form effective alliances with families, family advocates, and policy makers to foster family-centered policies, they will produce multiple innovations, which improve family well-being and enhance social and economic development. (4, 5, 6, 7, 8, 9)
- When professionals provide family-centered occupational and economic development supports, in addition to social and health services, family well-being will improve and so will social and economic development. (3, 4, 11)
- When professionals work with families to address patriarchy and democratize family relations, family well-being will improve. (2, 3, 4, 5, 6, 7, 8, 9, 11)
- When professionals receive family-centered, interprofessional education and training, they will be able to collaborate more effectively with each other and with families, integrate services more responsively and efficiently, and their results will improve. (5, 6)

- When professionals collaborate with one another and with families, their job satisfaction and effectiveness will improve and so will family well-being. (5, 6)
- When professionals collaborate with families, policy makers, and advocates, and employ strategic policy-practice skills, they will help organize and mobilize broad-scale support in service of family-centered policies and practices. (7, 8, 9, 11)
- When professionals understand globalization and its attendant processes and changes, their practice repertoires will expand, and they will seek strategic supports for their work from colleagues and families around the world. (10, 11)
- When professionals think globally and act locally, using existing action "scapes" and developing new "familyscapes," they will promote a new world ethic, one that will lead to improvements in family well-being, environmental quality, world peace and security, and sustainable living. (1, 11)

Collectively, these change propositions support twin conclusions:

- *The well-being of families must become a top national and international priority.*
- *Every year must be an international year of the family.*

TOWARD A NEW WORLD ETHIC

Beginning in the first chapter, several references have been made in this book about "a new world ethic." Such a new world ethic is a starting point for the kind of guiding vision described in chapter 6. It involves key shifts in thought, discourse, and planning frames. Table 12.1 identifies and summarizes some key shifts. These shifts help set the stage for a new vigil and action agenda for families.

FAMILYWATCH

Each policy maker, helping professional, family advocate, and citizen who enjoys the luxury of individual and family well-being can accept some responsibility for the world's families and act accordingly. A worldwide watch on the behalf of families and their well-being is needed. Familywatch is the label coined by the authors.

TABLE 12.1. Examples of Transitions in Support of a New World Ethic

FROM	TO
Self-interests and selfish interests are a primary focus of civil societies.	Individual and family well-being and sustainable living are the focus of civil societies.
Patriarchy dominates family and organizational life, and society in general.	Gender equity is the basis of family and organizational life, and society in general.
Unequal distribution of goods and services to family members based on gender and age.	More gender-equitable distribution of goods and resources to family members across the life span.
Unequal distribution of goods and services to families and individuals based on nationality, race, religion, ethnicity, income, and other indicators of social and cultural status.	More equitable distribution of goods and services to all members of communities, societies, and worldwide.
Democracy serves as a vague organizing term, and it is usually invoked by elite groups.	Grassroots, democratic practices are matched by global, cosmopolitan structures.
Economic competition and warfare dominate international discourse and exchanges.	Global accountability to families and succeeding generations, especially human survival, becomes the basis of international discourses and collaborative work.
Policy makers promote, or tolerate, unequal distribution of rights, goods, and services in families.	Policy makers promote equity as a foundation for sustainable family systems and societies.
Policy makers invest in strategies to combat escalating crime and terrorism, and, in support of jails and prisons, promote imprisonment.	Policy makers invest in prevention strategies and community development to promote family well-being.
Development agendas focus on large corporations and macroeconomic development.	Development includes more than economic factors; it is integrated with social development and addresses poverty and inequality.

continued

TABLE 12.1. (*Continued*)

FROM	TO
Economic development is measured exclusively in per capita income and the GNP.	Per capita income and GNP are viewed as imperfect proxy measures; development focuses instead on multiple, gendered, and women-centered indicators of well-being and sustainability.
Costs of production and prices do not include human and environmental harms; nor are these costs taxed.	True costs of production are added to the calculus of prices, and are taxed.
Individuals are prioritized.	Individuals and families are considered as interdependent entities; both are simultaneously considered and valued.
Linear thinking and categorical policies dominate; the frame remains the industrial nation-state in isolation or in competition.	Relational analysis and dialectical thinking, discourse, and planning dominate; the dialectic between national interests and global needs animates new governmental structures for international cooperation and decision making.
Vulnerable individuals are treated apart from their families, and both individuals and families are viewed in problem-oriented, deficit-based terms.	Individuals are viewed in the contexts of their family and community systems. Mindful of needs, build-from-strength and aspiration strategies are prioritized, along with empowerment and capacity building in support of families and communities.
Individual and family needs are viewed as private matters, as personal troubles.	Individual and family needs are viewed as public concerns, as social issues.
One person speaks for the family, typically a male.	All members have a voice, and norms support the elimination of family violence, abuse and neglect, and patriarchy.

Familywatch can be a springboard for local action and global advocacy. Just as members of Habitat for Humanity have used their weekends to build homes for the poor, so too are there opportunities with Familywatch for people to devote their discretionary time and efforts to a worthy cause. Familywatch volunteers may enhance, even save, millions of lives. Rather than remaining passive viewers of mind-numbing television news briefs and documentaries that merely describe problems and needs, pro-family advocates from all walks of life can do something about these problems and needs.

Family-centered policy and practice means creating the future, working hand-in-hand with families themselves. With relative ease, and without incredible sacrifices, individuals and families who enjoy well-being can join in for a day, a weekend, a week, a month, a year, or several years to address needs identified in Familywatch.

In one sense, advocacy and supports for the world's families are the most important democratic project for the twenty-first century. The world has become a smaller place. Interdependence is the norm. Family advocates from all walks of life may be asked to give, but in the global, interdependent world, they also get something back. The well-being of their families and their children's families depend on their firm commitments, strategic actions, and lasting achievements. Familywatch participants will be practicing the politics of generativity (Bellah, Madsen, et al., 1992), leaving a legacy for their children, their children's children, and other generations that follow.

NOTE

1. And, as chapter 5 suggests, implicit change-related assumptions are embedded in each proposition, assumptions that are structured in relation to the research and firm value commitments.

Appendix: Key Web Sites

Amnesty International: *www.amnesty.org/*
Bureau of Democracy, Human Rights and Labor Affairs:
    www.state.gov/www/global/human_rights/index.htm/#links
The Global Fund for Children: *www.globalfundforchildren.org/*
Center for Law and Global Justice: *www.usfca.edu/law/globaljustice/*
Global Exchange: *www.globalexchange.org/*
Global Education Associates: *www.globaleduc.org/*
Human Rights for Workers: *www.senser.com/*
Women's Environment and Development Organization (WEDO):
    www.wedo.org/
Journal of World Affairs and New Technology (WANT):
    www.world-affairs.com/
Green-Net: *www.gn.apc.org/*
Human Rights Web: *www.hrweb.org/*
Project Underground: *www.moles.org/*
Seva Foundation: *www.seva.org/*
World Organization Against Torture (WOAT): *www.omct.org/*
World Commission for Peace and Human Rights: *www.worphco.cjb.net/*
Peace Net—Women's Net—Eco Net—Antiracism Net: *www.igc.org/*
Feminist.com: *www.feminist.com/*
Global Fund for Women: *www.globalfundforwomen.org/*
Free the Children: *www.freethechildren.org/*
Human Rights Watch: *www.hrw.org/*
Anti-Defamation League: *www.adl.org/*
The American Anti-Slavery Group: *www.anti-slavery.org/*
Anti-Slavery International: *www.antislavery.org/*
National Council on Family Relations: *www.ncfr.com/*

United Nations: *www.un.org/* (Of interest may be the social development section. There is also a section within social development on aging issues and the International Year of the Older Person. Also of interest may be the human rights section.)

Welfare Information Network: *www.welfarinfo.org/* (National clearinghouse presenting information on a wide range of policy and practice issues regarding welfare and welfare reform.)

Habitat for Humanity: *www.habitat.org/*

Global Citizens: *www.globalcitizens.org/*

Global Service Corps: *www.globalservicecorps.org/*

Global Volunteers: *www.globalvolunteers.org/*

Cross-Cultural Solutions: *www.crossculturalsolutions.org/*

Partners of the Americas: *www.partners.net/*

Volunteer International (volunteer search site): *www.volunteerinternational.org/*

State of the World 2000: *www.worldwatch.org/*

Corporate Watch—The watchdog of the Web: *www.igc.org/*

Campaign for Labor Rights: *www.summersault.com/~agj/clr/index.html*

United Students Against Sweatshops: *www.umich.edu/~sole/usassy1/index.html*

United Nations Children's Fund (UNICEF): *www.unicef.org/*

American Refugee Committee: *www.archq.org/*

Witness: *www.witness.org/*

International Rescue Committee: *www.intrescom.org/*

Refugee International: *www.refintl.org/*

Student Action for Refugees (STAR): *www.star-network.org.uk/*

United Nations High Commissioner for Refugees: *www.unhsr.ch/*

Center for World Indigenous Studies: *www.cwis.org/*

Cultural Survival: *www.cs.org/*

International Rainforest Foundation: *www.savetherest.org/*

Survival International: *www.survival.org.uk/*

Poverty Net: *www.worldbank.org/poverty/*

Bibliography

Aaron, H., Mann, T., & Taylor, T. (Eds.). (1994). *Values and public policy.* Washington, DC: Brookings Institution Press.

Abramowitz, M. (1996). *Regulating the lives of women: Social welfare policy from colonial times to the present.* Boston: South End Press.

Adams, P., & Nelson, K. (Eds.). (1995). *Reinventing Human Services: Community and Family-Centered Practice.* New York: Aldine de Gruyter.

Adams, R., Dominelli, L., & Payne, M. (Eds.). (1998). *Social work: Themes, issues and critical debates.* London: Macmillan Press.

Alameda, T. (1996). R. A. I. N. makers: The consumers' voice. In K. Hooper-Briar & H. Lawson (Eds.), *Expanding partnerships for vulnerable children, youth and families* (pp. 46–56). Washington, DC: Council on Social Work Education.

Allard, M., Albeda, R., Colten, J., & Cosenza, C. (1997). *In harm's way? Domestic violence, AFDC receipt, and welfare reform in Massachusetts.* Boston: John W. McCormack Institute of Public Affairs, University of Massachusetts, Boston.

Alter, C., & Egan, M. (1997). Logic modeling: A tool for teaching critical thinking in social work practice. *Journal of Social Work Education, 33*(1), 85–102.

Alter, C., & Murty, S. (1997). Logic modeling: A tool for teaching practice evaluation. *Journal of Social Work Education, 33*(1), 103–118.

Anderson, B. (1994). *Imagined communities: Reflections on the origins and spread of nationalism.* London: Verso.

Anderson, S. A., & Sabatelli, R. M. (1995). *Family interaction: A multigenerational developmental perspective.* Boston: Allyn & Bacon.

Andrae, G., & Beckman, B. (1996). *Bargaining for survival: Unionized workers in the Nigerian textile industry.* Geneva: United Nations Research Institute for Social Development.

Annie E. Casey Foundation. (1995). *The path of most resistance: Reflections and lessons learned from new futures*. Baltimore: Author.

Annie E. Casey Foundation. (1999). *Kids count*. Baltimore: Author.

Appadurai, A. (1990). Disjuncture and difference in the global cultural economy. In M. Featherstone (Ed.), *Global culture: Nationalism, globalization, and modernity* (pp. 295–310). London: Sage.

Apple, K., Berstein, S., Fogg, L., Haapala, D., Johnson, E., Johnson, R., Kinney, J., Natoli, J., Price, D., Roberts, K., Robinson, K., Steele, T., Trent, E., Trent, M., Trent, V., Smith, R., & Vignec, R. (1997). Walking the talk in the neighborhoods: Building professional/natural helper partnerships. *Social Policy, 27*(4), 54–57.

Arendt, H. (1958). *The human condition*. Chicago: University of Chicago Press.

Argyris, C. (1996). Actionable knowledge: Design causality in the service of consequential theory. *Journal of Applied Behavioral Science, 32*, 390–406.

Argyris, C., & Schön, D. (1996). *Organizational learning II: Theory, method, and practice*. Reading, MA: Addison-Wesley.

Aronowitz, S., & DiFazio, W. (1994). *The jobless future: Sci-tech and the dogma of work*. Minneapolis: University of Minnesota Press.

Asay, S., & Hennon, C. (1999). The challenge of conducting qualitative family research in international settings. *Family and Consumer Science Research Journal, 27*, 409–427.

Asian and Pacific Development Centre. (1988). *The women in development programme*. Kuala Lumpur: Author.

Athanasiou, T. (1996). *Divided planet: The ecology of rich and poor*. Boston: Little, Brown.

Auster, B. B. (1997, February 10). And now, some banking tips from Bangladesh. *U.S. News & World Report*, p. 40.

Baber, K., & Allen, K. (1992). *Women and families: Feminist reconstructions*. New York: Guilford Press.

Baca-Zinn, M., & Eitzen, S. (1993). *Diversity in families* (3rd ed.). New York: HarperCollins.

Backman, G., & Sharma, S. (1998). Changing social welfare systems in the Nordic nations: Some observations and analyses. *New Global Development: Journal of International and Comparative Social Welfare, 16*, 34–45.

Baker, M. (1995). *Canadian family policies: Cross-national comparisons*. Toronto: University of Toronto Press.

Baker, R., Panter-Brick, C., & Todd, A. (1997). Homeless street boys in Nepal: Their demography and lifestyle. *Journal of Comparative Family Studies, 28*, 129–146.

Bales, K. (1999). *Disposable people: New slavery in the global economy*. Berkeley, CA: University of California Press.

Banfield, E. (1967). *The moral basis of a backward society*. New York: Free Press.

Barber, B. (1996). *Jihad vs. McWorld: How globalism and tribalism are reshaping the world*. New York: Ballantine Books.

Barnes, M. (1997). *Care, communities, and citizens*. New York: Longman.

Barsh, R. L. (1989). *The convention on the rights of the child: A reassessment of the final text*. New York: United Nations.

Barroso, C. (1994, March). Making grants across borders: Notes for presentation to International Committee of the Council on Foundations. Santa Monica, CA.

Bauman, Z. (1998). *Work, consumerism, and the new poor*. Buckingham, UK: Open University Press.

Becker, G. (1997). *Disrupted lives: How people create meaning in a chaotic world*. Berkeley: University of California Press.

Bellah, R., Madsen, R., Sullivan, W., Swidler, A., & Tipton, S. (1992). *The good society*. New York: Vintage.

Bello, W. (1996). Structural adjustment programs: "Success" for whom? In J. Mander & E. Goldsmith (Eds.), *The case against the global economy and for a turn toward the local* (pp. 285–296). San Francisco: Sierra Club Books.

Bello, W., Cunningham, S., & Rau, B. (1995). Market reforms are designed to prevent southern economic development. In J. Petrikin (Ed.), *The third world: Opposing viewpoints* (pp. 64–70). San Diego: Greenhaven Press.

Bender, W., & Smith, M. (1997). Population, food and nutrition. *The Population Bulletin, 51*(4), 1–48.

Bennholdt-Thomsen, V. (1991). When do housewives continue to be created in the third world too? In M. Mies, V. Bennholdt-Thomsen, & C. von Werlhot (Eds.), *Women: The last colony* (pp. 159–167). Atlantic Highlander, NJ: Zed Books.

Benoît-Guilbot, O. (1994). Introduction: Why are there so many long-term unemployed in the EU? In O. Benoît-Guilbot & D. Gallie (Eds.), *Long-term unemployment* (pp. 1–16). London: Pinter.

Benoît-Guilbot, O., & Gallie, D. (Eds.). (1994). *Long-term unemployment*. London: Pinter.

Berelson, B., Anderson, R. K., Harkavy, O., Maier, J., Mauldin, W., Parker, W., & Segal, S. J. (1966). *Family planning and population programs: A review of world development*. Chicago: The University of Chicago Press.

Beresford, P., Green, D., Lister, R., & Woodard, K. (1999). *Poverty first hand: Poor people speak for themselves*. London: Child Poverty Action Group.

Berger, M. (1989). Giving women credit. The strengths and limitations of credit as a tool for alleviating poverty. *World Development, 17*, 1017–1032.

Berger, P., & Luckmann, T. (1967). *The social construction of reality: A treatise in the sociology of knowledge*. New York: Anchor/Doubleday.

Berghman, J. (1997). The resurgence of poverty and the struggle against social exclusion: A new challenge for social security in Europe. *International Social Security Review, 50*(1), 3–21.

Berheide, C., & Chow, E. (1994). Perpetuating gender inequality: The role of families, economies, and the states. In C. Berheide & E. Chow (Eds.), *Women, the family and policy* (pp. 257–275). Albany: State University of New York.

Beuttler, William. (1990). *The family, the future: A bill of rights for children.* San Diego: Libra.

Blanchard, E. B. (1981). Observations on social work with American Indian women. In A. Weick & S. Vandiver (Eds.), *Women, power, and change* (pp. 96–103). Washington, DC: National Association of Social Workers.

Blank, R. (1995). Poverty and public policy in the 1990s. In G. Demko & M. Jackson (Eds.), *Populations at risk in America: Vulnerable groups at the end of the twentieth century* (pp. 60–76). Boulder, CO: Westview Press.

Blau, J. (1999). *Illusions of prosperity: America's working families in an age of economic insecurity.* New York: Oxford University Press.

Blumberg, L., Rakowski, C., Tinker, I., & Monteon, M. (Eds.). (1995). *EnGENDERing wealth and well-being.* Boulder, CO: Westview Press.

Boff, Leonardo. (1996). *Ecology and liberation: A new paradigm.* New York: Orbis Books.

Bohen, H., & Viveros-Long, A. (1981). *Balancing jobs and family life.* Philadelphia: Temple University Press.

Bolderson, H., & Roberts, S. (1997). Social security across frontiers. *New Global Development: Journal of International and Comparative Social Welfare, 13,* 7–23.

Booth, A., Crouter, A., & Lanvale, N. (1997). *Immigration and the family.* Mahway, NJ: Erlbaum.

Bosworth, B. P. (1993). *Saving and investment in a global economy.* Washington, DC: Brookings Institution Press.

Boulding, E. (1988). *Building a global civic culture: Education for an interdependent world.* New York: Teachers College Press.

Boulding, E. (1993). Ethnicity and new constitutive orders. In J. Brecher, J. Brown, & J. Cutler (Eds.), *Global visions: Beyond the new world order* (pp. 213–232). Boston: South End Press.

Bourdieu, P. (1986). The forms of capital. In J. Richardson (Ed.), *Handbook of theory and research for the sociology of education* (pp. 241–258). Westport, CT: Greenwood Press.

Boyden, J. (1993). *Families: Celebration and hope in a world of change.* London: Gaia Books and UNESCO.

Bradshaw, Y., & Wallace, M. (1996). *Global inequalities.* Thousand Oaks, CA: Pine Forge Press.

Braidotti, R., Charkiewcz, H., & Wireinga, S. (1994). *Women, the environment, and sustainable development.* London: Zed Books.

Brandon, R. (1996). The collaborative services movement: Implications for national policy makers. In K. Hooper-Briar & H. Lawson (Eds.), *Expanding partnerships for vulnerable children, youth, and families* (pp. 322–346). Washington, DC: Council on Social Work Education.

Bread for the World Institute on Hunger and Development. (1992). *Hunger. 1993. Uprooted people.* Baltimore: Author.

Brecher, J., Brown, J., & Cutler, J. (Eds.). (1993). *Global visions: Beyond the new world order.* Boston: South End Press.

Breton, D., & Largent, C. *The soul of economics: Spiritual evolution goes to the marketplace.* Wilmington, DE: Idea House.

Briar, K. (1983). Unemployment: Toward a social work agenda. *Social Work, 28*(3), 211–216.

Briar, K. (1988). *Social work and the unemployed.* Washington, DC: National Association of Social Workers.

Briar, K. (1990). Transforming human services with family support principles. *Family Resource Coalition Report 2, 6–7.*

Briar, K., & Kaplan, K. (1990). *The family caregiving crisis.* Silver Spring, MD: National Association of Social Workers.

Briar, K., & Ryan, R. (1986, spring). The anti-institution movement and women caregivers. *Affilia: The Journal of Women in Social Work, 20–31.*

Briar, K., & Welch, G. A. (1992). Strengthening families through international innovation transfer. *A guide to the Contact Family Program in Sweden.* Washington, DC: NASW.

Briar-Lawson, K. (1998). Capacity-building for family-centered services and supports. *Social Work, 43,* 539–550.

Briar-Lawson, K. (2000-a). Employment, economic supports, and family capacity building. In A. Sallee, H. Lawson, & K. Briar-Lawson (Eds.), *Innovative practices with vulnerable children and families* (pp. 13–31). Dubuque, IA: Eddie Bowers.

Briar-Lawson, K. (2000-b). The RAINmakers. In P. Senge, N. Cambron-McCabe, & A. Kleiner (Eds.), *Schools that learn* (pp. 529–538). New York: Doubleday.

Briar-Lawson, K., Alameda, T., & Lawson, M. (1997, May). *Empowering children to learn and develop.* Paper presented at International Conference on Families and Schools sponsored by Texas A&M University Institute on Race and Ethnicity, Mexico City, Mexico.

Briar-Lawson, K., & Drews, J. (1998). School-based service integration: Lessons learned and future challenges. In D. van Veen, C. Day, & G. Walraven (Eds.), *Multi-service schools: Integrated services for children and youth at risk* (pp. 49–64). Leuven/Appeldorn, The Netherlands: Garant.

Briar-Lawson, K., & Lawson, H. (1997). Collaboration and integrated, community-based strategies for individuals and families in rural areas. In S. Jones & J. Zlotnik (Eds.), *Preparing helping professionals to meet community needs: Generalizing from the rural experience* (pp. 111–126). Alexandria, VA: Council on Social Work Education.

Briar-Lawson, K., Lawson, H., Collier, C., & Joseph, A. (1997). School-linked comprehensive services: Promising beginnings, lessons learned, and future challenges. *Social Work in Education, 19, 136–148.*

Briar-Lawson, K., Lawson, H., Petersen, N., Harris, N., Sallee, A., Hoffman, T., & Derezotes, D. (1999, January). *Meeting the co-occurring needs of child welfare families through collaboration.* Paper presented at the Society for Social Work and Research, Austin, TX.

Briar-Lawson, K., & Wiesen, M. (2000). What hurts and what helps: Listening to families to build 21st-century child welfare reforms. In A. Sallee, H. Lawson, & K. Briar-Lawson (Eds.), *Innovative practices with vulnerable children and families* (pp. 229–244). Dubuque, IA: Eddie Bowers.

Brown, D. (1995). *When strangers cooperate: Using social conventions to govern ourselves.* New York: Free Press.

Brown, L., Brough, H., Durning, A., Flavin, C., French, H., Jacobson, J., Lenssen, N., Lowe, M., Postel, S., Renner, M., Ryan, J., Starke, L., & Young, J. (1992). *State of the world 1992: A Worldwatch Institute report on progress toward a sustainable society.* New York: Norton.

Brown, R. (1998). *Toward a democratic science: Scientific narration and civic communication.* New Haven, CT: Yale University Press.

Brown, J., D'Emidio-Caston, M., & Pollard, J. (1997). Students and substances: Social power in drug education. *Educational Evaluation and Policy Analysis, 19(1), 65–82.*

Bruce, I., Lloyd, C. B., & Leonard, A. (1995). *Families in focus: New perspectives on mothers, fathers, and children.* New York: Population Council.

Bruce, J. (1989). Homes divided. *World Development, 17, 979–991.*

Bruce, J. (1990, March/April). Fundamental elements of the quality of care: A simple framework. *Studies in Family Planning, 21(2), 61–91.*

Bruce, J., & Lloyd, C. B. (1992). *Finding the ties that bind: Beyond headship and household.* New York: The Population Council, International Center for Research on Women.

Bruner, C. (1991). *Thinking collaboratively: Ten questions and answers to help policy makers improve children's services.* Chicago: Family Resource Coalition of America.

Bruner, C. (1993). *Toward outcome-based accountability: Readings on constructing cost of failure/return on investment analysis of prevention initiatives.* Des Moines: Child and Family Policy Center.

Bruner, C. (1994). *Examining the costs of failure.* Des Moines: Child and Family Policy Center.

Bruner, C. (1996). *Realizing a vision for children, families and neighborhoods: An alternative to other modest proposals.* Des Moines: National Center for Service Integration, Child and Family Policy Center.

Bruner, C. (1997). *Realizing a vision for children, families, and neighborhoods:*

An alternative to other modest proposals. Des Moines: National Center for Service Integration, Child and Family Policy Center.

Bruner, C. (1998). Employing return on investment in policy making. *Georgia Academy Journal, 5*(4), 10.

Bullard, R. D. (1994). *Unequal protection: Environmental justice and communities of color.* San Francisco: Sierra Club Books.

Burggraf, S. (1997). *The feminine economy and economic man: Reviving the role of the family in the postindustrial age.* Reading, MA: Addison-Wesley.

Buvinić, M. (1989). Investing in poor women: The psychology of donor support. *World Development, 17,* 1045–1058.

Cahn, E. (1997). The co-production imperative. *Social Policy, 27*(3), 62–67.

Cahn, E., & Rowe, J. (1992). *Time dollars: The new currency that enables Americans to turn their hidden resource—time—into personal security and community renewal.* Emmaus, PA: Rodale Press.

Carlsson, M., & Humlesjo, E. (1992). *To be a light on the road.* Stockholm, Sweden: The Contact Family Program in Sweden.

Cass, B., & Cappo, P. (1995, February). *Families: Agents and beneficiaries of socio-economic development.* Paper presented at the United Nations Inter-regional Meeting of National Coordinators of the International Year of the Family, Bratislava, Slovakia.

Cassen, R., Wignaraja, G., & Kingdon, G. (1997). *Social investment, productivity, and poverty.* Geneva: United Nations Research Institute for Social Development.

Caughman, S., & Thiam, M. (1982). *The Markala cooperative: A new approach to traditional economic roles.* New York: SEEDS.

Center for Prevention and Early Intervention Policy. (1991). *Unit IV, Appendix: A guide for family identification of concerns, priorities and resources.* Florida: Florida State University Press.

Center for the Study of Human Rights. (1994). *Twenty-five human rights documents.* New York: Columbia University Press.

Center for the Study of Human Rights. (1996). *Women and human rights: The basic documents.* New York: Columbia University Press.

Center for the Study of Social Policy, Family Resource Coalition, Friends of the Family, on behalf of the State of Maryland, Harvard Family Research Project. (1989). *Colloquium on public policy and family support and education.* Annapolis, MD: Author.

Center for the Study of Social Policy, Family Resource Coalition, Friends of the Family, on behalf of the State of Maryland, Harvard Family Research Project. (1990). *Colloquium on public policy and family support: Helping families grow strong, new directions in public policy.* Annapolis, MD: Author.

Chandra, R. (1992). *Industrialization and development in the third world.* New York: Routledge.

Chang, H. N., & Bruner, C. (1994). *Valuing diversity: Practicing inclusion*. Des Moines: NCSI Clearinghouse.

Chapin, R. K. (1995). Social policy development: A strengths perspective. *Social Work, 40*(4), 506–514.

Charlton, S. E., Everett, M., & Staudt, J. (Eds.). (1989). *Women, the state, and development*. Albany: State University of New York Press.

Chattergee, P. (1999). *Repackaging the welfare state*. Washington, DC: National Association of Social Workers Press.

Chen, M. (1989). A sectoral approach to promoting women's work: Lessons from India. *World Development, 17*, 1007–1017.

Childers, E. (1997). The United Nations and global institutions: Discourse and reality. *Global Governance, 3*, 269–276.

Clayton, A., & Radcliffe, N. (1996). *Sustainability: A systems approach*. Boulder, CO: Westview Press.

Cohen, R., & Deng, F. (1998). *The forsaken people: Case studies of the internally displaced*. Washington, DC: Brookings Institution Press.

Cohen, D., & Kristen, S. 1984. *The next Canadian economy*. Eden Press.

Coleman, J. (1990). *Foundations of social theory*. Cambridge, MA: Harvard University Press.

Collier, J., Rosaldo, M., & Yanagisako, S. (1992). Is there a family? New anthropological views. In B. Thorne & M. Yalom (Eds.), *Rethinking the family: Some feminist questions* (pp. 31–48). Boston: Northeastern University Press.

Collins, D., Jordan, C., & Coleman, H. *An introduction to family social work*. Itasca, IL: F. E. Peacock.

Cooney, R., & Michalowski, H. (1987). *The power of the people: Active nonviolence in the United States*. Philadelphia: New Society.

Coontz, S. (1988). *The social origins of private life*. New York: Verso.

Council of State Policy and Planning Agencies. (1989). *A state policy academy on families and children at risk*. Unknown. Author.

Couto, R., & Gutherie, C. (1999). *Making democracy work better: Mediating structures, social capital, and the democratic prospect*. Chapel Hill: University of North Carolina Press.

Cowger, C. (1998). Clientilism and clientification: Impediments to strengths-based social work practice. *Journal of Sociology and Social Welfare, 25*(1), 25–38.

Crossette, B. (2000, January 14). U.N. studies how refugees qualify to get assistance. *New York Times*, p. A7.

Curtis, S., & Jones, I. (1998). Is there a place for geography in the analysis of health inequality? *Sociology of Health and Illness, 20*, 645–672.

Dade County Health and Rehabilitative Services System Task Force. (1991). Draft progress report to the Florida legislature. Dade County, FL: Author.

Dahl, A. (1996). *The eco principle: Ecology and economics in symbiosis*. Oxford: George Ronald; London: Zed Books.

D'Aluisio, F., & Menzel, P. (1996). *Women in the material world.* San Francisco: Sierra Club Books.

Daly, H. (1996). *Beyond growth: The economics of sustainable development.* Boston: Beacon Press.

Dangler, J. (1994). *Hidden in the home: The role of waged homework in the modern world economy.* Albany: State University of New York Press.

Danziger, S., & Gottschalk, P. (1995). *America unequal.* Cambridge, MA: Harvard University Press; New York: Russell Sage Foundation.

Darity, W., & Goldsmith, A. (1996). Social psychology, unemployment and macroeconomics. *Journal of Economic Perspectives, 10*(1), 121–140.

Dasgupta, P. (1995). Population, poverty and the local environment. *Scientific American, 272*(2), 40–45.

Dechungara, D. B., and Viezza, V. (1978). *Let me speak: Testimony of Domitila, a woman of the Bolivian mines.* New York: Monthly Review Press.

Degler, C. (1980). *At odds: Women and the family in America.* New York: Oxford University Press.

DeGraaf, P., & Ultee, W. (1994). The formation of a new underclass: Transitions to and from unemployment in the Netherlands. In O. Benoît-Guilbot & D. Gallie (Eds.), *Long-term unemployment* (pp. 153–164). London: Pinter.

Diamond, L. (1995). Third world civil society can promote democracy. In J. Petrikin (Ed.), *The third world: Opposing viewpoints* (pp. 151–159). San Diego: Greenhaven Press.

Diamond, L., Linz, J., & Lipset, S. (1995). *Politics in developing countries: Comparing experiences with democracy.* Boulder, CO: Lynne Rienner.

Dixon, J., & Macarov, D. (Eds.). (1998). *Poverty: A persistent global reality.* London: Routledge.

Djamiga, J. (1981). *Women and handicrafts: Myth and reality.* New York: SEEDS.

Dornbush, S., & Strober, M. (1988). *Feminism, children, and the new families.* New York: Guilford Press.

Doyal, L. (1995). *What makes women sick: Gender and the political economy of health.* New Brunswick, NJ: Rutgers University Press.

Dreman, S. (1997). *The family on the threshold of the 21st century.* Mahwah, NJ: Erlbaum.

Dryfoos, J. (1998). *Safe passage: Making it through adolescence in a risky society.* New York: Oxford University Press.

Dumon, W. (1991). *Les politiques familiales nationales des états membres de la cummunauté Europenne.* Bruxelles, Belgium: Commission des Communautes Europennes.

Dunleavy, P. (1997). The globalization of public services production: Can government be "best in the world?" In A. Massey (Ed.), *Globalization and the marketization of government services: Comparing contemporary public sector developments* (pp. 16–46). New York: St. Martin's Press.

Dunst, C., Trivette, C., & Deal, A. (Eds.). (1994). *Supporting and strengthening families: Vol. 1. Methods, strategies, and practices.* Cambridge, MA: Brookline Books.

Dunst, C., Trivette, C., & Hamby, D. (1996). Measuring the help-giving practices of human services program practitioners. *Human Relations, 6,* 815–835.

Durkheim, E. (1964). *Rules of sociological method.* New York: Free Press.

Dwyer, D., & Bruce, J. (Eds.). (1988). *A home divided: Women and income in the third world.* Stanford, CA: Stanford University Press.

Eade, J. (Ed.). (1997). *Living the global city: Globalization as local process.* London: Routledge.

Economist. (1999, November 27). Storm over globalisation, 15–16.

Economist. (1999, December 4–10). Clueless in Seattle, 17.

Economist. (1998, December 5). The conscience of mankind, 4–16.

Edelman, P. (1997, March). The worst thing Bill Clinton has done. *Atlantic,* 43–58.

Edin, K., & Lein, L. (1997). Work, welfare, and single mothers' economic survival strategies. *American Sociological Review, 62,* 253–266.

Eichler, M. (1997). *Family shifts.* New York: Oxford University Press.

Ellis, R., & Sumberg, J. (1998). Food production, urban areas, and policy responses. *World Development, 26,* 213–225.

Epping, R. C. (1995). *A beginner's guide to the world economy.* New York: Vintage Books.

Escobar, A. (1995). *Encountering development: The making and unmaking of the third world.* Princeton, NJ: Princeton University Press.

Ewalt, P. L., Freeman, E. M., Fortune, A. E., Poole, D. L., & Stanley, W. L. (1999). *Multicultural issues in social work: Practice and research.* Washington, DC: NASW Press.

Family Resource Coalition. (1990). *Statement of principles.* Chicago: Author.

Family Resource Coalition. (1995). *Report on culture and family-centered practice.* National Resource Center on Family Centered Practice. Chicago: Author.

Farber, B. (1973). *Family and kinship in modern society.* Glencoe, IL: Scott Foresman.

Farmer, P. (1996). Social inequalities and emerging infectious diseases. *Emergent Infectious Diseases, 2,* 259–269.

Featherstone, M., & Lash, S. (1995). Globalization, modernity and the spatialization of social theory: An introduction. In M. Featherstone & S. Lash (Eds.), *Global modernities* (pp. 1–24). London: Sage.

Feldman, R., Stall, S., & Wright, P. A. (1998). "The community needs to be built by us." In N. Naples (Ed.), *Community activism and feminist politics: Organizing across race, class, and gender* (pp. 257–274). New York: Routledge.

Felitti, V., Anda, R., Nordenberg, D., Williamson, D., Spitz, A., Edwards, V., Koss, M., & Marks, J. (1998). Relationship of childhood abuse and household dysfunction to many of the leading causes of death in adults. *American Journal of Preventive Medicine, 14(4),* 245–258.

Fellowship for Intentional Community and Communities Publications Cooperative. (1992). *Directory of intentional communities: A guide to cooperative living*. Rutledge, MO: Author.

Fetterman, D., Kaftarian, S., & Wandersman, A. (1996). (Eds.). *Empowerment evaluation: Knowledge and tools for self-assessment and accountability*. Thousand Oaks, CA: Sage.

Finch, J. (1989). *Family obligations and social change*. Cambridge, MA: Polity Press.

Fine, M., & Weis, L. (1998). *The unknown city: The lives of poor and working-class young adults*. Boston: Beacon Press.

Fisher, J. (1998). *Nongovernments: NGOs and the political development of the third world*. West Hartford, CT: Kumarian Press.

Fitzgerald, M., Guberman, C., & Wolfe, M. (1982). *Still ain't satisfied!: Canadian feminism today*. Toronto: Women's Press.

Folbre, N. (1991). *Women on their own: Global patterns of female headship*. New York: The Population Council, International Center for Research on Women.

Folbre, N. (1994). *Who pays for the kids? Gender and the structures of constraint*. London: Routledge.

Foldy, E., & Creed, W. (1999). Action learning, fragmentation, and the interaction of single-, double-, and triple-loop change. *Journal of Applied Behavioral Science, 35*, 207–227.

Foree, S. (1996). Who is this lady called "Mrs. G" and why does everyone call her for help? One community's story on parent advocacy. In K. Hooper-Briar & H. Lawson (Eds.), *Expanding partnerships for vulnerable children, youth, and families* (pp. 41–45). Washington, DC: Council on Social Work Education.

Foucault, M. (1977). *Discipline and punish: The birth of the prison*. New York: Vintage Books.

Fourth World Conference on Women. (1996). *Platform for action and the Beijing Declaration*. New York: United Nations Department of Public Information.

Fox, B. (Ed.). (1980). *Hidden in the household: Women's domestic labor under capitalism*. Toronto: Women's Educational Press.

Fox, B. (Ed.). (1993). *Family patterns, gender relations*. New York: Oxford University Press.

Freire, P. (1982). *Pedagogy of the oppressed*. New York: Continuum.

Friedman, J. (1995). Global system, globalization, and the parameters of modernity. In M. Featherstone, S. Lash, & R. Robertson (Eds.), *Global modernities* (pp. 69–90). Thousand Oaks, CA: Sage.

Friedson, E. (1994). *Professionalism reborn: Theory, prophecy, and policy*. Chicago: University of Chicago Press.

Fuchs, L. (1972). *Family matters*. New York: Random House.

Fukuyama, F. (1995). *Trust: The social virtues and the creation of prosperity*. New York: Free Press.

Gallie, D. (1994a). Conclusion: Toward a new underclass? In O. Benoît-Guilbot & D. Gallie (Eds.), *Long-term unemployment* (pp. 165–173). London: Pinter.

Gallie, D. (1994b). Social consequences of long-term unemployment in Britain. In O. Benoît-Guilbot & D. Gallie (Eds.), *Long-term unemployment* (pp. 121–136). London: Pinter.

Galtung, J. (1995). *On the social costs of modernization: Social disintegration, atomie/anomie, and social development*. Geneva: United Nations Research Institute for Social Development.

Gardner, S. (1999). *Beyond collaboration to results: Hard choices in the future of services to children and families*. Fullerton, CA: Center for Collaboration for Children, California State University and the Arizona Prevention Resource Center.

Garraty, J. A. (1979). *Unemployment in history: Economic thought and public policy*. New York: Harper & Row.

George, I. (1995). First world overconsumption causes third world poverty. In J. Petrikin (Ed.), *The third world: Opposing viewpoints* (pp. 26–33). San Diego: Greenhaven Press.

Gereffi, G., & Korzeniewicz, M. (Eds.). (1994). *Commodity chains and global capitalism*. Westport, CT: Greenwood Press.

Gerhart, J. (1989). Foreword. *World Development, 17,* 933–936.

Gerry, M. (1993). *A joint enterprise with America's families to ensure student success*. Washington, DC: Council of Chief State School Officers.

Gerson, D., & Van Soest, D. (1999). Relevance of Gandhi to a peaceful world society: Lessons for social work practice and education. *New Global Development: Journal of International and Comparative Social Welfare, 15,* 8–22.

Geyer, R., Ingebritsen, C., & Moses, J. (Eds.). (2000). *Globalization, Europeanization, and the end of Scandinavian social democracy?* New York: St. Martin's Press.

Ghai, D. (1997). *Social development and public policy: Some lessons from successful experiences*. Geneva: United Nations Research Institute for Social Development.

Giddens, A. (1990). *The consequences of modernity*. Stanford, CA: Stanford University Press.

Giddens, A. (1994). *Beyond left and right: The future of radical politics*. Stanford, CA: Stanford University Press.

Giddens, A. (1995). *Affluence, poverty and the idea of a post-scarcity society*. Geneva: United Nations Research Institute for Social Development.

Gil, D. (1970). *Violence against children: Physical abuse in the United States*. Cambridge, MA: Harvard University Press.

Gil, D. (1998a). *Confronting injustice and oppression: Concepts and strategies for social workers*. New York: Columbia University Press.

Gil, D. (1998b). Reframing political discourse: Politics of human needs. *New*

Global Development: Journal of International and Comparative Social Welfare, 14, 15–22.

Gil, D. (1999). Developmental social welfare services: A solution or strategy for the challenge facing social welfare globally. *New Global Development: Journal of International and Comparative Social Welfare, 15,* 1–7.

Ginsberg, H. (1983). *Full employment and public policy: The United States and Sweden.* Lexington, MA: Lexington Books.

Gittins, D. (1986). *The family in question: Changing households and familiar ideologies.* Atlantic Highlands, NJ: Humanities Press International.

Goldsmith, A. (1996). Seeds of exploitation: Free trade zones in the global economy. In J. Mander & E. Goldsmith (Eds.), *The case against the global economy and for a turn toward the local* (pp. 267–272). San Francisco: Sierra Club Books.

Goldsmith, E. (1996a). Development as colonialism. In J. Mander & E. Goldsmith (Eds.), *The case against the global economy and for a turn toward the local* (pp. 253–266). San Francisco: Sierra Club Books.

Goldsmith, E. (1996b). The last word: Family, community, democracy. In J. Mander & E. Goldsmith (Eds.), *The case against the global economy and for a turn toward the local* (pp. 501–514). San Francisco: Sierra Club Books.

Goldthorpe, J. (1996). *The sociology of post-colonial societies: Economic disparity, cultural diversity, and development.* Cambridge: Cambridge University Press.

Gonzalez, R. (1996). Distinctions in Western women's experience: Ethnicity, class, and social change. In L. Richardson, V. Taylor, & N. Whittier (Eds.), *Feminist frontiers IV* (pp. 9–17). New York: McGraw-Hill.

Goodfield, J. (1991). *An imagined world: A story of scientific discovery.* Ann Arbor: University of Michigan Press.

Gordon, L. (1998). How welfare became a dirty word. *New Global Development: Journal of International and Comparative Social Welfare, 14,* 1–14.

Gorman, D. (1998). The irrelevance of evidence in the development of school-based drug prevention policy, 1896–1996. *Evaluation Review, 22*(1), 118–146.

Goudzswaard, B., & deLange, H. (1991). *Beyond poverty and affluence: Toward an economy of care.* Grand Rapids, MI: Eerdmans; Geneva: WCC Publications.

Gouvernement du Quebec, Ministere des Relations Avec Les Citoyens et des L'Immigration. (1966). *Seminaire international sur les politiques et les plans d'action en matiere familiale.* Quebec: Gouvernement du Quebec.

Grace Hill Settlement House. (1995). *MORE: Member organized resource exchange.* St. Louis: Author

Graham-Gibson, J. K. (1996). *The end of capitalism (as we knew it): A feminist critique of political economy.* Cambridge, MA: Blackwell.

Greider, W. (1997). *One world, ready or not: The manic logic of global capitalism.* New York: Touchstone Books.

Griesgraber, J. M., & Gunter, B. *The world bank: Lending on a global scale.* London: Pluto Press.

Grown, C., & Sebstad, J. (1989). Introduction: Toward a wider perspective on women's employment. *World Development, 17,* 937–952.

Guba, E., & Lincoln, Y. (1989). *Fourth generation evaluation.* Thousand Oaks, CA: Sage.

Gusfield, J. (1996). *Contested meanings: The construction of alcohol problems.* Madison, WI: University of Wisconsin Press.

Guzzetta, C. (1998). The economy's global: Can social work education be global? *New Global Development: Journal of International and Comparative Social Welfare, 14,* 23–33.

Hall, E. (1988). *The Port Sudan small-scale enterprise program.* New York: SEEDS.

Halpern, R. (1995). *Rebuilding the inner city: A history of neighborhood organizations in the United States.* New York: Columbia University Press.

Halpern, R. (1998). *Fragile families, fragile solutions: A history of supportive services for families in poverty.* New York: Columbia University Press.

Halstead, T., & Cobb, C. (1996). The need for new measurements of progress. In J. Mander & E. Goldsmith (Eds.), *The case against the global economy and for a turn toward the local* (pp. 197–206). San Francisco: Sierra Club Books.

Ham, C. (1997). Lessons and conclusions. In C. Ham (Ed.), *Health care reform: Learning from international experience* (pp. 119–139). Buckingham, UK: Open University Press.

Handler, J. (1996). *Down from bureaucracy: The ambiguity of privatization and empowerment.* Princeton, NJ: Princeton University Press.

Hannerz, U. (1992). *Cultural complexity: Studies in the social organization of meaning.* New York: Columbia University Press.

Harding, L. (1996). *Family, state, and social policy.* London: Macmillan.

Harlan, J. (1998). *Feminism.* Santa Barbara, CA: ABC-CLIO.

Harrington, M. (1999). *Care and equality: Inventing a new family politics.* New York: Knopf.

Hartman, A. (1995). Ideological themes in family policy. *Families in Society: Journal of Contemporary Human Services, 76,* 182–192.

Hartman, A., & Laird, J. (1983). *Family-centered social work practice.* New York: Free Press.

Haruo, N. (1996). Planning for employment in the urban informal sector. *Regional Development Dialogue, 17*(1), 185–192.

Haspels, N., & Jankanish, M. (Eds.). (2000). *Action against child labor.* Geneva: International Labour Organization.

Haveman, R., & Wolfe, B. (1995). *Succeeding generations: On the effects of investments in children.* New York: Russell Sage Foundation.

Haynes, K. S., & Mickelson, J. (1999). *Affecting change: Social workers in the political arena*. New York: Longman.

Held, D. (1996). *Models of democracy*. Stanford, CA: Stanford University Press.

Held, D. (1997). Democracy and globalization. *Global Governance, 3,* 251–267.

Held, D., & McGrew, A. (1993). Globalization and the liberal democratic state. *Government and Opposition, 28,* 261–285.

Henderson, H. (1996). *Building a win-win world: Life beyond global economic warfare*. San Francisco: Berrett-Koehler.

Henderson, H. (2000). Transnational corporations and global citizenship. *American Behavioral Scientist, 43,* 1231–1261.

Hennon, C. B. (1981). The conceptualization of variant family forms. *Cybernetica, 24,* 199–214.

Hennon, C. B. (2000). *The family life education process*. Oxford, OH: Miami University, Family and Child Studies Center.

Hennon, C. B., & Arcus, M. (1993). Life-span family life education. In T. H. Brubaker (Ed.), *Family relations: Challenges for the future* (pp. 181–210). Newbury Park, CA: Sage.

Hennon, C. B., Brubaker, E., & Kaplan, L. (1991). Health, housing, and aging: Families as case managers. *Journal of Home Economics, 83*(1), 54–62.

Hennon, C. B., & Jones, A. R. (2000). Family-related economic and employment policies and programs in Central and Eastern European countries. In D. S. Iatridis (Ed.), *Social justice and the welfare state in Central and Eastern Europe: The impact of privatization* (pp. 132–150). Westport, CT: Praeger.

Hennon, C. B., Jones, A., Hooper-Briar, K., & Kopcanová, D. (1996). A snapshot in time: Family policy and the United Nations International Year of the Family. *Journal of Family and Economic Issues, 17,* 9–46.

Hennon, C. B., Jones, A., Roth, M., & Popescu, L. (1998). Family-enterprise initiatives as a response to socioeconomic and political change in Eastern and Central Europe. *Journal of Family and Economic Issues, 19,* 235–253.

Hennon, C. B., & Kopcanová, D. (1996). The International Year of the Family: Global efforts and a national initiative. In K. Hooper-Briar & H. A. Lawson (Eds.), *Expanding partnerships for vulnerable children, youth, and families* (pp. 362–390). Alexandria, VA: Council on Social Work Education.

Hennon, C. B., & Loker, S. (2000). Gender and home-based employment in a global economy. In C. Hennon, S. Loker, & R. Walker (Eds.), *Gender and home-based employment* (pp. 17–43). Westport, CT: Auburn.

Hennon, C. B., & Radina, M. E. (in press). Divorce and later life. In T. H. Brubaker (Ed.), *Family relationships in later life* (3rd ed.). Thousand Oaks, CA: Sage.

Hermans, H., & Kempen, H. (1998). Moving cultures: The perilous problems of cultural dichotomies in a globalizing society. *American Psychologist, 53,* 1111–1120.

Heying, C. (1997). Civic elites and corporate delocalization. *American Behavioral Scientist, 40,* 657–668.

Heyzer, N. (1989). Asian women wage-earners: Their situation and possibilities for donor intervention. *World Development, 17,* 1109–1124.

Himmelstrabd, K. (1989). Can an aid bureaucracy empower women? The case of SIDA. *Issue: A Journal of Opinion, 37*(2), 41.

Hirschmann, D. (1998). Civil society in South Africa: Learning from gender themes. *World Development, 26,* 227–238.

Hogg Foundation for Mental Health and World Federation for Mental Health. (1990). *Mental health of immigrants and refugees.* Austin, TX: Author.

Hoogvelt, A. (1997). *Globalization and the postcolonial world: The new political economy of development.* Baltimore: Johns Hopkins University Press.

Hooper-Briar, K. (1994). *Mission to Bratislava: Feasibility study on the affiliation of the Bratislava international centre for family studies with the United Nations.* New York: United Nations.

Hooper-Briar, K., & Lawson, H. (1994). *Serving children, youth and families through interprofessional collaboration and service integration: A framework for action.* Oxford, OH: Institute for Educational Renewal at Miami University and the Danforth Foundation.

Hooper-Briar, K., & Lawson, H. (1995). Families and social development. *New Global Development: International Journal of Comparative and Social Welfare, 11,* 1–26.

Hooper-Briar, K., & Seck, E. T. (1995). Jobs and earnings. *Encyclopedia of social work* (19th ed., pp. 1539–1545). Washington, DC: National Association of Social Workers.

Hosfeld, K. (1990). Their logic against them: Contradictions in sex, race, and class in Silicon Valley. In K. Ward (Ed.), *Women workers and global restructuring* (pp. 149–178). Ithaca, NY: ILP Press.

Hoy, P. (1998). *Players and issues in international aid.* West Hartford, CT: Kumarian Press.

Huntington, S. (1993). The clash of civilizations. *Foreign Affairs, 72,* 22–49.

Ibrahim, B. (1989). Policies affecting women's employment in the formal sector: Strategies for change. *World Development, 17,* 1097–1108.

Ife, J. (1995). *Community Building.* South Melbourne, Australia: Addison Wesley Longman.

International Council on Social Welfare. (1986). *Report from working group 9 on the unemployed: Policies and services.* Thirteenth regional symposium on social welfare, 9–14 June 1985. Turku, Finland.

International Labour Office. (1990). *International labour standards for development and social justice.* Geneva: Author.

International Labour Office. (1993). *World labor report 1993.* Geneva: Author.

International Labour Office. (1998). *World employment report 1998–1999. Em-*

ployability in the global economy: How training matters. Geneva: International Labour Organization.

International Network on Unemployment and Social Work. (1987). *INUSW Newsletter,* no. 9. Stockholm, Sweden: Stockholm University Press.

Isham, J., Kaufmann, D., & Pritchett, L. (1997). Civil liberties, democracy, and the performance of government projects. *World Bank Economic Review, 11,* 219–242.

Israel, A. (1987). *Institutional development: Incentives to performance.* Baltimore: Johns Hopkins University Press.

Jain, D., & Banerjee, N. (1985). *Tyranny of the household: Investigative essays on women's work.* Delhi: Shakti Books.

Jansson, B. (1998). *Becoming an effective policy advocate: From policy practice to social justice.* Pacific Grove: CA: Brooks/Cole.

Jeppesen, K. J. (1993). *A programme for development in Danish social policy.* Copenhagen: Danish National Institute of Social Research.

Jewell, K. (1988). *Survival of the black family: The institutional impact of U.S. social policy.* New York: Praeger.

Jiggins, J. (1989). How poor women earn income in sub-Saharan Africa and what works against them. *World Development, 17,* 953–964.

Johnson, A. (1999). Globalization from below: Using the Internet to internationalize social work education. *Journal of Social Work Education, 35,* 377–393.

Jordan, B. (1998). *The new politics of welfare.* Thousand Oaks, CA: Sage.

Kagan, S. L. (1996). America's family support movement: A moment of change. In E. Zigler, S. Kagan, & N. Hall (Eds.), *Children, families, and government: Preparing for the twenty-first century* (pp. 156–170). New York: Cambridge University Press.

Kagan, S. L., & Weissbord, B. (Eds.). (1994). *Putting families first: America's family support movement and the challenge of change.* San Francisco: Jossey-Bass.

Kagan, S. L., & Neville, P. R. (1994). *Integrating services for children and families: Understanding the past to shape the future.* Hartford, CT: Yale University Press.

Kahn, Alfred A., & Kamerman, S. (1975). *Not for the poor alone: European social services.* New York: Harper.

Kahn, A., & Kamerman, S. (1982). *Helping America's families.* Philadelphia: Temple University Press.

Kamel, W. (1997). Health dilemmas at the borders—a global challenge. *World Health Forum, 18*(1), 9–16.

Kamerman, S. (1996). Child and family policies: An international overview. In E. Zigler, S. Kagan, & N. Hall (Eds.), *Children, families, and government: Preparing for the twenty-first century* (pp. 31–48). New York: Cambridge University Press.

Kamerman, S., & Kahn, A. (1978). *Family policy*. New York: Columbia University Press.

Kamerman, S., Kahn, A., & Kingston, P. (1983). *Maternity policies and working women*. New York: Columbia University Press.

Kardam, N. (1991). *Bringing women in*. Boulder, CO: Lynne Rienner.

Kawewe, S. (1998). The inability of the United Nations to reform world practices endangering third world children. *New Global Development: Journal of International and Comparative Social Welfare, 14,* 46–61.

Kennedy, P. (1993). *Preparing for the 21st century*. New York: Vintage.

Kessler, R., Gillis-Light, J., Magee, W., Kendler, K., & Eaves, L. (1997). Childhood adversity and adult psychopathology. In I. Gotlib & B. Wheaton (Eds.), *Stress and adversity over the life course: Trajectories and turning points* (pp. 29–49). New York: Cambridge University Press.

Kessler, R. C., Mickelson, K. D., & Zhao, S. (1997, Spring). Patterns and correlates of self-help group membership in the United States. *Social Policy, 27*–46.

Khadja, K. (1999, February). Female genital mutilation. Special Interest Group Meeting, Council on Social Work Education, San Francisco, CA.

Kinney, J., Strand, K., Hagerup, M., & Bruner, C. (1994). *Beyond the buzzwords: Key principles in effective frontline practice*. Des Moines: National Center for Service Integration and National Resource Center for Family Support Programs.

Knapp, M., & Associates. (Eds.). (1998). *Paths to partnership: University and community as learners in interprofessional education*. New York: Rowman & Littlefield.

Kneerim, J. (1980). *Village women organize: Mraru bus service*. New York: SEEDS.

Knowles, C. (1996). *Family boundaries: The invention of normality and dangerousness*. Toronto: Broadview Press.

Korzeniewicz, M. (1994). Commodity chains and marketing strategies: Nike and the global athletic footwear industry. In G. Gereffi & M. Korzeniewicz (Eds.), *Commodity chains and global capitalism* (pp. 247–265). Westport, CT: Greenwood Press.

Kretzmann, J. P., & McKnight, J. L. (1993). *Building communities from the inside out*. Chicago: ACTA.

Krut, R. (1997). *Globalization and civil society: NGO influence on international decision-making*. Geneva: United Nations Research Institute for Social Development.

Kumpfer, K. (1999). Selective prevention interventions: The strengthening families program. In R. Asahery, E. Robertson, & K. Kumpfer (Eds.), *Drug abuse prevention through family interventions*. Rockville, MD: National Institute on Drug Abuse.

Kung, H. (1991). *Global responsibility: In search of a new world ethic.* New York: Crossroad.

Kunjufu, J. (1991). *Black economics: Solutions for economic and community empowerment.* Chicago: African American Images.

Kurz, K., & Prather, C. (1995). *Improving the quality of life of girls.* New York: United Nations Children's Fund Programme Publications.

Kuttner, R. (1997). *Everything for sale: The virtues and limits of markets.* New York: Knopf.

Lahav, G. (1997). International versus national constraints in family-reunification migration policy. *Global Governance, 3,* 349–372.

Langmore, J. (1998, January). *Globalisation and social policy.* Paper presented at the Second International Conference on Social Work in Health and Mental Health, University of Melbourne, Melbourne, Victoria, Australia.

Lawson, H. (1992). Toward a socio-ecological conception of health. *Quest, 44,* 105–121.

Lawson, H. (1998a). Academically-based community scholarship, consultation as collaborative problem-solving, and a collective-responsibility model for the helping fields. *Journal of Educational and Psychological Consultation, 9,* 195–232.

Lawson, H. (1998b, July). *Globalization and the social responsibilities of citizen-professionals.* Keynote address, AIESEP International Conference, Garden City, NY.

Lawson, H. (1999a). Journey analysis: A new methodology for integrating consultation and evaluation in complex change initiatives. *Journal of Educational and Psychological Consultation, 10,* 145–172.

Lawson, H. (1999b). Two new mental models for schools and their implications for principals' roles, responsibilities, and preparation. *National Association of Secondary School Principals Bulletin, 83*(611), 8–27.

Lawson, H. (2000). Back to the future: New century professionalism and collaborative leadership for comprehensive, community-based systems of care. In A. Sallee, H. Lawson, & K. Briar-Lawson (Eds.), *Innovative practices with vulnerable children and families* (pp. 393–418). Dubuque, IA: Eddie Bowers.

Lawson, H. (under review-a). *Feminist principles, theories of action, and policy-practice.* Manuscript submitted for publication.

Lawson, H. (under review-b). *The context of diversity and the diversity of contexts: Evaluating and enhancing the civil society-social capital framework for development.* Manuscript submitted for publication.

Lawson, H., & Barkdull, C. (2000). Gaining the collaborative advantage and promoting systems and cross-systems change. In A. Sallee, H. Lawson, & K. Briar-Lawson (Eds.), *Innovative practices with vulnerable children and families* (pp. 245–269). Dubuque, IA: Eddie Bowers.

Lawson, H., & Briar-Lawson, K. (1997). *Connecting the dots: Progress toward the integration of school reform, school-linked services, parent involvement and community schools.* Oxford, OH: Danforth Foundation and the Institute for Educational Renewal at Miami University.

Lawson, H., Briar-Lawson, K., & Lawson, M. (1997). Mapping challenges for vulnerable children, youth and families. *Universities and Community Schools, 5*(1–2), 79–94.

Lawson, H., Briar-Lawson, K., Peterson, N., and Harris, N., with Berns, D., Derezotes, D., Hoffman, T., Sallee, A., Boyer, R., Ynacay-Nye, R., Weisen, R., Western, P., Kean, L., Nelson, D., Kessin, D., & Garcia, J. (1999, April). *The development of an empowerment-oriented, interprofessional education and training model in response to the co-occurring needs of vulnerable families and the professionals who serve them.* Paper presented at American Educational Research Association Conference, Montreal.

Lawson, H., Briar-Lawson, K., Warner-Kearney, D., & Ynacay-Nye, R. (2000, January). *A new model for uniting, harmonizing, integrating, and promoting action research, advocacy, systems change, partnerships, and research innovation, dissemination, and utilization.* Paper presented at the Society for Social Work and Research, Charleston, SC.

Lawson, H., & Hooper-Briar, K. (1994). *Expanding partnerships: Involving colleges and universities in interprofessional collaboration and service integration.* Oxford, OH: Danforth Foundation and the Institute for Educational Renewal at Miami University.

Lawson, H., Petersen, N., & Briar-Lawson, K. (in press). From conventional training to empowering design teams for collaboration and systems change. In A. Sallee, H. Lawson, & K. Briar-Lawson (Eds.), *Innovative practices with vulnerable children and families.* Dubuque, IA: Eddie Bowers.

Lee, K. W. (1995). Racial inequality in Singapore. *New Global Development: Journal of International and Comparative Social Welfare, 11,* 56–73.

Leidenfrost, N. (Ed.). (1992). *Families in transition.* Vienna: International Federation for Home Economics.

Leonard, A., Landers, C., Arnold, C., Mejia, J., & Harego, A. (1991). *Child care: Meeting the needs of working mothers and their children.* New York: SEEDS.

Leonard, P. (1997). *Postmodern welfare: Reconstructing an emancipatory project.* Thousand Oaks, CA: Sage.

Lerner, G. (1986). *The creation of patriarchy.* New York: Oxford University Press.

Lerner, M. (1986). *Surplus powerlessness.* Oakland: Institute for Labor and Mental Health.

Levinson, D. (1989). *Family violence in cross-cultural perspective.* Newbury Park, CA: Sage.

Lewis, J. (1997). *Lone mothers in European welfare regimes: Shifting policy logics.* London: Jessica Kingsley.

Lind, A., & Farmelo, M. (1996). *Gender and urban social movements: Women's community responses to restructuring and urban poverty.* Geneva: United Nations Research Institute for Social Development.

Lindblom, C. (1990). *Inquiry and change: The troubled attempt to understand and shape society.* New Haven, CT: Yale University Press; New York: Russell Sage Foundation.

Link, G., & Beggs, M., with Seidermann, E. (1997). *Serving families.* San Francisco: Parent Services Project.

Lipscomb, A. (1996). Going the distance. A journey. In K. Hooper-Briar & H. Lawson (Eds.), *Expanding partnerships for vulnerable children, youth, and families* (pp. 57–64). Washington, DC: Council on Social Work Education.

Lusk, M., & Mason, D. (1995). Latin American street children: Action research with social work students. *New global Development: Journal of International and Comparative Social Welfare, 11, 15–25.*

Lynn, K., Kelly, E. M., Holley, L., & Zlotnik, J. (1994). *Strengthening families through international innovations transfer: Final report.* Washington, DC: NASW.

Lyotard, F. (1984). *The postmodern condition: A report on knowledge.* Minneapolis: University of Minnesota Press.

Madara, E. J. (1997, Spring). The mutual-aid self-help online revolution. *Social Policy, 20–26.*

Maguire, J. (1999). *Global sport: Identities, societies, civilizations.* Cambridge, UK: Polity Press.

Mah, A. Y. (1997). *Falling leaves: The memoir of an unwanted Chinese daughter.* New York: Broadway Books.

Mahler, S. (1999). Theoretical and empirical contributions: Toward a research agenda for transnationalism. In M. Smith & L. Guarnizo (Eds.), *Transnationalism from below* (pp. 64–102). New Brunswick, NJ: Transaction.

Mander, J., & Goldsmith, E. (Eds.). (1996). *The case against the global economy and for a turn toward the local.* San Francisco: Sierra Club Books.

Mansbridge, J. (1994). Public spirit in political systems. In H. Aaron, T. Mann, & T. Taylor (Eds.), *Values and public policy* (pp. 146–172). Washington, DC: Brookings Institution Press.

Marsh, P., & Crow, G. (1998). *Family group conferences in child welfare: Working together for children, young people, and their families.* Malden, MA: Blackwell.

Martin, P., & Widgren, J. (1996). International migration: A global challenge. *The Population Bulletin, 51(1), 1–48.*

Masland, T., & Nordland, R. (2000, January 17). 10 million orphans. *Newsweek,* pp. 42–45.

Mason, M., Skolnick, A., & Sugeraman, S. (1998). *All our families: New policies for a new century.* New York: Oxford University Press.

Massey, A. (1997). In search of the state: Markets, myths, and paradigms. In A. Massey (Ed.), *Globalization and marketization of government services:*

Comparing contemporary public sector developments (pp. 1–15). New York: St. Martin's Press.

Massiah, J. (1989). Women's lives and livelihoods: A view from the Commonwealth Caribbean. *World Development, 17,* 965–978.

Mastekaasa, A. (1996). Unemployment and health: Selection effects. *Journal of Community and Applied Social Psychology, 6,* 189–205.

Matsuoka, J., & Benson, M. (1996, February). Economic change, family cohesion, and mental health in a rural Hawaii community. *Families in Society: The Journal of Contemporary Human Services,* 108–166.

Mazur, L., & Sechler, S. (1997). *Global interdependence and the need for social stewardship.* New York: Rockefeller Brothers Fund.

McCroskey, J., & Einbinder, S. (Eds.). (1998). *Universities and communities: Remaking professional and interprofessional education for the next century.* Westport, CT: Praeger.

McKee, K. (1989). Microlevel strategies for supporting livelihoods, employment, and income generation of poor women in the third world: The challenge of significance. *World Development, 17,* 993–1006.

McKnight, J. (1995). *The careless society: Community and its counterfeits.* New York: Basic Books.

McKnight, J. (1997). A 21st century map for healthy communities and families. *Families in Society: The Journal of Contemporary Human Services, 78,* 117–127.

McMichael, P. (1996). *Development and social change: A global perspective.* Thousand Oaks, CA: Pine Forge Press.

Meenaghan, T., & Kilty, K. (1993). *Policy analysis and research technology.* Chicago: Lyceum Books.

Melaville, A. I., & Blank, M. J. (1991). *What it takes: Structuring interagency partnerships to connect children and families with comprehensive services.* Chicago: Family Resource Coalition of America.

Melaville, A. I., Blank, M. J., & Asayesh, G. (1993). *Together we can: A guide for crafting a profamily system of education and human services.* Washington, DC: Institute for Educational Leadership.

Mele, C. (1996). Globalization, culture, and neighborhood change: Reinventing the Lower East Side of New York. *Urban Affairs Review, 32*(1), 3–22.

Mengistab, K. (1996). *Globalization and autocentricity in Africa's development in the 21st century.* Trenton, NJ: Africa World Press.

Mercier, J., & Garasky, S. (1997). Introduction. *Policy Studies Journal, 25*(1), 69. On-line: *http: //www.microcreditsummit.org/declaration.htm.*

Microcredit Summit. (1998). On-line: *http: //www.microcreditsummit.org/declaration.htm.*

Midgley, J. (1997). *Social welfare in global context.* Thousand Oaks, CA: Sage.

Midgley, J. (1999). Growth, redistribution, and welfare: Toward social investment. *Social Service Review, 73*(1), 3–21.

Mies, M., Bennholdt-Thomsen, V., & von Werlhof, C. (1991). *Women: The last colony*. London: Zed Books.

Migdal, Joel S. (1974). *Peasants, politics, and revolution: Pressures toward political and social change in the third world*. Princeton, NJ: Princeton University Press.

Milardo, R. (Ed.). (1988). *Families and social networks*. Beverly Hills, CA: Sage.

Miller, S. M., & Collins, C. (1996, Summer). Growing economic fairness. *Social Policy, 41–55*.

Mills, C. (1969). *The sociological imagination*. New York: Oxford University Press.

Ministry for Home Affairs and Social Development. (1993). *The family law: A brief explanation of the bill amending the civil code*. Malta: Author.

Ministry for Home Affairs and Social Development, Malta. (1993). *World NGO forum: Launching the International Year of the Family*. Zabbar, Malta: Guttenberg Press.

Ministry for Home Affairs and Social Development, Malta. (1994). *Presentation of the Malta national committee for the International Year of the Family*. St. Venera, Malta: Author.

Minton, M. H., & Block, J. L. (1993). *What is a wife worth?* New York: McGraw-Hill.

Minuchin, P., Colapinto, J., & Minuchin, S. *Working with families of the poor*. New York: Guilford Press.

Miringoff, M., & Miringoff, M. L. (1999). *The social health of the nation: How America is really doing*. New York: Oxford University Press.

Mitzman, A. (1969). *The iron cage: An historical interpretation of Max Weber*. New York: Grosset & Dunlap.

Mizan, Ainon N. (1994). *In quest of empowerment: The Grameen Bank impact on women's power and status*. Dacca, Bangladesh: The University Press Limited.

Moghadam, V. M. (1992, March). *Approaching the family: Gender, development, and equity*. Prepared for the Second Ad hoc Interagency meeting on the International Year of the Family, Vienna, Austria.

Moghadam, V. M. (Ed.). (1996). *Patriarchy and economic development*. Oxford: Clarendon Press.

Mohan, B. (1992). *Global development: Post-material values and social praxis*. New York: Praeger.

Mohanty, C., Russo, A., & Torres, L. (1991). *Third world women and the politics of feminism*. Bloomington: Indiana University Press.

Molnar, A. (1987). *Forest conservation in Nepal: Encouraging women's participation*. New York: SEEDS.

Moore, M. (1988). What sort of ideas become public ideas? In R. Reich (Ed.), *The power of public ideas* (pp. 85–108). Cambridge, MA: Harvard University Press.

Moroney, R. (1986). *Shared responsibility, families and social policy*. Hawthorne, NY: Aldine.

Moser, C. (1998). The asset-vulnerability framework: Reassessing urban poverty reduction strategies. *World Development, 26*(1), 1–19.

Mosher, S. W. (1993). *A mother's ordeal: One woman's fight against China's one-child policy*. New York: HarperCollins.

Mungall, C. (1986). *More than just a job: Worker cooperatives in Canada*. Ottawa, Canada: Steel Rail Publishing.

Murray, C. J., and Lopez, A. D. *The global burden of disease*. Cambridge: Harvard University Press.

Nader, R. (1993). Introduction: Free trade and the decline of democracy. In R. Nader, W. Greider, et al. (Eds.), *The case against free trade: GATT, NAFTA, and the globalization of corporate power* (pp. 1–12). San Francisco: Earth Island Press and North Atlantic Books.

Naples, N. (Ed.). (1998). *Community activism and feminist politics*. New York: Routledge.

National Association of Social Workers' Presidential Project. (1988). *A national social agenda for America's families*. Silver Spring, MD: NASW.

National Association of Social Workers Strengthening Families Through Informational Innovations Project. (1993). *Effective strategies for increasing social program replication/adaption*. Washington, DC: NASW.

National Commission on Families and Public Policies. (1978). *Families and public policies in the United States: Final report of the commission*. Washington, DC: Author.

National Council on Family Relations. (1993). *One world, many families*. Minneapolis: Author.

National Governors Association (1989). *America in transition: Report of the task force on children*. Washington, DC: Author.

National International Year of the Family Committee/Family Student and Research Commission. (1993). *The family in the Maltese social structure*. Malta: Author.

Natoli, J. (1997, Spring). Self-help and the search for solutions in human services. *Social Policy, 68*–69.

Nelson, R., & Bridges, W. (1999). *Legalizing gender inequality: Courts, markets, and unequal pay for women in America*. New York: Cambridge University Press.

New Economy Development Group Inc. (1993). *Community economic development: A different way of doing things*. Ottawa, Canada: National Welfare Grants Program, Human Resources Department.

Newsletter of the Baha'i International Community. (1993, October–December). UNIFEM project to uplift women strikes a responsive chord. *One Country, 5*(3), 4–9.

Newton, K. (1997). Social capital and democracy. *American Behavioral Scientist, 40,* 575–586.

Nielsen, R. (1993). Woolman's "I am we" triple-loop action-learning: Origin and application in organization ethics. *Journal of Applied Behavioral Science,* 29(1), 117–138.

Norberg-Hodge, H. (1996). Shifting direction: From global dependence to local interdependence. In J. Mander & E. Goldsmith (Eds.), *The case against the global economy and for a turn toward the local* (pp. 393–406). San Francisco: Sierra Club Books.

Nuralamin, A. (1996). The informal sector paradigm: Analytical contributions and developmental role. *Regional Development Dialogue,* 17(1), vi–xxviii.

Oakley, Ann. (1974). *The sociology of housework.* London: Pitman Press.

O'Connell, H. (1994). *Women and the family.* London: Zed Books.

OECD. (1998). *Case studies in integrated services for children and youth at risk: A world view.* Paris: Author.

Ogbu, J. (1995). Cultural problems in minority education. Their interpretation and consequences, Part One. *The Urban Review,* 27, 189–205.

O'Keefe, M. (1995). Predictors of child abuse in maritally violent families. *Journal of Interpersonal Violence,* 10(1), 3–25.

Okin, Susan M. (1989). *Justice, gender, and the family.* New York: Basic Books.

O'Looney, J. (1996). *Redesigning the work of human services.* Westport, CT: Quorum Books.

Omari, C. (1986, August 30–September 5). *Strengthening the family and the community.* Paper presented at Twenty-Third International Conference on Social Welfare, Tokyo.

Ooms, T., & Binder, H. (1993). *Keeping troubled families together: Promising programs and statewide reform.* Washington, DC: AAMFT Research and Education Foundation.

Øvretveit, J., Mathias, P., & Thompson, T. (1997). *Interprofessional working in health and social care.* London: Macmillan Press.

Opotow, S. (1990). Moral exclusion and injustice: An introduction. *Journal of Social Issues,* 46(1), 1–20.

Osborne, D., & Gaebler, T. (1993). *Reinventing government: How the entrepreneurial spirit is transforming the public sector.* New York: Penguin.

Ostrom, E. (1990). *Governing the commons: The evolution of institutions for collective action.* New York: Cambridge University Press.

Otero, M., & Rhyne, E. (Eds.). (1994). *The new world of microenterprise finance: Building healthy financial institutions for the poor.* West Hartford, CT: Kumarian Press.

Ottone, E. (1993, August). Address at the opening meeting of the technical stage of the Latin American and Caribbean Regional meeting preparatory to the International Year of the Family, Cartagena, Colombia.

Ozawa, M. N. (1989). *Women's life cycle and economic security: Problems and proposals*. New York: Praeger.

Page-Adams, D., & Sherraden, J. (1997). Asset building as a community revitalization strategy. *Social Work, 42*(5), 423–434.

Parker, R. (1994). *Flesh peddlers and warm bodies: The temporary help industry and its workers*. New Brunswick, NJ: Rutgers University Press.

Peck, J. (1996). *Workplace: The social regulation of labor markets*. New York: Guilford Press.

Pede, J., & Glahe, F. R. *The American family and the state* (pp. 425–454). San Francisco: Pacific Research Institute for Public Policy.

Petrikin, J. (Ed.). (1995). *The third world*. San Diego: Greenhaven Press.

Pierson, C. (1996). *The modern state*. London: Routledge.

Pieterse, J. (1995). Globalization as hybridization. In M. Featherstone, S. Lash, & R. Robertson (Eds.), *Global modernities* (pp. 45–68). Thousand Oaks, CA: Sage.

Pietilä, H., & Vickers, J. (1996). *Making women matter: The role of the United Nations*. London: Zed Books.

Pinderhughes, E. (1995, March). Empowering diverse populations: Family practice in the 21st century. *Families in Society: Journal of Contemporary Human Services, 76*(3), 131–141.

Polak, F. (1973). *The image of the future*. San Francisco: Jossey-Bass; Amsterdam: Elsevier.

Popenoe, D. (1994). The family condition of America: Cultural change and public policy. In H. Aaron, T. Mann, & T. Taylor (Eds.), *Values and public policy* (pp. 81–112). Washington, DC: Brookings Institution Press.

Population Reference Bureau. (1999). *World population data sheet*. Washington, DC: Population Reference Bureau.

Potapchuk, W., Crocker, J., & Schechter, W. (1997). Building community with social capital: Chits and chums or chats with change. *National Civic Review, 86*, 129–139.

Premier's Council in Support of Alberta Families. (1994). *Family friendly community checklist*. Edmonton, Hilltop House: Alberta Family and Social Services.

Preskill, H., & Torres, R. (1999). *Evaluative inquiry for learning in organizations*. Thousand Oaks, CA: Sage.

Profeda-International Secretariate. (1994). *The family and human rights*. Madrid: Author.

Putnam, R. (1993). *Making democracy work: Civic traditions in modern Italy*. Princeton, NJ: Princeton University Press.

Putnam, R. (1995). Bowling alone: America's declining social capital. *Journal of Democracy, 6*(1), 65–78.

Putnam, R. (2000). *Bowling alone: The collapse and revival of American community*. New York: Simon & Schuster.

Radin, M. (1996). *Contested commodities: The trouble with trade in sex, children, body parts and other things.* Cambridge: Harvard University Press.

Ransom, J. (1997). *Foucault's discipline: The politics of subjectivity.* Durham, NC: Duke University Press.

Rao, A. (1990). *The women's dairy project in Thailand.* New York: SEEDS.

Rappaport, J. (1993). Narrative studies, personal stories, and identity transformation in a mutual help context. *Journal of Applied Behavioral Science, 29*(2), 237–254.

Rapping, E. (1997, Spring). There's self-help and then there's self help: Women and the recovery movement. *Social Policy, 56–61.*

Rawls, J. (1996). *Political liberalism.* New York: Columbia University Press.

Ray, D. (1998). *Development economics.* Princeton, NJ: Princeton University Press.

Reed, E. (1997). *Women's evolution: From matriarchal clan to patriarchal family.* New York: Pathfinder Press.

Reich, R. (1988a). Introduction. In R. Reich (Ed.), *The power of public ideas* (pp. 1–12). Cambridge: Harvard University Press.

Reich, R. (1988b). Policy making in a democracy. In R. Reich (Ed.), *The power of public ideas* (pp. 123–156). Cambridge: Harvard University Press.

Reich, R. (1993). *The work of nations: Preparing ourselves for twenty-first century capitalism.* New York: Knopf.

Reiman, J. (1995). *And the poor get prison: Economic bias in American criminal justice system.* Boston: Allyn & Bacon.

Reyneri, E. (1994). Italy: A long wait in the shelter of the family and of safeguards from the state. In O. Benoît-Guilbot & D. Gallie (Eds.), *Long-term unemployment* (pp. 97–110). London: Pinter.

Ridgeway, C. (1997). Interaction and the conservation of gender inequality: Considering employment. *American Sociological Review, 62,* 219–235.

Riessman, F. (1997). Ten self-help principles. *Social Policy, 27*(3), 6–12.

Rifkin, J. (1995). *The end of work: The decline of the global labor force and the dawn of the post-market era.* New York: Putnam.

Rights and Humanity. (1987, March). *Rights and Humanity Development Bulletin.* London: Author.

Riley, N. (1997). Gender, power, and population change. *The Population Bulletin, 52*(1), 1–48.

Riley, N. (1999). Challenging demography: Contributions from feminist theory. *Sociological Forum, 14,* 369–398.

Robbins, J. (1992). *May all be fed.* New York: Norton.

Robertson, R. (1992). *Globalization and social theory.* Thousand Oaks, CA: Sage.

Robertson, R. (1995). Globalization: Time-space and homogeneity-heterogeneity. In M. Featherstone, S. Lash, & R. Robertson (Eds.), *Global modernities* (pp. 25–44). Thousand Oaks, CA: Sage.

Rodwin, L. (1994). Rethinking the development experience: Aims, themes, and theses. In L. Rodwin & D. Schön (Eds.), *Rethinking the development experience: Essays provoked by the work of Albert O. Hirchman* (pp. 3–36). Washington, DC: Brookings Institution Press.

Rofe, N. (1993, February). Senegal loan officers pave way for success. *Frontlines, 33*(1), 4–5.

Rolfe, E. (1995). Personal communication to authors. June 1994, February 1995.

Rorty, R. (1998). *Achieving our country: Leftist thought in twentieth-century America.* Cambridge: Harvard University Press.

Rose, R. (1993). *Lesson-drawing in public policy: A guide to learning across time and space.* Chatham, NJ: Chatham House.

Rosecrance, R. (1986). *The rise of the trading state: Commerce and conquest in the modern world.* New York: Basic Books.

Roseland, M. (1998). *Toward sustainable communities.* Stoney Creek, CT: New Society.

Roth, K. (1998, March/April). Sidelined on human rights. *Foreign Affairs, 77*(2), 2–6.

Roudometof, V., & Robertson, R. (1995). Globalization, world-system theory, and the comparative study of civilizations: Issues of theoretical logic in world-historical sociology. In S. Sanderson (Ed.), *Civilizations and world systems* (pp. 273–300). Walnut Creek, CA: AltaMira.

Rudolph, H. (1994). Federal Republic of Germany: Change and diversity. In O. Benoît-Guilbot & D. Gallie (Eds.), *Long-term unemployment* (pp. 91–96). London: Pinter.

Rural and Appalachian Youth and Families Consortium. (1996). Parenting practices and interventions among marginalized families in Appalachia: Building on family strengths. *Family Relations: Journal of Applied Family and Child Studies, 45,* 387–396.

Salomon, J-J., & Lebeau, A. (1995). Internal conditions perpetuate third world poverty. In J. Petrikin (Ed.), *The third world* (pp. 43–51). San Diego: Greenhaven Press.

Sanders. J. M., & Nee, V. (1996). Immigrant self-employment: The family as social capital and the value of human capital. *American Sociological Review, 61,* 231–248.

Sanyal, B. (1996). Intention and outcome: Formalization and its consequences. *Regional Development Dialogue, 17*(1), 161–178.

Sassen, S. (1991). *The global city.* Princeton, NJ: Princeton University Press.

Schiel, T. (1984). Development and underdevelopment of household-based production in Europe. In J. Smith, I. M. Wallerstein, & H. Evers (Eds.), *Households in the world economy* (pp. 101–129). Beverly Hills, CA: Sage.

Schön, D. (1971). *Beyond the stable state.* New York: Random House.

Schön, D. (1983). *The reflective practitioner: How professionals think in action.* New York: Basic Books.

Schön, D. (1994). Hirchman's elusive theory of social learning. In L. Rodwin & D. Schön (Eds.), *Rethinking the development experience: Essays provoked by the work of Albert O. Hirchman* (pp. 67–95). Washington, DC: Brookings Institution Press.

Schön, D., & Rein, M. (1994). *Frame reflection: Toward the resolution of intractable policy controversies.* New York: Basic Books.

Schorr, A. (1997). *Passion and policy: A social worker's career.* Chesterland, OH: Octavia Press.

Schorr, L. B. (1989). *Within our reach: Breaking the cycle of disadvantage.* New York: Anchor Books.

Schorr, L. B. (1997). *Common purpose: Strengthening families and neighborhoods to rebuild America.* New York: Anchor Books.

Schreiner, M. (1999, October). Lessons for microenterprise programs from a fresh look at the unemployment insurance self-employment demonstration. *Evaluation Review, 23*(5), 504–526.

Schuler, M. (Ed.). (1992). *Freedom from violence: Women's strategies from around the world.* New York: United Nations Development Fund for Women (UNIFEM).

Schwartz, E. (1996). *Net activism: How citizens use the Internet.* Philadelphia: O'Reilly & Associates.

Schwartz, I., & Fishman, G. (1999). *Kids raised by the government.* London: Praeger.

Schweickart, D. (1996). *Against capitalism.* Boulder, CO: Westview Press.

Seabrook, J. (1995). External development strategies impoverish third world countries. In J. Petrikin (Ed.), *The third world* (pp. 34–42). San Diego: Greenhaven Press.

Secretariat for the International Fund for Agricultural Development. (1992). *The situation of the world's rural women. Banking on women: Facts and figures.* Summit on the Economic Advancement of Rural Women, Geneva, February 25–26, 1992: Author.

Secretariat for the International Year of the Family. (1994). *Inventory of national action* (2nd ed.). United Nations Department for Policy Coordination and Sustainable Development, Vienna: Author.

Sedt, A. (1993). The politics of family and immigration in the subordination of domestic workers in Canada. In B. Fox (Ed.), *Family patterns, gender relations* (pp. 278–296). New York: Oxford University Press.

Seidman, G. (1999). Gendered citizenship. *Gender & Society, 13*(3), 287–307.

Sen, A. (1999). *Development as freedom.* New York: Knopf.

Senge, P. (1990). *The fifth discipline.* New York: Doubleday.

Senge, P., Kleiner, A., Roberts, C., Ross, R., & Smith, B. (1994). *The fifth discipline fieldbook: Strategies and tools for building a learning organization.* New York: Currency Doubleday.

Shaw, D. (1997). World food security: The impending crisis? *Development Policy Review, 15,* 413–420.

Sheridan, M., & Salaff, J. W. (1984). *Lives: Chinese working women.* Bloomington: Indiana University Press.

Sherman, A. (1994). *Wasting America's future: The Children's Defense Fund report on the cost of child poverty.* Boston: Beacon Press.

Sherraden, M. (1991). *Assets and the poor: A new American welfare policy.* Armonk, NY: Sharpe.

Shore, L. C. (1987). Starting over (surviving a plant closure). Oakland, CA: Oakland Center for Working Life.

Shuman, M. (1994). *Towards a global village: International community development initiatives.* Boulder, CO: Pluto Press.

Sinclair, P. (1987). *Unemployment: Economic theory and evidence.* Oxford: Blackwell.

Sklar, H. (1995). *Chaos or community? Seeking solutions, not scapegoats, for bad economics.* Boston: South End Press.

Smith, M., & Guarnizo, L. (Eds.) (1999). *Transnationalism from below.* New Brunswick, NJ: Transaction.

Smith, R. (1995, April). Keynote address. Second National Interprofessional Conference, Los Angeles, University of Southern California.

Snyder, M. (1995). *Transforming development: Women, poverty, and politics.* London: Intermediate Technology.

Sokalski, H. (1993, November 18). *Statement before the conference on the family in the development process.* Moscow: United Nations.

Solomon, B. (1977). *Black empowerment: Social work in oppressed communities.* New York: Columbia University Press.

Solomon, R. (1974). *The international monetary system 1945–1976: An insider's view.* New York: Harper & Row.

Spakes, P. (1988, May 7). *National family policy and feminist social work practice: The incompatible pair.* Paper presented at the Council on Social Work Education Annual Program Meeting, Greensboro, University of North Carolina.

Spar, D. (1998, March/April). The spotlight and the bottom line. How multinationals export human rights. *Foreign Affairs, 77*(2), 7–12.

Sprey, J. (1969). The family as a system in conflict. *Journal of Marriage and the Family, 31,* 699–706.

Spring, J. (1998). *Education and the rise of the global economy.* Mahwah, NJ: Erlbaum.

Springer, J., & Phillips, J. (1994). Policy learning and evaluation design: Lessons from the community partnership demonstration project. *Journal of Community Psychology,* CSAP Special Summer Issue, 117–139.

Staggenborg, S. (1998). *Gender, family, and social movements.* Thousand Oaks, CA: Pine Forge Press.

Standing, G. (1989). Global feminization through flexible labor. *World Development, 17*, 1077–1096.

States at war. (1998, November 9). *Time,* 40–54.

Steady, F., & Touré, R. (Eds.). (1995). *Women and the United Nations: Reflections and new horizons.* Rochester, VT: Schenkman Books.

Steiner, G. Y. (1981). *The futility of family policy.* Washington, DC: Brookings Institution Press.

Stoesz, D., Guzzetta, C., & Lusk, M. (1999). *International development.* Boston: Allyn & Bacon.

Stoez, D., & Saunders, D. (1999). Welfare capitalism: A new approach to poverty policy? *Social Service Review, 73*(3), 380–400.

Strasser, S. (1982). *Never done: A history of American housework.* New York: Pantheon Books.

Stringer, E. (1996). *Action research: A handbook for practitioners.* Thousand Oaks, CA: Sage.

Takashima, S. (1988). *History and present situation of Japanese social welfare: In comparison with that of United Kingdom.* Japan: Nihon Fukushi University.

Tendler, J. (1989). What ever happened to poverty alleviation? *World Development, 17*, 1033–1044.

Thurow, L. (1996). *The future of capitalism: How today's economic forces shape tomorrow's world.* New York: Morrow.

Thursz, D., & Vigilante, J. (Eds.). (1975). *Meeting human needs.* Beverly Hills, CA: Sage.

Toharia, L. (1994). Spain: Modernization of unemployment. In O. Benoît-Guilbot & D. Gallie (Eds.), *Long-term unemployment* (pp. 111–118). London: Pinter.

Tönnies, F. (1974). *On social ideas and ideologies* (E. Jacoby, Trans.). New York: Harper & Row.

Tracy, M. (1998, March). *Comparative social welfare: Systematic policy models in social work education.* Paper presented to the Council on Social Work Education, Orlando, FL.

Tremblay, H. (1988). *Families of the world: Family life at the close of the 20th century.* New York: Farrar, Straus & Giroux.

Trost, J. (1996). Family structure and relationships: The dyadic approach. *Journal of Comparative Family Studies, 27*, 395–408.

Trzcinski, E. (1995). An ecological perspective on family policy: A conceptual and philosophical framework. *Journal of Family and Economic Issues, 16*, 7–33.

Tucker, S. (1996). *Benchmarking: A guide for educators.* Thousand Oaks, CA: Corwin Press.

UNICEF. (1993). *The state of the world's children.* New York: UNICEF House and Oxford University Press.

UNICEF. (1999). *State of the world's children.* Berlin: Author.

UNICEF, Development Programmes for Women Unit. (1993). *A time for action: Girls, women and human rights.* New York: UNICEF.

United Nations. (1975). *Poverty, unemployment, and development policy.* New York: Author.

United Nations. (1976). *Social welfare and family planning.* New York: Author.

United Nations. (1981a). *Integration of disabled persons into community life.* New York: Author.

United Nations. (1981b). *Popular participation as a strategy for promoting community-level action and national development.* New York: Author.

United Nations. (1984). *The family: Models for providing comprehensive services for family and child welfare.* New York: Author.

United Nations. (1985). *Administration of social welfare: A survey of national organizational arrangements.* New York: Author.

United Nations. (1986a). *Developmental social welfare: A global survey of issues and priorities since 1968.* New York: Author.

United Nations. (1986b). *Disability: Situation, strategies, and policies.* New York: Author.

United Nations. (1986c). *The family: Role of the family in the developmental process.* In report by Department of International Economic and Social Affairs and Centre for Social Development and Humanitarian Affairs (No. 2). New York: United Nations Publications.

United Nations. (1986d). *World survey on the role of women in development.* New York: Author.

United Nations. (1987). *The family, national family policies: Their relationship to the role of the family in the development process.* In report by Department of International Economic and Social Affairs and Centre for Social Development and Humanitarian Affairs (No. 3). New York: United Nations Publications.

United Nations. (1988a). *Action in the field of human rights.* New York: Author.

United Nations. (1988b). *Human rights: The international bill of human rights.* New York: Author.

United Nations. (1990, July). *Literacy: Tool for empowering women* (DPI/ 1075). United Nations Department of Public Information, New York: Author.

United Nations. (1991a). *1991 International Year of the Family,* "Building the smallest democracy at the heart of society." Vienna: United Nations Office at Vienna, Center for Social Development and Humanitarian Affairs.

United Nations. (1991b, July). *The quest for women's rights* (DPI/1144). United Nations Department of Public Information, New York: Author.

United Nations. (1991c). *Women: Challenges to the year 2000.* New York: Author.

United Nations. (1991d). *World economic survey: Current trends and policies in the world economy.* New York: Author.

United Nations. (1992a, May). *Changing the status quo: The United Nations' work for women* (DPI/1191). United Nations Department of Public Information, New York: Author.

United Nations. (1992b). *Family and crime* (Occasional Papers Series No. 3). Vienna: Author.

United Nations. (1992c). *Family matters* (Occasional Papers Series No. 1). Vienna: Author.

United Nations. (1992d). *Human rights: Summary or arbitrary executions* (Fact Sheet No. 11). Geneva: Author.

United Nations. (1992e). *Human rights: The rights of indigenous people* (Fact Sheet No. 9). Geneva: Author.

United Nations. (1992f). *Human rights: The rights of the child.* Geneva: Centre for Human Rights.

United Nations. (1992g). *Women 2000: Women in development.* Division for the Advancement of Women (No. 1). New York: Author.

United Nations. (1993a). Declaration of Valletta. United Nations and North America Preparatory Meeting for the International Year of the Family, Valletta, 26–30 April (V. 93–85478 9154T).

United Nations. (1993b). *Family as an environment: An ecosystem perspective on family life* (Occasional Papers Series No. 5). Vienna: Author.

United Nations. (1993c). *Family: Forms and functions* (Occasional Papers Series No. 2, V. 93–84799 9126T). Vienna: Author.

United Nations. (1993d). *International Year of the Family. Family enrichment: Programmes to foster healthy family development* (Occasional Papers Series No. 8, V. 93–90109). Vienna: C. Arp, D. Arp, & V. Mace.

United Nations. (1993e). *International Year of the Family. Family leave: Changing needs of the world's workers* (Occasional Papers Series No. 7, V. 93–88947). Vienna: E. B. Goldsmith.

United Nations. (1993f). *Older persons in the family: Facets of empowerment* (Occasional Papers Series No. 4). Vienna: Author.

United Nations. (1993g). *Partnership families: Building the smallest democracy at the heart of society* (Occasional Papers Series No. 6). Vienna: Author.

United Nations. (1993h). *United Nations publications catalogue.* New York: United Nations Publications.

United Nations. (1993i). *Statistical chart on world families* (ST/ESA/STAT/ SER.Y/7). New York: Author.

United Nations. (1993j). *World conference on human rights.* Vienna: Author.

United Nations. (1994a). *Development and international cooperation: An agenda for development* (Report of the Secretary General, May 6, A/48/935). New York: Author.

United Nations. (1994b). *International Year of the Family. Families and disabilities* (Occasional Papers Series No. 10, V. 94–23083). Vienna: P. Mittler & H. Mittler.

United Nations. (1994c). *International Year of the Family. Intersection of fam-*

ily, gender, and the economy in the developing world (Occasional Papers Series No. 9, V. 93–91378). Vienna: R. L. Blumberg & K. Pethan.

United Nations. (1994d). *International Year of the Family. Migration and the family* (Occasional Papers Series No. 12, V. 94–25200). Vienna: G. Hugo.

United Nations. (1994e). *International Year of the Family. Statistical chart on world families.* New York: Author.

United Nations. (1994f). *International Year of the Family. The elderly and the family in developing countries* (Occasional Papers Series No. 13). Vienna: Author.

United Nations. (1994g). *Reinventing fatherhood* (Occasional Papers Series No. 14). Vienna: Author.

United Nations. (1994h). *The concept of family health* (Occasional Papers Series No. 15). Vienna: Author.

United Nations. (1995a, November). *Compilation of family-specific recommendations of the global conferences of the 1990s.* Vienna: Author.

United Nations. (1995b). *Families function: Family bridges from past to future* (Occasional Papers Series No. 19). Vienna.

United Nations. (1995c). *International Year of the Family. Families, agents and beneficiaries of socio-economic development* (Occasional Papers Series No. 16, V. 95–51281). Vienna: B. Cass.

United Nations. (1995d). *International Year of the Family. Families in exile: Reflections from the experience of UNHCR.* (Occasional Papers Series No. 17, V. 95–51280). Vienna: Author.

United Nations. (1995e). *Indicative guide for action on family issues.* Vienna: Author.

United Nations. (1999, October). *Indigenous people: Mid-point of UN decade reflects action on indigenous issues.* New York: United Nations of Public Information.

United Nations. (2000). *The world's women 2000: Trends and statistics.* New York: United Nations.

United Nations Commission for Social Development. (1993). *World summit for social development: Draft resolution.* Vienna: Author.

United Nations Commission on Human Rights. (1989). *Convention on the rights of the child: Text of the draft convention as adopted by the working group at second reading.* New York: Author.

United Nations Commission on Human Rights. (1994). *A compilation of international instruments: (Vols. 1, 2). Universal instruments.* New York: Author.

United Nations Conference on Trade and Development (UNCTD). (1996a). *Globalization and liberalization: Effects of international economic relations on poverty.* New York: United Nations.

United Nations Conference on Trade and Development. (1996b). Conclusions and recommendations. In *Globalization and liberalization: Effects of international economic relations on poverty* (Interagency thematic contribution for the international year for the eradication of poverty) (UNCTAS/ECDC/ PA/4/Rev 1). New York: United Nations.

United Nations Department of Humanitarian Affairs. (1992). *Complex emergencies: A united approach*. Geneva: Author.

United Nations Department for Policy Coordination and Sustainable Development. (1994). *The United Nations system and the International Year of the Family*. Vienna: Author.

United Nations Development Programme (UNDP). (1994). *Human development report 1994*. New York: Oxford University Press.

United Nations Development Programme. (1995). *Human development report 1995*. New York: Oxford University Press.

United Nations Development Programme. (1999). *Human development report 1999*. New York: Oxford University Press.

United Nations Development Programme. (2000). *Women's political participation and good governance: 21st century challenges*. New York: Author.

United Nations Development Programme (UNDP) for Sustainable Human Development. (1998). *Poverty clock winning the fight against poverty. http:// undo.org/undp/povert/event.htm*.

United Nations Economic Commission for Latin America and the Caribbean. (1993, August 9–14). *Report of the Latin American and Caribbean regional meeting preparatory to the International Year of the Family* (93–9–1118). Cartagena, Colombia.

United Nations Economic and Social Council. (1986). *Declaration on social and legal principles relating to the protection and welfare of children, with special reference on foster placement and adoption nationally and internationally*. New York: Author.

United Nations Economic and Social Council, Commission for Social Development (1991, February 11–20). *Monitoring of international plan and programs of action. Preparation for and observance of the International Year of the Family: Report of the secretary-general*. Vienna: Author.

United Nations Economic and Social Council. (1992). *Monitoring of international plans and programmes of action. State of preparation for the International Year of the Family: Report of the secretary-general*. Vienna: Author.

United Nations Economic and Social Council, Commission for Social Development. (1993, February 11–20). *Monitoring of international plan and programs of action. State of preparations for the International Year of the Family: Report of the secretary-general*.

United Nations Economic and Social Council, Commission for Social Development, World Summit for Social Development. (1993, February 8–17). *Draft Resolution*, submitted by the Committee of the Whole on the World Summit for Social Development. Vienna: Author.

United Nations General Assembly. (1993). *Report of the preparatory committee for the world summit for social development*. New York: United Nations.

United Nations General Assembly Special Session on the Implementation of the Outcome of the World Summit for Social Development and Further Initiatives. (2000, June). *Social summit special sessions seeks solutions to globalization woes.* New York: United Nations Department of Public Information.

United Nations High Commissioner for Refugees, Centre for Documentation on Refugees and the Refugee Policy Group. (1991). *A selected bibliography on refugee health.* New York: Author.

United Nations High Commissioner for Refugees. (1993, April 19–30). *Status of preparation of publications, studies and documents for the world conference.* Contribution to United Nations World Conference on Human Rights Preparatory Committee. Geneva: United Nations.

United Nations IYF Secretariat. (1994). *The family. Bulletin on the International Year of the Family.* No. 2. Vienna: Author.

U.S. Department of Health and Human Services, Office of Human Development Services. (1988). *Social welfare developments in other industrialized countries: 2nd year report.* Washington, DC: Author.

U.S. Department of Health and Human Services. (1991). *Mental health services for refugees.* Washington, DC: Author.

U.S. General Accounting Office. (1995). *The foster care crisis.* Washington, DC: U.S. Government Printing Office.

Van Hook, M. D. (1987). Harvest of despair: Using the ABCX model for farm families. *Social Casework, 68,* 273–278.

Van Soest, D. (1997). *The global crisis of violence: Common problems, universal causes, shared solutions.* Washington, DC: NASW Press.

Van Wormer, K. (1997). *Social welfare: A world view.* Chicago: Nelson-Hall.

Van Veen, D., Day, C., & Walraven, G. (Eds.). (1998). *Multi-service schools: Integrated services for children at risk.* Leuven/Appeldoorn, The Netherlands: Garant.

Vickers, J. (1991). *Women and the world economic crisis.* London: Zed Books.

Vivian, J., & Maseko, G. (1994). *NGOs, participation, and rural development.* Geneva: United Nations Research Institute for Social Development.

Vosler, N. (1996). *New approaches to family practice: Confronting economic stress.* Thousand Oaks, CA: Sage.

Walby, S. (1999). The new regulatory state: The social powers of the European Union. *British Journal of Sociology, 50*(1), 118–140.

Waldfogel, J. (1997). The effects of children upon women's wages. *American Sociological Review, 62,* 209–217.

Wallerstein, I. (1974). *The modern world system I.* New York: Academic Press.

Ward, K. (1990). Introduction and overview. In K. Ward (Ed.), *Women workers and global restructuring* (pp. 1–22). Ithaca, NY: ILR Press.

Ward, K. (Ed.). (1990). *Women workers and global restructuring.* Ithaca, NY: ILR Press.

Waring, M. (1988). *If women counted: A new feminist economics*. San Francisco: Harper & Row.

Warness, K. (1983, August 23–27). *On the rationality of caring*. Paper presented at the International Conference on the Transformation of the Welfare State: Dangers and potentialities for women, Bellagio, Italy, Center of Women's Studies, Institute of Sociology University of Bergen.

Watt, V. (1999, December 16). Ugandan children abducted to perform acts of war. *USA Today*, p. 29A.

Watts, A. (1984). *Education, unemployment, and the future of work*. Milton Keynes, England: Open University Press.

Waxman, S. I. (1977). *The stigma of poverty: A critique of poverty theories and policies*. New York: Pergamon Press.

Wayson, W., & Cox-New, J. (1995). *Walking fine lines: A foundation and schools collaborate to improve education*. Little Rock, AR: Winthrop Rockefeller Foundation.

Weber, M. (1964). *The theory of social and economic organization*. New York: Free Press.

Weick, A., & Saleebey, D. (1995, March). Family strengths. *Families in Society*, 141–149.

Weiss, C. (1995). Nothing as practical as good theory: Exploring theory-based evaluation for comprehensive community initiatives for children and families. In J. Connell, A. Kubish, L. Schorr, & C. Weiss (Eds.), *New approaches to evaluating community initiatives: Concepts, methods and contexts* (pp. 65–92). New York: Aspen Institute.

Weiss, R., Forsythe, D., & Coate, R. (1994). *The United Nations and changing world politics*. Boulder, CO: Westview Press.

Welch, G., & Briar, K. H. (1991). *The Swedish Family Contact Program*. Silver Spring, MD: NASW Press.

Western, B. (1997). *Between class and market: Postwar unionization in the capitalist democracies*. Princeton, NJ: Princeton University Press.

Wetzel, J. W., & Campling, J. (1993). *The world of women: In pursuit of human rights*. London: Macmillan Press.

Wheatcroft, A. (1983). *The world atlas of revolutions*. New York: Simon & Schuster.

Whitchurch, G. G., & Constantine, L. (1993). Systems theory. In P. G. Boss, W. J. Doherty, R. LaRossa, W. R. Schumm, & S. K. Steinmetz (Eds.), *Sourcebook of family theories and methods: A contextual approach* (pp. 325–352). New York: Plenum Press.

White, M. (1994). Unemployment and employment relations in Britain. In O. Benoît-Guilbot & D. Gallie (Eds.), *Long-term unemployment* (pp. 34–53). London: Pinter.

Wilcox, R., Smith, D., Moore, J., Hewitt, A., Allan, G., Walker, H., Ropata, M.,

Monu, L., & Featherstone, T. (1991). *Family decision making, family group conferences: Practitioner's view.* New Zealand: Practitioner's Publishing.

Wilkinson, R. (1996). *Unhealthy societies: The afflictions of inequality.* New York: Routledge.

Wilkinson, P., & Quarter, J. (1996). *Building a community-controlled economy: The Evangeline co-operative experience.* Toronto: University of Toronto Press.

Williams, L. (1996, August 19). U.S. prison population doubles in 10 years. *Cincinnati Enquirer,* p. A1.

Williams, R. (1977). *Marxism and literature.* London: Oxford University Press.

Wilson, W. J. (1997). *When work disappears: The world of the new urban poor.* London: Vintage.

Wilson, W. J. (1999). When work disappears: New implications for race and urban poverty in the global economy. *Ethnic and Racial Studies, 22,* 481–499.

Windschuttle, K. (1988). *Education in the USA: Statistical comparisons with Australia.* Canberra, Australia: Australian Government Publishing Service.

Windschuttle, K., & Bufort, J. (1987). *Local and regional organizations: Their roles in fostering local employment initiatives* (Research Paper No. 2). Canberra, Australia: Australian Government Publishing Service.

Winfield, N. (1999). Orphans focus of AIDS day. [On-line] Associated Press, ABCNEWS.com: Orphans the Focus of AIDS Day. *http://abcnews.go.com/ sections/living/DailyNews/aids-world991201.html.*

Wolff, E. N. (1995). *Top heavy.* New York: New York Press.

Woodward, D. (1996). Effects of globalization and liberalization on poverty: Concepts and issues. In United Nations Conference on Trade and Development, *Globalization and liberalization: Effects of international economic relations on poverty* (pp. 25–128). New York: United Nations.

World Bank. (1999a). *Entering the 21st century: World development report 1999/2000.* New York: Cambridge University Press.

World Bank. (1999b). *World Bank atlas.* Washington, DC: Author.

World Bank. (1999c). *World development indicators.* Washington, DC: Author.

World Resources Institute, United Nations Environment Programme, United Nations Development Programme, and the World Bank. (1996). *World resources, 1996–1997.* New York: Oxford University Press.

Wronka, J. (1998). *Human rights and social policy in the 21st century.* Lanham, MD: United Press of America.

Wynn, J., Costello, J., & Halpern, R. H. (1994). *Children, families and communities: A new approach to social services.* Chapin Hall, University of Chicago.

Yaffe, J. (1998). *Quick guide to the Internet for social work.* Boston: Allyn & Bacon.

Zeitlin, M., Megawangi, R., Kramer, E., Colletta, N., Babatunde, E. D., & Garman, D. (1995). *Strengthening the family: Implications for international development.* Tokyo: United Nations University Press.

Zigler, E., Kagan, S., & Hall, N. (Eds.). (1996). *Children, families & government*. New York: Cambridge University Press.

Zimmerman, S. (1988). *Understanding family policy: Theoretical approaches*. Newbury Park, CA: Sage.

Zimmerman, S. (1992). *Family policies and family well-being: The role of political culture*. Newbury Park, CA: Sage.

Zlotnik, J. (1998). *Preparing the workforce for family-centered practice: Social work education and public human services partnerships* (report of the Ford Foundation Project). Washington, DC: Council on Social Work Education.

Index